COLOR PUBLISHING

On the Macintosh
From Desktop to Print Shop

KIM & SUNNY BAKER

RANDOM HOUSE
ELECTRONIC PUBLISHING

New York

Color Publishing on the Macintosh

Copyright © 1992 by Kim Baker and Sunny Baker

All rights reserved under International and Pan-American Copyright Conventions.

Published in the United States by Random House, Inc., New York, and simultaneously in Canada by Random House of Canada, Ltd.

Manufactured in the United States of America.

98765432 24689753 23456789

First edition

Library of Congress Cataloging-in-Publication Data

Baker, Kim, 1955-
      Color Publishing on the Macintosh: from desktop to print shop / by Kim Baker & Sunny Baker.
            p. cm.
      Includes bibliographical references and index.
      ISBN 0-679-73977-7 : $45.00
      1. Desktop publishing. 2. Macintosh (computer)—programming. 3. Color computer graphics. I. Baker, Sunny. II Title.
      Z286.D47B35 1992
      686.2'3042—dc20   91-47960
                                                                                        CIP

Credits
Book layout and production: Andrea Star Greitzer & Terry Kelley
PageWorks, Inc. 36 J. F. K. Street, Cambridge, MA 02138

Image on page 301 Copyright © 1989, 1990 by Teaching Publishing Services, Inc.

DEDICATION

This book is dedicated to the countless engineers, prepress professionals, service bureaus, print shops, and color publishers using their knowledge and hard work to produce quality color publications on the Macintosh. It's because of their efforts and dedication that the state of the art is continually advancing.

ACKNOWLEDGMENTS

The authors would like to give special thanks to the following people for their outstanding contributions to this book:

Michael Mellin, Publisher at Random House Electronic Publishing, Steven J. Bennett of The Bennett Information Group, and Mike Snell of the Michael Snell Literary Agency—for believing in this book and helping make it happen.

Julie Ann O'Leary and Jane Mellin, our editors at Random House, for their persistence and enthusiasm on the project.

The gang at InfoComp/Connecting Point in Chandler, Arizona, especially Jim Steinacker, Greg Larsen, and Tim Conrad, who provided technical advice, equipment loans, and speedy repairs.

Grant Hall of American Color, who really knows his stuff when it comes to electronic prepress.

Ellen Addington of Webcrafters, who helped with explanations on a number of real-world service bureau questions and problems.

Dave Shough of Digitech, who contributed his time answering a myriad of questions.

Steve Holliger of S. J. Pierce & Company and Michael Thorne of Technical Publishing Services, who both provided contacts and information, and answered obscure questions for us.

Woods Litho, and Frank Woods in particular, who brought a new meaning to the phrase "high-quality printing" with the company's 600-lines-per-inch printing process.

Colby Foote and Steve England of Color Masters, who put high-end prepress links into perspective for us.

Norm Atkin of LaserTypesetting for his insights on service bureau operations.

Julie Thompson, our efficient assistant, who helped assemble and proof the initial manuscript.

Sally, Kristy Jo, and Joe Staron—just for being there.

Our appreciation also goes to the many people in the companies listed in the *Sources* section at the back of the book, who contributed products, technical notes, and expertise.

Of course, for any omissions or inconsistencies in the book, we take full responsibility.

Contents

PREFACE

With *Color Publishing on the Macintosh,* we at Random House Electronic Publishing are offering you the *best* information available, in a form that brings you benefits not only at the first reading, but time and time again as you use the supplied software and consult the book as a reference.

We offer the best answers from the most knowledgeable authors, Sunny and Kim Baker. They've carefully translated their years of pioneering experience into a thoughtful, thorough, and engrossing book, a book designed to spare you all the time and money that newcomers spend when they take their first steps into a developing technology.

First, read the book carefully and follow the easy and gradual paths to successful color publishing; the extensive use of visuals will make new concepts crystal clear. As you go along, feel free to copy the checklists the Bakers have created to help you remember all the little details at key points in the process. Look at the helpful tips and sidebars that give you essential cautions and additional information. Feeling lost as you discuss a project with a printer or service bureau? *The Color Publisher's Glossary* offers a complete reference to the technical terms you'll confront. And the software supplied on the disk gives you a leg up with special Macintosh utilities and the practical experience that comes with using them. As you work with the Bakers at your side, always friendly and supportive, you'll thank them for helping you avoid the potentially expensive pitfalls of the complex but rewarding desktop color publishing experience.

What Kim and Sunny offer you is control over your work: You can translate your ideas into effective, hard-hitting color publications—directly, right at your own Macintosh. But what else makes this book so different?

The answer lies not only in the invaluable content, but in Random House Electronic Publishing's unique presentation. This is a *readable* book, a book that not only contains the answers you need, but presents them in an effective way, reflecting the expertise of the country's leading reference publisher. Note the thoughtful use of a second color to highlight information and help you find the section you're searching for. Need to find something fast? Check out the thorough index at the back. And the book lies flat, so you can set it open by your computer at the page you need. This is a book that invites you to read and refer.

Finally, this book was created by the very methods you'll read about, by people who care about your future in this exciting arena. As fellow pioneers in the world of desktop color publishing, we wish you the best of luck. Read and enjoy.

— Michael Mellin
Publisher
Random House Electronic Publishing

INTRODUCTION

NOW, CREATE COLOR DOCUMENTS RIGHT ON YOUR DESKTOP!

Every major visual communication technology has eventually advanced from black and white to color. Just as in movies and television, where color has become the standard for reproduction, desktop publishing on the Macintosh is now a world of color.

The Mac's WYSIWYG (What You See Is What You Get) capability and sophisticated page layout tools have been extended to handle the manipulation, definition, and production of full-color documents. Desktop designers can now design with color right on the screen, using the same "what if" capabilities they have learned to depend on for type and illustrations. Sophisticated color effects can be created with a click of the mouse. The color and cosmetics of an ad, brochure, product package, catalog, annual report, or direct mail piece can be experimented with and fine-tuned for maximum impact.

While on-screen color is not yet fully accurate, new color standards and calibrators are working toward this goal. With the addition of advanced color separation and image manipulation software, affordable color scanners, improved color printers, and more accurate high-resolution image-setters, color desktop publishing is coming into its own. In fact, color publishing on the Mac has evolved so quickly and become so compelling that daily newspapers, wide-circulation magazines, award-winning design firms, and the creative departments in advertising agencies are abandoning time-tested drafting board techniques and moving full speed into color desktop publishing—without so much as a glance in the rearview mirror. As a result, color desktop publishing on the Mac is becoming the standard, instead of the exception, for professional publishing.

What *Is* Color Desktop Publishing?

You become a color desktop publisher when you produce a job that finishes at a print shop and uses two or more colors of ink. For the purposes of this book (and from a print shop's point of view), black and gray are colors just like orange and red. If you print a document with a dark gray and a light gray, that's color publishing. If, however, you print a document that employs only blue with no other colors, that's single-color publishing and for the purposes of this book, not considered color desktop publishing.

The process of designing and producing single-color or black and white documents is already covered in a variety of well-written books, available at most bookstores. This book covers black and white technology when necessary, as a foundation for understanding and implementing color publishing, but the primary focus is on the production of materials that will print in more than one color.

Color Publishing Has Levels of Complexity

The simplest color publishing project is a document that employs black plus one or two solid (spot) colors. These two- or three-color projects can be developed by relatively inexperienced color publishers working on monochrome Macintoshes. The limited number of colors does not limit the design possibilities—some of the most stunning projects are designed with only two or three colors.

The next level of color publishing complexity involves working with process color, also called four-color process. Process color is required when you want to include full-color photographs and illustrations in your documents. Process color technology (in theory anyway) allows you to specify any color as a mix of dots made up from the process inks: cyan, magenta, yellow, and black.

One of the reasons producing process color documents is complicated is that the colors are made up of dots of various sizes, using only four inks. If these dots change size, the color shifts. This color shift can cause the face of an attractive model to appear too red or greenish and sickly. Fortunately, with care and practice this kind of disaster can be avoided.

The most complex color publishing, typical of elaborate annual reports and brochures, incorporates spot colors in combination with four-color process colors. Additional special treatments such as varnishes and foil-stamping further complicate the production of expensive color pieces. The technology isn't much different than handling process and spot colors on their own, but because of the added number of elements there are more variables to control and a greater possibility that problems will creep in.

Color Separation

When you print color images, the photo or illustration must be broken down into the four process colors so that a lithographic press can print them. This is called *color separation* and can be handled on the Macintosh with special software, on dedicated prepress systems from Scitex and Crosfield, or through conventional means, depending on your quality requirements and experience. If handled conventionally, the separation is completed by a color separation house or a well-equipped print shop.

For now, it is enough to know that the process of color separation results in four pieces of film—one for each of the four process colors—that must align perfectly when printed. Problems may also occur when the dots used to create the colors change in size or shape, or when alignment between film layers is incorrect. Problems can be caused by software, improper color specification, or the incorrect output of film layers. These problems are not inherent in single-color printing because only one piece of film is required. Color separation is the most complex aspect of color publishing, and three chapters in this book (Chapters Seven, Eight, and Nine) are dedicated to various aspects of the separation process.

Another technical aspect of color publishing is the process called *prepress,* which means converting the job to film, ready for plating. Conventionally, this involves stripping the film into assembled masks that are used to create printing plates. Stripping requires expert personnel, steady hands, and specialized equipment. On the Macintosh, most prepress functions can be handled with software, or by processing Mac files on a high-end, dedicated prepress system when large, high-resolution images and complex print treatments are used.

All these issues—choosing colors, color separation, and prepress—are unique to the color publishing world. So even if you are already an expert in using page layout software and producing black and white designs, there's a lot to learn if you want to print your documents in full color.

In-House Color Publishing Saves Time and Money

Color photo reproduction has become possible on the Macintosh within the last couple of years; this fact, coupled with the ability to produce finished publications without sending out for type or color separations, provides complete control over the entire design and production process. Where the color separation of photos and illustrations once required the use of an expensive outside firm or the purchase of a million-dollar piece of equipment, Mac publishers can now, within limits, handle the color production processes directly on the desktop. They can even perform color correction and retouching with the click of a mouse!

For high-quality color reproduction, the Mac's page designs can be directly imported into professional prepress systems. Many magazines, including *Fortune* and *Playboy,* are now produced on Macs connected to high-end prepress systems that cut production time and improve creative control of projects. This reduces or eliminates the time-consuming *stripping* process for getting documents ready to print. As *Macworld* put it in a 1989 article on color publishing, "No more stripping at *Playboy!*"

Best of all, desktop publishing now allows designers to create publications with extensive use of screened colors and fancy typography—options that were cost-prohibitive before the new generation of desktop publishing tools. Designers were once restricted to designing pieces with only a handful of colors because of limited printing budgets—yet by using Mac-based color, a single publication can contain twenty different screened colors at almost no extra cost. Elaborate type treatments, once dependent on the skills of a $100-an-hour type designer or a shop with special camera equipment, can now be completed in seconds right on the desktop by a beginner.

These new color tools and capabilities provide publishers much greater latitude when designing eye-catching ads, brochures, catalogs, annual reports, and direct mail pieces. And, because the charges for expensive outside services for color separation and typesetting are reduced or eliminated, the cost of producing quality publications is also reduced and the turnaround time minimized as well.

It's Not All a Bed of Roses

Today, almost anyone with an eye for aesthetics can sit down in front of a Macintosh and, with a little practice, begin to produce quality color publications. This is not to say that Mac-based color publishing is without its pitfalls. For example, a color image that looks fine on screen may produce surprises in the form of improper color balance and other problems when run out on an imagesetter. Or, a publication may look fine in film, but still cause grief for the print shop because of hard-to-recognize problems such as *dot gain* and *hairline misregistration*. (Ways to find and eliminate these problems will be presented in the book.)

There are a number of other issues that cause problems with Macintosh color desktop publishing, though most of these can be worked around. Improvements to color publishing hardware and software are gradually fixing the glitches. Print shops are also learning about computer-based color publishing and as a result are developing an eye for problems and evolving solutions for dealing with them.

Start Publishing in Color Today!

This book is designed not only to show how to assemble color publications on the Mac, but also to provide a color publishing methodology that allows you to sidestep the most common problems and get the best results from the color publishing process. We'll help you understand the process by explaining each task step by step.

Use this book to learn to take color publications from desktop to print shop with the least amount of time and effort. The book will help you make the best use of the service bureau that does your imaging and the print shop that prints your publications. We'll also show you how to choose the hardware and software tools of the trade and how to select the right service bureau and print shop. If you're an experienced desktop publisher working in black and white, this book will help you advance your present level of publishing expertise to the next logical step—color—naturally.

> ### Tip: There's a Color Publisher's Glossary at the Back
>
> To help you understand color publishing from desktop to print shop, we've included a glossary at the back of the book. If a word or phrase appears that you aren't familiar with, look it up in the glossary for quick help.

Who Should Read This Book?

This book will not teach you how to run a Macintosh computer. It will not teach you the basics of design, nor provide screen-by-screen instructions for operating page layout programs or color painting programs. There are instruction manuals provided by product manufacturers to explain the mechanics of such applications and plenty of books on these topics available at any well-stocked bookstore. Instead, this book provides an explanation of the basics of producing color documents with a Macintosh and taking them into print. It explains the terminology, processes, tools, and production options you will encounter in the world of color publishing on the Mac.

Color Publishing on the Macintosh is intended for people with some black and white desktop publishing experience who want to move into color. It is also for those desktop publishers who have already made the transition to color but are encountering problems. The book provides practical advice on Macintosh color publishing techniques and issues, to fill the gap between information in the manuals and real experience.

This book is also of use to designers, ad agencies, training and documentation groups, and corporate communications departments interested in moving into color publishing on the Macintosh. For them, it will explain the basics of color publishing, introduce the tools of the trade and how to choose them, and show what can be done on the Mac and what can't. And, most importantly, this book demonstrates that sophisticated color publishing is within reach of just about anyone who can afford a Macintosh—and that includes almost everyone.

CHAPTER

I

THE COLOR DESKTOP PUBLISHING PROCESS

"Freedom of the press belongs to those who own one."

—A.J. Leibling

Just three or four years ago, desktop publishing on the Macintosh was primarily a black and white technology. Only a handful of adventurous publishers attempted to employ elaborate color in their desktop designs because of serious limitations in the computer's ability to represent and reproduce color images. Today, one by one, these technical roadblocks are being removed, and color publishing on the Mac is becoming a powerful alternative for producing a variety of full-color publications.

The artful use of color is one of the most effective and powerful tools for getting a publication noticed. Coupled with striking photographs, illustrations, and engaging design elements, color can make ordinary desktop publishing projects come alive. Full-color production is already standard in the desktop publication of magazines, advertising, direct mail pieces, and brochures, so a knowledge of color publishing techniques on the desktop is a must for any designer who plans on replacing the conventional drafting board with the power of a computer.

You Are Here

In this chapter we'll look at the color publishing process and compare Mac-based color publishing with traditional color publishing. The chapter also provides four step-by-step growth paths into color publishing on the Macintosh. By starting with Path One (the easiest) and working up, you will build color publishing skills in a logical sequence, avoiding technological risks that may lead to a catastrophic project failure. Study these paths carefully. Choose the one that best matches your current level of "color expertise," and start enjoying color publishing on the Macintosh.

Conventional Color Publishing versus Mac Color Publishing

Out with the Old...

The process of creating color documents *conventionally* takes a long time because so many steps are involved. In conventional color publishing, type has to be set and corrected several times, and photos and illustrations must be broken down into a format compatible with the printing press. The print shop then spends a couple of weeks assembling the job and readying it for press. Inserted into this lengthy cycle are numerous client revisions, which usually add several additional weeks to the process while the changes are made and incorporated into the film.

A typical four-color brochure project, handled conventionally, takes about a month from completion at the designer's shop to actually reaching press, assuming no serious mistakes were made that required time-consuming corrections. This is added to the time needed to create the job *before* it reached the print shop. A typical (expensive) brochure project we handled for a large microprocessor manufacturer took a total of five months from initiation to finished copies. While some of this time was spent in approval cycles with senior management, even without those delays the project would have required about three months for writing, design, photography, illustration, production, and printing.

Now, due to the advanced color technology available with the Macintosh computer, all aspects of color publishing from simple spot color to color separation and image retouching, can be handled right on the desktop. Most professional-level Mac programs support the Pantone Matching System, a world-wide standard for specifying spot color, allowing a designer in New York to choose a color that a print shop in Japan can match almost exactly.

Powerful color paint programs are also available for the Mac, offering a color palette of up to 16,800,000 colors—more than twice as many hues as a trained human eye can differentiate. And, illustration programs allow almost anyone to produce unique designs using complex typography and easy-to-manipulate curves and shapes.

Best of all, color power on the Mac is available at a moderate price. Ten years ago the equipment and software for computerized color publishing cost millions of dollars and took up a room the size of a small warehouse. Today, the tools to produce adequate color page layouts, complete with photos, charts, illustrations, and type, can be had for less than $6,000. This equipment is small enough to fit comfortably on a desk while still allowing room for standard office paraphernalia.

A combination of affordability and compact size puts the power of color publishing into the hands of just about anyone who wants or needs it. Today, freedom of the color press has become a reality, and most people find color publishing on the Macintosh more fun than work!

There's No Going Back

Because the conventional process takes a long time and results in large bills for design and production time, computer-based color publishing is quickly replacing traditional methods. If clients compare estimates from Macintosh-based designers to those from shops still working on drafting boards, the choice becomes obvious. A Macintosh-based designer can complete the work much faster than one still pasting up type on a drafting table, and the resulting invoice is generally 25 to 60 percent lower.

In with the New!

Today, a complex color brochure job can be accomplished on the desktop in a week or two (barring lengthy approval cycles). Computer-based publishing has introduced an entire generation to graphic design and typography without an intermediate stop at the drafting board. If you are one of the many designers making the transition from board to Mac, you'll experience a new sense of freedom from problems such as crooked paste-ups and three-day waits for type to come back from the typesetter.

Unlike working on a drafting table, where most design experiments must be carried out during the tissue or thumbnail phase, using Mac-based color publishing tools you can perform change after change and still have your original version available through the "Undo" or "Revert" commands. Try different type sizes, faces, and leading right on the screen. Play with different page layouts. Add sophisticated type treatments. Choose alternate color combinations. If an experiment doesn't work out, in seconds you can always go back to where you started.

If you are using a reasonably color-accurate monitor and professional-level software, you can experiment with Pantone colors, screens, and screen tints. Is PMS 404 the right gray or would 417 look better? If you have access to a color printer or color proofing system at a service bureau, you can produce instant comps from the same document that will be used to produce the final, printer-ready output. Good-bye to hours of drawing comps with smelly marker pens!

Illustration becomes easier too. While the color pencils and opaque watercolor paints familiar to all designers aren't at hand, software functions that substitute for these tools are available on the Mac. Variable pressure watercolor brushes, airbrush tools, colored pencil, and even charcoal and pastel, can all be simulated. Effects such as computer-perfect linear gradation of color can be achieved in seconds, and complex curves and polygons can be adjusted as many times as needed. One illustration

Conventional Color Publishing versus Mac-based Publishing

Step	*Conventional Method*	*Mac-based Method*
Copywriting	Copy typed on typewriter. Client changes entered by marking up copy or completely retyping the document.	Copy is entered on the Mac or an IBM-PC compatible. (Most Macs can read both kinds of disks). Client changes are easily made by simple editing of saved document on the computer.
Tissue/ Thumbnails	Designer lays out design ideas on tissue or paper and then copies them over and over to refine layout.	Designer lays out actual publication and then revises it on screen, sometimes saving several different versions to show to client. Thumbnail sketches can be printed directly from most page layout programs.
Typesetting	Type entered by typesetter.	Copy imported into the design automatically by the page layout program.
Comp Produced	Time-consuming process involves drawing the comp using solvent-based markers and pasting down photocopies. Changes are difficult.	Layout is printed on color printer or color proofing system. Changes are easy to make on the Mac.
Illustrations Produced	Illustrator commissioned or a designer may handle the process.	Commissioned illustrator uses computer-based or conventional tools, or designer may handle the process on the Mac.
Photos Produced	Photographs commissioned.	Photographs commissioned, or designer may scan photos on Mac-based scanner.
Mechanical Produced	Laborious assembly of type, color breaks and other elements onto illustration board.	Final layout is output onto film with an imagesetter, ready for the printer.
Halftones/Color Separations	Print shop may handle in house or send out to color separator.	Handled on Mac prior to film output.
Screen Tints/Process Color Breaks	Designer builds layers of rubylith indicating breaks for stripping room.	Handled directly as part of design on screen and output in layers of film automatically.
Stripping	Print shop stripping department burns all tints and assembles mechanical elements into film and then into masks to create plates.	When making optimal use of an imagesetter, stripping is nonexistent. Printer burns plates from film, although a simple mask may still be required. (New technology is allowing plates to be "burned" directly from the imagesetter.)

program, Aldus Freehand, allows up to 99 levels of Undo—so a mistake made hours ago can be easily corrected.

While you may at first miss your hand tools, this feeling gradually fades as the possibilities of desktop design become apparent and the results bear fruit. Your transition is much like the trek that writers began making more than ten years ago—from chattering typewriter to silent, efficient word processor. Even if you try to avoid the transition from drafting board to computer, or intend to mix board-based design with Macintosh publishing, you will eventually spend a greater share of your time on the Mac than at your board.

Introducing Macintosh Color Publishing into Your Work Environment

While the Macintosh is regarded as the standard environment for color desktop publishing because of the number and quality of sophisticated color applications available, introducing a Mac to your work environment requires some thinking and planning. The purchase of a complete Mac color system can seem expensive to the uninitiated, and a number of people inside your company may have to approve the decision before you can proceed. Keep the following traps in mind and deal with them before installing Macs and after they are in operation:

1. The Toy Computer Bias

At its introduction in 1984, the Mac was undeservedly labeled as a computer for crackpots and people who couldn't use a *real* computer (whatever that is). While some of this was justifiable because the first Macs were little more than a whisper of what was to come, today this attitude is totally unjustified, particularly in the area of color publishing. You may need a Mac to produce quality color publications, but because of the "toy computer bias" you may find a 286-clone computer with 640 KB of memory, DOS, and a copy of WordPerfect thrust upon you by a purchasing agent who doesn't know any better. These products have their place, but not as a substitute for Mac color.

Deal with this by documenting your case for a Mac purchase. First, document pricing information. The prejudice that a Mac costs more than a DOS machine doesn't hold up once you start talking about a machine with a large color monitor, networking capabilities, and advanced graphics software. Second, call local service bureaus and get quotes from them on their opinions regarding graphics on the two platforms. (Only a small percentage of service bureaus support color publishing on other computer platforms, so the comments will be mostly pro-Mac.) Third, take the decision maker to a store that handles both DOS/Windows machines and Macs and demonstrate the difference between them.

2. Color Mac Overload

The introduction of a color Macintosh into many company environments is a much-ballyhooed event. Everyone will want to take a turn with the new computer to see the great on-screen graphics and play with sounds like the Wild Eep. Since many companies are largely equipped with DOS/Windows machines, the quality and consistency of the Mac's output will seem superior for the majority of graphic applications, and you may find all the work of a visual nature coming your way, everything from annual reports to Christmas party invitations.

Deal with this problem by developing a system for approving the projects in advance. You or your boss, if you have one, should decide what work will be done on your Mac and what won't. Consider using the demand for Mac-based projects as an opportunity to justify additional Macs and software.

3. More than You Can Chew

Since the Mac is known as a powerful platform for graphics and color publishing, you may get pushed into producing complex color projects before you have the experience/equipment that you need to be successful. Pressure to produce more than you can handle may be justified by your bosses because of the large amount of money spent on the equipment and software. People mistakenly believe the system should start producing a return on investment from Day One.

Manage this problem by putting together a written plan for taking on projects in a logical sequence. Start out with easy ones and move forward in complexity over time. Next to each project list the skills you will acquire during the project. When you demonstrate that you must acquire training and experience and are quite willing to do so, your managers and co-workers will (hopefully) realize that it takes time to fully understand and use the power of the new machine. A second tactic is to acquire software and peripheral equipment only as you need it. If you haven't purchased a sophisticated illustration program, such as Adobe Illustrator, no one can expect you to produce elaborate color illustrations.

4. Cutting Corners

A common mistake made by companies purchasing computers for color work is the assumption that cutting corners in order to buy more Macs is better than purchasing one or two full-powered systems. While it's true that color publishing can be done on a black and white Mac with a 9" screen—it's extremely difficult. Color painting can be accomplished on a Mac capable of only 256 colors, but when separations are produced the results may be less than satisfactory. Large, two-page layouts can be handled on a 13" monitor, but it takes more time and effort to get elements to balance properly and it's frustrating to spend time scrolling around the screen instead of designing.

Solve this problem by purchasing professional-quality products and systems. Yes, a 19" monitor with a fast 24-bit color card that does 16.8 million colors is expensive, but in order to get professional results, you need to be able to see what you are doing. If you must cut corners, buy the system in pieces as you can afford them, instead of purchasing inferior or limited tools that will only lead to frustration. Since color publishing work often entails tight deadlines, compromise equipment inevitably slows throughput and increases the possibility of making time-consuming, costly mistakes.

Get Started in Color Publishing the Right Way—Slowly

While it's theoretically possible to take on a 40-page, eight-color annual report with 70 charts and photos and produce reliable output with little color publishing experience, chances are that the project will run into serious problems right from the start. Mistakes in color publishing are expensive, because the printer's bill will still have to be paid if an undetected problem makes it into print. The film output alone costs fifteen to twenty dollars per color, per page. If a mistake in the film is made by you and not the service bureau running the job, the film is yours and so is the bill.

If you're lucky, the mistakes may be detected by an eagle-eyed print shop employee, but it may cost so much to fix them that the price/speed advantage of color publishing goes out the window.

Use This Book to Build Your Skills

Like learning to drive a car, the best way to learn to produce color publications is to start out slowly and build knowledge and experience. Your first driving lesson probably wasn't held on a busy freeway. By analogy, don't take on a six-color project, with complex registration and extensive use of color photos, for your first desktop color publishing project. Instead, take on simple projects at first and gradually build your expertise and confidence with each software product. There are a number of color publishing traps that novice publishers can fall into unwittingly; the best way to avoid these problems is to start slowly and gradually increase the complexity of projects as experience is acquired. Let others blaze the trails while you build a steady path to your long-term color publishing goals.

By starting off slowly with relatively simple color projects created without tight deadlines, you'll quickly pick up the experience necessary to tackle more complicated jobs. Never take on a multi-color, rush project that requires you to use untested, untried technology. If the rush project hits a technological brick wall, you'll be forced to waste time and money recreating it from scratch using conventional methods.

Tip: When in Doubt, Ask!

In the world of color printing, terminology is bantered around by just about everyone. When you start adding computer jargon to design and printing lingo, the mix can be downright intimidating. Don't just pretend to understand, because you may find yourself agreeing to a process, change, or specification that you may regret later. One of the best ways to cut through jargon is to ask for an explanation of every phrase. Ask enough times and the purveyors of technical or cryptic language will stop using it in your presence. In the meantime, you'll learn the meanings and can yourself begin bantering the terminology around.

If you have the opportunity to work with experienced color publishers, question them on their methods and ask them to review your projects for potential problems. Another useful source of advice is your service bureau. Service bureaus are companies that take your page layout file and output it on a high-resolution printer called an imagesetter (see Chapter Ten for more information on this topic). Any worthwhile service bureau will have one or more Macintosh color publishing gurus who will make an effort to answer your questions and give you credible advice. Because service bureau personnel work daily with color publishing programs and problems, they are often an excellent source of practical expertise.

The Four Paths to Color Desktop Publishing

Depending on your experience in desktop design, the sophistication of your Macintosh publishing system, and the budget available for your projects, you may take on all or only part of the color publishing steps, leaving the really technical aspects of the color separation and production to your printer, service bureau, or color separation house. There are four paths to color publishing available to you:

- The *first path* is for novice color publishers or those using monochrome Macintosh systems to produce simple color documents.
- The *second path* is oriented towards more experienced color publishers (working on Macs with color monitors), who do not want to tackle the complexities of desktop color separation.
- The *third path* is for users planning to have their Mac documents processed on a high-end prepress system.
- The *fourth path* is for the experienced publisher capable of handling the entire process from start to finish, including color separation on the desktop.

While the Mac is becoming increasingly capable of producing high-quality color separations, the knowledge and equipment to handle such tasks is beyond the scope of all but the most experienced and best-equipped Macintosh color publishing professionals. Thus, most color publishers will begin at levels one or two to produce quality documents with predictable results.

Work up through the Levels as You Acquire Experience

Instead of trying to tackle complicated color publications with no color publishing experience, start by producing Path One publications and work up. The purpose of explaining these four paths is to provide you with a roadmap to follow to learn Macintosh-based color publishing. Once you are regularly achieving expected results using Path One procedures, jump to the next level and begin learning the new processes. By working through the paths gradually, you'll master the trade and will discover how to avoid the alligator traps that await the unwary.

Path One: Create Black and White Layouts

At this level, you create a piece by using a page layout program in black and white. Boxes are used to indicate where black and white and color

Color Publishing on the Mac - Start Simple and Build Your Skills

Your Level of Experience	Project Complexity	Kinds of Projects	Goals and Objectives
You are new to color publishing, but have at least some experience with laying out pages on the desktop.	Use spot colors for your first color documents. Limit the number of colors to three or less to keep things simple.	Take on small, simple ads, mailers, or brochures. Make sure the schedule is loose so you can fix problems conventionally if necessary.	Learn how to specify color, how to apply it to objects, and consider applying your own traps as explained in Chapter Seven. Have all color images handled by your print shop. Move up to the next level of complexity after two or three successful projects.
You have experience specifying spot color from the desktop.	Begin adding screen color to your work. Limit the number of colors.	Continue with small, simple ads, mailers, or brochures.	Learn how screen colors are used and study the color results you achieve on press. Move up a level when you are capable of achieving predictable screen color every time you apply it.
You have experience handling both spot and screen color from the desktop.	Design color illustrations with Illustrator or Freehand and begin including them in your color projects.	Attempt full-size ads, brochures, and other full-color print projects.	Learn how to create illustrations within Freehand or Illustrator. Use both spot and screen color where appropriate and add trapping. Move up a level once you have achieved consistent results in several publications.
You have experience with both kinds of color and know how to assemble and color separate color illustrations.	Begin using scanned and paint-type images in your publications. Color separate them on the desktop.	After running tests with proofs to test your skills (and your service bureau's), attempt full-size ads, brochures and other print projects. At first, take on projects without tight deadlines.	The most complex element in color publishing is the scanning and separating of color images. This requires patience on your part to learn how to treat each image. Learn color separation by scanning and separating small images and have color proofs made to see how things look. Once you become adept at the mechanics of separation, you've joined the élite group of color publishers working entirely on the Mac!

images will be added into the document by the print shop. This is a great way to learn the basics of assembling a color job with none of the risks.

The pros and cons of this approach are:

Pros

- Is easy and requires a minimal knowledge of color publishing on the desktop
- Can be accomplished with a minimum of color publishing software and other tools
- Can be readily accomplished using a monochrome Macintosh.

Cons

- Costs more, because it requires substantial work on the part of the print shop and color separation house
- Doesn't allow you to take advantage of desktop-generated special effects and screen tint colors, which can be produced at a fraction of the price of having your print shop do it.

Path Two: Create a Color Layout with Photos and Illustrations Scanned for Placement

At this level you create a piece by using a color page layout program that allows you to specify individual colors, handle the black and white photos, and design all aspects of the job. Color photos and illustrations can be scanned in for placement. However, color separations are handled conventionally.

The pros and cons of this approach are:

Pros

- Relatively easy for simple color projects
- Cuts the time from desktop to print because less work is required on the part of the print shop. This results in cost savings as well.
- Allows you take advantage of most of color desktop publishing's inexpensive special effects and screen tint color.

Cons

- May produce surprises at the service bureau for the novice color publisher trying out new effects and software tools. However, the right service bureau can help you solve most of these problems.
- Requires the use of reliable page layout software to take full advantage of special treatments and prevent surprises at the service bureau and print shop.

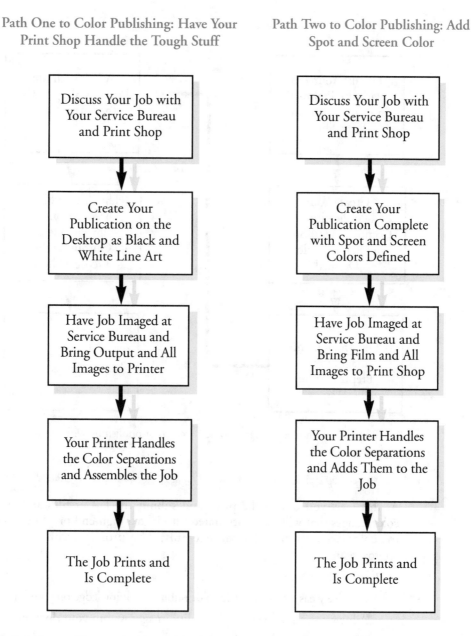

Path One to Color Publishing: Have Your Print Shop Handle the Tough Stuff

Path Two to Color Publishing: Add Spot and Screen Color

Path One:

Discuss Your Job with Your Service Bureau and Print Shop

↓

Create Your Publication on the Desktop as Black and White Line Art

↓

Have Job Imaged at Service Bureau and Bring Output and All Images to Printer

↓

Your Printer Handles the Color Separations and Assembles the Job

↓

The Job Prints and Is Complete

Path Two:

Discuss Your Job with Your Service Bureau and Print Shop

↓

Create Your Publication Complete with Spot and Screen Colors Defined

↓

Have Job Imaged at Service Bureau and Bring Film and All Images to Print Shop

↓

Your Printer Handles the Color Separations and Adds Them to the Job

↓

The Job Prints and Is Complete

If you're new to color publishing, follow Path One to explore the basics. Path Two lets you familiarize yourself with spot and screen color in page layouts.

Path Three to Color Publishing: Connecting to a Prepress System

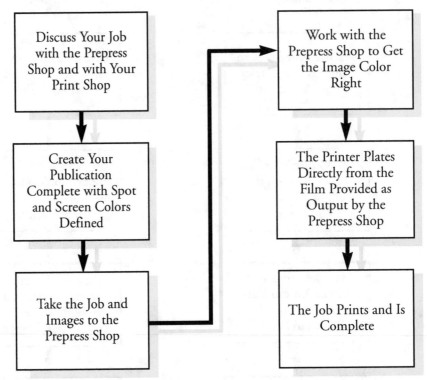

Path Three shows how to integrate Mac-based color publishing with high-end prepress systems.

Path Three: Hand the Desktop Design over to a High-end Prepress System for Color Separation

At this level you design the piece and submit the layout files and any color images that will be incorporated into it to a high-end prepress shop for color separation and final assembly. The pros and cons of this approach are:

Pros

- Relatively easy, requires little color publishing knowledge on your part
- Allows you to use very high-quality images within your document
- Eliminates most surprises because the prepress system operator knows how to assemble your work and fix any problems. In addition, color separations are produced with predictable results. The quality of the separations will be a level above those produced by all but the most experienced Mac users.

Cons

- High-end prepress time is expensive, although when used properly, quite cost effective.

- May slow down your job because you must work to the prepress shop's schedule and wait for the shop to get around to your project—unless you are willing to pay rush charges (potentially *very* expensive).

Path Four: Handle the Entire Job Yourself, Including the Color Separations

At this level you create a piece using a page layout program and handle your own color separations using Macintosh programs designed for this

Path Four to Color Publishing: Handling Your Own Color Separations

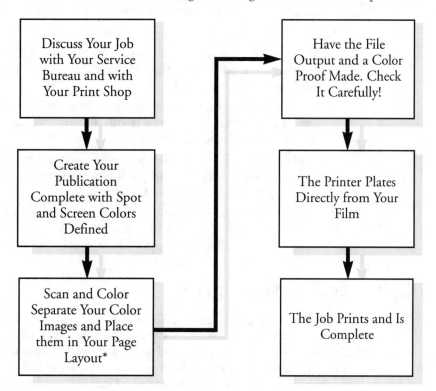

If your program has a color separation module, separations are made after the layout is assembled.

As you hone your color publishing skills, you may want to handle the entire color publishing project from the desktop. This chart of Path Four shows the steps for complete color document creation on the desktop.

purpose. You scan and correct images before they are color separated, just like the high-end prepress systems do. (You may have someone with a quality scanner scan the image but you generate the color separations.) After the film is imaged on the imagesetter, the finished job is ready for the printer to create press plates.

The pros and cons of this approach are:

Pros

- Provides complete control over the entire project from the desktop to the print shop

- Cuts the time from desktop to print because less work is required on the part of the print shop. This results in significant cost savings as well.

- Allows you take advantage of all of color desktop publishing's special effects, screen tint color, and photo-retouching capabilities.

Cons

- May produce surprises at the service bureau for all but the most experienced desktop publishers. However, the right service bureau can help you solve the problems.

- Requires the use of a well-equipped Macintosh color publishing system and sophisticated page layout and color separation software—these tools are relatively expensive.

- For best results this should be attempted through a print shop that is familiar with color desktop publishing issues and will take the time to check the work for trouble spots.

- If your job arrives at the printer's shop full of problems and they (hopefully) catch the errors, the charges for ACs (author's corrections) may outweigh the savings of desktop color publishing.

The Color Desktop Publishing Process

Because of the expense of producing and printing a color document, it's important to treat color publishing projects with the care and respect they deserve. Murphy's Law is alive and well when you produce color jobs of any kind, whether on the desktop or through conventional means. That means keeping a weather eye on projects to identify mistakes and potential problems before they make it into print. Treat the creation of color publications as a process that follows an established series of steps, rather than just throwing something together on a Mac and hoping the service bureau and printer will sort out and fix any problems.

Quality Levels in Process Color Separation

When you read this book you will run across several vague terms describing printing quality. These terms are vague because in the world of color publishing there is a considerable range in project quality. For example, you can print a brochure on a four-color press, using Mac-produced separations from uncorrected scans, on expensive dull-coated paper and call it high quality, even though the results may look horrendous. The resulting printing bill will be the same as that for a truly high-quality brochure printed with the finest separations. To clarify the topic somewhat, here are definitions of commonly used terms:

- **Newsprint Quality** This is the easiest of color publishing because of its relatively low resolution. The emphasis within newspaper publishing is on low cost and fast production. Newspapers are printed at low resolution on a very absorbent paper that stretches considerably as it speeds through the press. Because of these limitations, color separations that wind up on newsprint aren't that critical, because they invariably print out of register and fine detail is lost. So, when printing at low resolutions, great detail and clarity are actually negatives, because too much information simply comes out murky in print. Color isn't critical either—problems such as yellow casts become irrelevant on paper that's already yellow anyway.

- **Magazine Quality** The next level up in quality is magazine quality. While some magazines use high-resolution printing, the majority are printed at around 133 lpi (a medium line-per-inch resolution). Most magazines are printed on smooth uncoated or coated paper, so color becomes more critical and detail can be accurately reproduced. With practice, adequate color separations for this level are possible on the Macintosh by the average publisher willing to learn the trade.

- **High Quality** This level of publishing is the most difficult, yielding separations and print quality found in the finest magazines, annual reports, and brochures. With screen resolutions at 200 lpi or higher, this kind of printing invariably shows off separation flaws originating from anything less than the best quality scans and impeccable separations. To attain this level of quality requires an intimate knowledge of printing and color separation, and very high-end Macintosh equipment. Plus, it helps if you don't mind waiting around for images to process, because the higher the resolution, the more time it takes to get the film.

The process of creating a color publication varies little from document to document, although complex projects obviously take longer and may employ more tasks than a simple project. Here are the steps that most color publishing projects go through on their way to print. Most are discussed in greater detail in the following chapters, but the basics are as follows:

1. The Project Is Defined

Project definition involves specifying objectives for the piece as well as describing the physical format of the printed document, developing a timeline for completing it, and estimating a budget. A more detailed explanation of the steps at this stage follows.

> **Tip: Use Your Service Bureau's Knowledge to Build Your Skills**
>
> If you're new to color publishing but can't wait to tackle complicated color projects, consider learning the ropes by watching a pro in action. Depending on the project and the technical expertise of your service bureau, you can have your SB handle the complex aspects of the project for you, including the scanning and color separation of photographs. While this may not save you any money over conventional methods (most bureaus charge by the hour for such services), if you ask, they may let you watch the process and be willing to answer your questions while they work. This is about as close to a free color publishing education as you'll ever get!
>
> If this sounds appealing, try to find a bureau that will cooperate with you and doesn't mind your presence in their work room. A really large, busy service bureau is probably the wrong choice for such an exercise. Instead, look for a small but very experienced shop that regularly handles color projects.

A. Define the Format

The format definition involves specifying the size of the document, the color treatments that will be used, and the number of photos and illustrations to be included. Is the piece a two-color, eight-page brochure or a one-page, four-color ad? In addition, specify whether any special print

Creating Color Documents Step-by-Step

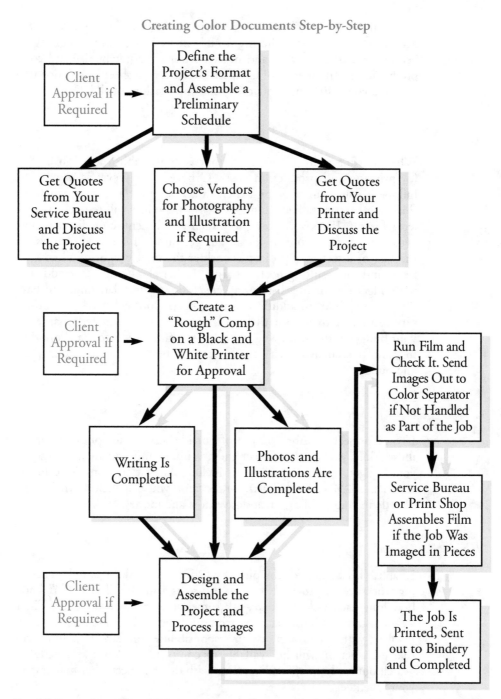

In addition to the color publishing steps carried out on the desktop, most projects follow a series of steps similar to those used in the conventional publishing process.

treatments such as foil stamping or die-cutting will be required. If the project is an ad, select the media it will run in before designing it, because various magazines and newspapers have different size and color production requirements. In Chapter Twelve a worksheet is included that will help you define the format for color publications of all kinds.

B. Get Price Quotes

When starting a document, it's important to establish a rough budget for printing and production costs. Otherwise, whoever is paying the bill, be it you, your boss, or a client, may be in for a surprise when the final numbers are tallied. In many cases the budget will restrict the project's format. If it's a printed piece such as a brochure or direct mailer, get quotes for printing. If it's an ad, get quotes for media charges. In the case of direct mail projects, consider the total weight of all components and the resulting postal charges. Other charges must be added to the budget for mailing list rental, envelope stuffing, labeling, and handling, if required. In addition to these costs, you will need to choose a service bureau to output film and include their estimated charges in your budget. After reviewing your options and quotes for media, printing, and miscellaneous services, choose the best vendors for your needs and budget.

C. Select Outside Creative Vendors If Needed

If your project requires the use of outside services for photography or illustration, you need to select these vendors and add their charges to your budget. If your requirements include illustration, consider using an experienced Mac-based illustrator, because you can include their work directly in your publication and save time and money.

D. Schedule the Project

Establish a schedule for the piece by listing each task. A sample scheduling worksheet is provided for you to use as a model. If you don't know how long each task will take, ask someone who has experience. Then, assign a start and finish date to each task. If more than one person will be involved with the project, assign responsibilities for each task and verify that each person will be available to complete the work as scheduled. Watch out for holidays and conflicts with other projects that may impact your schedule.

Project Scheduling Worksheet				
Task Name	*Duration*	*Start Date*	*Finish Date*	*Person(s) Responsible*

2. Create a Comp for Approval

Depending on the project and the required approvals, you may want to design a "rough" version of the piece with your page layout program, using horizontal lines or old word processing files to designate where the copy will go. This is called a *comp* (for comprehensive) and gives a client a rough idea of what the finished piece will look like. If you have access to a color printer, computer-produced comps can be made to look very much like a finished document. Best of all, unlike drafting board design where the comp is a project in itself, the work you put into creating a comp on the computer can be used as the template for the finished piece.

3. Write and Design the Piece

Sometimes a writer will be used to develop the headlines, body copy, and captions for photos and illustrations, while you design the piece on the Mac. Although historically the design and writing have been separate tasks accomplished by two or more people, many desktop publishers now double as both designer and writer and add their copy as they lay out the document. This has significant advantages, because the copy can be written to precisely fit the layout and the layout can be designed to accommodate the copy.

During the design process, the following color publishing steps will be accomplished:

A. Create the final page layout.

B. Specify any spot or custom colors to be used in the document.

C. Scan the photos and illustrations to be incorporated into the design.

D. Incorporate scanned photos and illustrations. If you will be color separating the images on the Macintosh, these scans may need to be modified and manipulated before color separation, using color retouching and image manipulation software. Then they are separated using color separation software. Spot colors are separated when the file is imaged with the imagesetter.

E. If the images are to be separated conventionally, the scans and illustrations are used to establish placement only. These placement-only images will be color separated and incorporated by the print shop later.

F. Integrate final type and design elements.

G. Proof the piece by printing it out on a laser printer or color printer.

H. Make final adjustments to the piece after proofing.

I. Prepare the files for imaging on the imagesetter.

4. Output the Film

After the writing and design are complete and approved, the job files from the Mac go to a service bureau to be run out as film (unless you are fortunate enough to have your own in-house imagesetter). If the images were not separated on the desktop, photos and illustrations must be sent out separately to a color separator (a special company or print shop that will produce the color-separated images using conventional technologies).

5. Assemble the Job for Print

The film is delivered to the printer, or in the case of an ad, it's sent to the publication that in turn sends it to their print shop. The print shop uses the film to create press plates through a process called stripping. The trend in the 1990s is to eliminate stripping by handling the plate production process directly at the service bureau. In the future, the service bureaus (inside print shops) will produce the ready-for-press plates directly from the computer files.

6. Have the Job Printed and Send It to the Bindery

The job is printed and then assembled into its final form, be it brochure, magazine, ad, newspaper, direct mailer, catalog, etc. The color publisher usually attends a press check to verify the colors and printing quality before the entire job is run. After printing, if services such as special trimming (die cutting), unusual binding, or other special treatments are required, the job may go to a shop called a bindery for final assembly. When the assembly of the piece is complete, the job is shipped to you for distribution.

Talk to Your Print Shop

Before beginning any kind of color publishing project, discuss the job with your print shop. Printers know what can and can't be accomplished in print. On your Macintosh it's easy for you to assemble a job that can't be printed. You can specify twenty solid spot colors, design a document for a paper size that wastes half the sheet, or make any one of a hundred other serious (expensive) mistakes. That's why all color work should be discussed up front with a printer. A good printer can explain how the job should be set up, help you match the right paper to it, and provide parameters for dot gain and trapping. (Dot gain and trapping are discussed in Chapters Seven and Nine.)

Producing Color Ads Is a Different Process

Producing ads is slightly different than producing print projects such as catalogs, brochures, and datasheets, because you lose control of production before the ad reaches the print shop. For that reason, extra care must be taken that no mistakes creep into the Macintosh files you create.

Instead of the output from the imagesetter going to a printer's stripping room for conversion into press plates, an ad is produced as film, according to the specifications provided by the media the ad will appear in. Depending on the complexity of the ad, the film will need to be assembled into finished format with the color separations, copy, and other elements already in place. Some publications will do this assembly for you, just like a print shop, but they charge for this service, and the results may be substandard or incorrect. For this reason, you are better off having the assembly done locally where you can keep an eye on it.

Provide whoever will output the job with the publication's specifications so that they use the right resolution for the photos. For the assembly, have either your service bureau, a properly-equipped print shop, or a color separation house handle this for you. Again, make sure you provide them with the publication's technical specifications before they start the job. If your ad will run in more than one place, provide the specs for each magazine or newspaper, because adjustments may need to be made to the film to accommodate different page sizes and print specifications. You will also need multiple copies of the film— one for each publication—unless the specs are identical and there's time to ship the film from place to place.

Once the film is created, you will want to see a proof of the job to ensure that everything is correctly assembled and appropriately color balanced. Have two copies of the proof made, one for you to inspect (and keep), and one to be sent along with the job so that the publication's print shop can match the color.

The best way to initiate this discussion is to assemble a small sketch of each page. Show how many photos will be used, specify how many colors are desired, and specify any large solid areas of color in the design. Review this with your printer and ask his advice. At this point you should discuss paper as well. This same sketch and the specifications can be used by your print shop to produce a quote for the job. By involving a print shop up front in your project, it will go smoother and you can use expert advice to create a printable job at the right price.

Talk to Your Service Bureau

Along with being unprintable, some jobs can't be run out at a service bureau because of incorrect or ungainly specifications. While you'll get a better understanding of this topic as you read the book, show the same sketch you took to the print shop to your service bureau. In addition to going over the sketch, bring in a list of software and fonts you plan to use and discuss the schedule.

This is important, because while your page layout program will allow you to place an 11" by 17" color separation, a service bureau will look at your sketch and tell you to have it separated conventionally because they can't or won't handle it. So, to avoid wasting your time assembling a layout that can't be imaged, review the project with your service bureau before starting work—particularly if the job is complicated or incorporates process color separations.

What Macintosh Color Desktop Publishing Can't Do (Yet)

Almost anything possible on a drafting board or in the stripping room of a well-equipped print shop is possible on a Macintosh with the right software and peripherals. Still, the very high end of the publishing scale—where large, high-resolution photos are common—is out of reach to all but the best-equipped and most knowledgeable color desktop publishers. The following limitations are based in technology and budgets and will likely disappear as technologies improve.

- **Storage Limitations** Large images take up huge amounts of disk space, even when stored using compression systems that shrink file sizes.
- **Computer Speed Barriers** Processing large, high-resolution images eats CPU time and ties up expensive imagesetter time during output. (Most service bureaus charge by the minute after a set

amount of time has elapsed for imaging. See Chapter Ten for more details.)

- **Scanner Limitations** The scanning equipment required for capturing and saving high-quality color images is very expensive, although time on high-quality scanners can be rented at a service bureau that has such equipment at its disposal. Less expensive scanners produce images too murky for use in high-quality publishing without time-consuming image correction.

- **Color Accuracy Problems** If an image is important enough to print at high resolution, color balance and accuracy are also critical. To produce quality color designs, a monitor with near-perfect color accuracy is required, but unfortunately such a beast does not yet exist. While current calibration tools partially fix this problem, the perfect color monitor has not yet arrived.

- **Imagesetter Limitations** To achieve truly accurate color, the imagesetter must be perfectly calibrated to a degree that few service bureaus bother to attempt. The machine must also be a recent, top-of-the-line model, because older equipment inherently lacks the precision and resolution necessary for accurate color and proper screen angles. In addition to this problem, the RIP processors that convert the Mac's output into a format for imaging are too slow for really large jobs.

On the bright side, many of these problems are being addressed with improvements to Macintosh color technology, and the Mac itself is gaining in processing power with each new model. The problems of desktop color publishing can be worked around by using conventional methods to process large high-resolution images, using smaller image sizes, or enhancing scans through programs such as Photoshop, Cachet, or ColorStudio. And, as mentioned earlier, color publishing projects initiated on the Macintosh can now be exported to professional prepress environments such as the Crosfield and Scitex systems. These systems are fully capable of scanning, manipulating, and storing large, high-resolution images of all kinds.

Outside of these limitations, there are few other aspects of color publishing that can't be achieved with the Macintosh. While specific capabilities differ between software packages, popular page layout programs such as QuarkXPress and PageMaker can be used for almost any kind of publishing—from creating dazzling color posters, to complete books (with photos and illustrations), to six-color brochures. Also coming to market are special-purpose packages that fulfill special color publishing needs. For example, Posterworks is capable of creating billboard-sized ads, and

Desktop Packaging Plus can be used to create color product packaging in complex shapes and sizes.

Tip: The Size Barrier

While there is no hard ceiling to any aspect of Mac color publishing, unless you're a high-end publisher (see Chapter Thirteen), you will probably run into a practical size barrier when attempting to process color images that take up more than 30 megabytes on disk. Images this large choke imagesetters and result in such monstrous bills—for overtime charges and rerunning defective film—that conventional separations may be cheaper and easier. Depending on the model and configuration of the Mac driving the imagesetter, the imagesetter's capabilities, memory capacity, and a number of other factors, running giant files may crash the system, produce poor quality images, or result in unusable output.

Can this limit be worked around? Yes, most likely, but these monster files are better handled by high-end prepress systems (also described in Chapter Thirteen). Using a professional system is expensive and probably means yet another stop on the way to the print shop. However, using a system designed to handle giant files will not only give you better results, but will ultimately save you money because the file won't need to be run more than once to get usable film.

In this chapter you have learned how to get into color desktop publishing by taking it slow and acquiring experience gradually as more complicated projects are addressed. You have also been introduced to the process of color desktop publishing and the steps required to bring a project from concept to print, be it an ad, brochure, catalog, mailer, or datasheet.

In the next two chapters we'll show you how to choose the hardware and software tools for effective color publishing. If you already own a complete color set-up with software tools, skip to Chapter Four, where we start getting into the mechanics of color publishing. Keep Chapters Two and Three in mind, however, and refer to them when the need for a new tool arises.

CHAPTER
2

CHOOSING THE HARDWARE TOOLS OF THE PUBLISHING TRADE

"The buyer needs a hundred eyes, the seller not one."
— George Herbert

One reason that color publishing on the Macintosh is improving and expanding rapidly is the wide variety of hardware and software available for high-quality color design. This makes the Mac publishing market very competitive, with manufacturers adding new functionality to products and holding down prices in order to attract and keep customers. Unfortunately, the sheer number of products can be daunting to the novice publisher, who must choose equipment and software amid conflicting claims and outright misrepresentations. The lack of product knowledge of many computer salespeople further complicates the problem. In order to choose the right tools, you need to do a little research on your own, rather than relying on the recommendations of people who have never used color publishing tools outside of a five-minute sales demo. Use this chapter and Chapter Three's advice to choose a system that's just right for your color publishing requirements, budget, and work habits.

You Are Here

In this chapter, we present the issues you should be concerned with when evaluating color publishing hardware, including the Mac itself, scanners, and printers. It will help turn you into a David Horowitz of color publishing, capable of evaluating the right hardware for your color publishing needs. If you already have a complete color Macintosh with all required peripherals, skip to either Chapter Three to learn about purchasing software, or to Chapter Four if you are already familiar with the software options.

Buy One Piece at a Time to Test Quality and Compatibility

Rome wasn't built in a day, and a color Macintosh publishing system shouldn't be either. When purchasing a Mac system and software for color publishing, buy it a piece at a time whenever possible. That way you can evaluate the merits of each new item and test it carefully to see if it works as claimed and integrates smoothly with the rest of your system. Because the best color publishing tools are invariably expensive, building a complete system with a large color monitor is not a purchase to be taken lightly. In addition, the prices of color publishing products are falling and, at the same time, their capabilities are improving; so waiting a few months to buy a new color scanner or an accelerated 24-bit color board may allow you to purchase a superior product at a lower price.

Finger-pointing is another problem to be dealt with when purchasing color publishing products. The manufacturer of a product that appears to be giving you problems will inevitably blame the problem on another company's product, thereby absolving the company of responsibility. If you buy components one at a time, it is easier to identify the real culprit.

Consider purchasing hardware and software from a store or mail order house that gives you at least a week to test the product before losing your return privileges. Test each item from start to finish and put it through all of its paces. If a product will be used to take publications through to print, take a sample project through to the proofing stage to see if it produces results as expected. (See Chapter Ten for information on color proofing systems.)

If a purchase is unusually expensive, such as a high-resolution scanner or a pricey product employing new technology—then further research is necessary before signing on the dotted line. If possible, use the product at the dealer's or manufacturer's site and test it thoroughly. Then, if you like what you see, get the names of at least three users and call them for a recommendation. Take any comments other than a glowing tribute to mean that the product is either not as useful as anticipated or has untoward problems.

Another factor when purchasing professional-quality equipment for color publishing is that it's often more difficult to install and use than less expensive gear. Many professional products are designed for very experienced users and come equipped with brief or cryptic manuals and user-hostile software that circumvents the Mac's friendly user interface. For example, installing an inexpensive color scanner designed for the casual user is a simple matter of connecting a plug and a cable to your system and dumping a software file into the Mac's system folder. Installing a professional scanner may require the manufacturer to send out an installation team to set up and calibrate the hardware. Then, a board must be added to your Mac and a number of oddly-named files scattered through the System Folder to make the scanner run.

Don't Rely Solely on Magazine Reviews for Purchase Decisions

One of the best sources of information on new releases of color DTP products is found in the Macintosh-oriented magazines. These reviews cover a wide range of products, and most of these magazines have either a regular feature dedicated to some aspect of publishing or run special issues on the topic on a regular basis. These reviews are important tools for identifying useful new products because the reviewers report how well each product performs, how well it stacks up against the competition, and any problems encountered in testing.

Unfortunately, some reviewers are more thorough than others. Many of them don't take output from tested products through to print before writing a review. For example, one page layout package (Ready-Set-Go) received adequate reviews, but in our experience in 1988 with versions 4.0 and 4.5, the program didn't produce reliable results when run out at a service bureau. Instead, it typically failed to image one or more elements and arbitrarily shifted type. Several years of magazine write-ups failed to disclose these serious shortcomings.

Professional Desktop Publishing Products and You

When choosing products for color desktop publishing, it's tempting to take the less expensive route wherever possible. Unfortunately, with the exception of a few programs and hardware tools that are legitimate bargains, taking the inexpensive route can lead to disaster.

You can purchase a 400 dot-per-inch hand-held color scanner for a fraction of the price of a transparency-capable scanner; however, even with steady hands, it will be difficult, if not impossible, to get adequate image quality from it. For color publishing you should use professional-quality tools and avoid the temptation to purchase something that's "almost as good as the real thing."

Who Ya Gonna Call?

When evaluating color publishing products, consider warranty and service availability, particularly when purchasing equipment such as a 21" color monitor that weighs close to a hundred pounds. If it dies, even within warranty, you'll have a monster shipping bill, a sore back, and possibly a long wait if the service center is located in a distant city.

Also consider the technical support. Is it free, or does it only last 90 days unless you pay an annual fee? (Companies selling expensive items such as imagesetters and high-resolution scanners may charge significant fees for a support and service contract, but in the case of a device that costs $50,000 to purchase and requires regular maintenance, this may actually be a bargain.)

Look for support on a toll-free phone number. This may save big bucks on your phone bill, because many hardware and software companies have installed "windbag" phone answering equipment. Some of these systems try to shunt you through a nearly useless automated support system with canned replies before providing access to a live body. Ask associates who already use the product not only about how well it worked, but whether or not the technical support people were accessible, helpful and courteous, or hard to reach, inept, and indifferent.

Study the product's manuals before you buy. Almost every computer product comes with one or more lengthy manuals, and since these are your first line of defense when learning a new product or attempting to find out what a *"– 43 Print Driver Error"* is, they should be well-organized, complete, and to the point. Any manual (except tutorial books) over 25 pages should have both a table of contents and a credible index.

Tip: Product Registration Cards

Though it's officially against most software manufacturers' policies, many hardware and software products *can* be returned for credit, refunds, or exchanges within a short time after purchase. When testing a new product, don't return the registration or warranty card until you are satisfied with it. A product that hasn't been registered can often be returned if it doesn't meet your needs. Once the card is mailed, however, the product is usually yours for keeps. *Do* return the warranty or registration card as soon as you decide to keep a product. These cards are important because many companies use them to mail you update notices, free bug fix releases, and company newsletters. Your registration record is also used to notify you if problems or safety issues are discovered with a hardware product. (And you *do* want to hear about those!)

When purchasing a product, either through mail order or from a store you know little about, use a credit card whenever possible to order products. That way if the merchandise doesn't turn up or proves unworkable, you have at least the credit card company to complain to in an attempt to adjust your bill. Before taking the mail order route, keep in mind that while it may cost more to purchase from a local computer dealer, it's a good feeling to have someone to call when you encounter a problem— particularly if the trouble involves hardware. While many mail order companies claim to provide technical support on the products they sell, their idea of technical support and your idea of technical support may differ markedly.

Color Publishing Technology as an Investment

When purchasing technology of almost any kind—from consumer electronics to color publishing equipment—it's important to buy only what you really need. While a car purchased today will, if properly maintained, be worth at least ten percent of its original purchase price ten years down the road, today's hot new color hardware product becomes tomorrow's boat anchor or high-tech paperweight in as little as four years. And, software has virtually no resale value once it leaves the store or arrives in the mail.

Because the technology is evolving so fast, consider the direct return on investment instead of the item's asset value before purchasing computer equipment and software. For example, if you purchase a $15,000 Mac system, how long will it be before it pays for itself? This should be stated as a tangible benefit such as "it will produce $150,000 worth of advertising art within two years," or "it will save $30,000 in production costs over conventional methods within six months."

While color publishing equipment may have tangible value if sold two years from the date of purchase, in five to eight years it will be mostly obsolete—as are the Mac 128K, the Fat Mac, the 512KE, and the dinosaur. Because professional color publishing requires a substantial investment in systems that will likely become outmoded, always buy tools that will be of immediate use rather than ones to "grow into." (Avoid the opposite mistake of purchasing a system that's wholly inadequate and needs immediate upgrading or replacement.) And, whenever possible, spend a little more to purchase today's hot new model rather than getting a discount on last year's close-out.

Always try to choose technology with a growth path. For example, where the once-popular Mac Plus has little future for the color desktop publisher, the original Mac II series computers continue to be upgradeable to near-current standards. This goes for software as well. Mainstream software is usually upgraded on a regular basis by its manufacturer, whereas small market, garage-based products may be discontinued.

By carefully selecting equipment that has a bright future, you will get the best value for your money and avoid the technology quagmire common to these kinds of investments. It will also provide you with the tools appropriate for your level of experience and needs, thereby maximizing productivity while minimizing cash outlay—the best situation when buying tools that decline rapidly in resale value.

The Standard Components of a Color Desktop Publishing System

There are three basic components to any color publishing system—the computer system itself, the software you use to design publications, and the imagesetter system used to image and output your film to take to the print shop. You may not own all of the individual parts of the color publishing system, but these are the tools used to get your document to print. In the case of the imagesetter, most color publishers rent time on a service bureau's system rather than buying or leasing this expensive and quirky equipment themselves.

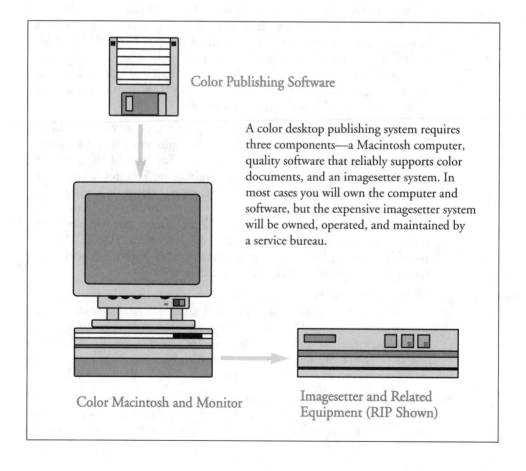

Color Publishing Software

A color desktop publishing system requires three components—a Macintosh computer, quality software that reliably supports color documents, and an imagesetter system. In most cases you will own the computer and software, but the expensive imagesetter system will be owned, operated, and maintained by a service bureau.

Color Macintosh and Monitor

Imagesetter and Related Equipment (RIP Shown)

Choosing a Macintosh CPU and Monitor—the Heart of Your Color Publishing System

When selecting a Macintosh computer for color publishing, the criteria are simple—you want the fastest machine possible with as much memory and as large a hard disk as you can afford. Whenever possible, purchase a Mac that is designed for color publishing professionals—that means one with a fast microprocessor and multiple expansion slots, and preferably 8 MB of RAM or more. You can take advantage of virtual memory (where the Mac treats part of your hard disk as internal RAM memory) to make up for a lack of internal memory, but this is *much* slower than using actual RAM.

Your Mac also needs a large hard disk. If you plan to work with color images, they take up considerable disk space. Keep in mind that in addition to disk-hogging page layout and image-processing programs (Page-Maker alone uses 5 MB if you install all of its files), you will also need adequate space for fonts, images, the Mac's increasingly large operating system, and other programs such as word processors, paint and illustration programs, and compression routines.

In addition to the Mac CPU, most color Macs require the selection of a keyboard. For publishing, select the more costly Expanded Keyboard that includes function keys (F-Keys). These keys automate cutting and pasting and other functions such as page-up and page-down. The F-Keys can be programmed with macro software to perform common DTP operations that would otherwise require taking your hands off the keyboard to grab the mouse.

Unfortunately, your budget may severely limit purchase possibilities. Below are a few of the tradeoffs to consider if your budget is tight.

- **Few Expansion Possibilities**   If you choose the least expensive color models with one or no expansion slots, the jury is still out as to whether Apple will provide long-term future upgrades or faster boards for these machines. More importantly, without some kind of expensive add-on box, your computer will be unable to handle both a board to drive your monitor and a card for a scanner or other device.

- **Incompatibility Risks**   Buying a Mac that can't normally handle color and then adding non-Apple boards or software to add color capability may trap you into a system incompatible with future Mac operating systems and future releases of color publishing software.

Checklist for Purchasing a Mac for Color Publishing

Use this checklist for comparison shopping when evaluating a Macintosh system for color publishing. Filling out a copy of this form will help you evaluate different Mac models, options, and prices.

Macintosh CPU

CPU Model_____ Is it a current model? Yes ☐   No ☐

Microprocessor Model? _____ (68030 and 68040 are superior to 68000 or 68020)

How fast is the microprocessor's clock speed (ask the salesperson)? _____ MHz

Chips

Math Coprocessor? Yes ☐ (Better)   No ☐ (If No, how much does one cost? $_____)

Is a PMMU included? (A PMMU is a paged memory management unit. It assists in processing memory intensive tasks.)

Yes ☐ (Better) No ☐   How much does one cost? $_____

Color

How many colors can it produce on a monitor without an add-on board?

Number of Colors _____ On How Large a Monitor? _____ (inches)

Expansion Possibilities

How much RAM memory can it hold? _____

(There may be variations in the amount of RAM memory individual units hold. One unit may take eight megabytes and another nine megabytes.)

5 MB RAM $_____ 8 MB RAM $_____ 16 MB RAM $_____ 32 MB RAM $_____

How many expansion slots does the Mac have? _____ (Two or more slots is better.)

Is an extra board required to add a NuBus Card ? Yes ☐   No ☐

If Yes, how much does this board cost? $ _____ Is it available now? Yes ☐   No ☐

Disk Storage

How many hard drives can the machine handle internally? _____

How large is the hard disk? _____ MB

Who manufactures it? _____ How long is the hard disk's warranty? _____

How fast is its access time? _____Milliseconds (A smaller number is better.)

Miscellaneous

Extended Keyboard? Yes ☐ No ☐ Is it an Apple keyboard or made by a third party? ___

Dealer

Dealer Name_____ Salesperson Name_____Phone #_____

Is there a return policy? Yes ☐ No ☐ Quoted Price $_____
Is set-up included? Yes ☐ No ☐

- **Hard Disks Mean Limited Image Capacity**   Small hard disks are obviously less expensive than large-capacity hard disks, but when you consider that a 6" by 6" full-color image takes up approximately 13 MB of space, you may run out of room before completing your first color project. Serious color publishing with scanned images is nearly impossible with a disk smaller than 80 MB. A smaller hard disk will work if you don't plan to include images in your work (or if you have them handled by the print shop) or if they are limited to sizes not much larger than a commemorative postage stamp.

Mega-Storage Systems

Large, high-resolution color images use up a lot of hard disk real estate—as much as 70 MB or more in the case of a large image scanned on a high-end prepress system and imported to the Mac color publishing environment. Obviously, large, high-capacity storage systems are required to handle anything more than a handful of such images. There are five high-volume storage options:

- Large Hard Disks
- Optical Storage Systems and WORMs
- Tape Storage Systems
- Removable Media Hard Disk Systems
- Silicon Hard Disks.

Of these storage possibilities, the most obvious choice is a large-capacity hard disk, and that's all that is required for most color publishers. Expensive disk systems are available that handle more than 1,000 MB (called a gigabyte)—a huge amount of storage! Other alternatives include optical disk storage and tape systems that can be used for general storage and are ideal when archiving images for future use. Tape is also useful for automatically backing up hard drives; most tape units are sold with software specifically designed for this purpose, such as Dantz Development's Retrospect.

These high-volume technologies have their own advantages and disadvantages. For example, optical disks can handle vast amounts of data but are slow, and those with both read and write capabilities are expen-

Continued

sive. (Optical drives called WORMs for "write once, read many" times are also available and are less costly.)

Tape systems that hold 150 MB per tape are available for around $1,000 and with each new $20 tape purchased, another 150 MB of storage is at hand. Larger DAT-based (digital audio tape) and 8mm systems hold more than 1,000 MB and don't cost much more. On the downside, tape is sequential in nature, and relatively slow, so locating an image and then loading it from tape to the system takes time.

There are also removable hard disk systems, such as the SyQuest, which allow you to use multiple disk packs in the same drive. These are relatively fast and convenient and the drives are reasonably priced. But the replacement packs are expensive, limited in storage capacity when compared to tape and optical storage, and prone to damage if accidentally dropped during handling. Removable hard disk systems that we've worked with are also unusually noisy when in use.

One high-end solution, for working with large images or complex programs that swap chunks of an image out to disk, is to purchase a silicon hard disk (very expensive). These units use a collection of RAM chips that simulate a hard drive to your Mac. The speed of one of these "drives" is blinding—but when you shut the thing off, or if the power fails, the contents of the "disk" are irretrievably lost.

When shopping for a flexible storage solution, the tradeoffs are speed, storage capacity, and price. Don't settle for a system that meets one of these criteria at the expense of another, unless you are really short of money or don't mind waiting twenty minutes for an image to load and then another 30 minutes to save it. If you settle on a system that's lean on capacity because of price, you may save money, only to have to spend it on an additional system in the near future when you run out of space. Other systems for handling large images, compressing them, and transporting them are discussed in Chapter Ten.

Color Monitors for Color Publishing

One of the most expensive purchases for color publishers is an adequate color monitor system. The choice of monitor is particularly important to the serious color publisher, because if you produce publications eight hours per day, you want a monitor that's easy on the eyes and represents color and shapes as accurately as possible.

Macintosh monitor and card combinations come in several flavors: monochrome; 4, 16, and 256 grays; and 256 and 16.8 million colors. The choice for professional color publishers is the "full-color" monitor and card with 16.8 million colors, because only in this mode is accurate on-screen color possible.

256-color monitors provide plenty of lively color, since all 16.8 million colors are available but only 256 can appear on screen at one time. In the case of colors above and beyond the available 256, the Macintosh creates patterns with the available colors to simulate them (called dithering). When using precision color painting programs, the intricate patterns representing missing colors give the image a granular look that makes painting accuracy difficult. If, however, most of your work is limited to simple color design and you plan to have color separations handled by someone else, you may be able to get away with just 256 colors.

Color is controlled through the Macintosh's Monitor Control Panel. Any number of colors/grays can be selected from the maximum number possible on a given monitor/board configuration, all the way down to black and white. This control is important because some programs will not run in full-color mode and some people prefer switching their color monitor into gray mode for lengthy word processing sessions. **Note:** To run in full-color mode on older Mac II series computers with pre-System 7 operating systems, a file called 32-Bit QuickDraw must be present in the System Folder. Without this file, only 256 colors are possible, even on systems capable of full color.

Depending on the model Mac you choose, in addition to a monitor you will need a NuBus card (a printed circuit board) that goes inside your Mac to drive the monitor. Newer Macs have built-in color capabilities, but some still require an add-on card to handle full color. Since the card often costs as much as a monitor, you'll want to carefully select the most capable, cost-effective monitor/card combination for your budget.

Macintosh monitors also come in many sizes, from a 9" monochrome to 36" full-color behemoths for use at trade shows and conferences. If you have the budget, it's easiest to design color publications on 21" desktop monitors (diagonal measurement). A monitor this size displays two 8½" by 11" pages almost to the edges, with room left over for the Macintosh menu bar and page layout rulers.

When choosing a monitor for color publishing, buy the largest screen size you can afford so you can see as much of a layout as possible at one time. After choosing a size, choose a card to drive the monitor. For example, if you choose a 19" monitor, inexpensive cards won't drive it because they only support 13" monitors. The card also determines the number of colors that can be displayed. The best cards include an on-board accelerator that speeds up screen redraw when working in full-color mode. You will want this accelerator to speed up the otherwise slow process of redrawing full-color images as you manipulate them.

When choosing a monitor and card, leave the screen lit for at least fifteen minutes to stabilize the temperature. Make sure the system is set to full-color mode (**Millions** on the Control Panel). Then, look for the features discussed below. We have provided a checklist to help you recall the selection parameters when you go to the computer store.

Geometry and Focus

The rectangular image shown on the monitor should indeed be rectangular with almost no bowing of the edges of the image around the border of the screen. By first drawing a simple grid of horizontal and vertical lines on the screen, look for bending or waviness in these lines toward the edges of the screen. Also, study the ends of lines to see if there is any fuzziness that indicates a focus problem. The larger the monitor, the more difficult it is for the manufacturer to maintain adequate focus and geometry. Because color monitors use the individual red, green, and blue (RGB) guns to create all other colors, try the tests with lines made from purple, orange, brown, and yellow to check that focus is maintained when the three color guns in the monitor combine to create other colors.

Brightness and Color Balance

A color monitor should have a bright image when viewed in a normally lit store environment. An easy way to compare brightness is to take two monitors you are considering and put them next to each other (not too close or they'll magnetically interfere with each other), then use their brightness and contrast controls to create a bright image that doesn't go out of focus. The image shouldn't become so bright that the black edges around the screen image are no longer black. While one monitor may be slightly dimmer than another and still be acceptable, if one is noticeably dimmer or can't become nearly as bright as the other without substantially lightening the black areas, it's not bright enough.

Color balance is somewhat harder to judge than brightness because color is so subjective. One way to test color balance is to scan an 8" by 10" color photo and then put a copy of the scan on the monitors under consideration. Open the scans in the same image-processing or page layout program on both monitors and compare the on-screen results. (Store personnel can help you do this. Make sure that no color calibration is enabled on either system.) While the scanner will influence the color quality of each image, you can still compare it to the original and look to see how far out of balance red, green, and blue are from one monitor to the other. A monitor that's too far out of range has leanings toward one color range at the expense of others. For example, your test image may look oddly bluish. While no monitor has perfect color, the problems can be minimized with a color calibrator (discussed later in the chapter).

Flicker

An annoying problem common to monitors is *flicker*. Large monitors suffer from this problem more than small ones. Look for monitors with a high vertical screen refresh rate (ask the store or the manufacturer for this number). 60 Hertz is acceptable but a higher number is generally better. 72 is the current standard. To subjectively measure your personal sensitivity to flicker, walk about ten feet from the monitor and turn your head 90 degrees away from the image area. Then study the monitor from the corner of your eye using your peripheral vision. If you notice the image flickering or jittering significantly, this may not be the monitor for you.

Resolution

Standard Mac screen resolution is 72 dots per inch. If you choose a monitor with higher resolution (more dots per inch), it simply means that the image will appear slightly smaller and will no longer be WYSIWYG. You will lose the important 1:1 size ratio of on-screen display to print-out. Choosing a monitor with less resolution means that the image will appear slightly enlarged and possibly grainy.

Speed

If you are considering monitor/board combinations from different manufacturers and with built-in acceleration, compare the systems side by side. With the systems set in full-color mode, open the hard disk window on each one and make the windows similar in size. Drag these windows around on the screen to see how fast the image is recreated. A really fast accelerator will result in no perceptible time lag from window drag to redraw. A slow board may take several seconds to accomplish the same thing.

Checklist for Purchasing a Monitor and Card

Use this checklist for comparison shopping when evaluating a monitor and monitor card option for color publishing.

Monitor

Brand_____ Model _____ Has it been discontinued? Yes ☐ No ☐

Color or Grayscale ? Grayscale ☐ Color ☐ Is the screen glare-resistant? Yes ☐ No ☐

How large does it measure diagonally? _____

Does it have a stand that tilts and swivels? Yes ☐ No ☐

How much does it weigh? _____ If it weighs more than thirty pounds, and you plan to put it on your Mac, you'll need a metal stand.

Stand Model _____ Stand Price $_____

What ratings does it have for ELF emission? _____ Milligauss
(A smaller number is better. You may need to get this information from the manufacturer. Some comparisons are available in the Mac press.)

Monitor Resolution (dots per inch) _____ (72 dpi is standard for Macintosh monitors.)

Screen Refresh Rate _____ Hertz

Rate the monitor from 1 to 5 on the following (5 is better): _____

Geometry and Focus____ Brightness and Color Balance ____ Minimum of Flicker _____

Monitor Warranty _____ (Years)

Does the monitor have to be shipped back to the manufacturer for service? Yes ☐ No ☐

Card

How many colors can it handle? Grayscale ☐ 256 Colors ☐ Full Color ☐

If it provides full color (24-bit color), does the card have an on-board accelerator? Yes ☐ No ☐

Rate the accelerator's screen refresh speed from 1 to 5 (5 is better):_____

Can the card drive several makes and models of monitors? Yes ☐ No ☐

Card Warranty _____ (Years)

Software

Does the card require a potentially troublesome System Extension to operate? Yes ☐ No ☐
(Some non-Apple cards include a System Extension but can operate without it.)

What software does the manufacturer include?

Pan and Zoom ☐ Tear-Away Menus ☐ Testing and Calibration Software ☐ Other: _____

Dealer

Dealer Name_____ Salesperson Name_____ Phone #_____

Is there a return policy? Yes ☐ No ☐ Quoted Price $_____

Driver and Utility Software

The monitor/card's software is important too, be it routines that install off your Mac's hard disk or software built into the monitor's NuBus board. If it isn't kept up to date, you may end up with a monitor that won't work. Models that perform fancy tricks, such as rotating the screen or changing resolutions, depend heavily on the viability of this software. Any bugs or incompatibilities may cause you considerable problems, because color publishing products push the Mac's resources to the limit. Monitor manufacturers have been known to be tardy when delivering updates compatible with new releases of the Mac's operating system.

Tip: Don't Choose a Monitor System on the Basis of Free Software That Comes with It

Most non-Apple monitor systems come with two sets of software routines. One set actually runs the monitor; the other consists of tools and utilities for tearing off menus, creating desktops bigger than the monitor, and other neat tricks. Since the most important aspect of a display is to reliably render images on screen, this should be your primary concern when choosing a monitor. Don't allow software toys to persuade you unless you absolutely can't live without one of their functions.

One reason to ignore these perks is because many of them don't work properly. Incompatibility with popular software packages is common, and each new release of the Mac operating system renders many of these tools useless until an update appears. For example, SuperMac's freebie pan and zoom software caused major but hard-to-trace problems when System 7 was released. In the past Radius has thrown in tear-away menu software that in many cases leaves an inoperative menu on the screen until the system is restarted—even when other programs are launched with completely different menus. Their software that enlarges pull-down menu names didn't work right either when we last tried it.

Color Calibrators—Tools for Matching Monitor Color to Printed Output

For now, fully accurate color display on a monitor is not available. Even the most expensive calibration systems may perform a "calibration" that is only vaguely related to what shows up in print. Calibration systems do, however, provide correction to serious Macintosh monitor shortcomings such as white and cyan balance. Running a calibration system also provides day-to-day color monitor consistency and allows you to match a system with two color monitors so that they display color consistently.

A variety of automatic calibration systems are available for the Mac. None of these systems currently produces a completely color accurate monitor, but they do make improvements.

All but the most expensive Macintosh monitors have a serious problem producing the color cyan (sort of a medium light blue). This color is usually represented on screen as a bright turquoise far removed from the real color. Since monitors create all colors from just three guns, the cyan/blue problem throws most of the spectrum off. Because of this flaw with blue, achieving true white on the display is also a problem.

Fortunately there are ways of partially adjusting color inaccuracy with software and hardware calibration to ensure more accurate color. Software-only color calibration systems come free with a number of high-end color painting and image manipulation software packages. These systems operate by having the user adjust software-based controls until the screen image matches one supplied in hard copy form with the software package. While these programs can be used to calibrate a monitor, they are limited in their capabilities, because matching a printed sample color to bright on-screen colors is difficult even for a trained eye. Even the subtle changes in room lighting as the sun moves during the course of a day will produce very different "calibration."

A second and easy-to-use tool for calibration is a hardware device that attaches to monitor screens through a suction cup and measures and adjusts monitor color to one of several standards, using software to control the color output of the guns. This kind of tool, combined with a high-quality monitor, provides partial color calibration when used on a regular basis, although it may still take some experimentation to get the monitor color to begin to match what is seen in print. Chapter Six provides more information on calibration and color standards.

Introducing the Input and Output Tools of Color Publishing

In addition to acquiring a Macintosh CPU and monitor for color publishing, you will need a device for capturing color photos and illustrations (a scanner), unless you plan to handle images with an illustration program, use clip art, copy files scanned elsewhere, or have the pictures added to the job by a print shop, service bureau, or high-end prepress system.

You will also need a PostScript printer to print either color or black and white proofs to check your designs. Hard copy output is vital for proofing text. You can read it on the monitor, but for some reason typos are easier to find on a printed page than on screen.

Color Scanners—the Eyes of the Macintosh

One of the most powerful tools for color publishing is a color scanner. With a scanner of adequate quality (potentially expensive depending on the quality required), you can take images through to print without the expense of using an outside color separation house. Black and white images can also be handled with a color scanner.

Color scanners vary considerably in resolution capabilities, color accuracy, scan-size limitations, and price. At the low end of the scale are hand-held color scanners that offer shaky output and only handle images about four inches wide. You can "stitch" individual scan passes together to form larger images. (Good luck if you attempt this.) At the high end are drum-based scanners that rotate an image on a drum while a laser reads the color. Manufactured by companies such as Scitex, Howtek, and Optronics, these systems are similar to ones used by professional color separation houses and priced accordingly.

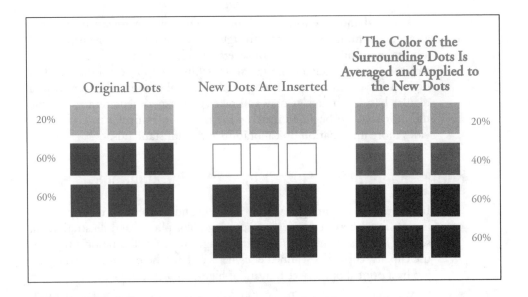

Interpolation Simplified: When an image is enlarged, new dots must be added. To do this, the scanner software or application creates the new dots and inserts them into the image. To determine the color for the dots, the software looks at the neighboring dots, averages their color values, and assigns the averaged color value to the new dots in that part of the image. Packages like Adobe Photoshop provide several methods for interpolation within the General Preferences dialog.

There are many available scanners that only handle grays, and while there is a way to make them do color by using multiple passes with colored plastic film, this is definitely not the way to get acceptable results.

Color scanners are rated for resolution in dots per inch (dpi), with a scanner capable of high resolution being more expensive than one of lesser resolution. Color scanners are also priced according to the image size they can handle, how well they can capture color and detail, and what kind of software they are bundled with.

In addition to the scanner's actual resolution, there may be a higher resolution that the scanner can create by interpolating dots to simulate higher resolution. (When shopping for a scanner, check that the resolution figure quoted is actual resolution and not interpolated.) To create this "higher resolution," the scanner's software typically doubles the actual resolution and then guesses the color of the new dot in between each scanned dot, or the scanner looks at a group of dots and averages them. This average is then used for the new dots in that vicinity.

Because the "guess" dots are usually halfway between the real dots in color value, with smart interpolation software the effect works reasonably well. If a scanner is not equipped with software to handle this trick, image-retouching software that comes with it may be able to do it through resampling. Resampling is the process used by an image-retouching program that converts an image from one resolution to another. This involves algorithmic-based guessing or interpolating of the color of the dots that aren't directly available in a scanned image.

Four Kinds of Scanners and Their Uses

Scanner	*Use*	*Don't Use*
Flatbed Scanner	Images contained in unflexible formats such as illustrations on cardboard and pictures in books. Acceptable for newsprint and some magazine reproduction.	High-quality color reproduction. Most flatbed scanners don't produce great color, and the layer of glass between the scanning optics and the object to be scanned loses detail information.
Drum Scanner	Use drum scanners when top-quality color is required. Drum scanners work best at scanning transparencies.	Don't use a drum scanner when high quality isn't required. A scan on such an expensive piece of equipment is costly.
35mm Slide Scanner	Use 35mm slide scanners for high-quality image captures from slides.	Don't use a 35mm slide scanner for images larger than 5" by 7" when enlarged. Beyond that point, the tiny 35mm image doesn't contain adequate detail for further enlargement.
3-D Scanner	Use 3-D scanners for scans of physical objects. For example, if you were assembling a book on butterflies, specimens could be directly scanned on a 3-D scanner.	Don't use a 3-D scanner for transparencies or when high quality is required. These scanners can be painfully slow as well.

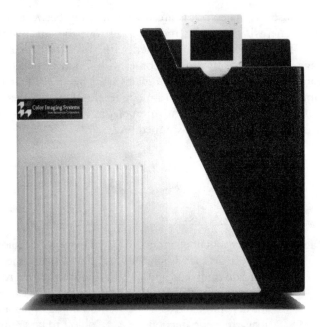

Most slide scanners accept only 35mm slides. The best of these units are capable of relatively high-quality image capture.

The very best scanners are drum-based. The image, be it a photographic print or a transparency, is wrapped around the drum. The drum rotates at high speed while the image is scanned by a laser. Drum scanners provide professional-level results but also require professional-level expertise and knowledge to get the best results. For example, transparencies are often coated in oil before scanning to reduce the possibility that a tiny physical scratch will show in the scan.

In addition to the hand-held and drum scanners already mentioned, color publishers may come across or use the following types of scanners:

- **Flatbed Scanners**   Color flatbed scanners use a moving light bar that scans and captures the image in one or more passes. Flatbed scanners are the most common for color publishing because of their affordability, ease of use, compact size, and relative flexibility.

- **Sheetfed Scanners**   To input an image into a sheetfed scanner, it is fed into a slot, moved over a light bar, and then exited from the machine. Sheetfed scanners are very limited in the media they accept because the scanned document must be flexible and small enough to fit through the machine. For example, to scan a picture in a book, you would have to first cut the page out before feeding it through the scanner.

- **35mm Slide Scanners**   Capable of excellent color and resolution, though still not quite as good as drum scanners, 35mm slide scanners provide cost-effective, quality scans and take up little physical room on a desk. Their major limitation is that all input media must be in 35mm slide format, and these images can't be enlarged past a certain point because there's only so much information contained in a tiny 35mm slide.

- **3-D Scanners**   These scanners use an image-sensing camera positioned over a flat bed and surrounded by high-intensity lights to capture images. These scanners are designed to create two-dimensional images from three-dimensional objects.

- **Other Scanned Image Sources**   Scans can also be captured from video sources, and digital cameras allow direct digital capture of a photograph in a format readable by the Mac.

When you're shopping for a scanner, there are some critical performance features to consider, including the ones described below.

Adequate Resolution

Scanner resolution directly relates to the quality of the images when they are resized, output, and printed. For magazine publishing needs (except high-resolution publications like National Geographic), 300 dpi is adequate. For higher quality publishing, the sky's the limit, although 400 to 600 dpi is more than adequate for all but the most demanding resolution requirements, such as scanning line art and type (see Chapter Five) or for scanning small and enlarging later. In the case of 35mm slide scanners, higher resolution is standard; otherwise a 1½" slide image scanned at 300 dpi and blown up to 5" by 7" in a publication would result in a horribly grainy picture. Slide scanner resolution must be at least 1,000 dpi, and 2,000 or 3,000 dpi is much better, unless you plan to print the image at the same size as the slide (unlikely).

Clean Color

Scanners vary considerably in their ability to interpret color images and accurately record them. Where one scanner produces crisp, clean images with lively color, another may produce images that can only be described as murky. As scanners increase in price, their color recording ability improves (most of the time anyway). A problem with scanner color is that in addition to the overall loss of information, cross-contamination of colors can occur. A photograph of a bright red maraschino cherry may become contaminated with blues and greens. It doesn't take much contamination to reduce the bright red to a dull red and make an image look flat and uninteresting. While professional color separators can compensate for this problem and clean up the red, you want to start with a color-correct image to avoid the extensive learning curve associated with color balancing. Professional color separators can make the cherry's image look more vibrant in color than the actual cherry!

Because the nature of scanned images varies due to different kinds of film and other factors, some scanning software packages include options that compensate for color shifts in order to produce more accurate results. In the case of a flatbed scanner, the color balance must be accurate both in the middle of the scanner bed and toward the edges. All colors must be balanced, with no unnatural leanings toward light or dark, nor toward any individual color such as yellow, red, or blue. To really test a scanner, color separate the scanned images and have a color proof produced to compare the results. The steps to handle this task are explained in subsequent chapters.

Good Detail Resolution

You may run across scanners that offer good color balance at the expense of detail resolution capabilities. (You may also run across ones with good detail resolution but poor color balance.) Detail resolution is a scanner's ability to resolve the fine points of an image and to make even color transitions. For example, in an image of a woman wearing an intricate lace dress, the dress may look like lace when scanned on one scanner and appear as haze on another.

Checklist for Purchasing a Color Scanner

Use this checklist to choose a color scanner for your Macintosh color publishing system.

Scanner

Brand_____ Model _____ Has it been discontinued? Yes ☐ No ☐

Type of scanner: Flatbed ☐ Drum ☐ 35mm Slide ☐ 3-D ☐ Warranty _____

What size media can it accept? _____ " x _____" 35mm Slides Only ☐

What physical media will work (check all that apply)? Flexible Paper Media ☐

Flexible Transparent Media ☐ 35mm Slide ☐ Rigid Media (Books, Illustrations on Board, etc.) ☐

Maximum Resolution _____ dpi Maximum Resolution with Interpolation _____ dpi

What kind of calibration does it use? None ☐ Automatic ☐ Test Image ☐

How does it connect to a Mac? SCSI Port ☐ NuBus Board ☐ GPIB Board ☐

If it uses the SCSI Port, is there a SCSI output connector? Yes ☐ No ☐

If it uses GPIB board, how much does this cost? Price $_____

Rate the scanner from 1 to 5 on the following (5 is better):

Clean Color _____   Detail resolution in the shadow, highlights and midtones _____

Exact Registration of Color _____ Liveliness of Color (Saturation)_____

Test scanning speed by scanning a test image in color. Time to scan your test image _____

Scanner Software

Can it scan line art? Yes ☐ No ☐ Can it scan grayscales? Yes ☐ No ☐

Is a color separation package included? Yes ☐ No ☐ Name and Version _____

If yes, is it a full version of the software? Yes ☐ No ☐

What file formats can it save in? TIFF ☐ PICT ☐ EPS ☐ Other _____

How large is the preview window? ___ " x ___" Is it a "live" preview window? Yes ☐ No ☐

Is there a gamma control? Yes ☐ No ☐
Can you set the highlight and shadow points? Yes ☐ No ☐

Does the scanner or software require a potentially troublesome System Extension to operate? Yes ☐ No ☐

Dealer

Dealer Name_____ Salesperson Name _____Phone #_____

Is there a return policy? Yes ☐ No ☐ Quoted Price $_____ Price for GPIB Board $_____

Another common scanner detail problem is found in the highlights and shadows of an image. Some scanners produce otherwise clear, crisp images, but lose highlight or shadow detail. Make a point of checking the highlights and shadows of a test scan against the original image. Yet another detail problem is found in images with smooth color transitions that must be resolved properly to appear natural, a particular problem with skintones.

Exact Registration

Color scans are made up of three colors (red, green, and blue) assembled on top of each other to create the impression of full color. If one layer is placed slightly off center to the others, it results in an image that looks out of focus. Many flatbed scanners make one pass for each color layer. If the scanner's light bar incorrectly places one layer in relationship with another, a fuzzy scan results. Watch for this effect not only before purchase, but as repeated use wears the scanner's mechanism. Test for color registration by scanning a drawing of several black lines drawn diagonally on a piece of white paper. If, after scanning and magnifying the image, you can see lines with individual red, green, and blue components or edges, then the scanner has registration problems. (See Chapter Seven for more information on registration.)

Definition: Banding

A problem common in computerized image processing, and with scanned images in particular, is banding. For example, if you place an orange on a tabletop with the sun coming into the room from one window, the side of the orange facing the window will be a bright orange color; then there is a smooth transition of color from bright to dark as your eye moves around the orange to the side facing away from the window. Banding occurs when a computer is unable to make this transition evenly and instead skips from one color to several darker (or lighter) shades without showing the colors in between. It results in images that look unnatural and computer processed. Banding occurs in scanners with limited grayscale or color capabilities and with defective imagesetters—watch for it!

Continued

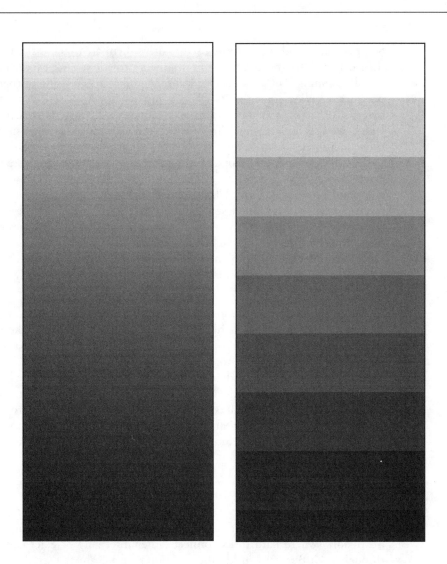

Banding. Banding occurs when an input device such as a scanner, or output devices such as printers or imagesetters, are unable to make smooth color transitions. In this example, the normally smooth transition at the left is shown again with severe banding at the right. Banding may be even across the spectrum, resulting in bands of equal width (as in this example), or noticeable only in the light or dark areas of an image.

Useful Software

Some scanners and the software used to drive them are much easier to use than others. The most convenient scanners provide a desk accessory to handle scanning, but a standalone scanning and color correction program provides superior color results when compared to most desk accessory-based scanner drivers. For example, we own an Epson color scanner, which we use for scanning "for position only" images for inclusion in color documents. This scanner ships with ColorStudio, which can directly drive the scanner and works well with it. It also ships with a scanner driver package called ScanDo, which works as either a desk accessory or as a standalone application. Unfortunately, for such a comparatively simple program, it's the buggiest product we've ever worked with outside Microsoft Word for the Mac version 3.00. In eight bug fix releases over one and a half years (that we know of), it still doesn't work correctly. Early versions crashed both the scanner and the Mac, or created "scan" files containing no information. More recent versions conveniently crash only the scanner.

Before purchase, test these kinds of applications that drive scanners by scanning large images at high resolution to see if they can take that level of punishment. Then open the resulting scan files in a paint or image-retouching program to see if the scan was correctly saved. There should be no "noise" at either the top or bottom of the image. Noise looks like the screen of a television tuned to a channel where there is no broadcast signal. It indicates that the scanning software improperly wrote the file to disk and means serious problems exist with the product. You also may wish to scan and save images in all of the file formats supported by the software.

Connectivity

Depending on the scanner's price, it may either connect through the SCSI port (where hard disks connect either internally or externally) or through a NuBus card inside the computer. If a scanner uses the SCSI port, choose one that has an input SCSI connector as well as an output hookup. Some scanners have only one connection; the manufacturer assumes the scanner will be the last piece of equipment daisy-chained on the SCSI bus. That's fine, but if you end up owning two such devices, each with only one SCSI hookup, you'll have to power everything down and switch devices when you want to use the one that's not hooked up.

If you are purchasing a scanner that uses a NuBus card, it will either take the form of a proprietary board that comes with the scanner, or a GPIB (General Purpose Interface Board) that must be purchased separately. If the scanner uses a card, you'll need room for it inside your Mac. In the case of the GPIB board, it may not be included in the quoted price of the scanner and may add five to 25 percent to the purchase price.

Tip: A Deal on Image Correction Software

Because the trend in color scanners is to package standalone image processing software with a scanner (and this software is quite expensive when purchased separately), it may be an important consideration in your decision. (This software may also include a convenient driver program to operate the scanner.) Thoroughly investigate the software options to determine if the bundled software is useful to you. Is the color correction and separation tool a full version or a "limited" one chopped off at the knees? How difficult is it to scan line art? Do you have enough memory to run a memory-intensive color separation program bundled with the scanner? What kind of adjustments does the program allow before scanning? How old is the scanner's software? Will it run on the current operating system? (See the section in the next chapter on image-processing software for more information on what this software should be able to do.)

Poor Construction or Design

A few flatbed scanners offer add-on light bars so they can scan transparencies. While unable to handle 35mm slides with any credibility, these systems can work with transparencies of larger sizes. The problem with most of these systems is that the light bar is not really a part of the scanner, but instead is attached with two-sided tape or other unsuitable methods. Consider such a system only after running test scans with the light bar and finding the results satisfactory and the set-up easy to master.

Finally, before shelling out several grand on a color scanner, read *A Weak Link* at the beginning of Chapter Five to get a more realistic idea of what a scanner can or can't do for you. Depending on your needs, you may want to buy the cheapest junker you can get your hands on to scan images for position only, and then rent time on a high-quality scanner at a service bureau or color separation house. Otherwise, you may spend a large chunk of money on a scanner that really can't do what you need done.

Printers—Black and White and CMYK All Over

Like most other products used in publishing, color printers, along with black and white ones, have fallen in price while they have improved in power and capability. While the first color printers (ignoring the lowly ImageWriter II) were capable of printing muddy colors on an area of only 6½" by 9", today's printers are capable of fairly accurate color and print areas up to 11" by 17". Some of the printer manufacturers we know are listed in the *Sources* section at the end of the book.

There have been improvements in the capability of black and white printers as well. Not only are they faster than the ones of yore, many models now offer high-resolution plain paper output good enough to print from—if you're not too picky about the way screens and small type looks (not good enough for serious color publishing, however). New smoothing technology, first developed by Hewlett-Packard and copied by other manufacturers, allows even 300-dpi printers to produce clean-looking type by adding small extra dots in between what would otherwise be a jaggy curve on a letter.

Far greater color accuracy is becoming possible on printers, and new technology allows Macs to drive machines capable of producing proofs that look almost identical to the finished piece. This enables designers to show clients how an ad or brochure will look before it goes into print. Calibration is possible on some models also, assuring more accurate color output of images and color matching systems such as Pantone.

In the color printer world, there are several kinds of technology for producing color output from the Macintosh. The results from these various systems look distinctively different. Even a company's own implementations of the same technology produce color printers with strikingly different output. Before purchasing a color printer, it's best to shop around to find the output quality you prefer at a price you like.

The most common color printing technologies in use today include thermal wax, ink-jet, dye sublimation, and solid toner systems.

- **Thermal Wax Printers**   Colored wax is forced off four panels (one each for cyan, magenta, yellow and black) in a roll of clear plastic onto the paper to create an image. Thermal wax printers produce shiny images rich with color, although most models produce obnoxious patterning when they mix colors.

- Ink-Jet Printers   A carefully measured spray of ink is applied to specially made paper through multiple passes to each page. The newest ink jets produce colors not only by regulating dot sizes, but also by adjusting how much ink is sprayed onto the paper. Ink-jet printers often require special paper to get the "best" output, but even on these expensive papers the ink spreads when it hits the surface. This spreading causes ink-jet output to have a slightly fuzzy or out-of- focus appearance.

- Dye Sublimination Printers   A solid dye is changed into a gas to create an image on special paper. The best of these printers produce results that look almost as good as a photograph, because the printed image isn't made up of observable colored dots or dither patterns like ink-jet and wax technology-based printers. Unfortunately, while these printers produce beautiful color images, some do an inept job of reproducing text.

- Solid Toner Printers   A powdered "ink" is used to create a colored image in much the same way a laser printer or photocopier works. In fact, color copiers using this technology produced by Canon and Kodak take output directly from a Mac and produce dazzling 11" by 17" color images. These printers may be connected to the Mac via systems provided by the manufacturers or by EFI's superior Fiery ColorLaser controller, which provides better resolution and faster processing than the controllers provided by Canon or Kodak.

PostScript and Printers

The standard in color publishing is currently the PostScript-based printer because most color publishing projects are ultimately run out on a PostScript-based imagesetter. Running a job on a PostScript printer gives a good indication what the final results will look like and how long the job will take to image at the service bureau. The output produced by printers using other imaging "standards," such as QuickDraw, may not resemble what will print from the imagesetter. (QuickDraw is discussed briefly in Chapter Four.)

For printers that don't directly support PostScript output, software-based PostScript interpreters such as Freedom of Press are available to handle the job, although these are usually slower than direct PostScript support.

There are several factors to consider, as described in the next few pages, when choosing any PostScript printer, be it black and white or color. We have again provided a checklist to remind you of these features when you begin your quest for a printer that will meet your proofing requirements when working on color projects.

- PostScript Compatibility   Does it use true PostScript or a Post-Script clone? PostScript clones use a completely different set of software code that emulates the real PostScript developed by Adobe Systems. While some of these implementations work fine (some are much faster than PostScript), others are reportedly full of bugs and problems. PostScript is relatively bug free, because the massive installed base of users has provided a steady stream of feedback to Adobe concerning problems, and because Adobe is continuously updating the technology.

- PostScript, Level 1 or 2?   Which version of PostScript does it use? Newer printers incorporate PostScript Level 2, which has significant advantages for memory management and the handling of large files. In the case of color PostScript printers, there are many improvements in PostScript Level 2 to support accurate color output.

- Paper Flexibility   Ideally, a black and white printer should provide crisp output on a variety of papers. Many color printers, however, still require specially manufactured paper.

- Paper Sizes Supported   If you plan to print two-page layouts, get a printer that can handle 11" by 17" pages so you don't waste time taping pieces of paper together. While these printers are more expensive, they have greater flexibility when it comes to large or unusual-sized layouts.

- Speed   Processing speed is important, particularly if you share the printer on a network with other users or regularly print complex jobs. A printer with a slow microprocessor (like the slug we own) can take an hour to print one 8½" by 11" page if it contains large scans and complex page layout information. Published page-per-minute ratings are suspect for PostScript printers, because these speeds are only realized when you print multiple copies of the same page. Try printing a complex image at the store to get a real idea of the speed you can expect. (Adobe has announced a PostScript coprocessor that will speed up text-only output, but it probably will do little to speed up more complex output consisting of page layout elements and images.)

Checklist for Purchasing a Color Printer

Use this checklist for comparison shopping when evaluating color printers. Much of it is applicable to purchasing black and white printers as well.

Printer

Brand _____ Model _____ Has it been discontinued? Yes ☐ No ☐

What kind of color printer is it? Ink Jet ☐ Thermal Wax ☐ Die Sublimination ☐ Solid Toner ☐

What size media can it accept using paper trays? ___ " x ___ " Manual Feed? ___ " x ___ "

Does it use special paper? Yes ☐ No ☐

How much does the paper or imaging material cost? $_____ per_____

How much does ink or color media cost per 100 pages of output? $ _____

Maximum Printer Resolution _____ dpi Microprocessor _____
Running at what speed? _____

How much does the printer weigh? _____ How long is the warranty? _____

Can it be serviced on site or must it be returned to the dealer or manufacturer?
On-Site ☐ Return ☐

Connectivity and Expansion

How much memory does the printer have? ___ MB How much memory can it hold? ___ MB

Which version of Postscript does it use? None Level 1 ☐ Level 2 ☐

PostScript Clone ☐ PostScript Software Clone such as Freedom of Press (slow) ☐

How does it connect to a Mac? SCSI Port ☐ LocalTalk ☐ Other _____

Can multiple users share it? Yes ☐ No ☐

If it uses the SCSI Port, is there a SCSI output connector? Yes ☐ No ☐

Can it connect to a hard disk for font handling and spooling? Yes ☐ No ☐

Output Quality

What calibration methods or color standards does it employ (if any)? _____

Rate the printer from 1 to 5 on the following (5 is better):

Clean Color ___ Type output quality at 12 points ___ Lack of noticeable patterning ____

Time to print a test image (print the same file on other printers under consideration) _____

Dealer

Dealer Name _____ Salesperson Name _____ Phone #_____

Is there a return policy? Yes ☐ No ☐ Quoted Price $_____

- **Color Media Replacement**   Ask to see how the toner or "ink" is replaced. Some models of ink-jet and toner-based printers are fully capable of spilling color media and making a permanent mess. While this in itself may not be a reason to reject such a unit, you should at least be aware of this possibility before you buy so you can choose a suitable location for the printer away from carpet and furniture. While the salesperson has the door open to show you the gory ink-changing details, study the mechanism. If it looks on the flimsy side and you plan to print 20,000 pages per month, this is not the printer for you.

- **Color Balance**   If you are sizing up color printers, look for color-balanced output that shows as little patterning or dithering (also called "doilies" because of the lacy look of a bad or overt dither) as possible. Look also for an image with strong, bright color, rather than a slightly murky look that is shifted slightly towards yellow, red, or blue. Some color printers consistently produce color that looks dull or shifts toward one color or another. The best way to test this is to bring your own color scan and use it to produce output from the same program on each color printer under consideration. You may be surprised at the variation in the color between technologies and individual printer models.

- **Type Output Quality**   When shopping for color printers, study the quality of black type printed on a white page. The best printers produce twelve-point type that looks almost as good as that of a 300-dpi black and white PostScript printer. Printers that produce grainy looking, hard-to-read type at twelve points are difficult to use for proofing. In other than dye sublimation printers, which provide great color images but sometimes lousy type output, this may also point to a fundamental weakness in the printer's design that will result in soft-looking images.

- **Consistent Color Output**   If you are considering a solid toner-based color printer, run your sample and then wait a week or two and run it again on the same kind of paper. (Hopefully the printer will get used during this period.) Then compare the two samples. If the color has shifted significantly between the two tests, then the printer may produce variable results according to the humidity and amount of day-to-day use. That makes it of little use to a color publisher concerned with consistent results.

- **Color Standard Support**   Another factor in selecting a color printer is to evaluate any and all color standards and calibration systems it may employ or be compatible with. Currently there are a patchwork of color standards, such as TekColor, Eport color technology, and Pantone, for matching on-screen color to printer color. A printer that accurately supports the color system you use will be a real boon to your color publishing efforts.

Tip: Less Than Meets the Eye

When shopping for a color printer, do more than look at the ads. And don't rely on the sample output produced by the printer's manufacturer. When producing samples for use in ads or as part of a demo, some manufacturers cheat by carefully designing a document that doesn't show the weaknesses of the printer's dithering routines or inadequacies of color balance. Take, for example, an ad run for a thermal wax printer that showed stunning clarity of color without the visible dot patterns endemic to these machines. Careful study of the ad revealed why this was so: the drawing created for the ad almost exclusively used cyan, magenta, yellow, and black—colors the printer could produce as solids without mixing! This same printer, when put through its paces with other images, produced unsightly dot patterns just like other printers of its kind.

The Other "Hardware" Tools You'll Need

In addition to a Macintosh and a printer, there are several items you will need for checking work on press and understanding and selecting process colors. Available from art supply stores that cater to graphic designers (not weekend artists), these tools are inexpensive but important. The following are some of the basics we recommend for your toolbox.

A Magnifying Loupe

To evaluate photo quality before scanning and for checking jobs on press, buy a magnifying loupe. (The press personnel treat you with new respect when you bring out your loupe to examine dot registration.) While precision Nikon loops are expensive, most art supply stores carry workable models for $15 to $45.

Don't buy a *linen tester*, however. These are sold as substitutes for loupes, but lack the magnifying power required for serious color work.

To evaluate a loupe, study a page of fine type with each model. Look for crisp, strong magnification. Make sure the loupe also takes in plenty of ambient light for easy viewing.

Two Rulers

Purchase an accurate metal ruler for checking art. Also purchase a precision film ruler; these are printed on transparent film and show measurements down to tiny fractions. Rulers are important for checking alignment on final output.

Color Charts

You'll want to purchase color charts from one or more color matching systems, including Pantone, Focoltone, and TruMatch. There is more information on these color systems in Chapter Six.

There may be other tools you'll need as you go along, but the ones we've covered here should get you started in color publishing. As you read the book, you'll get a deeper understanding of the process and the tools required to understand and evaluate output.

Now that you've met the hardware tools you are most likely to own and understand the importance of other pre-purchase considerations, including technical support and integration with other tools, in the next chapter we'll look at the software tools used in color publishing.

CHAPTER

3

SELECTING COLOR
PUBLISHING SOFTWARE

"When a man is trying to sell you something,
don't imagine that he is that polite all the time."

—Edward Watson Howe

There are a vast number of software packages for color publishing on the Mac. Programs are available for developing color page layouts, creating illustrations, and incorporating unusual type effects. Because these products vary in their features, ease of use, and price, you will want to make your selection carefully and only after testing several programs.

The most important software decision you will make is the choice of a page layout program. It is within this program that color publishers spend most of their time assembling type, illustrations, and design elements into a finished document. A page layout program is at least partially responsible for the reliability of output produced at the service bureau. The wrong package may cause a host of time-wasting problems in the form of useless film from the imagesetter. Some programs offer superior color handling abilities too, saving you the cost of purchasing a separation package.

Depending on the complexity and size of the art you plan to create on your Macintosh, and whether you want to handle your own color separations, you may need to buy other packages as well. A variety of options are described in this chapter.

You Are Here

In the last chapter you read about the hardware required for color publishing. This chapter describes the software you will use in color publishing. Tips are provided to assist you in making the correct decisions regarding an application that you may literally have to live with eight hours a day for several years.

Choose each software package carefully, because purchasing the wrong one can cause hours of frustration while you try to figure out how it works (or doesn't). Follow the advice in this chapter and read up on purchases in the Macintosh and prepress magazines (listed in the back of the book) to keep tabs on new developments. This way you'll have a head start in acquiring the best software tools for your needs.

There Are Three Grades of Color Publishing Software

With the plethora of software on the market, particularly in the page layout and color paint program categories, it's easy to be taken in by advertising hype and misinformation. When evaluating products, keep three categories of software capabilities in mind. They will make it easier to recognize the kind of product you are evaluating.

The Toy Program

Toy programs are common among the applications available for color publishing. Toy programs look like real products, but aren't as reliable as those designed for professionals. The reason for toy programs is simple—everyone wants to create neat graphics and play with letters on screen. After finishing the "layout," the fruits of their labor are "imaged" on an ImageWriter II with a color ribbon to take to school or tack up on the fridge.

These programs should be avoided by serious color publishers at all costs, because the files they produce may fail to image at the service bureau. Or, the service bureau operator may chuckle when he hears what was used to design the job and then refuse it. Outside of a few legitimate bargains, these programs are recognized by the large number of features at a price much lower than a professional version of similar software.

On Press with a Toy Page Layout Program

A designer working with a tight budget for a color Mac publishing system decided to cut corners by purchasing an inexpensive page layout program. The package selected was less than half the price of the "big boys," and it was easy to use. According to the literature, the package included all the features of the more expensive programs.

After assembling a three-color direct mail piece with the program and outputting it as film at the local service bureau, everything looked fine. The colors registered properly with each other and the black and white photos looked crisp and clean on film.

Off the job went to the printer, who assembled the masks and produced press plates. When the job was ready for print, the designer was there to check it. On press everything looked fine, and after making a

Continued

couple of minor adjustments to one color, the designer proudly walked out the door with a copy of the freshly printed mailer in hand. Walking across the print shop's parking lot to grab lunch at a local restaurant, she glanced at the photos on the inside of the piece. Suddenly realizing that one of the photos was crooked, she rushed back into the shop to abort the print run before the job was complete and the expensive paper wasted.

That afternoon, the job was sent back to the printer's stripping room to correct the crooked photo. It turned out that the inexpensive page layout program had ever so slightly added curves to the straight lines that ran above and below the photos. The printer manually added new lines and the job was soon back on press. The total bill for wasted paper, extra press time, and the changes came in at $2,344—a sum that would have purchased a professional-quality page layout program three times over!

The Color Publisher's Program

Usually priced between $500 and $1,000, there are programs specifically engineered for serious color publishers. The majority of these tend to be easy to use, but offer an advanced feature set you can grow into as you acquire prepress skills. Recognize these packages by their price, a long list of features (usually), and their relative ease of use. QuarkXPress and PageMaker are the most widely used of this type of program on the Mac.

Professional Users' Programs

For the serious color publisher with a background rooted in color separation and/or printing, packages are available that offer sophisticated control. These are not programs that you'll be able to learn in a few hours. Often priced above the $1,000 level, many of the programs cost several thousand dollars or more. Recognize these products by the price and through an inspection of the manuals. If the terminology loses you after page three, then you are probably looking at a package designed for the "power color publisher." Quoin is an example of a page layout program in this category. These are not programs to start with; they are programs for color experts. If you purchase one of these packages, you may find it so hard to decipher and use that you give up color publishing altogether.

However, once you get some experience, you may find yourself demanding the power and precise control these programs provide.

> **Tip: Keep Your Applications Up-to-Date**
>
> Because your color publishing files will be imaged at a service bureau or sent to a high-end prepress system using the latest software, it's important that you keep your applications current. Stories abound of would-be color publishers who attempted to image files created by older applications and were disappointed when a file imaged incorrectly or not at all.

Page Layout Environments for the Macintosh

There are a wide variety of programs available for the Mac that allow you to combine type, pictures, and design elements on the printed page. Mac page layout software is based on two different metaphors. (A metaphor is the way a page layout program imitates drafting board design.) Both metaphors provide color publishers with very different work environments and for most publishers, once a metaphor is learned, it is relatively difficult to change to another. You need to choose the one that feels the most natural to your style of assembling publications and accommodates the kinds of projects you plan to produce.

The Paste-board Metaphor

The page layout program, PageMaker, uses a paste-board metaphor. This allows designers to freely place a variety of elements on a desktop "pasteboard" that faintly resembles a drafting table surface with a piece of layout board mounted down on it. The paste-board metaphor allows the introduction of visual elements (type, pictures, lines, and boxes) that can be freely arranged in almost any fashion. Around the edges of the layout surface, PageMaker provides a large empty space representing the surrounding surface of a drafting board, useful for temporarily "pasting" type and other elements before mounting them down to the layout. PageMaker handles blocks of text in type holders—tools reminiscent of the type chases used to set obsolete lead-based hot type.

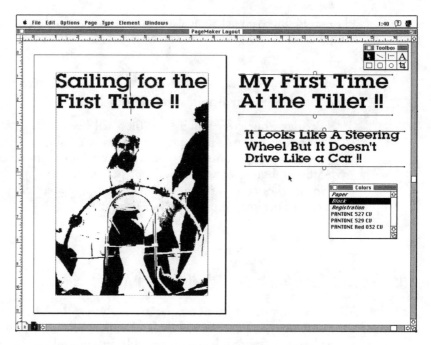

PageMaker handles type in unique type holders that resemble the mechanical tools used for traditional hot lead type.

The Box-based Metaphor

The "box-based" metaphor is the most commonly used approach in Mac-based color programs. Most desktop publishing programs (except Page-Maker), use boxes to delineate the position of type and pictures in a lay-out. To add text to a page, you draw a box where you want the type and then key it in or import it from a word processing file. Boxes can also be used as place holders for pictures or filled with color to create solids.

Professional Page Layout Programs That Support Color Publishing

Page layout programs differ from each other in features, type handling and manipulation, large document management capabilities, color handling abilities, ease of use, reliability in producing color-accurate output, and of course, price. The ones discussed here include several popular "serious" publishing packages, as well as three special-purpose products— one designed for creating large posters, one that excels in assembling ad layouts, and a program for creating color product packaging.

PageMaker

The first page layout program to reach the market was designed by Aldus Corporation. PageMaker is oriented towards free-form document design and is capable of handling long documents requiring automatic generation of tables of contents and indexes. Many designers moving from drafting table to desktop initially find PageMaker's environment more comfortable than the box-based metaphor used in other page layout programs, because it resembles the familiar drafting table. Aldus now includes its Aldus Pre-Print package, a color separation program, with PageMaker.

QuarkXPress

QuarkXPress, developed by Quark, Inc., appeared after PageMaker and attempted to take page layout in a much different direction. QuarkXPress is oriented towards sophisticated color publishing and provides very fine control of type and item positioning within a layout. Quark has close ties to several high-end prepress systems and offers precise control of color specification through several color models and systems. QuarkXPress was also the first general-purpose page layout program to offer color trapping and extensive on-screen color capabilities. (Trapping is explained in Chapter Seven.)

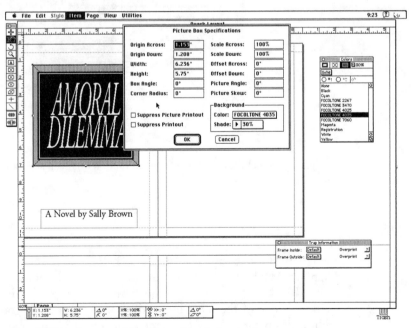

QuarkXPress uses precision boxes for placing both type and pictures.

Quark, Inc. also pioneered the trend to customize and enhance its QuarkXPress product for specific applications by introducing Xtensions. Quark's Xtensions technology allows capability to be added in separate modules. These modules are available from Quark and a number of third-party software developers. Xtensions range in functionality from simple routines, like one for importing odd files, to complete systems for automating the creation of books and manuals. Recently, PageMaker has been provided some extension capability through the recently developed Aldus Additions technology—though there are more sophisticated and diverse Quark Xtensions available at this writing.

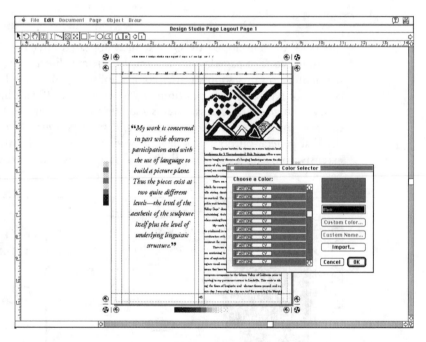

DesignStudio includes a color separation module that can separate process color images.

DesignStudio

DesignStudio is a page layout program from Letraset and Manhattan Graphics. Manhattan Graphics also created the still-popular low-end program, Ready-Set-Go, one of the first desktop publishing packages. Letraset is one of the most innovative forces in modern graphic arts. In addition to being part of the same company that invented the Pantone

Matching System (no small accomplishment), Letraset has for years provided rub-down sheets of type (called *press type*) in a large variety of faces that allow designers to assemble layouts by hand. Letraset also offers a large library of symbols, colored papers, films, and other products for creating professional presentations and architectural layouts.

The first "general-use" page layout program to include its own color separation routine for images, Letraset's professional-quality page layout program, DesignStudio, is similar in orientation to QuarkXPress. It provides a platform for color publishing and fine control of type and item positioning in a layout. Plus, its color separation module allows control of screen color as well as images.

Ventura Publisher and FrameMaker

Ventura Publisher shares the box metaphor, was designed by Ventura Software Inc. (a division of Xerox), and is one of the most popular publishing environments in the IBM PC-compatible world. Designed for the production of long documents, Ventura Publisher is capable of building complex tables and equations required for publishing technical manuals.

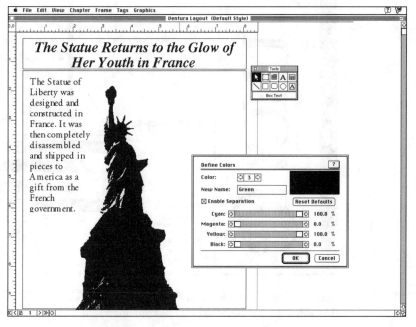

Unlike the IBM PC version, the Macintosh version of Ventura Publisher has fairly limited color support.

FrameMaker is similar in functionality and orientation to Ventura in its support for long documents. Produced by Frame Technology of San Jose, California, FrameMaker, like Ventura Publisher, offers limited support for color, but can work with images that have been color separated in other programs.

Quoin

A powerful color publishing environment that's more expensive than the previous packages is Quoin from Quoin Publishing Systems. (The name is pronounced *coin,* like a quarter. A quoin is a wedge used to lock lead-based type in a chase for printing.) Quoin is a European import, and it supports traps and has extensive customization features similar to those found in professional document management packages. A Quoin-customized keyboard is available to speed typesetting and document processing. Quoin allows the generation of sophisticated tables for type management and can color separate images.

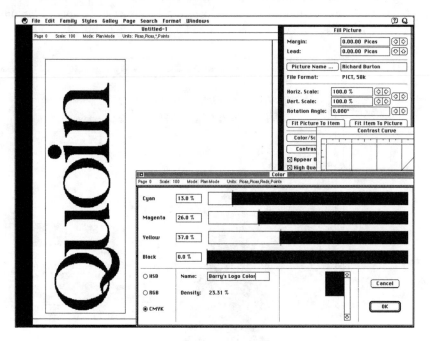

Quoin is a powerful page layout package with color support. It's more expensive than other general-purpose programs discussed in this chapter.

Three Special-purpose Color Publishing Programs

Multi-Ad Creator

A powerful special-purpose color publishing product, Multi-Ad Creator, was developed by Multi-Ad Services. This page layout program is used to create single ads rather than produce multiple-page publications. Creator is optimized to make the designing, copyfitting, and assembly of ads as simple as possible. Creator also offers built-in separation routines, trapping facilities, and the ability to handle complex PostScript type manipulations such as gradations and other effects.

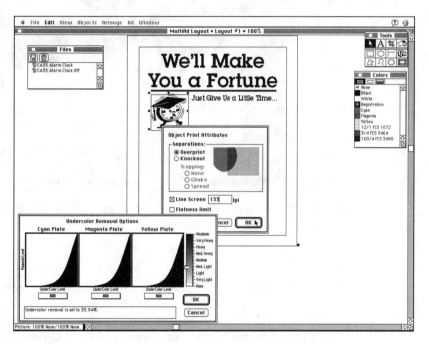

Multi-Ad Creator is a powerful package for creating ad layouts.

PosterWorks

Another special-purpose color page layout program is PosterWorks from S.H. Pierce and Company. Designed for assembling large color documents such as posters and poster-sized ads, it includes advanced capabilities for color separation and other prepress requirements. Fully capable of producing billboard-sized ads, PosterWorks can also be used to produce posters on a black and white or color printer, a page at a time. The resulting pages, called "tiles," can then be assembled into a finished document, or the files can be output on an imagesetter for assembling and printing a large poster at a print shop.

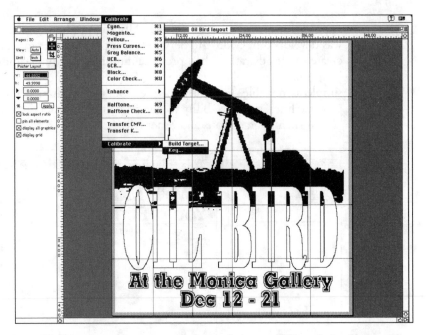

PosterWorks can create one-page layouts as large as a billboard. It offers sophisticated process color output controls.

Desktop Packaging Plus

Desktop Packaging Plus is a powerful (and expensive) program for creating color packaging on the desktop. It can be used by itself or in conjunction with a computer-aided design (CAD) program for precision physical design requirements. Supporting a variety of formats including DDES2, a file format standard for the packaging and laser die-making industry, Desk-top Packaging Plus handles the process of creating packaging from desktop to print shop.

Choosing a Color Page Layout Program

To select the color page layout package that's right for your needs, consider the kind of documents you plan to assemble and evaluate your work habits. If most of your work consists of long, heavily structured documents with limited use of color, choose a product that excels in this area, such as FrameMaker. If your work centers around ads, then QuarkXPress or Multi-Ad Creator may be the right package for your work. If you spend most of your time designing brochures and color direct mail pieces, consider PageMaker, DesignStudio, or QuarkXPress.

Select a program with the right kind of functionality for all of your needs. The professional page layout programs described above all have their strengths and weaknesses—ones that you must weigh carefully before purchase, because these packages are priced at as much as $995 or more. (Desktop Packaging Plus and Quoin are substantially more expensive.) You can buy two or more programs to meet the needs of different kinds of projects, but this is expensive. Not only that, but you'll have two different environments to explore and two sets of experiments to make in order to learn how to get the best color results from each one.

When choosing a page layout program that's right for you and your color publishing needs, evaluate the features and capabilities described in the next few pages. A checklist is provided in the chapter to help guide your purchase decision.

Color Publishing Capabilities

In order to handle complex color publishing projects, you'll need a program that provides support for color images of all kinds. Preferably it should also provide color trapping capabilities that work correctly, so less stripping time is required from your print shop if you plan to handle the entire color publishing process yourself.

The program should also support several kinds of color specification systems including Pantone, Focoltone, TruMatch, and CMYK (all explained in Chapter Six) and provide consistent and quality results from the imagesetter. When in doubt, check with service bureaus or run tests yourself.

In addition to producing graceful color output, some page layout programs are superior to others in their ability to render accurate color on screen. A program with poor on-screen color representation becomes problematic if you design in color, because what you see on the screen will have little to do with what makes it into print. While an experienced designer may be able to visualize the actual look in his or her mind and ignore what is seen on screen, most people can't. To evaluate a program's color display capabilities, place a color scan into two programs under consideration and then open them side by side on the same large monitor—you may be surprised at the difference. (Make sure that the format used for the pictures is supported in high-resolution mode. For example, one program may show only low-resolution representations of TIFF format files to speed display time, while another package may display TIFFs in high-resolution formats.)

Another test is to acquire a Pantone Swatch Book and use it to check Pantone colors on screen. Open the program's Pantone color picker and compare the on-screen Pantone colors to the ones in the swatch book. On an uncalibrated monitor, these colors should look at least remotely like the swatch book colors. On a recently calibrated, high-quality monitor, each color should appear to be within the ballpark, if not nearly identical.

Tip: Choose a Page Layout Program Supported by Several Service Bureaus in Your City

While there are a number of page layout programs to choose from, not all of them are fully supported by all service bureaus. So, if you choose a powerful but not very popular package, you may need to bring not only your data file to the local SB, but also your program disks so they can temporarily load your program to output your files.

You *can* create a PostScript file and avoid this problem, but unless the file images perfectly the first time, any problems will have to be resolved by you and then the file must be rerun—your service bureau will be unable to fix a file in PostScript format. Bringing your page layout software to an SB is not a good idea either, because under the terms of most software licenses, this is illegal. Second, a service bureau that is not intimately familiar with a product through daily use won't know how to get the best results from the software—a potentially serious problem in the case of a file that has color accuracy problems or causes other grief when output. Third, some SBs will simply refuse to handle your work, having had problems with unfamiliar programs in the past. Fourth, it's important that more than one SB fully support your program, because you may want to change service bureaus if the level of service drops, their equipment becomes obsolete or their pricing uncompetitive.

Color Separation Capabilities

Depending on your needs, you will want a program that can at least separate spot and screen colors elegantly. See Chapter Seven for the low-down on color separation.

Checklist for Purchasing a Page Layout Program

Product _____ Version # _____ Has it been discontinued? Yes ☐   No ☐

How long does the manufacturer provide free technical support for the product? _____

Program Uses Box Metaphor ☐   PageMaker Metaphor ☐

What will it be used for? Multi-page Documents ☐   Single Page Ads/Posters ☐

What file formats does the program accept images in? TIFF ☐   PICT ☐   RIFF ☐   EPS ☐

What is the zoom range for documents?____% to ____% Maximum page size _____" x _____"

How many master pages can the program handle? ___ Maximum number of pages per document __

Can graphics be automatically updated? Yes ☐   No ☐   Can items be grouped? Yes ☐   No ☐

Is there layer control? Yes ☐   No ☐ Can items be duplicated automatically? Yes ☐   No ☐

Rate the program from one to ten for screen redraw speed _____ (ten is fast).

Type Features

Can fonts be searched for and replaced automatically? Yes ☐   No ☐

 Font sizes: Minimum ___pt   Maximum ___pt Can stories be updated automatically? Yes ☐   No ☐

Can styles be searched for and replaced automatically? Yes ☐   No ☐

Can type be rotated? 90° Increments ☐   Unlimited Rotation ☐

Kerning Support? ☐   Tracking Support? ☐   Horizontal Scaling Support? ☐

Are tabs easy to set and use? Yes ☐   No ☐ Automatic support for drop caps? Yes ☐   No ☐

Is there built-in support for tables? Yes ☐   No ☐ Is there built-in support for fractions? Yes ☐   No ☐

Is vertical justification supported? Yes ☐   No ☐ Can hyphenation be set manually? Yes ☐   No ☐

Does the program provide a useful speller? Yes ☐   No ☐   Thesaurus? Yes ☐   No ☐

Support for Index ☐   TOC ☐

Color Support and Color Separation

Spot Color - Pantone Yes ☐   No ☐ Focoltone Yes ☐   No ☐ TruMatch Yes ☐   No ☐

Process Color - RGB Yes ☐   No ☐ CMYK Yes ☐   No ☐ HSB Yes ☐   No ☐

Pantone Process Color Simulation Yes ☐   No ☐ Other Color Models Supported _____

Process color image separation module included? Yes ☐   No ☐

Does the program directly support spot color separation? Yes ☐   No ☐ Trapping ? Yes ☐   No ☐

Can output resolution be set by the program? Yes ☐   No ☐

Can the program accept color separated images? Yes ☐   No ☐

Dealer

Dealer Name _____ Salesperson Name _____ Phone # _____

Is there a return policy? Yes ☐   No ☐ Quoted Price $ _____

Features Required to Meet Your Needs

Study each package under consideration by sitting down with it in a store and using it to create a document. If your work involves substantial text, expedite this process by bringing in a word processing document on a disk for import into the program. Keep in mind that some special-purpose functions that are not imbedded in the program may be available at a reasonable cost from another company. QuarkXPress, for example, encourages other software houses to create QuarkXtensions—programs that add power and special-purpose functionality to QuarkXPress.

Speed and Ease of Use

All page layout programs differ in their operation. You may find that for personal reasons, you like the "feel" of one over another. You may also find that for the kind of documents you handle, one program is much faster with screen redraws and navigation than another. While this may seem unimportant if you're new to color publishing, a really hard-to-get-around-in program or one that takes 30 seconds to redraw the screen every time you change a word or two, adds a layer of frustration to projects on tight deadlines.

Painting, Image Processing, and Illustration Tools

The Mac provides a full complement of tools for manipulating images brought in from the outside world via scanners, as well as programs for desktop painting and illustration that allow you to create images of your own from scratch. Scanned images can also be brought into Mac painting and illustration programs and then manipulated into completely new composite images.

Using the power of the Mac, you can scan an old black and white family photo and colorize it, then lifting only the people, you can place them in a landscape taken by the Mariner space probe's visit to Mars. Next, add a few custom flying saucers overhead drawn in a Mac illustration program and paste in road signs reading, "Next Exit Luna City 60,000,000 Miles - Exiting Traffic Keep Right." The possibilities are endless, and the environment is extremely flexible and entertaining to work in. Best of all, programs for creating quality color illustrations like this on the Mac are available for under $200.

Photo #1 + Photo #2 =

Composite Photo of Birthday Photo and Buddha

Combining images is relatively easy with retouching programs. Just think of the "travel" pictures—like this one—that you can assemble!

There are three kinds of programs for creating and manipulating images. As the price and functionality of the products increase, the lines begin to blur between the product types. The standard classifications of programs include paint programs, illustration programs, and photo-retouching and color separation software, described in the following pages.

Paint Programs

A variety of software is available for "painting" on-screen with paint brushes, airbrushes, and a bucket for dumping "paint" into large areas. There are even charcoal, colored pencil, and transparent watercolor effects available in some packages. Most high-end paint programs have built-in color separation capabilities as well. Some paint programs include Painter, PixelPaint Professional (currently up for sale to another company), and Oasis.

Illustration Programs

Different than paint programs, illustration programs provide tools for using the computer to draw precision curves and irregular shapes that can be readjusted as many times as desired. Because these programs also support elaborate color type effects, they can be used to create crisp logos, complex design elements, and almost any kind of illustration possible on a computer. Most of these programs directly support color separation through an integrated color separation utility. Adobe Illustrator and Aldus Freehand are two popular illustration packages.

Photo-retouching and Color Separation Software

Photo-retouching software is used to enhance and modify scanned photographs and can be used for Mac-based retouching. These packages can also color separate scanned photos and images created in paint programs. Not all color separation programs support retouching and painting functions, but most do. Three notable programs in this category are Adobe Photoshop and Letraset's ColorStudio. For image correction and color separation only, there's Cachet from EFI, Color Access from Barneyscan, and SpectrePrint Pro from PrePress Technologies.

Other Software

In addition to these three categories of software, there are also *draw programs, CAD programs*, and *rendering software*. Draw programs work much like illustration programs with more emphasis on precision and less on professional quality color illustration. To the color publisher they are less expensive and easier to learn. You may use them, but because of their limited support for color, illustration programs are more appropriate for advanced color graphics.

CAD (computer-aided design) programs are used to create mathematically precise images required for architectural work, product design, and for specifying mechanical parts and assemblies. They can also be used to create three-dimensional "frames," and then a rendering program can be used to add a skin over this frame to make a solid-looking object, complete with color, texture, and illumination from a properly positioned light source. This software may be used within the framework of color publishing to create ultra-realistic images and product packaging. The 3-D effects are unimportant in most other color publishing documents.

Evaluating Full-color Paint Programs

There are a variety of paint programs for the Macintosh capable of handling high-resolution 32-bit color (full color). These programs vary considerably in their functionality, features, and ease of use. The most basic ones offer limited toolbox options and lack sophisticated features, but still allow the creation of dazzling color images on the Mac's screen.

The more powerful paint programs offer masking capabilities. In conventional terms, a mask is a layer of material that blocks paint. When using a real airbrush, an adhesive plastic material (the mask) is carefully cut and laid down on the surface where paint is not desired—much like a stencil. In computer terms, masks work much the same way, except that you can also create a mask that allows an entire image to be pasted down on top of another image. With a Mac you have full control of where an image shows and where it doesn't. Ghost-like effects are possible too, by creating a mask that allows only a percentage of an image to be laid on top of another image—a very elegant tool.

While almost anyone can fully explore the tools available in color paint programs in minutes, it takes practice to become proficient. The ordinary mouse that comes with every Mac becomes awkward when used as a brush or pencil within a color painting program. In fact, most serious Mac-based illustrators use an electronic tablet of one kind or another to give them greater control over the painting process.

Tablets can be used with a more natural stylus-like device for drawing and painting. You can also place an image on a tablet surface and then trace its image directly into the computer. A new generation of pressure-sensitive tablets such as the Wacom Tablet (affectionately known as the "Whack 'Em Tablet" in the industry) responds to the pressure of the stylus as you draw. Depending on how it's set up, it either draws darker and/or wider lines as you push harder on the surface of the tablet. Pressure-sensitive tablets are also available from Kurta and other manufacturers.

Photo #1   +   Mask   +

Photo #2   =

The mask controls the combination of image elements.

Masks can be used to control the way one image element is added to another.

When used with programs such as Oasis from Time Arts, a pressure-sensitive tablet can provide effects that look amazingly like conventional tools. Within Oasis, you can build watercolor washes of differing densities and even produce dry brush and other painterly effects through the tablet. This combination of hardware and software can also mimic pastel, charcoal, and colored pencil textures and densities.

Tip: Use Talc to Make Drawing Easier

When using a Wacom or another tablet to draw or trace images, one of the stickier points is the way your hand starts and stops because of skin moisture as it moves across the tablet face. To fix this problem, lightly dust your hands with talcum power before and during work sessions. Pool players use talc to make the cue glide smoothly in their hands, so why shouldn't you? (Don't, however, use talc for the same purposes with a mouse. It may cause slippage of the mouse's movement sensors or obscure the movement-reading optics.)

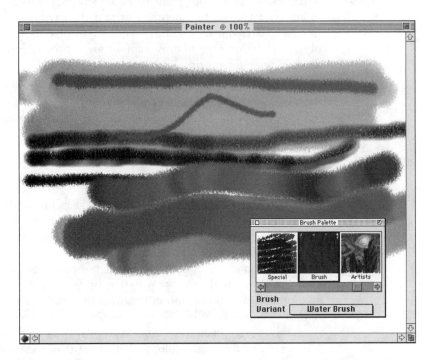

Watercolor effects are possible on the desktop with color blends and brush-like textures, as shown in this desktop "wash drawing" test done with Painter.

Oasis also provides the watercolorist's dream, paint that dries slowly according to how the controls are set. One of the prettiest effects possible with conventional watercolors is to work wet-in-wet, that is to lay down a color on a wet paper surface and then add a second color, so the two blend in a controlled manner. Unfortunately, because of variables such air temperature, paper surface, and a hundred other factors, keeping one color evenly wet long enough to add another is not always possible. With Oasis and similar programs on the Mac, the color *never* has to dry if you don't want it to!

The criteria for choosing a color paint program include those detailed below.

- **Ease of Use** Most color paint programs are quite intuitive, but a few have odd tool boxes or effects hidden in layers of commands. Try out the tools and controls to see what kinds of effects are possible. Does each function work as expected, or are some tools hard to handle? Mixing, choosing, and saving custom color palettes are easier in some programs than in others.

- **High-resolution Capabilities** Inexpensive color paint programs support a resolution of only 72 dots per inch. If you plan to color separate and print your paint-based illustrations, this is inadequate unless you paint a big picture first and then reduce the image to increase its resolution. Though your monitor only displays at 72 dpi, your paint program must support greater resolution in order to look convincing in print.

- **Support of Pressure-sensitive Tools** Since this is the wave of the future, you will want a program that supports pressure-sensitive tablets even if you don't plan to use this capability immediately.

Tip: If Only a Chef's Hat Could Make You a Chef…

When considering a color paint program, keep in mind that the sample illustrations you see in product ads and promotional literature are almost always rendered by professional illustrators. You may not be able to duplicate their level of skill without years of serious study and practice. While this is not meant to be discouraging, sit down with a color program under consideration and attempt to create an illustration typical of the kind you plan to use in your documents. While there's no question that the computer offers advantages over traditional methods, such as instant and near-perfect gradations of color and an eraser that doesn't scuff the drawing surface, computerized painting tools require time and practice to master, just like the conventional ones do.

Definition: Anti-aliased

Sounding rather like a procedure for removing Martians from city streets, this is actually a system of eliminating a computer-based weakness when drawing angles and curves. Aliasing is a problem that crops up when a complex angle or curve is rendered by a computer without enough resolution to handle the job. Visible to the eye in the form of stair-step lines and jagged curves, aliasing can be reduced and nearly eliminated by PostScript. Some software packages compensate by softening the line by adding dots to the edge halfway between the line's color and the background color. This "softening" of the hard edge makes problematic lines and curves look natural and removes the "jaggies" from type and object edges.

Aliased line with prominent
stair-stepping

Anti-aliased line without
stair-stepping

- **File Format Compatibility** The Mac supports several different file formats (see Chapter Four for the options). Check to see what formats a prospective paint program can open and save in. Make sure that these are compatible with other software you plan to use.

- **Adequate Speed** While largely a function of the Mac's CPU and video board, some programs are far faster than others when recreating the screen after changes. A slow paint program takes the fun out of building elaborate color images. If you spend more time twiddling your stylus while waiting for a screen redraw than you do painting, the program is not for serious color work.

- **Useful Features** Check for anti-aliased brushes and type (if you aren't using a routine such as Adobe Type Manager to smooth type edges). Anti-aliasing features create type and brush edges that appear without jagged edges. Also look to see if a masking layer, perspective plane, or other extras come with the package.

- **Color Separation Support** Depending on your needs and the other software you own or plan to acquire, you may want to purchase a paint program that can handle its own color separations.

Evaluating Illustration Programs

Illustration programs such as Freehand and Illustrator provide powerful tools for creating professional-quality illustrations, even if you're a novice illustrator. In paint programs, once an element is drawn on the screen, it becomes a permanent part of the image unless it's carefully erased. Illustration programs, on the other hand, maintain each line, shape, and piece of type as individual elements that can be moved, changed, or deleted, without affecting the rest of the image. (This is explained further in Chapter Four.)

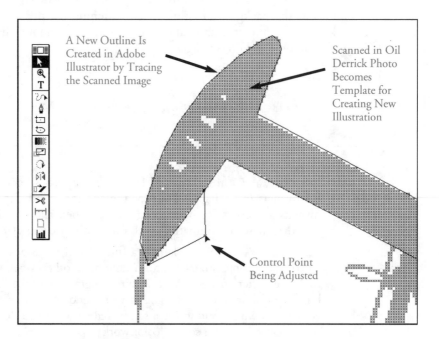

A New Outline Is Created in Adobe Illustrator by Tracing the Scanned Image

Scanned in Oil Derrick Photo Becomes Template for Creating New Illustration

Control Point Being Adjusted

In this example, the pump head scan has been used as a template. Then new lines are drawn around it. These lines can be fine-tuned to fit, as shown.

These programs come with a built in "cheat sheet"—the ability to take a scanned image and then build a new illustration on top of it while correcting mistakes and adding entirely new elements. Color, textures, and other effects can be composited as required. In addition, new items can be created by using the drawing tools built into the program. After the redrawing process is complete, the original scanned image is removed, leaving a fresh new illustration in its place. Paint images can also be imported into illustration programs, where they become objects that can be moved around and resized to fit the space at hand, but can't be otherwise manipulated.

Within these programs, complex curves can easily be adjusted by grabbing any point on a curve and dragging it to a new position (called Bézier points and Bézier curves). This is a powerful feature for the "I-can't-even-draw-a-straight-line-with-a-ruler" crowd. The Mac automatically handles the mop-up operations on the geometry while you go on with the next drawing operation.

Illustration programs are fully capable of handling complex type effects and manipulating text in complex arrangements. Colored type, graduated shadows, and a variety of other effects are not only possible but simple. With Illustrator, you can take the outlines of existing type characters and modify them into a completely new typeface.

When choosing an illustration program, you want to carefully study the functionality, because the range of features, as in page layout programs, is extensive. Practice with one of these programs to see if you can relate to the system of Bézier curves and points that are the heart of this software—some people find this technique impossible. Instead they fall back on paint programs or conventional illustration techniques. In addition to a comfortable interface, quick screen redraw, and support for several compatible file formats, look for:

- **The Right Feature Set** Choose a program with a feature set that most closely meets your needs. In the case of Illustrator and Freehand, the companies that created them are constantly playing a game of leapfrog to add functionality and new tools, so make sure you are working with the latest version during evaluation.

- **Accurate Color, both on Screen and at the Imagesetter** For color illustration, you need a program that produces accurate on-screen color on a color-calibrated monitor and predictable color results when output at the service bureau. Ask your SB for advice in this regard. If you don't own a color separation program, choose an illustration package that includes a color separation module in the purchase price.

- **Speedy Assembly** If you are forced to specify colors through lengthy command sequences or to go to Preview Mode to see what your drawing looks like after making a minor change, this significantly reduces your throughput and makes drawing a lot less fun. Test the kind of work you plan to do with the program and see which product lends itself best to the job and your working style.

Evaluating Image-retouching and Color Separation Programs

Programs that allow you to take a scanned image, retouch it, and create color separations ready for the printer (via a service bureau) are the most technical and sophisticated tools in the color publishing toolbox. With the right package, you can drive your scanner directly with an add-on scanner driver, providing instant image enhancement capability without changing programs and wasting time.

Color separation-only programs are the most basic products in this group and usually offer color correction and only a limited set of filters for fixing images. The full-feature image-retouching and color separation programs have a more robust toolbox and a larger set of filters and effects. Most of these programs contain drawing tools that allow you to add elements to images or create completely new illustrations, similar in power to a well-equipped color paint program. In addition, these image programs can color separate scans and images created in other programs. The two kinds of programs are differentiated as follows:

- **Color Separation Programs**   These programs color separate images and offer color correction and filtering facilities to improve image quality.

- **Image-retouching and Color Separation Programs**   In addition to color separation, these packages allow extensive "repairs" to be made to damaged images. They also support the application of special effects filters capable of a wide range of transformations (such as converting a color image into something that looks like a stained glass window). These programs have a toolbox for touching up and adding new elements to an existing image or painting a new image from scratch. The most tool-laden program, ColorStudio, provides color separation capabilities and a complete toolbox like a color paint program.

A fundamental requirement for these programs is the ability to produce high-quality color separations (at the service bureau) that also look good on press. To check this, use the programs under consideration to color separate a couple of scanned photos and have proofs made to check color. (We cover proofs in Chapter Ten.) Talk with service bureaus and print shops for recommendations as well. Because these are powerful programs with considerable engineering and testing behind them to ensure reliable output, they tend to be on the expensive side.

Photoshop is a popular and powerful image-retouching and color separation program. Both Photoshop and its competitor ColorStudio can run a color scanner directly with the right software "plug-in" module.

In addition to a comfortable interface and quick screen redraw, listed below are some other features to look for when choosing an image manipulation and color separation program. (If you don't understand all the terminology used here, don't worry, it will be discussed later in the book. If you have that lost feeling, use the glossary or read the sections on using these programs in Chapters Seven, Eight, and Nine.)

- **Extensive Color Handling Capabilities**   These programs should allow color to be adjusted with predictable and repeatable results. If you're new to color publishing, consider a package with "automatic color enhancement features." While these don't provide the quality available from a knowledgeable color separator who can make superior adjustments manually, the automatic features are easy to use and improve images significantly over doing nothing.

- **Useful Features**   Depending on your needs, you will want a program that supports advanced features such as masking and alternate image channels, as well as offering anti-aliased brushes and type capabilities similar to those found in color paint programs.

- **An Easy-to-understand Feature Set**   Most of these programs have elaborate feature sets that vary in accessibility and ease of use, so the documentation is more important for this software than for any other Mac-based color publishing product. Check out the manual to see if it's straightforward in its explanation of each feature; if it looks and sounds like it's written for a brain surgeon, keep looking. Beware of very brief manuals accompanying one of these programs. It either means that the program doesn't do much or, more likely, that you'll have to figure out how to use it through trial and error.

- **Flexible and Useful Filters**   Most photo-manipulation programs offer "must have" effects such as *Unsharp Masking* and softening. (*Unsharp Masking* is explained in Chapter Eight.) Others offer a wide variety of special effect functions in addition to the standard ones. Most of these sound neat but never get used.

- **Color Model Conversion and Support for CMYK Editing**   You want the capability to convert an image built in one color model to another. For example, a RGB color image created in a paint program must be converted to CMYK color to print it. Newer programs offer direct editing of images in CMYK mode on screen, reducing surprise color shifts during conversions. (See Chapter Six for details on color standards.)

- **Resampling Tools (Resizing Tools)**   Resampling tools allow you to resize an image by having the program "reconstruct" it rather than simply shrinking or enlarging it. Resampling can also be used to change an image's resolution within the program by adding extra dots through interpolation when necessary. Resampling is accomplished by using a "Resizing" command in most programs.

- **Compatibility with Other Programs and Prepress Systems**   You want to ensure that an image program works well with file formats you plan to use. Most of these packages are quite flexible in their support for file formats.

- **Support by Several Local Service Bureaus**   Choose a package that is supported and recommended by several service bureaus in your city. That way, if there's a problem, they can add an experienced hand to help you sort it out.

- **Handling of Black and White Images Directly**   If your work includes the processing of black and white images, choose a package that gracefully handles both color and black and white. Otherwise, you will need to purchase and learn an additional grayscale manipulation program, such as ImageStudio or Digital Darkroom, to handle non-color images.

Original Image

Add Noise Filter

Emboss Filter

Twirl Filter

Mosaic Filter

Pointillize Filter

Examples of Photoshop and ColorStudio filter effects

- **Support for Pressure-sensitive Tablets**   If you plan to use the program for serious painting as well as color correction, retouching, and separation, you'll want access to pressure-sensitive tablet technology.
- **A Scanner Driver Compatible with Your Scanner**   If you're purchasing the program to use with a specific color scanner, see if there's a driver available that allows you to scan directly from within the program.

Type Manipulation Tools

Many general-purpose and specialty page layout programs are capable of subtle manipulation of type used in headlines and body copy. But, when it comes to really elaborate effects such as those used in logos, posters, and some ads, type manipulation software is required. Formerly the domain of expensive script artists, type designers, and typographers with special equipment capable of distorting type with special lenses, many elaborate type effects can now be accomplished by a novice on the Mac using programs designed for this purpose.

Unlike page layout programs intended to handle large volumes of text, these programs are designed to manipulate small amounts of type—usually no more than several words. However, the range of effects available within these programs is startling, with the ability to distort, enhance, and reshape letters, and add visual elements and color. A complex logo that might once have cost thousands of dollars in design and production costs can now be produced in less than an hour.

Not to be confused with programs such as Fontographer, which are used to design new typefaces, type manipulation programs offer the color publisher incredible flexibility to manipulate existing fonts. More importantly, depending on the package selected, color separation is possible and a variety of typefaces can be employed—including fonts that come with the program and Abobe-compatible fonts available from other sources. Two popular type manipulation tools are TypeStyler from Broderbund Software and LetraStudio from Letraset.

Now you know what tools are available for Macintosh publishing and what to look for when choosing color publishing tools for your toolbox. While the sheer number of products available is substantial, and more are coming to market, after reading these last two chapters you should be able to evaluate products and select the ones that best meet your needs.

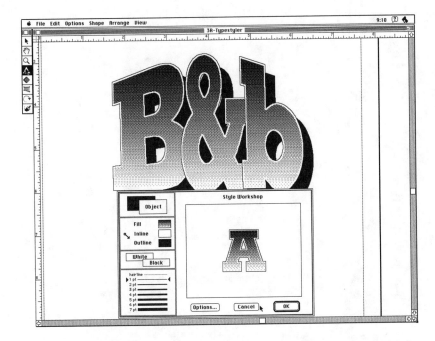

Produced conventionally, such a complex logo may take days and hundreds of dollars. With TypeStyler, it can be created in minutes, complete with color.

In the next chapter, we'll look at Macintosh file formats and other conventions and standards you need to be aware of for color publishing. Important environments such as PostScript will be explained and the nuts and bolts of color publishing techniques will be presented. We also look at alternative sources for images to be used in color publishing documents.

CHAPTER

4

MACINTOSH STANDARDS
AND FORMATS FOR
COLOR PUBLISHING

"An expert is someone who knows some of the worst mistakes that can be made in his subject and how to avoid them."

— Werner Heisenberg

In conventional color publishing, a designer takes physical components such as type and glues them down to a board to create a mechanical. The mechanical is used by the printer to create the film that will then be converted into press plates for printing. Mechanicals consist of a bottom layer of illustration board and layers of film and tissue overlays on top. The bottom layer contains the elements that print as black, such as type and lines. Each layer of film represents one color, and the elements pasted down on each layer will print that layer's color. Illustrations that consist of simple line art are mounted to the mechanical for direct processing. Photos and complex illustrations are not directly incorporated into the work. Instead a photocopy or sketch is mounted where the art should be added by the print shop, and color separations are made later.

Developing a traditional mechanical requires expertise in setting and specifying type, manually indicating color breaks, creating overlays, and assembling the paste-ups. The tools and materials required include rubylith (transparent red adhesive-backed material), rubber cement or wax, X-acto knives, and burnishing tools, in addition to a drafting table and a parallel rule.

On the Mac many of these mechanical processes are automated. Instead of a physical mechanical, the Macintosh creates the final document on screen and an imagesetter produces film directly from the Macintosh file. The film replaces the mechanical and is much closer to being ready for plating than traditional mechanicals. If color separations are included in the output film, the printer can create plates without any further assembly.

Macintosh automation does not mean that special expertise is no longer required to get to print, however. To assure that the imagesetter output produces accurate film for printing, the color desktop publisher requires a basic but intimate knowledge of how the Mac represents publishing information internally. Desktop designers must exchange their knowledge of *repro* and paste-up techniques for expertise in specifying files, operating software, integrating graphic elements from different programs, and managing the files used to create color documents on the Mac.

You Are Here

This chapter presents several fundamental aspects of the internal operations and file representations that are central to color production on the Mac, including:

- The differences between the formats used to create drawings and illustrations and what each format is best used for

- The formats used to represent black and white, grayscale, and color images, and information on the impact these formats may have on the quality of the final document

- The various ways type can be represented and the advantages of each

- The different file conventions used by the Mac to represent images and the considerations in using one file format as opposed to another

- Memory management considerations that will make manipulating images and documents easier and faster

- How to fix the frequent and unexplained system crashes that can occur when using complex software to manage large documents.

Why should you read about these seemingly technical and uncolorful topics? Well, if you save a color scan as an EPS file rather than a TIFF, it will take up substantially more disk space and memory and may be impossible to manipulate from the desktop. Or, if you design with "harmonized" fonts in a program that uses font ID numbers to identify the typefaces in your document, you may pick up a job from your service bureau with clunky Courier substituted for graceful Garamond. You will need to redo the film as a result. These small but annoying problems go on and on—especially if you aren't familiar with important Macintosh internal structures and standards.

Even though you want to start choosing colors, playing with effects, and designing stunning publications on the desktop, invest the time to read about these mundane issues before you do. Your work will go faster, and you'll produce more consistent results in the long run.

Paint-type Graphics versus Object-oriented Graphics

In color publishing, there are two kinds of graphic representations for manipulating scans and creating illustrations. They are dissimilar in structure and have very different applications in Macintosh color publishing. These two formats are paint-type graphics and object-oriented graphics.

Paint-type images are comprised of dots or dot structures. These dots may represent simple black and white, grays, or colors. Object-oriented graphics are composed of individual "objects" and each one remains a separate entity that can be individually manipulated. Unlike paint-type graphics where the image is described by dots, each object is described mathematically to define its shape, angles, and fills. These representations are also called draw-type graphics or vector-based graphics.

Paint-type Graphics

Because paint-type graphics are made from a combination of dots, the quality and detail of these images are a function of their resolution, which is specified as "dots per inch" or "dpi." Images made up of a larger number of dots per inch have greater clarity and detail.

Paint-type graphics are used on the Mac for "painting" images in programs such as Painter, DeskPaint, and PixelPaint Professional, among others. When you paint a line in a paint program, you are adding a series of dots to the image. If the new line overlaps a previously drawn element, the first element is partially replaced by the new one. Paint-type images are also used for scanned images and as a result, a scan can be retouched dot by dot.

Here's when to use and when not to use paint-type images in your color work:

Pros

- Paint-type images are the only way to represent a scanned image on the Mac. A properly scanned paint-type image can be extensively retouched, added to, pasted into another image, or completely changed from within a paint or retouching program.

- Paint-type graphics are used for all Mac painting programs because color changes and editing can be made one dot at a time. The image can be magnified on screen to retouch glitches in scans and to identify and fix rough edges and stray dots. Paint programs employ dot structures because they allow textures similar to those created with conventional brushes and paint to be produced.

Cons

- Don't use paint-type graphics for images that must be extensively resized. Resizing black and white-only images (no grays or colors) results in unattractive patterning. Resizing other paint-type images within a page layout program is a time-consuming process on an imagesetter and may precipitate an imagesetter crash in extreme circumstances. This won't win you any popularity contests at your service bureau.

- Paint-type graphics may not be suitable for drawings that contain a large number of hard-edged lines. When paint-type images are output at high-resolution on the imagesetter, edges of circles and diagonal lines may appear stair-stepped or rough. This can be worked around to some degree by painting or scanning at a high resolution.

As mentioned, improperly reducing or enlarging paint-type black and white-only images can result in unattractive and unexpected results. (These images are called bitmaps and are discussed later in this chapter.) When reducing a black and white-only bitmapped graphic, the Mac samples every four pixels to make one, and to enlarge such a graphic, every one pixel becomes four. Thus, for best results paint-type images must be reduced and enlarged in multiples of four dots.

For example, a bitmapped image scanned at 400 dpi and then reduced to 211 dpi has either too many or too few dots to evenly spread over the space (see example). This results in an unattractive patterning that resembles a cheap plaid sports coat. If this same image were reduced to 100 dpi, the Mac could accurately display the image without patterning because the ratio of dpi in the first image compared to the desired dpi is a 4:1 ratio. (Because a 4:1 ratio is may be too deep a reduction or enlargement, 2:1 works almost as well for many images.) Printing a bitmapped graphic can also cause problems, because a 220-dpi image output on a 300-dpi laser printer will not provide the right number of dots for the printer to distribute correctly on the paper.

In conclusion, paint-type images are used for scans and painting programs. They are good at representing continuous tones and colored textures. Their limitations are apparent when working with line art and images that need to be resized. Object-oriented images, described next, eliminate these problems, but can't be used for the same images that paint-type graphics are best at.

Resizing black and white paint-type graphics may introduce unsightly patterning if the four-to-one rule is ignored. Odd reductions such as 67.5% cause the most severe problems.

Object-oriented Graphics

Object-oriented drawing programs use mathematically defined "objects" rather than dot structures to define images. This method of representing images is very powerful for creating detailed illustrations of all kinds, especially those comprised of hard-edged lines that employ precise color fills and carefully defined variations in color. Instead of drawing a line consisting of a series of dots, object-oriented programs draw a "100 percent black line, 1/64" wide from Point A to Point B."

Because the line is a set of mathematical instructions rather than a series of dots, the line actually appears more solid as it is printed at higher resolutions. And, because the line exists as a command, if the size of the image changes, the algorithms used by the program will automatically specify where the line will be drawn and how big and wide it is in proportion to the new dimensions. Of course, you aren't aware of these calculations being generated by the computer. That is handled transparently as you draw, resize, and otherwise modify an object-oriented image.

Unlike paint programs, where each new element becomes integrated on one layer as part of the total image, in an object-oriented program (such as Illustrator) each object remains a separate entity, fully capable of being moved, changed, or discarded without affecting other objects. Object-oriented programs, including illustration programs and page layout programs, use multiple layers to represent a document or image. Each object floats either in front, behind, or on the same layer as all other elements and remains independent. In a paint program, when something is removed it must be erased dot by dot, leaving blank space where the element used to be. The image must then be fixed or modified in the erased areas. When an element is erased from an object-oriented image, the rest of the drawing remains intact.

Here's when to use and when not to use object-oriented images in your publications:

Pros

- Object-oriented drawing formats are standard in Mac-based illustration programs. Paint-type images can be imported into these programs, but there they become an object incapable of further editing. The drawing and type placement tools within page layout programs are all object-oriented.

- Use object-oriented tools for any drawing that requires extensive resizing. Because "objects" exist only as mathematical descriptions, resizing is exact and automatic. For example, if you create a new logo for a company, the same art used on business cards can be imaged at a size large enough for a small lighted sign by simply specifying a larger size.

Cons

- Don't attempt to use object-oriented illustration programs for manipulation of scanned images. About all you can do is resize, crop, and float new objects in front of the scan.

- For freestyle painting, object-oriented illustration programs are slow to work with and too constrained. Their strengths are handling line illustrations and manipulating text. Subtle manipulation of color tints is best left to paint programs. Object-oriented illustration programs do not support paint-type tools like brushes and airbrushes.

Bits, Bytes, and Color—How Images Use Memory

When using color images in your documents, it's important be aware of the way they use memory. This knowledge allows you to maximize image quality while minimizing storage space and imaging time. Black and white bitmapped images take up much less memory and hard disk space than grayscale or color representations. This is because a black and white image requires substantially less information to "describe" it than a color one does.

Macintosh computers represent black and white, grays, and color within memory by structuring images according to the number of colors they contain. As you probably know if you've been using a Mac or other computer for a while, most computers use binary (base-two) numbering for all of their memory functions because this system lends itself nicely to electrical systems. Like a light switch on the wall, each memory unit in the Mac's RAM is either on or off. Each of these on/off units within memory is called a *bit*. The combination of on and off bits is used to represent different data.

A single bit can only represent two colors because it can only be on or off. Thus, one bit is required to represent a black or white dot. *On* represents black; *off* represents white. Groups of bits are used to handle grays and more complex colors. Eight of these bits are called a *byte*, and four bytes (32 bits) is a Macintosh *word*. Computers process information in word sizes—the bigger the word, the more information that can be processed at one time.

Black and White Bitmapped Images

The simplest images are composed of black and white dots with no grays in between. These images are called bitmaps. Each bit within a bitmap can be either black (on) or white (off). These kinds of images are the most compact when stored in memory or on a hard disk. They are also the most limited in their ability to be manipulated.

This bitmapped image of an old photo is made up of black dots of various sizes to simulate the range of grays.

This is the same image scanned and manipulated as a grayscale on the Mac. Note how much better it looks than the previous bitmapped image.

Grayscale Images

The next step in image complexity is the grayscale. Grayscales are made up of as many as 256 different grays. Instead of just a single bit representing black or white, grayscales use one byte (eight bits) to hold a number that corresponds to the correct shade of gray. Gray number zero is white. Gray number 256 is black. The numbers in between represent the various gradations from black to white. Eight bits (a fourth of a word) are used because in base-two numbering (binary) the maximum number that can be represented with eight bits is—you guessed it—256. This also means that an eight-bit grayscale image consumes approximately eight times more memory than a simple black and white image.

Eight-bit Color or Indexed Color

The Mac also offers eight-bit color that works in much the same way as grayscale. Up to 256 colors can be represented in eight-bit mode because that is how many colors can be represented within eight bits in memory. Each number refers to a different color. This is also called *indexed color* because a number is assigned to each color, like an index or look-up table. This index is used by the computer to identify the colors and to create each specified color on screen or in the document.

Full Color, 24-bit Color, and 32-bit Color

The next and final level in image complexity is full color. Full-color representations use a full word of Mac memory to represent each dot or pixel within an image. Full-color images use 24 bits to specify the number representing each color. In base-two numbering, 24 bits can represent almost seventeen million numbers—plenty of color choices! But wait, if each word contains 32 bits, why are only 24 used? Well, an untrained human eye as owned and operated by the man on the street can only distinguish around 1.5 million colors. The trained eye of a custom ink mixing specialist can distinguish around 7.5 million colors. So, more than seventeen million color choices would be pointless. The remaining byte in the Mac word is either ignored or used by software to represent other data about the image.

Full color is also called 24-bit and 32-bit color by product manufacturers, but these terms refer to almost identical systems of color representation. We have used the term "full color" throughout the book for consistency.

You may also hear terms such a *pixel depth* and *image depth* used to refer to the storage of color data. These terms refer to a theoretical "depth" where each dot in eight-bit color is eight bits deep. A black and white image is only one bit deep because only one bit is required to describe each black or white dot. A full-color image is 24 bits deep. (Really 32 bits deep, but only 24 bits are used to represent the color.)

The reason you need to understand color representation in memory is because full-color files are huge due to the amount of memory required to store each pixel in the image. Storage and memory are always at a premium in a computer system. The smaller the files, the faster you can process them. However, the large color files hold more information in the form of more colors or more pixels for a larger image. As a color publisher, you must balance these requirements to make maximum use of your system resources. If you scan a black and white image in full-color format, it will take up as much room as a four-color image, even though there are really only two colors in the image. The resulting file will be approximately 32 times larger than it needs to be, a waste of storage and processing capability.

On the other hand, if you have a full-color photograph for use in a high-quality brochure, you must use full 32-bit color to store the image, because this is the only way to represent the full spectrum of colors in the photo. If this file were saved as eight-bit color, it would look dithered and unnatural, even though the file would be smaller and easier to store and image. Eight-bit color should only be used for screen representations or for files that will not be color separated. Eight-bit color does not have enough information for adequate color separations.

Memory and Color Publishing

As one of the most memory-intensive uses of the Macintosh, color publishing stretches most Macs to the limit, sometimes causing crashes when pushed too far. As a color publisher you can do a few things in order to cut down system bombs and manage your memory more efficiently.

Your first line of defense is to have a machine with enough RAM memory, as we discussed in Chapter Two. The Mac's operating system continues to grow in size, as do the sophisticated application programs used for color page layout and illustration. These programs and color page layout and image files use up a lot of RAM when you create and modify documents. The more RAM you have, the bigger the files and programs you can work with simultaneously.

Your second line of defense is to give each application the room it needs to breathe easily while carrying out its work. Mac software publishers, in their zeal to keep their products "compatible" with older Macs' limited memory resources, often specify their product's memory requirements on the low side. For example, one large page layout program sets the memory to a default of 1.5 MB. Then, as soon as purchasers load the program and can't get it to print, they call the company's technical support line. The company's technicians, already intimately familiar with this problem, instruct the users to set the memory up to at least 2.5 MB if they plan to incorporate images and multiple typefaces (and how many desktop publishers don't?).

Tip: When Weird Problems Occur, Rebuild the Desktop

Color publishing often involves huge hard drives with a large number of files. One of our 200 MB hard disks has more than 1,500 files on it, as the tape back-up system regularly reminds us. With a large number of files, the hidden **Desktop** file that keeps track of what's where may become corrupt. One sign is the system telling you that a closed application is busy or the application that created a file can't be found. Fix this by rebuilding the desktop. To rebuild, reboot your Mac while holding down the **Option** and **Command** keys. Once you see the "Are you sure you want to rebuild the desktop?" dialog box, release the keys and click **OK**.

Signs that an application needs more memory include: frequent unexplained crashes when working on large files; extremely slow response when making changes and carrying out commands (often accompanied by lengthy hard disk activity); and obviously, any "Out of Memory" dialog boxes that appear on screen.

The memory available to Mac applications is controlled in the *Get Info* box. To check on memory settings for an application, click once on its icon to select it and select **Get Info** available under the Finder's **File** menu. A box will appear, showing you the manufacturer's memory recommendation and below it the current memory setting. To change the setting, simply select the numbers in the box below the recommended memory and enter a new value. How much should you increase an application's memory? A good rule of thumb for applications exhibiting the problems described is to add a quarter to a third more memory and see if the symptoms disappear.

The memory allocated to applications can be adjusted in the Get Info box.

If Problems Are Frequent or Insurmountable

Some color publishing problems are difficult to work around. When using a color Mac hooked to scanners, calibrators, video boards, and extra drives, and using large, complex applications, a lot can go wrong. One high-quality scanner we used regularly produced oddly misregistered scans. A typical scan produced color that was normal on the left side of the image but became increasingly misregistered toward the right side. The manufacturer spent considerable time with us on the phone but we got nowhere. Finally, when we took the unit to an Apple dealer and ran it on their machine, it performed flawlessly. The actual problem? A loading order conflict between the machine's System Extension and a recent update to a virus control program.

Frequent unexplained crashes may be the result of a corrupt system file, incompatible *System Extensions* and *Control Panels,* a corrupt application, or failed hardware. If an application crashes frequently and its manufacturer's technical support department isn't able to solve the problem, do the following:

- **Move All Non-Apple System Extensions and Control Panels** Put all non-Apple System Extensions and Control Panels into a folder on your hard disk outside the System Folder and restart. If the problem goes away, add the Extensions and Control Panels back into the System Folder one at a time, rebooting as you do. If the problem suddenly recurs, then the last Extension or Control Panel is incompatible with the application and is causing the problems. Or, it's incompatible with some section of the Mac's operating system. Extensions and Control Panels sometimes also have conflicts with each other. If this doesn't solve the problem then…

- **Reload the Problem Application**   Try replacing the application with a fresh copy from a locked disk. Erase the *preferences file* the application may have placed in the system file as well. (The application will replace the preferences after reloading. But, if substantial work has been put into it, such as custom color palettes or kerning tables, move the file into an unused folder for later retrieval.) If this doesn't solve the problem then…

- **Reload the System**   A variety of gremlins can corrupt the Mac's operating system. Try replacing it using the System Installer, after throwing out the current System Folder. If you keep a large number of fonts in the system itself, back these up first. If this doesn't solve the problem then…

- **"Zap" the PRAM**   Most Macintosh models have a tiny area of memory called PRAM (Parameter RAM). This memory stores information on the Mac's settings and maintains this information even when the machine is shut off or unplugged. Because this memory never changes unless you change the settings, should it become corrupt, it can cause a wide variety of strange problems and crashes. Check with your dealer on how to clear this memory if your machine has it. You may need to reset some of the Control Panel settings after doing it. If this doesn't solve the problem then…

- **Try the Offending Application or Hardware Elsewhere**   Bring your application or hardware into a sympathetic Apple dealer and attempt to make it run on one of their systems. If it operates fine there, consider having your Mac checked out for bad memory chips, bad sectors on your hard disk, SCSI problems, or power supply failure. If this doesn't solve the problem then…

- **Get a Fresh Copy of the Application or Acquire New Hardware** Occasionally master disks go bad, or manufacturers quietly update software to fix bugs and incompatibilities that produce unexplained crashes. Hardware simply fails from the normal causes—poor design, excess heat, old age, or mishandling. Static is a notorious enemy of interface boards like those commonly used to connect scanners to Macs. Replacement will either fix the problem or demonstrate that it is lurking elsewhere in your system. Keep in mind that newly released hardware and software may have problems that are not fixable by you. If you have just purchased a new product that doesn't work, return it ASAP or put pressure on the manufacturer and dealer to get the mess straightened out. If this doesn't solve the problem then…

• Consider reviewing your family lineage for curses inherited down through the generations.

System 6.X Users

There are still users working with versions of System 6 of the Mac's operating system because they like its smaller size and its tried and true compatibility with certain applications. If you are one of these people, there are a few things you may need to do on your Mac in addition to implementing the advice above.

First, if you use more than a couple of system extensions (called "Inits" in System 6), you may need to use Heap Tool on the supplied disk to modify your system's heap size. The heap size is the amount of memory allocated to the operating system by System 6. When too many inits are installed, the system may attempt to use more memory than allowed, precipitating sudden crashes.

To identify this problem, use the **About the Finder** command under the **Apple** menu. If the bar that represents the system's memory usage is more than eighty percent black (memory used) you need to remove inits or use a program such as Heap Tool to adjust the amount of memory available to the system.

In addition to adjusting your system's heap size, if you use Suitcase II or a similar program to manage your fonts and have more than a handful of font families in use at one time, you may want to provide the program with more memory as well. To give Suitcase II more space, click on the **Settings** button and then click on the **Power User** button. Once open, this option allows you to change the *Boot Blocks*. Changing this number to twenty from its default of twelve will usually solve the font management problems that may manifest themselves as printing errors.

Last, make sure you are using the final version of System 6—6.07. It has the best chance of being compatible with newer versions of color publishing software. Some products won't run with a version older than 6.04, or if they do run, they may crash more often than you'd like.

Updates to your system software (up to 6.07) are available from your Apple-authorized dealer for free if you supply the disks and do your own disk copying. If your system is numbered lower than six and you intend to work in color, update your system as quickly as possible. Don't even try any of the newer color-based programs until you do.

PostScript, QuickDraw, ATM, TrueType, and You

There are three major standards used on the Macintosh to describe page layouts and type—PostScript, QuickDraw, and TrueType. These standards usually go unnoticed unless one of them causes a problem or fails to perform as expected. As a color publisher you need to be aware of them in order to get the best results on screen, at the imagesetter, and when dealing with devices that don't employ Mac standards.

PostScript—the Standard that Defines the Page and the Type across Platforms

The standard that helped put Mac publishing on the map is a page description language called PostScript. Developed by Adobe Systems (Apple Computer was once a major shareholder in Adobe), PostScript provides a consistent platform for handling images and imaging needs on the Mac and other computers. PostScript is actually a programming language for defining pages.

Adobe Systems licenses PostScript interpreters to companies that manufacture output devices such as printers and imagesetters. When an image is saved in PostScript format it is converted into a long series of commands (a program) that describes how to redraw the image. Then a device, equipped with a PostScript interpreter, be it imagesetter, laser printer, or other system, reads and interprets the commands (or programs) that are stored in the PostScript files and uses them to recreate the image. The PostScript interpreter then *rasterizes* the code into an image that can be output in finished form. (Rasterization is the creation or recreation of an image line by line from top to bottom. Your monitor is constantly rasterizing the Mac's display line by line but does it so fast that you can't see it.) There are other file formats, such as those produced by QuickDraw (discussed next), that can be interpreted by PostScript.

The power of PostScript is that it is capable of accommodating a wide variety of images and is "device independent." Device independence is one of PostScript's greatest advantages. This means that once a file is created in this format, it can be output on any device with a PostScript interpreter, and the file will image correctly (within limits), regardless of the output device's resolution and color capabilities. The same PostScript file that produces a page at 300 dpi on a laser printer can be produced on an imagesetter at 2,400 dpi. PostScript is device independent on the input side as well, and a variety of computer programs on various computer platforms are capable of generating PostScript-compatible files.

```
%!PS-Adobe-2.0
%%Title: Untitled-1 [draw]
%%Creator: PrintMonitor
%%CreationDate: Monday, May 6, 1992
%%Pages: (atend)
%%BoundingBox: ? ? ? ?
%%PageBoundingBox: 125 130 2425 3170
%%For: Mr. Bear
%%DocumentProcSets: "(AppleDict md)" 71 0
%% © Copyright Apple Computer, Inc. 1989-91 All Rights Reserved.
%%EndComments
%%BeginProcSet: "(AppleDict md)" 71 0
userdict/LW{save statusdict/product get(LaserWriter)anchorsearch
exch pop{dup length 0 eq{pop 1}{(Plus)eq{2}{3}ifelse}ifelse}{0}ifelse
    exch restore}bind put
userdict/downloadOK known not{userdict/downloadOK{systemdict dup/eexec
    known exch/cexec known and LW dup 1 ne exch 2 ne and and vmstatus exch
    sub exch pop 120000 gt and}bind put}if
userdict/type42known known not{userdict/type42known systemdict/
    resourcestatus known{42/FontType resourcestatus{pop pop true}
    {false}ifelse }{false}ifelse put}if
type42known not downloadOK and {userdict begin /*charpath /charpath load
    def/charpathflag false def/charpath{userdict/charpathflag true put
    userdict/*charpath get exec userdict/charpathflag false put}bind def
    end}if
userdict/checkload known not{userdict/checkload{{pop exec}
    {save 3 dict begin/mystring 6050 string def
exch/endstring exch def{currentfile mystring readline not{stop}if
    endstring eq{exit}if}loop end restore pop}ifelse}bind put}if
userdict/LW+{LW 2 eq}bind put
userdict/ok known not{userdict/ok{systemdict/statusdict known dup{LW 0 gt
    and}if}bind put}if
systemdict/currentpacking known{currentpacking true setpacking}if
/md 270 dict def md begin
/av 71 def
/T true def/F false def/mtx matrix def/s75 75 string def/sa8 8 string
    def/sb8 8 string def
/sc8 8 string def/sd8 8 string def/s1 ( ) def/pxs 1 def/pys 1 def
/ns false def
1 0 mtx defaultmatrix dtransform exch atan/pa exch def/nlw .24 def/ppr
    [-32 -29.52 762 582.48] def
```

Sample PostScript Code (beginning of file)

In addition, PostScript provides benefits to desktop publishers in the form of improved font quality. Font libraries have been created especially for manipulation by PostScript interpreters. PostScript font representations require only one example of each typeface to be stored for use by the PostScript interpreter. Any point size specified can be derived mathematically by PostScript. This saves memory over systems that require each font size to be stored separately. A font defined for PostScript applications ensures that font quality will be the best possible at that resolution.

There are more fonts available for PostScript than for any other standard. PostScript fonts are currently produced by Adobe, Bitstream, Linotype, and other established typographic companies. This makes the typographic choices available to desktop publishers almost limitless.

Adobe has created a standard (called Type 1) for describing PostScript fonts; it optimizes their representation by PostScript devices. Fonts that are specified as Type 1 are the easiest to use. PostScript will optimize the placement and arrangement of the dots on the page so that each character in each font remains highly readable and truly represents the original typeface design.

Like most software, PostScript is constantly undergoing major and minor revisions to improve its speed and to fix bugs and problems. The first major revision in PostScript code, PostScript Level 2, was released in 1991. The newer version offers better support for color and a number of other enhancements.

The advanced color publisher may choose to write PostScript programs, using strings of PostScript commands, by entering them as text in a word processor. (Save the file as ASCII to strip out the word processor codes.) These programs can then be interpreted just like other PostScript files. PostScript as a computer language uses commands that are fairly simple to learn, and with a little practice you can create stunning type effects and add borders and other effects to PostScript-based images stored in EPS format (described later in the chapter). Some knowledge of PostScript code also allows you to open a PostScript file and study the code to identify errors that are causing problems at the imagesetter or to fix minor inconsistencies in code coming from another computer platform.

It is not necessary to learn the PostScript language to gain the benefits of its precision and flexibility, however. Most color publishers let their application programs create the PostScript files. But, if there is a problem with outputting a PostScript file, a knowledgeable operator at a service bureau or other PostScript expert might be able to fix the file to print the way you want it to, for an appropriate fee of course.

QuickDraw—the Mac's Screen Drawing Routine

QuickDraw is the Macintosh's internal screen-drawing language, developed by Apple and used for representing type, images, and the Macintosh desktop on Mac monitors. QuickDraw's primary purpose is to represent information on screen, but it can also output images to printers and other devices. Its representation system can interpret screen-related events, such as moving a mouse or scrolling throughout a document, quickly and accurately. QuickDraw translates this information into representations compatible with a video display. QuickDraw can represent complicated images on the screen, but is not as powerful or accurate for printing documents as PostScript. QuickDraw does not create files that can be manipulated like PostScript files.

QuickDraw also has "hooks" into PostScript that allow non-Postscript files to be rasterized by a PostScript interpreter. When something like a plain vanilla PICT-format file needs to be printed, it is first loaded into memory and turned into a QuickDraw representation on screen. When you print this image, QuickDraw sends commands to the PostScript interpreter to create the output representation. Thus, a PostScript-based device can still print a non-PostScript file with quality representation. (PICT files are described later in the chapter.) Instead of creating "pure" PostScript files, many programs send QuickDraw representations to a PostScript interpreter, where they are then translated into PostScript output.

QuickDraw can also be used to directly drive printers and other devices that do not have a PostScript interpreter, but for the color publisher, the results printed with QuickDraw on a non-PostScript device may be substantially different than what is produced by the PostScript-based imagesetter, making QuickDraw inappropriate for color publishing. Some programs have a hard time producing reliable output when their files are printed with QuickDraw and may produce unexpected results.

ATM—No More Jagged Type on Screen!

ATM, the acronym for the product named Adobe Type Manager, accurately renders compatible typefaces on a Macintosh monitor the same way they will print. QuickDraw without ATM cannot render most typefaces smoothly or accurately. ATM is a free System Extension that replaces QuickDraw's type rendering commands with its own. (Apple reportedly plans to build ATM into the operating system sometime soon.) Before ATM, only a handful of Mac programs could render type on screen with any accuracy. While twelve-point type looked quite readable inside word processing software, larger sizes, italic faces, and fonts with characters made up of swirls and flourishes were barely readable.

ATM changed all that. With ATM installed, all Type 1 fonts become fully readable in all sizes and formats. Type 3 fonts (the non-Adobe PostScript font description standard) are not enhanced by ATM. (In case you're wondering, there is no Type 2 PostScript font description standard in practice. The standard was never commercially implemented. Type 3 is a dying standard, and most type foundries are moving their fonts to Type 1 compatibility.)

ATM is important to color publishers because it allows you to experiment with colored type on a colored field and get a much better idea of how type elements balance against other elements in the design. Without type enhancement technology like ATM, 30-point gold-colored italic text displayed against a dark blue background appears as a yellow-brown smear. In addition, kerning large typefaces (moving individual letters closer together to make headlines easier to read and more elegant) was impossible on screen before ATM because the letters were so hard to differentiate. ATM eliminates most of these problems.

This Is a Screen Shot of Type Drawn without Font Outlining Technology

This Is a Screen Shot of the Same Type Drawn *with* Font Outlining Technology

Bitmapped type versus outline fonts

The principal behind ATM is similar to the one used to render type in PostScript. Instead of having a bitmap of each character in each point size in memory, a mathematical description of the outline shape of each character is represented only once. This outline can be scaled to larger or smaller sizes in the same way object-oriented drawing programs scale elements in an illustration.

With QuickDraw, fonts are represented as bitmaps. When using bitmapped fonts, a different "picture" must be created from dots for each character in each size. Resizing a bitmapped font causes a visual mess unless the 4:1 ratio for resizing bitmaps is observed, as explained earlier in the chapter. Fonts created from bitmaps became increasingly rough as resolution increases because the dot structure becomes apparent.

Fonts represented by ATM can be resized in tiny increments, and because of this they are often called "scalable" fonts. Because these fonts are drawn with outlines instead of dots, they become cleaner as the resolution increases.

ATM is important for printing on non-PostScript devices, because it can be used to replace QuickDraw's font routines and produce smooth output for Adobe Type 1 Fonts. As a color publisher, you probably won't create much final output on non-PostScript devices, but if you produce color presentations on a non-PostScript film recorder used to create 35mm slides, ATM is a must for producing good-looking type.

TrueType

TrueType was the product of a joint venture between Apple Computer and Microsoft Corporation. TrueType is a font outline technology that works like ATM, although it supports fonts created using different standards than Adobe uses. TrueType comes free with new Macintoshes, Apple's non-PostScript printers, and Microsoft's Windows environment for IBM-PC compatible computers. It's advantages over ATM are not obvious. For handling type, it conceptually works the same way and has most of the same features. (Because Apple now bundles ATM in with its system software for the Mac, the future of TrueType looks questionable, though we aren't placing any bets on its demise yet.)

Since you will be working with service bureaus that have invested heavily in Adobe and other Type 1 fonts, TrueType may not allow you to create documents with fonts directly supported by your favorite SB. Some service bureaus are refusing documents with TrueType because they have experienced font substitution problems. Check with your service bureau to discover their feelings toward accepting and imaging documents with TrueType fonts. If you are considering mixing TrueType fonts with other kinds, such as Adobe Type 1 fonts, think twice, because fonts may be substituted incorrectly at the imagesetter.

Keeping Your Fonts in Harmony

Macintosh fonts are specified either by their name or by a number. This causes two problems for the desktop publisher that must be dealt with before heading for the service bureau. The best way (or at least the one that precipitates the fewest problems) is to use applications that manage fonts by name rather than by number. Most professional page layout programs work this way and use the actual name of the font instead of the number.

Some programs, such as Ventura Publisher, are for some undisclosed reason limited to using font names with only 30 characters or some other arbitrary length. Thus, if you use these programs with fonts with long names (rare) the font must be renamed within *ResEdit* (not fun).

Programs that rely on numbered fonts instead of named fonts can be a real problem when imaged. Macintosh fonts often have duplicate numbers, because there is no master scheme for font manufacturers to use when numbering their products. This is complicated by the fact that Apple didn't realize that there would be a literal explosion in the number of fonts designed for the Mac and provided only a limited number of possibilities when the computer was introduced and subsequently upgraded. Not only was the original font numbering system limited, it was also complicated and one of the few places where the Macintosh engineers lacked vision for future growth.

Today, fonts are referenced by a number between 1 and 32,767 (some numbers are reserved for use by Apple). Unfortunately, some fonts may attempt to use the same number if you have a large selection of fonts from several sources. One font is selected and a different one displayed. Fonts can also be incorrectly substituted on the screen if you move files from one Mac to another. One way to fix this problem is to put fonts in separate suitcases (using a program like Master Juggler) and then open only the font suitcases you need for specific documents.

Another method is to use a program such as Font Harmony, included with Suitcase II, to do the job. Font Harmony looks at all fonts stored in suitcases and then renumbers the ones with duplicate numbers. This works well on your system, but if you transport a file that uses harmonized font numbers to a service bureau's computer for imaging, their font numbers may not match your numbers. If one of their fonts used in a program that refers to fonts by number is not numbered the same way as yours, their font will replace your desired font when your job is output. If you don't use these programs, this isn't a problem.

If no font with the same name or number is available, Courier is usually substituted. (Courier is probably substituted because it is easy to notice on a page and acts like a red flag, informing you that font substitution has occurred. Pray that you notice it at the service bureau and not on press!)

Here are several ways to deal with font identification problems:

- Ask your service bureau to check and fix any problems. Bring a proof and a list of fonts so they can check the job on screen. There may be an extra charge for this service.

- Convert the document into PostScript and completely avoid the risk of such a problem.

- Only use software that references fonts by name, not by number. Apple has requested that all software developers reference fonts by name in future releases. Eventually they will all comply.

- Use recent versions of fonts from the same manufacturer and choose a service bureau that does the same. Newer font families from the same source use carefully chosen font ID numbers so there's no risk of font conflicts from the same manufacturer.

Font problems also occur when bitmapped fonts are specified within a document to be run out at the imagesetter instead of the ImageWriter they were designed for. (The ImageWriter was a low-cost, low-resolution dot matrix printer from Apple.) Because no PostScript outline font is available for bitmapped fonts, an unsightly dot-by-dot representation of the font is imaged or sometimes nothing is output at all. Bitmapped fonts look terrible when printed on imagesetters.

Macintosh Image File Formats

There are a number of file formats employed by the Macintosh for storing and transferring graphics files. Each of these has advantages and disadvantages, and some support color publishing better than others. In addition, not all programs support all formats, or they provide support that is limited, only partially compatible, or unpredictable. You should be aware of the strengths and weaknesses of each file type so that you don't run into problems using a file format that isn't the best choice for your work.

Mac File Formats

Formats	Use for	Advantages	Disadvantages
MacPaint	Not Recommended	—	Limited to 72 dpi
TIFF	Bitmapped, grayscale, color images, color separations	Relatively compact, stable, compatible with almost all Mac software	Multiple TIFF file formats not compatible with all programs
PICT	Object-oriented graphics, images where appropriate	Compact size	May move objects around. When object-oriented graphics are moved between programs, images may appear resized
RIFF	Images used with Letraset and Manhattan Graphics programs	Compact size, reliable	Not compatible with many programs
EPS	Grayscale, color images, object-oriented graphics from programs such as Adobe Illustrator, color separations	Reliable (usually)	Large file sizes are difficult to store and transport, image files may not be opened for changes
Proprietary File Format	Images that will be manipulated or imaged within the specific program	Saves and opens fast, may be other advantages particular to the specific program	Files not compatible with other software in many cases

Surprisingly, there is considerable misinformation on file formats and are differing opinions on which format produces the most reliable and consistent results. For example, one recent publication advises against using high-resolution PICTs because they are too unstable. Another recommends PICT files over TIFF files for the opposite reasons. An informal poll of ten West Coast service bureaus revealed that when queried about their preference for representing paint-type images, four favored PICT format files, another four favored TIFF, and two liked both formats equally. Which should you use? Well, it depends on the project and which formats are best supported by the color publishing software tools you are using.

Proprietary File Formats

Most applications have a proprietary file format, called a *native format*, that is all their own. Without a file translation program, a file saved in a proprietary format is inaccessible by other programs. Programs that use such a format also have a "Save as Other" option that allows you to save the file in a standard format for use by other programs. Here are the advantages and disadvantages of saving images in native format:

Pros

- When putting a job away for further work, a program's proprietary format may offer distinct advantages, including faster speed when making changes, access to features not available in other formats, and quicker screen redraws. In many cases these files open and save faster too, because the program does not have to do a conversion during the process. Programs such as Photoshop create compact files that open and close faster than TIFF or PICT-format files—a major advantage when working with giant color images.

Cons

- Files saved in native formats cannot be directly accessed by other programs in most cases. This can be a major problem when attempting to open an old but important file saved with an older program that no longer works with the current operating system. For common formats, translators may be available—but don't count on them if you don't have to.

MacPaint Format

Originally developed for the revolutionary MacPaint program, this format is the great grandaddy of all Mac illustration and painting formats. Things have come a long way since 1984 (fortunately), and this now-clunky format supports only 72 dpi and is useless for color publishing unless you are looking for a grainy black and white image.

You may come across MacPaint images in clip art and company files, however. You can make them look better by scaling the art down to 24 percent to increase the resolution, using another paint program such as Zedcor's DeskPaint. This will result in a physically smaller image, but it will have enough dots (300 dpi) that you may be able to use the image for something. If you save the new image as a PICT or TIFF you can colorize it. You can also convert the image, using Adobe Streamline, into a more modern image format capable of higher resolution and enhancement. Streamline is discussed in Chapter Fourteen.

When working in grayscale or color, avoid saving anything in this format even though it is still an option within many Mac graphics programs. If you convert a file into MacPaint format, you will lose most of the detail and all of the color because the MacPaint format caters to a low-resolution black and white world. The final advice on saving images in MacPaint format is *don't*—unless you plan to use the image only for screen display or as a muddy, for position only (FPO) marker to show where you want an image placed. MacPaint files are extremely compact, but that's because they contain such a small amount of information.

TIFF: Tagged Image File Format

The TIFF file format was developed by Aldus, makers of PageMaker, to replace the late but unlamented FOTO format used by PageMaker 1.2. Currently capable of supporting grayscales and full color at nearly any resolution, TIFF is a standard that has been adapted to other computers including IBM PC compatibles. (These formats are not exactly identical and require a translator to transfer most images.) TIFF is strictly a paint-type format, and many scanners and paint programs use TIFF as their default representation. TIFF, along with EPS format (described later) is the standard for files that will be color separated.

There are variations in this standard, and TIFF file formats are classified by letters. Class B TIFF supports only black and white images; Class R supports full-color images. The other classes are not important for color publishing. Most up-to-date software supports the current full-color standard. If in doubt, create a simple file with a couple of colored lines in it and then attempt to place the file in another color program or two. If it opens and the color looks right, it's probably fine. If not, then you may see a message like the one shown.

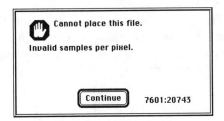

Importing an image in an incompatible file format into a page layout program will usually produce an error message.

The advantages and disadvantages of saving images in TIFF format include:

Pros

- TIFF is very useful for scans. It produces compact files, usually produces predictable results, and gets the job done relatively quickly.

- TIFF is the file format of choice for handling bitmapped images within PageMaker. TIFF images can also be displayed at high resolution within PageMaker, if you don't mind the wait for screen redraws. This format was originally designed by Aldus for PageMaker, and the two get along well together. PageMaker is also capable of reading a wide variety of TIFF implementations.

- TIFF is supported by most Mac graphics applications. Files saved in this format are compatible with all page layout programs, retouching programs, and most paint programs. Files saved as TIFFs can also be moved to other computer platforms like IBM PC compatibles, although translation may be required, depending on the TIFF standard employed and individual application program capabilities.

- TIFF offers easy compression of large images if the LZW (Lempel-Ziv-Welsh) compression option is selected in the originating program. This kind of compression is "lossless," so the entire file is maintained with no data compromises, although files compressed with this option remain more than half their original size. This does save some hard disk space, but not all programs can directly open compressed TIFFs.

- Many page layout programs allow single-color colorization and brightness and contrast adjustment of TIFF images.

Cons

TIFF is not completely standard, and there are rumored to be more than 32 minor and major variations in TIFF formats. Fortunately, the most common formats are created and supported by the most popular Mac graphics software.

PICT File Format

It's hard to say whether TIFF or PICT is the most popular graphic file format in the Macintosh world. PICT supports full-color bitmapped images, just like TIFF does. PICT also supports object-based draw images created by MacDraw and most illustration packages. As one of Apple's first image formats (along with MacPaint), it has been enhanced to handle color on Mac II series machines. In this format, it's called

PICT2, although when you save in a color program, the "2" doesn't appear. PICT is not widely used for creating color separations, however.

The advantages and disadvantages of saving images in PICT format include those listed here:

Pros

- PICT files support object-oriented drawing with great precision.

- PICT files tend to be more compact than either uncompressed TIFF or EPS graphics. This means that they take up less hard disk space and often image faster at the service bureau.

- PICT files can be opened by almost all Mac graphics and page layout programs. With a translation program, they can be imported into the IBM PC environment.

Cons

- PICT images used in some programs produce unexpected on-screen results. The rendering may appear much larger than the measurements specified within the application or scanning software. This occurs because the program displays the PICT at 72 dpi regardless of the file's actual physical size and resolution. When this occurs, the higher the resolution, the larger the on-screen image appears to be. While this makes retouching, accurate cropping, and resizing difficult, the picture will usually print and image at the correct size. To check the results of a resize operation, print a copy of the image on a PostScript-based laser or color printer—in most cases, it will turn out fine. If you are experiencing problems, check the program manuals for details concerning importing PICTs.

- A potential problem with object-based drawings saved as PICTs can occur when a drawing is moved between applications; some items may move around on the page, change their appearance slightly, or disappear altogether. This usually requires only minor fixes although major surprises do occur. One drawing we imported looked fine on screen, but imaged upside down for reasons unknown. As you work with PICTs, you'll learn which programs transfer PICT files best and where problems will creep in.

RIFF File Format

Raster Image File Format (RIFF) was developed by Letraset as an alternative file format for supporting grayscale and color images. It has alternate forms as an eight-bit format for handling grayscale images and as a 32-bit file format for specifying full-color images. RIFF files were designed to be compact, and they are useful for storing images on a cramped hard disk full of color images. There are advantages and disadvantages to saving images in RIFF format:

Pros

- RIFF files support both grayscale and color with good results.

- RIFF offers built-in compression that saves substantial disk space. These files are extremely compact compared to other formats.

- RIFF directly supports the transfer of large files to multiple floppy disks—a capability that makes transferring color images from Mac to service bureau much easier.

Cons

- RIFF is supported by only a few programs outside the Letraset product line. QuarkXPress, for example, supports grayscale RIFF files but produces a "Bad File Format" error if you attempt to place a color RIFF.

- Service bureaus may show a reluctance to deal with RIFFs because their experience with the format is limited. If this becomes a problem, look for another service bureau or save your files as TIFFs or EPS and not RIFFs.

> **Tip: Save a Copy of the Original Image in a Format That Can Be Opened!**
>
> When converting files or color separating scans or paint-type images into EPS format, it's a good idea to save a copy of the original document as either TIFF, PICT, or RIFF, in case you need to make changes or corrections. Once saved as EPS, other applications cannot open the file for changes. Without a copy saved in another format, you'll be forced to recreate the image from scratch.

EPS File Format

EPS, also known as EPSF, stands for Encapsulated PostScript. Probably the most powerful (although not always the easiest to use) file format for color publishing, encapsulated PostScript provides a vehicle for producing highly detailed images that are portable across a wide range of computer systems and output devices.

Reportedly developed by Altsys (not Adobe, the maker of PostScript), EPS files are built from the kinds of PostScript commands described earlier in this chapter. These commands can be stored as either regular text (ASCII) or in the language of computers (binary or hexadecimal numbers), although not all programs that support EPS files can read all three formats.

Unlike TIFF and PICT files, EPS files are written descriptions of the contents of a file. To display an EPS file of a scanned image, the Mac would need to interpret the PostScript code and rasterize it for the screen—a feat which, at this writing, no Macintosh program can do for scans saved as EPS. To compensate for this disadvantage, EPS files are often saved together with a low-resolution PICT file that represents the image. This is called a PICT preview image and allows an EPS file to be placed and cropped within a page layout program.

In most cases, the PICT preview file can be specified at a low resolution to save memory, or this representation can be skipped completely. If the PICT file is not saved with the EPS file for use in placing the image in a page layout program, a gray box appears with the name of the file and little more. This box can be cropped and the image reduced and rotated like any picture, though you won't be able to see what you're doing until you print a proof on a PostScript printer or imagesetter. When the file is printed or otherwise output on a PostScript device, this PICT representation will be replaced with the actual EPS image.

EPS, like other file formats, has specific advantages and disadvantages:

Pros

- EPS files are stable and produce predictable results when outputting a wide variety of images. This format handles bitmaps as well as object-oriented illustrations with equal aplomb.

- EPS files can be easily moved across computer environments and output devices. For example, it's possible to take an EPS file created on an IBM PC and print it directly on an imagesetter driven by a Mac. (Some minor conversions may be required.)

- EPS files saved as ASCII (not binary, thank you), can be edited by a knowledgeable user to add effects and delete elements. EPS files can also be edited to fix errors that are only evident when outputting the file.

Cons

EPS files can be extremely large. EPS files saved as ASCII-format text are even bigger than their binary equivalents. It takes a lot of commands to describe an image. A picture really is worth a thousand words when described in PostScript! The use of the optional PICT preview image eats up additional space. Large EPS files present logistical problems for small or congested hard disks and make transporting files from Mac to service bureau unlikely on a floppy disk, even if a compression routine is used.

Tip: Use EPS to Import Page Layouts

Occasionally you may want to place a page or chart created in a page layout program into another kind of page layout program, or you may want to take an entire page and reduce it. To do so normally requires adjusting every element on the page—a time-consuming chore. Instead, save the page as EPS, then import the page into an application that supports the format. QuarkXPress, for example, has a **File** menu item for creating EPS files and also saves a preview PICT format file so you can see and manipulate the page within another application. This allows you to crop, rotate, and resize the page in another program, but you cannot edit its text or make other changes.

Scitex CT (Contiguous Tone) File Format

There comes a time when a project is best finished on a high-end prepress system, or when a high-quality scan created on a high-end system must be brought into a Mac color document. The format readable by some Mac programs and most high-end prepress systems is called Scitex CT. Scitex is a major manufacturer of prepress systems, and this format is reserved for handling high-quality color images. Because of the cost associated with using high-end prepress systems, processing grayscales is rarely justified in this format—it's too expensive.

Scitex CT format provides some unique challenges. First, color images moved from Scitex to Mac are often gargantuan. The transfer challenge is further complicated because prepress systems use awkward nine-track tape as a transfer medium. To get around this problem, ask your prepress operator for advice. Most shops that do a lot of file transfers from Mac to prepress systems and back offer the usual service bureau alternatives for file exchange. (See Chapters Ten and Thirteen for more advice.)

Transporting Image Types between Computer Platforms

Working with files received from or destined for other kinds of computers can be daunting for the color publisher. There are a wide variety of formats in use and with the exception of TIFF and Targa (a format used in high-end illustration programs on IBM PCs), little direct compatibility exists. Besides simple compatibility problems, importing images for color publishing on the Mac is complicated, because the foreign file format is structured differently and may contain more or less information than is desirable for serious publishing.

The easiest way to transfer images from another platform is through a program that supports a wide variety of image types, like ColorStudio or Photoshop. These packages do a reasonably good job of reading and writing a number of different formats. Some Macintosh page layout packages offer direct transfer from DOS to Mac and back as well.

MacLink Translators (discussed in Chapter Fourteen) and other similar packages allow cross-platform transfer of images through the Apple File Exchange utility or by connecting a cable between the systems. Files can then be shipped by either floppy disk or via a network adaptation package, like those offered by Sitka or NOVELL, that allows Macs to transfer files to non-Mac computers on the network.

If your work includes a substantial number of images imported from other computer environments, look for software that directly supports the other platform and then test to see how well it works. If you plan on moving files through a translation program, test the results thoroughly as well. Some translators bring over most of the information but may not handle variations in file formats, or they may strip out material deemed unnecessary by their maker. When in doubt about the quality of a translation, have the file run out on an imagesetter to see if there are problems that appear in film and are invisible on a monitor.

In some cases, the application program on the non-Macintosh computer may produce such poor-quality graphics that conversion is a waste of time. If this is the case, consider importing the image as a template into an illustration program such as Freehand and then building a clean new drawing on top of it.

Using Clip Art for Your Images

Clip art consists of drawings and illustrations produced by various illustrators and assembled into a collection for resale on diskettes or CD-ROM, or available for downloading from bulletin board systems. Familiar images such as people working behind a desk, maps, symbols, and many other pictures are available as clip art. All you have to do is select the image you want and then paste it into a page layout or drawing program, where you can modify it if you want to.

Unfortunately, clip art varies considerably in quality. Many clip art images are low-resolution MacPaint files and are of little use to the serious publisher. The poorer quality packages suffer from inept drawing, cliché images, and limited choices. There are, however, sophisticated grayscale and color clip art packages available, and many of these contain object-oriented art saved in EPS or PICT format. These illustrations can be modified within an illustration program or resized within a page layout program to suit your needs. Though they cost more than MacPaint-based clip art packages, these professionally rendered drawings don't suffer from the cheap or trite appearance of other clip art drawings.

If you use clip art in a document that enjoys a widespread distribution, some of your readership may have seen the same image used elsewhere. Anyone purchasing the package can use the same art you used. However, if your drawing skills are limited, high-quality clip art collections can provide you with a valuable alternative for adding interest and a professional touch to your color publications. Or, you can use them as templates within Illustrator or Freehand to create a new, less hackneyed image.

Books: The Original Clip Art Source

In addition to software-based clip art, there are a variety of books available that contain either public domain art or illustrations created specifically for incorporation into other publications at no charge. These images can be scanned for use in your documents. The purchase price of the book gives you license to reuse the work in any way you see fit. Check the copyright page to see what uses are specifically allowed. Some books allow only one or two images to be reproduced. Others allow their entire contents to be used as frequently as needed. If the art has been printed using screens, read *Scanning Printed Images* in the next chapter before purchasing the book. Clip art books are available at art supply stores and frequently in the "Art" section of regular bookstores.

Other Ways to Acquire Images

There are a number of sources for collecting images that are not copyrighted. The federal government maintains huge archives of photos that can be had for a minimal fee. These images cover diverse subjects, ranging from space shots to oil pipelines. The archives of most libraries are other sources of public domain images, primarily historical photos, but sometimes other general-purpose images are available.

You can also acquire images for a (usually) reasonable fee from stock photo houses found in the *Yellow Pages* under *Photographs-Stock*. The companies maintain large libraries of images in a variety of formats, produced by professional photographers covering a wide range of subjects. You select the image you want from an inventory numbering in the thousands and then pay a fee for *one-time use*. This fee may range from almost nothing to thousands of dollars, depending on how you plan to use the image. If you are assembling a magazine article for a charity, the fee may be surprisingly low. If it will be used in a massive ad campaign for a major corporation, then the fee will be substantially larger. Note that while you can rent the use of these images, they are still copyrighted, and stock photo houses take a dim view of unauthorized reuse of their photos.

In this chapter you have learned some of the underlying mechanics of Macintosh color publishing. While some of this material may be instantly forgotten, keep it handy for future reference—then when you need to decide on what file format to use, have a problem with printing bitmapped fonts, or need to find out the difference between 24-bit and 32-bit color, just turn to Chapter Four.

In the next chapter, we will look at ways to get new images into the Macintosh for inclusion in your color documents—this is done through scanning. You will learn how to get the best from scanners and scanned images and explore some of the tools for fixing and manipulating scanned images for impressive results.

CHAPTER

5

SCANNING PHOTOS
AND ILLUSTRATIONS FOR
COLOR PUBLICATIONS

"Without good input, good color is impossible."

— Joe Matazzoni
discussing scanners and
Mac-based prepress in *MacWorld*

If a picture is worth a thousand words, it's because a well-chosen image gives an idea, process, event, or person a life that words alone cannot convey. Pictures catch the eye and supplement the text with additional detail that makes it easier to understand and livelier to read. For the desktop color publisher, the ability to add images to designs is vital to creating work that catches and keeps the attention of the reader.

For the color publisher who doesn't plan to use clip art or add images created directly on the Mac with an illustration program, access to an accurate color scanner capable of capturing quality images is a must. Unfortunately, good scanners are expensive. You can bypass ownership by renting time on one owned by a service bureau, but it still helps to understand the issues surrounding scanning so that you can explain what you want to the bureau and rectify any problems that crop up.

You Are Here

The various kinds of scanners were discussed in Chapter Two. This chapter explains how to get the best results from these machines and presents techniques for scanning in order to achieve the best results in color publications.

In any project, you must decide whether or not to handle your own color image capture and processing or have it done professionally. The section titled *Scan It Yourself or Have Someone Else Do It?* explains the issues associated with desktop scanning versus professional scanning, to help you make the appropriate decision for your documents. The rest of the chapter discusses the mechanics of scanning, including preparation of images, choosing scanner settings, and working with the scan after it's created.

A Weak Link in the Macintosh Color Publishing Chain

Image capture (scanning) is probably the weakest link in the Mac color publishing process. There are two problems associated with color scanning that affect color publishing projects: inadequate hardware and inadequate experience.

1. Inadequate Hardware

Mac-compatible scanners suffer from a variety of problems when capturing images. At the high end, drum-based scanners are adequate for any level of publishing, but few Macintosh-based color publishers can afford equipment of this caliber.

The inexpensive scanners that most of us and our companies can afford are not good enough for serious color work. While an inexpensive scanner produces color scans suitable for newsprint-quality reproduction and some magazine work, its output may appear flat and lifeless when printed at higher resolutions on quality paper. Some of these problems can be corrected through image-retouching software such as ColorStudio and Photoshop, but generally speaking, miracles are in short supply when attempting to fix scans that must be printed at high resolution and are lacking in color and detail.

Images that appear clean and crisp on the Mac's 72-dpi screen may look murky and dull in print. This is much more than just a resolution issue. You get an adequate scan for color work at less than 300 dpi, the entry-level resolution for color flatbed scanners in the Mac market. But, other problems, such as an inability to capture detail, dull color, and/or a lack of information at the extreme ends of the brightness scale, make such scans look unattractive and murky in print. Manually reworking images to fix these problems takes so long that it's not practical in a busy agency or production department.

2. Inadequate Experience

A period of trial and error is required to identify the kinds of images that can be scanned without requiring substantial correction. Unfortunately, the only way to test scanner results is to color separate the output and have color proofs assembled. This gets expensive, unless you have access to such tools and processes within your company.

Consistent, predictable results are always the goal of any color publisher. It takes time and effort to get quality results from a color scanner. However, you can shortcut this entire process by using the scanning knowledge and equipment of a well-equipped service bureau or color house, as explained in the next section.

Scan It Yourself or Have Someone Else Do It?

As we mentioned before, depending on the nature of your project, be it a budget newsletter or a sophisticated brochure, you need to decide when to handle your own scans and when to have someone do it for you on their professional equipment. There are four options to choose from when handling and incorporating scans in your work.

Tip: A Certain Magic

People with normal eyesight are extremely critical of printed pictures. We spend most of our waking time using our eyes as the primary sense for tracking events in the outside world. A poorly printed image catches the eye quickly because the brain subconsciously evaluates and measures the printed images against those in the real world. You may decide a color separation looks "good enough," but in print the image may stick out like a sore thumb. Why? Because on paper there is enough discordant information to tell the brain that something is amiss.

There's a certain magic that goes into any quality printed image to make the right connection with the brain. Catching the eye with poor quality is not the way to get noticed. Understanding how to create the magic takes time and practice—but it's ultimately worth it.

---

1. Scan for Position

You can scan images to show their position inside your documents. These "for position only" (FPO) scans show your printer where the conventionally processed images will go, how they should be cropped, and how to reduce or enlarge the photographic image, if necessary. Of course, if you have a printer do it, there will be a charge for separating and stripping the images, plus your job will take a little longer to prepare for press.

2. Scan and Manage the Images Yourself

You can scan your own grayscale images and handle your own color scans if you and your equipment are up to the task.

3. Have a Service Bureau Handle the Scanning

Many service bureaus will scan images for you, for a price. Their charges may include color correction and separation, as well. Before taking this route, compare the cost of having the images handled conventionally by experts at a color separation house. The savings in using a service bureau may be meager and the results mediocre, unless the bureau is well-equipped with a transparency or drum-based scanner and the operators have the experience and know-how required.

4. Have the Images Scanned into a Prepress System

Depending on the charges for the work, having images scanned on a high-end prepress system provides good results if the company with the prepress system is credible. This is easiest if the rest of your job is ultimately headed into the same prepress system for final production. The scanned files created by a high-end system may be so large as to be unmanageable on a Macintosh. Depending on who does the scanning, it may be less expensive and certainly less hassle to have separations produced by the prepress system. In this case, scan your images for position only.

There is a point where you have to ask yourself whether desktop-produced color scans and the color separations created from these scans make economic sense over conventional techniques. If your scan takes too long to image on the imagesetter, you may receive a bill approaching that from a high-quality color separation house. You have to add up the cost for four pieces of film and the extra imagesetter time when making this determination. You must also consider that quality professional scans are available from color houses with free color correction in most cities for as little as $30 to $50, but a competent scanning system is entry-level priced at $5,000, and a good one is priced from $15,000 to $70,000. It takes a lot of scans to make a machine like that pay for itself, plus you have to manipulate and correct the images and then live with the results.

When you work with a color house, you get to see proofs and have an opportunity to make color corrections before accepting the finished film. When you do it yourself, you may not even see the problems until the job is ready for the press. Changes at this point are expensive, and you'll have to pay to rerun the film again. When you use professionals to handle your scans, you can let them work around thorny issues such as scan to print resolution, UCR and GCR, dot gain, and a number of others.

Our first rule when using scanned images is: *When in doubt about the quality of your scans and separations, have proofs made to see what they really look like before proceeding into print* (see Chapter Ten).

The Steps for Scanning

Scanning photos and illustrations follows a predetermined set of steps in order to capture a quality image for subsequent manipulation and output through the Macintosh. The steps for scanning are described in detail in the next pages.

1. **Select and Prepare the Image**   Choose the image you want to scan and inspect it for dust and contaminants. If the image is dirty, look for a clean one or clean it if possible.

2. **Warm up the Scanner**   Turn on the scanner and let it stabilize. Turn it on *before* starting your Mac if the scanner is connected to your computer's SCSI port. All SCSI devices must be ready before a Mac can be started, or your hard disk may not come on line.

3. **Preview the Image**   Scanning software allows you to take a low-resolution snapshot of your image so you can crop and resize it before the final scan is made. After making the preview scan, check to see if the image is correctly aligned horizontally and vertically.

4. **Set the Controls**   Set the resolution, cropping, resizing, and imaging mode (line art, grayscale, color, etc.). If your scanner allows settings for highlight and shadow, set these after a preview is scanned for measurement. After setting the controls, check that there is enough disk space to accommodate the image. (Changes made with the controls to adjust resolution, size, and color mode will alter the memory required for the scan.)

   Choose also the kind of file format appropriate for the software you plan to process or place the image with. (File formats were discussed in Chapter Four.) The format of choice is usually TIFF, because most applications support it. TIFFs can be extensively manipulated and, while not in the most compact file format, they are reasonably efficient.

5. **Scan**   Capture the image and inspect it on your monitor. Do not remove the image yet. Check the scan first to see what you actually captured. Scan again if necessary.

6. **Fix the Image**   If necessary, manipulate and repair the image within a paint or (preferably) an image-retouching program until you get exactly what you want. (See Chapter Eight.)

The Scanning Process Step by Step

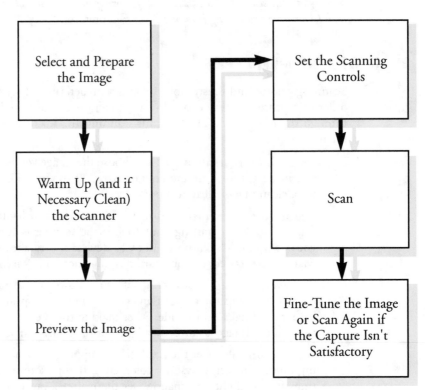

Follow these steps for scanning and repeat the process until you are satisfied with the final image quality.

Choosing Images for Scanning

Good Scans Start with Clean Images

The computer industry cliché that says "garbage in, garbage out" is nowhere truer than in the case of converting photos and illustrations into digital images with a color scanner. If you scan a murky, underexposed print, it will come out even murkier. While brightness and contrast controls within a scanner or a retouching program can compensate for some of the lighting problems, information that's barely visible in an image to start with won't magically appear, no matter how you set the controls.

To get good scanning results, start with an image that's better in quality than one you will accept as the end result—that way you won't be disappointed by what you see in print. This is true not only with scans handled by Macs but when using conventional techniques as well. The original image is *always* better than the printed one, and in the case of desktop-produced scans, even more so. The only exception is an image processed by a professional using a retouching program. In this case, a photo that is unacceptable because of poor photography, inept processing, or overt physical damage can be revived to appear significantly better than the original. This work isn't easy, however.

Evaluating the Image

The best scans come from photos and transparencies with good color, crisp focus, and clear detail. Because the scanning process tends to lose information, starting out with a photo that's already fuzzy will result in a very fuzzy scan. When evaluating an image for scanning, look for the characteristics described here and follow the steps we've discussed already for making a test scan.

A Clean Image

The image should be free from scratches or other damage from faulty processing or mishandling. Dust should be carefully removed with a special brush or pressurized air available at photo stores. Damaged images should be replaced or retouched within an image-retouching program. In the case of 35mm slides that will be enlarged, dust and scratches can be serious impediments to achieving clean scans. A dust particle that is nearly invisible on a slide may appear the size of a boulder after the image is enlarged and sharpened.

A Sharper Image

Study small details under a magnifying loupe to make sure the image is sharply focused. If it is not, reduction during scanning may help. However, in the case of a small image (such as a slide) that must be enlarged, no amount of post-scan processing will completely repair the problem. Severely out-of-focus images are difficult to fix because the color may look washed out even after enhancement. Also, keep in mind that it's common when working with photos for one area in an image to be sharp while another is soft. To work with such an image, you may be able to enhance the fuzzy area with retouching software so it begins to match the rest of the photo.

Appropriate Exposure

Study the image to see if it is too light or too dark. If so, consider making changes to the scanner's settings to partially correct the problem and then finish the job within color separation software. By making a partial improvement on scanning, you have a better chance of capturing detail that may otherwise be lost.

Scan and Compare Results

Scan the image and compare the results with the original. Look closely for loss of detail in the brightest and darkest regions. Watch for major color shifts. Rescan on another scanner if the results are significantly out of balance or if detail is clearly present but simply can't be captured with the scanner you are using.

Put the Cat out

When handling a rush job with numerous black and white photos, a designer decided to send the images out for scanning to a service bureau because of the job's complexity and the short schedule. Receiving the images back on disk two days later, he began final assembly of the project to get it ready for imagesetter output. On screen, everything looked fine, until he found an image that looked like there was a small hair in it. When he examined the remaining images, they all had the same hair in approximately the same place. Curious and now worried, he magnified an image to get a better look. At 400 percent it was obvious that the defective images all had this anomaly. At 800 percent it was possible to identify different different colors in the hair. A call to the shop revealed the problem. The owner had recently taken in a stray tabby cat and this pet liked to spend his days sleeping on the lid of the warm flatbed scanner. Moral of the story: If you must send a rush job to a service bureau, make sure they put the cat out.

Scan in the Best Light

If you use a scanner with a light source that is constantly on (many only light while scanning), leave it on for at least fifteen minutes so that the light source can stabilize. A cold scanner may produce slightly different colors than a warm one. Conversely, don't leave these models on all the time, because the light source will age, and this also alters color accuracy.

If you use a flatbed scanner, the placement of the image on the bed may affect the final quality of the scan. It's always most convenient to line up a rectangular image along the top corner of the bed because it can be easily placed against the metal edges. The best color quality (which may not be all that good), however, is almost always obtained in the middle of the glass where the light is most even.

Taking Photos for Scanning

You probably know that different kinds of cameras and films produce varying results. As film goes, different brands and types have different color balance. If your scanner software has the ability to automatically compensate for color shifts by brand, and if you take your own photos, consider using a film the scanner software can balance. The owner's manual will list the films supported by your scanner software.

You may also need to use two or more kinds of film to get the results you want. For example, a film that takes great shots in daylight may be too slow for indoor or night work, so you may select a "faster" film for such shots. Don't use fast films for all jobs however, because as a film's ASA (speed) rating number increases, the images become grainier and color quality diminishes. So, ASA 1000 film in bright sunlight may not produce as good an image as film rated at ASA 64, even though the faster film is more expensive.

The size of the original image is an important factor and something to consider when choosing film and print sizes, as well. Larger film formats, like 2½", capture more detail. Smaller formats, such as 35mm, capture less information. Because scanning tends to lose detail, the more information there is in the original image, the more will remain after scanning. Larger images can be reduced effectively during scanning. Enlarging images is problematic.

The very best images are created from transparencies—film positives that show the image in the way a color print does but are transparent. (You are probably familiar with transparencies as 35mm slides.) The reasons are simple: Not only is film more sensitive to detail and the tonal range from dark to light than photographic print paper, but a transparency is first generation—a color print is second generation.

A photographer shooting transparency film develops it, and the process is complete. To make a print, a film negative must be made and then a print made from it, a two-step process. Each time an image is reproduced, it loses some detail. Prove it to yourself on a photocopier. Take a magazine photo and copy it. Then take the copy and copy it. Keep copying the copies long enough, and the resulting image will grow increasingly fuzzy and will gradually move toward an even gray.

Tip: Bracket Your Shots for the Best Choices

When commissioning photos or handling the job yourself, have several shots made of the same subject with half f-stop adjustments made in both directions from the mythical *perfect exposure.* (This is called "bracketing.") This is a simple trick that allows you to choose among photos for the one with the most detail and the right brightness and contrast.

Unfortunately, many inexpensive color scanners can't handle transparencies, and the ones that do often have trouble maintaining detail in the darker areas of an image. If you are shopping for a scanner that will handle transparent media, watch out for this problem.

Choosing Illustrations and Printed Pictures for Scanning

Reflective art is simply a photographic print, an illustration on illustration board, or a printed picture from other sources. These media are called "reflective," because unlike a transparency where light penetrates the medium to expose the target image, light reflects from a print to reveal the image. Reflective art is more difficult to reproduce than transparent media because less detail is captured when reflective art is scanned. Therefore, your selection of an illustration or printed image for scanning requires careful consideration.

Most illustrations and printed images, like photos, are easily scanned. The same criteria described for selecting photos for scanning should be applied to these images. In the case of drawings produced by professional illustrators, problems may creep in without special handling. Pros work in a variety of media and on surfaces of different kinds. While it's easy to scan a compact pen and ink drawing on illustration board onto a flatbed scanner, drawings that employ pastels can create a big mess, resulting in

damage to the drawing and pastel dust inside your scanner (and on carpet, walls, clothes, etc.). You must take care not to materially damage an
illustration done by someone other than yourself, because unless otherwise arranged, the creator owns his creation. If you damage it, you'll be
on the hook to have it fixed or replaced.

The best way to avoid these problems is to commission illustrations in
formats that lend themselves to scanning or convert drawings to formats
that do. For example, if the job involves messy charcoal, have a photo
shot of the drawing and scan that. While a second generation photo will
lose some of the information contained in the original, it's much better
than losing the entire drawing and ruining your scanner in the process.

If you plan to scan an illustration with a drum scanner that requires
the image to be wrapped around a drum, commission the work on a flexible medium rather than conventional illustration board. Professional
color scanning houses have perfected a technique for taking just the top
layer off the cardboard, but this is tricky, and it takes considerable practice to avoid picking up too much material or tearing the illustration.

Some illustration styles are problematic as well. One popular technique is to cover canvas with a thick layer of *gesso* (gesso looks like white
paint but has the texture of a milkshake) and then glue down other elements—such as tinted photocopied pictures, glass beads, cardboard letters, three-dimensional design elements—even doll heads and broken
china. The only way to handle such an image is to either demand that
the surface elements do not become so thick as to be unscannable or to
take it to a photographer to have a manageable print or transparency
made. If you use a 35mm transparency scanner, then photography is the
preferred way to handle such a beast.

Tip: Dull, Dull, Dull

The texture of photographic print paper limits the quality of a
scan. Glossy papers are particularly troublesome on some scanners. The highly reflective surface of such paper reflects light so
that the scanner doesn't see the image, creating color shifts and
washed-out areas. If your scanner has problems handling "glos-
sies," visit your local art supply store and purchase a can of *dulling
spray.* Applied evenly, it eliminates the gloss but doesn't alter the
image. Be aware that although some dulling spray brands are
"removable," you'll find it impossible to get off the sensitive surface of a print.

Size can also be a problem. Many illustrators create large drawings, assuming their work will be photographically reduced to fit. That's fine if you plan to photograph the piece before scanning or happen to own a scanner with a large scan bed, but otherwise, commission work to fit your scanner and reduce it from there if necessary. On the other side of the coin, small illustrations, like small photos, are difficult to enlarge past a certain point. The images ultimately become diffuse or fuzzy as they are enlarged.

Scanning from pictures reproduced in books and magazines is another problem because the dot patterns in the printing may make the scan appear muddy or grainy. The reproduction limitations make the use of scanned pictures undesirable, unless it is absolutely necessary to capture a particular image that doesn't exist in another format. We have included a special section on scanning printed pictures in this chapter, for those of you who find yourself forced into this situation.

Scanners and Calibration

All scanners have characteristic inaccuracies in how they "see" color. Two scanners of the same model just off the assembly line will respond to color differently. Scanners also change in color accuracy as their optical elements age. For these reasons, many scanners require calibration of some sort to maintain color accuracy. Some scanners perform automatic calibration on power up without your knowledge. A Howtek flatbed we tested said nothing in the manual about calibration, but a call to Howtek technical support revealed that the unit calibrates itself from the white plastic on the bottom of its lid. (Better not leave a photo in the scanner when turning it on!) Other scanners use a routine that allows you to scan a test image to perform calibration.

Some scanners have no calibration mechanism at all, instead relying on settings made at the factory. Short of tearing such a unit apart and twiddling with trim pots (don't!), your only calibration alternative is to use a third-party software solution or live with the default settings.

It's much easier to start with color-accurate scans than to fix color within a color separation program later. In addition to the calibration options provided by the manufacturers, there are a variety of third-party methods for calibrating scanners, including software and special hardware combined with software. Unfortunately, any calibration scheme that requires matching scanned colors on your monitor to sample swatches is an exercise in futility, since your monitor's color isn't correct to begin with. Only consider one of the color matching calibration systems if you have an accurately calibrated monitor (currently unavailable).

Line Art, Continuous Tone, Halftones, Grayscale, and Full-color Images

There are several different kinds of image formats and terms for images used in color publishing. Because they sometimes get confused, we explain them here briefly.

Line Art

Line art is just that—illustrations or pictures made from solid lines and shapes. Line art is black and white only, with no grays, shadings, or colors in between. Sometimes line art is printed as a single color, such as red or blue, but the art source is always a black and white line drawing. The text you are reading is line art—it's fully black with no shades of gray or color.

Continuous Tone

When you take a photo, the resulting image is *continuous tone.* To your eye, the picture contains even transitions of color across its surface. Curved elements are smooth in their transition from light to dark. In the the case of a close-up photo of a young girl's face, there is no noticeable jump in color between the top and bottom of her cheeks. This natural-appearing graduation is called continuous tone because the color transitions are even and smooth. Photographs are actually made up of dots like a computer image, but these tiny particles are so numerous, random, and small that they are undetectable without a strong magnifying glass.

Halftones

Unfortunately, the most popular printing technology of today, the lithographic press, can only print a solid dot or no ink at all. To print a continuous tone photograph, a solution had to be devised that would allow continuous tones (grays in our example) to be printed as a series of dots. The solution is simple—to produce a gray, print only part of a dot and leave part of it white. That way, the paper shows through next to each dot. To the eye, this mix of white paper and a black dot appears as a gray. To create a darker gray, bigger black dots let less white show through. To make a lighter gray, smaller black dots let more paper show though. This is called halftoning—a term you'll hear frequently in publishing both on and off the desktop.

In conventional printing, halftones are produced by putting a screen in front of the image and then shooting a picture of the dot patterns created by the screen. Screens are rated by the number of lines per inch. A screen suitable for converting images for use in newspapers has fewer and larger openings. Screens for high-quality brochure and annual report reproduction have much smaller dots and more of them per inch. As the screens become finer, their presence is less noticeable in the printed image. Study any printed document with black and white photos through a magnifying loupe, and you will see the halftone dots. Notice that lighter grays have smaller dots and darker grays use larger dots. Study both the coarse screens used for newspaper photos and the finer screens used in magazine photos.

The enlarged halftone on the left was produced conventionally using a traditional halftone screen to break the image into dot structures. The enlarged halftone on the right was produced by a computer. Note how the dot structures look slightly different.

Grayscale Images on Your Monitor

Grayscales are images composed of continuous grays. Unlike a halftone, where the image is made from dots composed of varying amounts of black and white, grayscales are made of actual grays. Grayscales displayed on a monitor with 256 grays are as close to a continuous tone black and white photograph as the computer world gets. High-resolution grayscale (and color) scans can be quite convincing, showing their structure only with magnification. All grayscales are converted to halftones when output by the imagesetter so they can be printed by lithographic presses. We cannot show you a true grayscale here because this book is reproduced using lithographic printing technology.

Full-color Images on Your Monitor

Full-color images displayed on a computer monitor consist of red, green, and blue components that on screen appear to the eye as continuous tones unless the images are magnified. Each color component on a monitor is like a grayscale—it appears on your monitor as a solid color. When printed, color images must be converted to cyan, magenta, yellow, and black (CMYK) dots (like halftones), which are recombined on press to create a convincing representation of the original image. (See Chapter Eight for more information on *process color.*)

Because scanned images may appear as grayscales or full-color RGB representations on screen, they may look different when separated and printed. Thus, evaluating a scan on screen is not an accurate way to determine the quality of the scan. A color proof must be used (see Chapter Ten).

Resolution, LPI, and DPI

An understanding of resolution is central to effective scanning. The standard measurement of resolution in the computer world is dots per inch, or dpi. This number specifies the number of dots scanned, displayed or printed within a square inch. A Macintosh screen has a resolution of 72 dpi, which means that each square inch is composed of 72 by 72 dots (when discussing monitors, these dots are also called *pixels)*. Most laser printers print at 300 dpi and imagesetters "image" at 1,270 to more than 3,000 dpi.

It is sometimes confusing to the color publisher that there are several different dpi ratings that must be considered. There are four kinds of resolution measurements you will be faced with when scanning and printing color images:

1. Input Resolution

When scanning, the input resolution is the precision at which an image is captured. This resolution is set before the scan is made, although the resolution can be changed within color separation programs if necessary.

2. Screen Resolution

The Mac's screen resolution is always 72 dpi. So, if you are looking at a color image scanned at 300 dpi on screen and displayed at actual size, you aren't really seeing all of the information, because the Mac's monitor can't display it. (If you enlarge the image, then you can see more information.)

3. Output Resolution

The *output resolution* is specified when the image is output to film on an imagesetter. This resolution is specified in dpi. Different models of imaging equipment are capable of different levels of resolution, starting at 1,270 dpi and going beyond 3,000 dpi. You can output a scan at a higher resolution than it was scanned with, but the result looks flat because the additional dots are created through interpolation, a mathematical guessing process.

4. Lines-per-inch Resolution

The *lines-per-inch* rating is used to specify the resolution at which the image will print when on press. This setting determines how large or small the dots are and how close together they appear when printed. The specification for this setting is largely determined by the paper the image will be printed on. For example, if the image is destined for newsprint, a low lpi specification, 65 lpi for example, will be used, because newsprint supports only coarse (large) dots. The very best printing is possible at 600 lpi with new technology, but resolutions from 100 to 200 lpi are typical for most color documents. When your files are imaged, your SB will want to know the desired lpi for your file if it contains images or colors made of screens. Ask your printer what the output lpi should be before you have your file imaged.

How to Determine Scanning Resolution

So, what resolution should you use for your scans? Well...it depends on the size of the image, the size you plan to reproduce it at, the level of reproduction quality required as explained in Chapter One, and what your scanner is capable of.

You probably recall our first rule of scanning, from earlier in the chapter: *When in doubt about the quality of your scans and separations, have proofs made to see what they really look like before proceeding into print.*

Now, here are the rest of the rules for getting predictable results from scanned images used in color publications.

The second rule of scanning is: *Your scans must have enough resolution so that there are a minimum of 1.5 dots per inch (dpi), though not more than 2 dpi, for every line per inch (lpi) specified for the printed image.*

The third rule of scanning is: *If you are enlarging a scanned image that cannot accommodate the second rule of scanning, then you must settle for less enlargement, settle for lower reproduction quality (fewer lines per inch), or find a scanner capable of higher resolution than the one you are using.*

The fourth rule of scanning is: *Scanning with too much information is a waste of time. A file that reaches the imagesetter with a dpi:lpi ratio of more than 2:1 contains information that is unused and will slow down processing of the job. It will also make the file more difficult to transport because of the storage the extra information requires. Therefore, don't scan files at resolutions higher than required to meet the terms of the second rule of scanning.*

The reason for these rules is simple. When an image is output on an imagesetter, the system takes every 1.5 dots to 2.0 dots and interpolates them into 1.0 line of output resolution. If you use less resolution (fewer dots), the imagesetter does not have enough information to produce quality output, and the image may look flat or grainy (but potentially okay for some applications). As the ratio of dots to lpi gets closer to 1:1, the resulting image will appear "pixelized" with the individual dots noticeably visible in the output.

Enlarging Images

Wherever possible, the ideal scanning solution is to scan images at the size and resolution that is required for print. (See *Should You Resize While Scanning?* later in this chapter.) But sometimes this isn't possible because your scanner may lack the resizing and resolution capabilities required for the job, or you may be working with a scan that originated elsewhere. Determining the appropriate enlargement possibilities for scanned images can be complex because if the scan is enlarged too much, it may not contain enough information to reproduce properly in print. While the underlying rules are simple enough, actually putting them to work becomes more complicated when you are enlarging an image scanned without enough dots to make the minimum 1.5:1 ratio of dpi:lpi.

Tip: The Magic Formulas

To determine the optimum scanning resolution (dpi) for scanning an image at 100 percent of its original size to be enlarged or reduced, the following formula can be used:

Screen frequency (lpi) x *a number between 1.5 and 2.0* (depending on print quality desired) x *the final width after resizing ÷ the original width = optimum scanning resolution (dpi)*

If the results of this calculation are more dpi than your scanner can handle, refer to the third rule of scanning in this chapter.

When resizing an image that is already scanned, there is a (relatively) simple formula for figuring out the resulting dpi:lpi to see if the new size of the image will have enough information to image and print with adequate quality. Just compare the desired lpi of your printed image to the results of the following formula:

dpi after resizing = scanning resolution ÷ (original width ÷ desired width)

If the resulting ratio of dpi:lpi is within the rules, great. If not, consider another enlargement or reduction factor or resample the scan in a color separation program like Adobe Photoshop.

For example, if you have a 300-dpi scan of an image you want to reproduce in a magazine and you need to enlarge it from 2" by 2" to 6" by 6" (a 300 percent enlargement), you shouldn't do it because you're breaking rule number two. A 300-dpi scan enlarged to 300 percent reduces the dots per inch to 100 dpi, because the same number of dots covers an area three times as large. To print this 100-dpi image and keep the ratio of dpi:lpi at 1.5:1, this image could only be printed at 75 lines per inch, a resolution adequate for a newsprint job but not good enough for higher quality publications.

If the same image had been scanned at 600 dpi, the enlargement would work fine. A 600-dpi scan enlarged 300 percent produces an enlargement with 200 dots per inch of effective resolution. Using a ratio of dpi:lpi of 1.5:1, this image can be printed at 150 lpi—adequate quality for most magazine work and mid-quality brochures.

Reducing Scanned Images

Reduction with low resolution scans (and scanners) is much easier. For a reduction, the ratio formula simply works in the other direction. For example, if you were to scan a 2" by 2" image at 200 dpi and then size it down to a postage stamp size of 1" by 1", (50 percent reduction), you would have a 400-dpi image. If you want to print the image at 100 lpi, this produces an ungainly ratio of 4:1, which is too high. However, the image can be easily scanned with less resolution, or it can be resampled to a lower resolution (using your color separation software) to remove the excess information.

Extra Information Does Not Always Mean Extra Quality

Remember: Breaking the fourth rule of scanning with too much extra information won't improve image output quality. If you scan an image at 200 dpi and leave it the same size (100 percent of original size), the 200-dpi scan at 100 percent of size printed at 100 lpi produces a 2:1 ratio, which is at the top of the ratio for quality at this lpi level. But, if the same scan was captured at 300 dpi, the ratio of dpi:lpi comes out to 3:1. This extra information will not make your output quality any better. Service bureaus frequently see files with ratios of 4:1 or more coming in the door and bills for substantial imagesetter overtime going out the door. Scans with too much information may fail to image or crash the imagesetter.

Which Ratio Is Best?

The usual guideline is that images should be scanned with a ratio of scanner dots per inch to lines per inch when printed within a range of 1.5 dpi:1 lpi to 2 dpi:1 lpi. The higher 2:1 ratio is optimal for high-quality work, but 1.5:1 is adequate for most color publishing projects. The reason that there is a variation in these ratios and no hard, fast rules is because of the tradeoff between image quality and image size. For images destined for newsprint, lower ratios approaching 1:1 may work, although you may have to experiment to get a handle on problems such as grainy (coarse-looking) output. One advantage of a low dpi to lpi ratio is that file size and imaging time is reduced considerably.

In an image composed of soft shapes and color transitions, such as a landscape with sky and mountains, you may be able to use a resolution ratio as low as 1.3 dpi:1 lpi, even for high-quality printing. The image won't look much crisper at a higher resolution if all of the color transitions are relatively smooth and no hard edges are present. If, however, hard edges or diagonal lines are present, then scanning at a higher resolution is required to assure that the edges are clear and crisp in print. If you are in doubt about the quality of your scan or the ratio to use, always remember the first rule of scanning and have a proof made.

> ### Tip: Breaking Rule Number One
>
> If you find yourself in a position of having a scan with inadequate resolution for a required enlargement, there is a workaround, although we don't recommend it for high-quality requirements. Use ColorStudio or another application that provides interpolation and that offers an unsharp masking filter. (Interpolation and unsharp masking are explained in Chapter Eight.) Enlarge the image to the size you require with interpolation smoothing out the process. This will allow the software to intelligently add extra dots to the image to preserve its visual integrity. Then apply unsharp masking to reduce the flat look of the resized image. While this technique won't produce as good an image as resizing during scanning or enlarging an image containing the right number of dots for enlargement, it can save the day when no other alternatives are available.

Should You Resize While Scanning?

In most cases it is best to resize the image during the scan at the resolution appropriate for the lpi you will specify for output when the color separation is produced. This is the simplest way to capture and manipulate the image, as long as your scanner supports the degree of resizing required to produce adequate resolution. Enlarging images after scanning is not the best approach because it often produces an image that looks lifeless or flat, unless you scanned it with enough extra resolution to accommodate the resizing, as we've discussed already.

Reducing images after scanning is fairly straightforward, though it adds an extra step to the production process. If, however, the image must be severely reduced, it may be better to accomplish as much of the reduction as possible with the scanner, then finish with an image-retouching program.

Scan at Higher Resolution If You're Unsure What Size the Finished Image Will Be

It's not uncommon in the graphic arts to redesign a publication at the last minute before heading for the service bureau. If you work in an indecisive organization or for clients who often change their minds, scan with the worst-case enlargement in mind and then reduce resolution when the design is approved. Don't, however, resize and resample the original scan! Use a copy in case another revision is forthcoming.

Imagesetter Resolution and Color Capability

How you scan grayscales directly affects the resolution that can be realized from imagesetter film. This is because of the way digital halftones are produced. Imagesetters can only duplicate a fixed number of dots per inch, based on their specifications and the settings. Therefore, if you use dots for detail (resolution), you can't use the same dots to represent colors or grays. Keep in mind that colors image as black and white halftones on four pieces of film. Quite simply, the more color or gray information that is present in an image, the less the resolution possible. With more resolution, fewer grays and colors are possible. As the resolution of the imagesetter output goes up, however, this becomes less of a problem, because there are more dots to play with.

Eight Computer-produced Halftone Dots

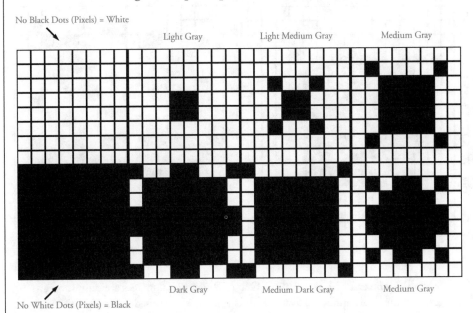

No Black Dots (Pixels) = White

Light Gray   Light Medium Gray   Medium Gray

Dark Gray   Medium Dark Gray   Medium Gray

No White Dots (Pixels) = Black

Computer-generated halftones are composed of halftone cells. Each cell is composed of individual pixels. Cells with fewer black pixels appear white to medium gray. Cells with more black pixels appear dark gray or black. In this example, the halftone cells contain 64 pixels, making them capable of representing 64 different shades of gray.

Continued

When creating a halftone image conventionally, a screen is placed between a continuous tone photo and the imaging media. This screen breaks the image down into dots of varying size, with light colors represented as tiny dots that look almost white and dark colors as large dots that look black. This allows dots to be created in any gray, ranging from white to solid black and in a theoretically infinite number of sizes.

Computers, on the other hand, have no problems with solid black and white, but only a limited number of "gray" choices in between. This is because an imagesetter, or laser printer for that matter, can produce only a certain number of dots per square inch, and these dots can either be used for higher resolution or more grays but not both.

More Levels of Gray But Less Resolution   More Resolution But Fewer Grays

256 Levels of Gray Possible   64 Levels of Gray Possible

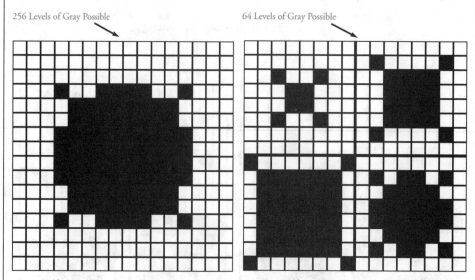

Halftone Cell Composed of 256 Dots (Pixels)   Four Halftone Cells Composed of 64 Dots (Pixels)

More Resolution versus More Levels of Gray: When digital images are output on an imagesetter, the total number of available dots (pixels) can be used to provide either more resolution or a greater number of grays, but not both. As shown in this example, the number of dots used to create an image can be used to produce halftone cells with 256 dots (256 grays), or to produce a larger number of total halftone cells carrying more detail (resolution). This problem can be solved by outputting files on imagesetters that offer higher resolution than older, less expensive models.

Continued

When an imagesetter produces a halftone, it groups dots into halftone "cells" to simulate the variable-sized dots of a traditional halftone. When a grayscale or color image is halftoned, the available output dots are used to form halftone cells. Each cell represents one printed dot. A cell that contains more grays is made of more imagesetter dots to represent the larger number of possible grays. This reduces the resolution because more of the imagesetter's total available dots are being used to make these bigger cells. These cells determine the size of the pixels, and the number of pixels determines the resolution. The more pixels, the higher the possible lpi resolution.

To increase output resolution, the dots must become smaller, so fewer imagesetter dots are used to make each cell. Because these cells are smaller and contain fewer dots, fewer are available to represent grays, so resolution goes up, but the total number of possible grays goes down.

If you need both high resolution and the maximum number of colors possible, which you usually do when working in color, you need to output your images at 2,540 dots per inch or more (imagesetter resolution). This allows you to use a 160-lpi halftone resolution (or more if the imagesetter has even higher dpi capabilities). This gives you 256 grays, or approximately 16.7 million colors in the case of color separations (256^3 each for red, green, and blue) and a fairly high lpi resolution—good enough for all but the highest quality color publications.

Don't Resize Images in Page Layouts!

Avoid using your page layout program's "Resize" function for scanned images, especially for large ones. If you resize an image within a page layout program, it may crash the imagesetter, and the service bureau people will not appreciate the extra time your job takes to handle the resizing. Expect an extra charge for imagesetter overtime if a scan is substantially resized. If your file precipitates a crash, expect incomplete film or none at all.

Use the Right Crop to Make Sure the Image Fits

When scanning an image, competent scanner software allows you to preview the image and then allows you to select only the part of the image you plan to use. The part you select is called the "crop." If you plan to scan close to the finished size, make the crop about two to three percent

larger than what you actually need. This "slop factor" ensures that when
you place the image in your design, no white space shows around the
edges of the image. Otherwise, when you place the image in a box, upon
output (or worse, at the print shop), you may find a gap on one or more
sides between the image and the inside edge of the box.

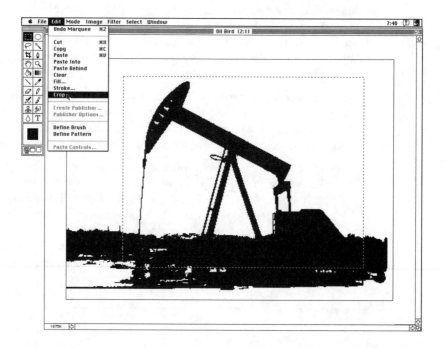

Cropping an image allows the reader to see only what you deem important and
can strengthen the impact of photos. It also results in smaller file sizes and
faster imaging.

Scan It as Halftone or Grayscale?

Black and white images are usually scanned as grayscale images, even
though some scanner software allows you to create "halftones" directly. The
reason for this is simple. Grayscale images can be extensively manipulated,
retouched, and within limits, resized on the Macintosh, using software for
this purpose. An image saved as a grayscale can then be screened on output
to meet various resolution needs. For example, an image used in an ad can
be output at 85 lpi for a newspaper and later output at 133 lpi for use in a

magazine version of the same ad. Scanner-produced halftones, while taking up substantially less disk space, can only be cropped or rotated—any other manipulation introduces problems. In addition, the halftones produced with scanner software are really dither patterns that don't reproduce well. And, unless you scan halftone images at screen resolution (72 dpi) they will be nearly illegible on screen, making cropping difficult. Of course a 72-dpi halftone is useless, because the resolution is too low for most printing.

Working with Brightness, Contrast, and Gamma Correction

Scanning black and white images is quicker and easier than color scanning. To produce quality color scans, you must first understand the black and white scanning issues, including brightness, contrast, and gamma correction. This section of the book is intended to get you up to speed in evaluating images in general and making pre-scan corrections to black and white (gray) adjustments where appropriate. In many cases, you'll want to make these black and white adjustments as part of the color balancing discussed in Chapter Eight, rather than making these changes before scanning.

Brightness and Contrast

All images, whether color or grays, share two characteristics—brightness and contrast. An image's brightness is how light or dark it is overall. For example, overexposing a photo in bright sunlight produces an image that's too light. Or conversely, underexposing a photo during a sunset may produce an image that's too dark. Ideal brightness is achieved when the darkest elements are nearly black and the brightest elements are nearly white. All other elements in the image should fall evenly between these extremes.

Contrast is the difference in the degree of brightness between elements in an image. Images are said to lack contrast when too many elements are approximately the same brightness. A "contrasty" image is one where each element stands out distinctly because of strong differences in brightness. For example, in a photo of a woman wearing a gray dress taken against a background of a gray wall, there may be little contrast between the dress and the wall. A photo of the same woman wearing a white dress photographed against a black wall has considerable contrast. Sometimes extreme contrast is desirable; other times it is inappropriate. This depends on the purpose of the photo and the look you are trying to achieve in your design. For example, images with wide variations in brightness lend themselves to newsprint publishing, because the absorbent paper tends to reduce contrast. The same images may look harsh or flat when printed on high-quality coated paper.

Undesirable contrasts, whether too much or too little, can be caused by subject matter, inept photography, and processing errors. Some films and print papers are more "contrasty" than others, as well.

1.   Too Light   2.   Too Dark

3.   About Right

Color and black and white photo images may suffer overall from being too light or dark. An image that's too light will appear washed out, as in image 1. Photos that are too dark have areas of shadow that reproduce completely black, as shown in image 2. This problem image contains areas of deep shadow contrasted with bright sunlight, making it difficult to fix quickly on the desktop.

Definition: Highlights, Midtones, and Shadows

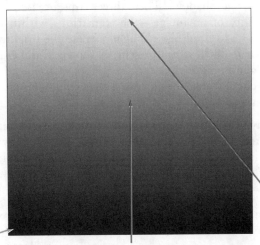

Shadows Print as a Nearly
Black Color Such as Blue-
Black or Very Dark Gray

Midtones Print as Middle Range
Colors or Grays. Most Images Are
Comprised Largely of Midttones

Highlights Print as a Nearly
White Color Such as Pale
Cream or Very Light Gray

All images have a "range of contrast" consisting of highlight, midtone, and shadow colors. Images that contain black and white and color information that fails to span the entire range of contrast often look artificial to the human eye. For example, color photographic images reproduced in newspapers look unconvincing because newsprint takes so much ink that no true white is possible without manipulation of the range of color in the picture.

Continued

Three terms you will run into frequently in color publishing product manuals and at the print shop or color separator are Highlights, Midtones, and Shadows. These three terms are used to define the contrast quality of an image—the transitions within the image from bright white to dead black. Highlights are the brightest portion of an image where detail is still present, as shown in the example. Midtones include almost all of the detail in a properly balanced image. Shadows are the darkest areas of an image that while approaching black, still contain some detail.

You may also hear of quartertones and three-quartertones. A three-quartertone is simply three-quarters of the way toward black from white; this equivalent to a dark gray. A one-quartertone is one-quarter the way toward black from white, and thus a light gray.

The Tonal Gradation - Highlights to Shadows (approximate)

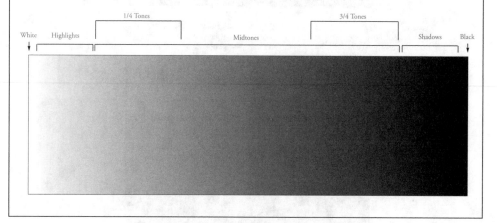

Brightness and contrast are important to color publishing, because during scanning, imaging, and printing, the brightness and contrast of an image tend to move toward the middle gray region. As images are processed, they tend to lose brightness, detail, and contrast (just as in the photocopier experiment suggested earlier in this chapter). An image with proper brightness and contrast lends itself to color correction better than one with problems, because the overall gray balance will ultimately affect how the color will look when printed.

If an image is too bright or dark, you can compensate for it when scanning or within an image-retouching program. Remember, however, that areas of an image where the detail has blended into dark shadow or bright white can't be corrected. If the information is barely present in the original, it will be lost during scanning. Also keep in mind that if an image is mostly too dark but has some light areas, increasing the overall brightness will lighten the dark areas but may also turn the light areas to pure white. This problem is dealt with more effectively with *gamma* controls, described below.

Too Little Contrast

Extra Contrast

About Right

Images without enough difference from the darkest color to the lightest are said to lack contrast. In print, they usually look murky and uninteresting. "Extra contrast" is used for images reproduced on inexpensive paper. This process compensates for the contrast lost when printing on such papers.

Contrast Extremes

For images lacking contrast, experimentation is in order when scanning. While most scanner software, image-retouching programs, and even page layout programs allow contrast adjustment, if an image requires substantial adjustment it may be irreparable. Images with extreme contrast or little contrast usually contain little detail.

Check the results of contrast changes carefully to ensure that no area has lost detail or moved too much toward light or dark. Extreme contrast changes should be avoided, unless you are looking for an unusual effect or making an image suitable for reproduction on newsprint.

Contrast May Affect Special Effects Filters

You may also need to make an image extremely "contrasty" before putting it through a special effects filter within an image-retouching or color separation program. Filters that cause substantial changes to an image, such as Photoshop's **Emboss** filter, are often triggered by the contrast in an image. Thus, extreme contrast causes more pronounced filtering.

Gamma Correction

Gamma correction adjusts the gray balance of a scanned photo to compensate for inherent problems—areas that are much brighter or darker than the rest of the image. For example, if you shoot a photo of a storefront with a bright sky behind it, the camera's automatic exposure system may produce an image where the storefront appears dark and the sky behind it nearly white. If the detail of the storefront is still present in the image (extreme problems can't be fixed with gamma), you can use gamma correction to fix the problem. With gamma correction, an algorithm is used to change the brightness curve of images in a non-linear fashion. Instead of simple overall changes to brightness and contrast, gamma correction changes only the problem areas in the mid-tones, leaving the extreme shadow and highlight areas alone.

In the storefront example, you might set the gamma to brighten the darker parts of the store while leaving the bright sky alone. Correctly applied, you will have a new image of an appropriately lit storefront against a slightly brighter sky. Shadows that should remain dark will still appear appropriately deep.

 Uncorrected Scan   Improper Correction with Brightness Adjustment

Scan Adjusted with Gamma Correction

Gamma correction repairs images where the midtones are too light or too dark. In this scan, inept photography has produced an image in which the sky is appropriately bright but the foreground too dark. Adjusting only the brightness helps the faces but lightens the shadows and highlights. Gamma correction is capable of changing only the midtones, leaving the shadows and highlights alone. As a result, the sailors' faces and clothing and the wheel are brightened, while the dark clothing and the black section of the wheel post remain appropriately dark.

Gamma correction is something you get better at with practice. Like contrast adjustments, gamma adjustments should be made carefully with judicious checking of the entire image to ensure that the wrong areas don't shift in brightness. For example, in the case of the dark storefront with gamma applied indiscriminately, areas that should remain dark may become unnaturally bright—making the image look washed out or supernatural.

When Should You Make Brightness, Contrast, Gamma, or Color Correction Adjustments?

The adjustments described above for brightness, contrast, and gamma correction can all be made *before* the scan if the scanner's software is equipped with these controls. (**Note:** Gamma correction is not supported on many inexpensive scanners. It may also be partially replaced with another process or through the automatic color correction within some color separation programs.)

Even when these adjustments are available in the scanning software, the best time to manipulate the image is still after the scan. Why? Because changing control settings and studying the resulting changes within a dinky preview box in the scan software won't tell you much about what's really going on. Making changes while scanning may require you to make multiple scans until you get the right results. That can take time, particularly if you are scanning a large image with a slow scanner. There are three exceptions to this rule:

1. **If the Highlight and Shadow Can Be Set**   If your scanner allows highlight and shadow points to be set, this should be done at the time of scanning. (See *Correcting Color* in Chapter Nine.)

2. **Production Scanning**   Make adjustments at the time of scanning for grayscale images required in a hurry. If you are working in a quick-turnaround production environment, printing at relatively low resolution, and aren't too worried about quality, you can develop a practiced eye to make rough adjustments when scanning. Scanning software with a large preview window makes this considerably easier. (*Never* do this with images that you plan to color separate!)

3. **Extreme Problems**   Images with extreme brightness, fuzziness, gamma, or color problems should be at least partially corrected during scanning. Try making halfway corrections while scanning. This preserves detail and makes your job of post-scan correction an exercise in fine-tuning rather than a hatchet job.

Scanning Line Art

As described earlier, line art is simply a drawing in black and white, with no colors or grays. Line art is an important component of color publishing, because simple sketches can be made outside the computer, scanned, and then colored and enhanced with a Mac paint, illustration, or re-touching program. Other line art applications include scanning logos and symbols for use in ads and literature.

For the best results when scanning line art, remember the following tips.

- **Darken the Scanner's Brightness Setting for Best Results**   A simple trick for getting cleaner line art is to set your color scanner's brightness down a step or two toward the dark side. Color scanners sometimes have a problem capturing line art, particularly with images where the black isn't all that black. Experiment to see what works best for your scanner. If the image includes extremely thin lines, this technique is particularly helpful.

- **Use Acetate between the Art and the Scanner**   A trick used by printers to thicken lines is to place a layer of clear acetate over the image to thicken lines when photographing line art. You can use this technique when scanning too. By sandwiching a layer of acetate or mylar between the image and the scanner's sensors, the line will thicken because the plastic slightly diffuses the line's image and the scanner sees it as being wider. Using increasingly thick acetate increases this effect, like a magnifying glass.

For line art that requires substantial modification, a low-resolution scan may be adequate, but for more critical applications, you'll want to scan with as much resolution as possible. Otherwise, diagonal lines, hard edges, and curves will appear jagged when you output the image. Type is particularly difficult to scan and is best avoided except as a template for a font manipulation program, where new letters will be created and the scan thrown away.

Useful when converting colored logos or other art to black and white, some image-retouching programs come with a *threshold* control. This allows you to set the point at which a color or gray becomes 100 percent black or 100 percent white, with no gradations in between.

Working with Color Images

Practice Makes Closer to Perfect

Scanning color images and getting good results is substantially more difficult than scanning grayscales. First, the issues explained to this point for scanning black and white photos still apply. Then, on top of that, you must deal with color balance and large file sizes. In addition, your faithful service bureau may be adequate when handling black and white scans but may stumble on producing color. You may not discover this until you've wasted a lot of money on inept color separations.

When scanning color images in preparation for color separation, the rule is simple—if the job will finish on newsprint and you have a decent scanner, you can probably achieve adequate results with a little practice. If, however, your plans include magazine-quality reproduction or above, then you need to experiment with different kinds of images and image processing to learn how to get good, repeatable results. Part of this process is also learning what kind of images to attempt. If you plan on achieving very high-quality color separations, at some point you'll need to head for a high-end prepress system or use a service bureau equipped with a drum scanner.

When learning to scan and manipulate color images, take on projects without tight deadlines. Until you get a feel for making things work, it may take you several trips through the imagesetter for new sets of negs (negatives) and color proofs to check results before printing. Also, limit your work to small images. They scan, process, and output much faster than large images. Plus, a 2" by 3" separation with mediocre color may be acceptable for publication, whereas a larger image with easy-to-see flaws won't be.

Image evaluation is important too. People are the most difficult subjects to reproduce in color, because a slight color shift can make a face look oddly green, blue, or red. A similar small shift in color may not materially affect a landscape. If you are just getting started, practice with people photos, but don't plan on taking the results to publication right away. Chapter Eight discusses color balancing and separation techniques in detail, and Chapter Ten explains proofing systems that will help you evaluate your progress and success.

Scanning Printed Images

Printed images, like those found in books, magazines, and newspapers, are composed of a dot structure. Because of these dots, scanning printed images and then breaking them into dots again for printing may result in odd and unattractive patterns called moirés. (See *Moiré Patterns* in Chapter Nine for more on this.)

There are several techniques for avoiding this problem, although the best route is to get a copy of the original photo or illustration instead of scanning the printed version. Many publications will allow you to use an original image as long as you give them appropriate credit. Also, before printing, consider running a test of the image to make sure that patterning, though invisible on the screen, doesn't appear in the printed output. Some scanners, such as the Agfa models, claim to be able to drop out the patterning, but we've never tried it.

We recommend trying the following workarounds that may help you reproduce printed black and white or color images with better results:

- **Apply a New Screen Angle**   Although technically involved, the best way to handle scanned printed images is to apply a new screen angle that will complement the existing one(s). (Screens and screen angles are explained in subsequent chapters.) Or, process the image conventionally and let your printer struggle with rescreening the image. In the case of images using low-resolution screens (such as those found in newspapers), this is pretty much the only way to fly, although the results of rescreening may be ugly.

- **Reduce the Image**   If you substantially reduce the size of the image during scanning, the scanner will see less detail and minimize the dot patterns. This only works when a significant reduction is possible and the image was printed at high resolution. Newspaper photos must be reduced so much that this approach doesn't help much.

- **Defocus the Image**   High-end scanner software and photo retouching/separation programs allow you to "soften" or defocus images. This reduces the patterning, and if the image was adequately softened, sharpening can then be applied without regaining the dot patterning. Experimentation will disclose the right amount of softening and then sharpening to use for a given image.

- **Redraw the Image**   Use the scan as the template for a new drawing to be created within Freehand or Illustrator.

- **Use a Filter**   Filters can be applied in retouching and separation programs to materially change a scanned image and add special effects. For example, if you create a diffusion image (also an option in most scanner software), the dot structure will be lost. Some paint programs offer a variety of filters that may work nicely for this purpose, as well.

In this chapter, we've discussed scanning on the Mac, with an eye toward practicality and the problems that make high-quality scans difficult without a good scanner, extensive practice, and a large-capacity hard disk. In the next chapter, we'll discuss color on the desktop and how to add color to desktop-produced layouts and designs.

USING COLOR TO DESIGN ON THE MACINTOSH DESKTOP

"It is vital that you understand the magic and trickery of color. Color is always seen in its surroundings. What it is near and how much of it there is affects how it looks."

—Jan White
Color for the Electronic Age

In order to take a color project into print, it's helpful to understand the color systems used for both color publishing and printing. Color science is very technical, but for Macintosh color publishing many of the complexities are automated with hardware and application software, so you don't have to become deeply involved in the technology. If, however, you find color as fascinating as we do, you may want to supplement this chapter with a book on color theory available from an art supply store or the local library. Classes in color science and color theory are also offered by colleges and universities with large art departments.

You Are Here

At this point in the book, you have a Macintosh system and the requisite color publishing software (or are at least considering the purchase) and are ready to begin assembling color publications. This chapter explains the basic mechanics of color on the desktop, including color models, color standards, calibration, and the incorporation of color into Mac color publishing projects.

Assembling color publications requires an understanding of the realities of color printing. There are many design possibilities that simply can't be printed, although your page layout program won't stop you from assembling these ideas. That's why, as recommended in Chapter One, you should discuss color projects with your printer before embarking on a job that otherwise may require substantial revision before printing. Hopefully, the information in this chapter will give you some idea about the limitations as well.

Color Design Considerations

For those new to designing with color, there are a few guidelines to follow that will help you produce better looking projects while you build experience. Designing with color offers new opportunities to the desktop publisher who has mostly worked in black and white. Color can be used to set a mood for a publication, be it quiet and classy or eye-popping. Color is a powerful tool for making brochures, direct mail pieces, and ads stand out from the competition. Color can also be overused, used ineffectively, or used incorrectly, negating its value and the extra cost of producing a color piece. There are a myriad of wonderful books on color design, so we won't try to duplicate the information here, but to get you started, here are several "designing with color basics" for you to keep in mind:

- **Choose Colors for Maximum Impact**   When designing with color, keep in mind that some colors are more "optical" than others. A bright red catches the eye much faster than a pale blue. Using the pale blue for a key headline and the bright red for an unimportant detail will result in the secondary item getting more notice than the primary message.

- **Colors Go in and out of Style**   Like clothes, colors go in and out of style. People quickly embrace fresh-looking color combinations and gradually tire of them. Using an out-of-style color combination instantly makes your publication appear behind the times. This is okay if you are assembling ads for a historical society, but not a good idea for a cutting-edge computer product brochure. If you are new to color design, pick up recent design and advertising annuals like those produced by *Communications Arts* and study the colors used in the award-winning work. Study older issues for a comparison if you want to learn how color preferences change over time. (The address for *Communications Arts* is listed in the *Sources* section of the book.)

- **Some Colors Should Be Avoided**   Unless you are printing posters for Saint Patrick's Day or packaging frozen peas, take care when using green. Research shows that it is the least favored color. So, while a leprechaun green may grab the eye, the subconscious won't be receptive to the message. For similar reasons avoid chocolate browns, murky tans, and too much hot pink.

Continued

- **Use Fewer Colors**   While it's true that one of the key advantages of Mac-based color publishing is that a large number of screen colors can be incorporated into a single document at no additional cost, that doesn't mean you should do it! Unless you are very knowledgeable about color design, too many colors can confuse the reader's eye and tire the mind. (This applies to using too many fonts as well—a common desktop publishing mistake. Just because you have them doesn't mean you have to use them.)

- **Choose Colors under Several Light Sources**   If you are deciding on a Pantone or Focoltone color, study the swatch book under several light sources. If you pick a color under incandescent light and your finished piece will be read in an office, study the swatch under fluorescent lights as well—you will be amazed how light sources shift the perception of the color. A bright yellow that looks conservative in normal room lighting may scream if used in large quantities on a sun-lit billboard. (Of course, you can't account for everything in the target environment when choosing color—even wallpaper, furniture, paint, and carpet can shift the perceived color of a printed piece to a point where it looks only vaguely like the intended choice.)

- **Use the Right Dose**   Use loud, bright colors in small amounts. Use light, pale colors in larger areas.

- **Make Type Easy to Read**   Yes, you can print text in fluorescent red to catch the eye, but if there's much more than a sentence of copy in this color, people will have a hard time reading it or may not bother to try. Text is easiest to read when printed in black or dark gray.

- **Leave White Space!**   When designing with colors, particularly bright ones, leave lots of white space in your publication. This allows the eye to rest while looking at the piece. White space also makes the colors seem fresh and crisp.

- **Be Aware That Some Colors "Vibrate"**   When bright red and bright blue touch in print, the eye has difficulty determining where one color stops and the other starts; thus the colors seem to vibrate. Green with red and some other combinations have the same problem. While this can be used as a design element on rare occasion, weigh this kind of impact carefully.

Continued

- **Medium Blues Are Most Popular**   People generally like blues. For this reason, blue gets used too often. Publications that rely heavily on blues may look like one of the crowd and lack impact as a result.

- **Gray Is Universal**   The grays, including black and white and shades in between, work with all other colors.

- **All Rules Can Be Broken**   Rather than prescriptions, these comments are simply suggestions. Should you decide to break any one of the "rules," study your creation carefully before going into print—what looks fresh and inventive on screen may look clumsy or incompetent in print—be careful!

Color and Color Models

Color models are systems for explaining how one color relates to another. You learned a simple color model in kindergarten—red and blue makes purple—blue and yellow makes green—red and yellow makes orange. Unfortunately, in the world of color printing and publishing, color models are more complex than this.

There are a variety of color models that have been established over the centuries, growing in sophistication as science began to better understand light and perception. As a color publisher, you don't need to be aware of all the models, though it is important to understand some of the possibilities for color mixing.

The reason that there is more than one color model is simple—none of the models can accurately reflect all the relationships among the entire range of color possibilities without being too convoluted to understand and apply. A model that best suits the immediate need must be selected. Computer monitors use the red, green, and blue (RGB) model, because it provides bright color on a video display and is easily compatible with the technology of color video devices. Four-color printing on offset lithographic presses uses three colored inks—cyan, magenta, and yellow—with black as the fourth color. (Called the CMYK model—the K in CMYK refers to the printer's word for black, *key*.)

Both the RGB and CMYK color models are important to the color conversion performed in order to move an image from the RGB world of computers to the CMYK environment of the four-color press.

Red-Green-Blue Color

The most familiar color selection model on the Macintosh is found in the Apple Color Picker—used to specify color within some programs, as well as choose highlight colors for the Mac's Finder. The RGB model is used in the Color Picker and refers simply to the red, green, and blue guns that light a color monitor. (The Color Picker also uses the Hue, Saturation, and Brightness model explained later.) As we said in Chapter Two, the guns light the phosphor on the inside of the screen to make it glow. The three guns' colors can be mixed to simulate a wide variety of colors. When no gun is lighting an area of the screen, it appears black, even though most monitors appear dark gray or green when turned off. The guns can be combined at varying levels of output—this is how other colors are created.

You can experiment with the RGB model by selecting the Color Control Panel and then selecting **Other** for the highlight color to display the Color Picker. Setting the three RGB numbers to zero produces black—no light from the RGB guns inside the monitor. Setting the three values to the maximum (65,535) produces bright white because all three guns are firing at their maximum in the center of the color wheel. The Color Picker with its color system is shown in the *Color Section* of this book. See Figure C-1.

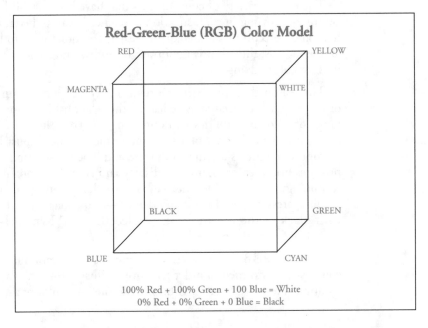

Red-Green-Blue (RGB) Color Model

100% Red + 100% Green + 100 Blue = White
0% Red + 0% Green + 0 Blue = Black

RGB is the color model that lends itself naturally to color televisions and monitors.

Process Color or CMYK

The four-color printing technique using *process color* or *CMYK color* is employed to print full-color images (explained in more detail in Chapter Eight). Images are broken down during *color separation* into cyan, magenta, yellow, and black components. These are the process colors. When recombined on press, these process colors are printed as combinations of dots to give an approximation of the original color and detail. Much in the way RGB works, the colors cyan, yellow and magenta are capable of representing (almost) any color when mixed together in varying amounts. The color recombination is limited only by color separation quality, printing, and paper quality.

Using the CMYK process color method, some colors (such as peach) shift into other related colors, but the finished printed image generally looks very much like the original. CMYK colors also relate fairly well to RGB colors: red in RGB becomes a combination of magenta and yellow in CMYK; green in RGB is composed of yellow and cyan in CMYK; and blue in RGB is made up of cyan and magenta in CMYK.

Black is used in CMYK because, while in theory solid cyan, magenta, and yellow will produce black when mixed together equally, in practice they create a brown. Black adds crispness to shadow areas and makes the image more convincing on paper. As explained in Chapter Nine, black also reduces the total amount of ink required on press—making the printing process more manageable and predictable. A true black is not available in the RGB system. Black is actually the color of the monitor screen when it is off—and this varies from dark gray to green.

Additive Color and Subtractive Color

One of the issues that affects Mac color publishing on a fundamental level is the incompatibility of Mac screen color with printed color. The RGB colors on a Mac's screen are created by adding light to change a black-appearing screen, whereas four-color printing uses colored inks to partially obscure the paper's white surface and subtract reflection of certain colors so the desired color is visible. These two different systems are called *additive color* and *subtractive color*.

The Mac's screen is *additive color* because light is added to create color. The press uses *subtractive color* because inks are used to partially block the reflection of light. Obviously, the Mac's screen can represent brighter colors than the print process because the white on the screen is much brighter than the white of a sheet of paper held up to it. For this reason,

RGB color on a monitor can create a number of strong colors that can't be reproduced in print.

On the monitor when all guns are firing at full strength, red, green, and blue equal white. In fact, on monitors that allow separate electrical inputs for red, green, and blue, you can switch the connectors (with the power off, please) so that red goes into green, blue into red, and green into blue; the screen colors will be completely wrong, but white will still look white, because at full output the addition of the gun colors is always the same.

Could you print RGB color in theory? As a laboratory experiment, you could probably start with black paper and then add semi-opaque red, green, and blue to create process color. Just as CMYK color uses black to compensate for the imperfections in the color model, you might have to use white as a fourth color to brighten light areas of the image. Is it practical? Not really.

A conversion from RGB to CMYK is necessary, therefore, because of the different ways colors are created on a monitor and on a printing press. To compensate for these differences, a CMYK simulation mode is available within some programs for direct manipulation of images. The advantage of working directly in this mode is that there are fewer surprises when converting RGB images to CMYK images. Some CMYK simulations limit the number of RGB colors that can be created, so unprintable ones are not available. In our experience, the disadvantage of these simulations is that they slow painting down measurably.

Screen Color and Spot Color

In addition to being able to simulate full-color, continuous tone images, CMYK colors can also be used to print "solid" colors. By mixing different percentages of the four colors together, a large number of colors can be created. This technique is called *screen color*, because screens of each process color are used to create a new color. The screens of each process color are varied by a set percentage to each solid color possibility. So, screens consisting of ten percent cyan, 90 percent magenta, 50 percent yellow, and ten percent black create a deep, burnt red in print. Screen color samples can be found in the back of the Aldus PrePrint manual. For an example of screen mixes, see Figure C-2 in the *Color Section* of this book.

> ## Tip: Experiment with a CMYK Color Wheel
>
> Most art supply stores sell a color wheel consisting of four trans-
> parent mylar wheels mounted one on top of another. Each wheel
> represents one of the four CMYK colors and is imprinted with
> screens of each color ranging from ten to 100 percent. By rotating
> the wheels in various combinations, you can see what the different
> percentages of each color look like when mixed. This wheel can be
> used to help you specify CMYK color if you are working on an
> uncalibrated monitor. These wheels are available in both fine and
> coarse (suitable for newsprint) screen values, though you may have
> to call around to find both versions.

The ability to add screen color to publications is a powerful aspect of
Mac-based color publishing. Screen color gets expensive when handled
conventionally because of the labor and film required to "burn" each
screen layer—one each for cyan, magenta, yellow, and black. On the
Mac, you can easily use as many screen colors as you want because,
instead of using physical screens requiring time-consuming assembly, the
imagesetter creates them electronically with no extra effort.

Another way to create colored solids and type is to print a *spot color*.
Unlike screen color, where the mix of process inks is used to build a new
color on press, spot colors are simply solid color inks laid down on paper.
Spot colors are usually specified through the Pantone Matching System
or Focoltone swatch books. (These color systems are explained later in
this chapter.) Solid color inks produce more optically convincing solids
than do screened colors.

Because screened colors are made from two to four inks (you don't
have to use all four), they sometimes look murkier than a spot color
equivalent. Some colors are essentially impossible to render through
screen color because of the limitations inherent in the process color
model. This makes solid spot colors necessary for critical applications of
color. Spot colors can be custom mixed to match any color perceptible to
the human eye. Because each spot color requires its own press plate, each
is output on the imagesetter as a separate piece of film for making plates
at the print shop.

Be careful not to confuse four-spot colors with four-color process
printing. Four-color process printing requires that the press be inked with
the standard CMYK inks. These are used to simulate the entire color

spectrum when printing images and screen colors derived from the process colors. A four-spot color job means that four individual colors are loaded onto the press. These colors print as separate colors in designated areas and will not be combined. It is possible to combine process printing with spot color printing. It's only a matter of press time and your budget. Figure C-3 (*Color Section*) shows the difference between spot color, screen color, and process color images.

The Pantone Matching System

The most widely used system for mixing spot colors is the Pantone Matching System (PMS). Until this system was introduced in the early 1960s, color specification was handled with swatches of colored fabric, paint chips, and other hard-to-match color samples. With the introduction of Pantone matching, a universal color matching system for spot color was finally achieved. From just a handful of individual Pantone inks, hundreds of colors can be created. This system allows you to specify a color on your computer that a print shop in a remote city can match almost exactly.

The Pantone system provides swatch books of colors for designers to choose from. Once selected, the printer mixes or buys the correct color and attempts to match it on press as closely as possible. Because colored inks look different on different kinds of paper, Pantone sells swatch books for coated and uncoated papers and newsprint. Each color is referred to by its PMS number.

Many Mac software developers license the Pantone Library and include these colors in their programs. Then you can choose the color you want by clicking on an on-screen swatch book showing the color and its number. Choosing a color will place a spot-color overlay of that color in your design; it will be output on the imagesetter as a piece of film ready for press. On the downside, even with the recent additions to the Pantone system (more colors, pastels, metallics, etc.), there are many colors it doesn't offer.

Pantone colors within many applications can also be specified as process colors. This means that instead of outputting and printing with the actual Pantone-matched ink, the color will be simulated as a screen color. To create Pantone color simulations, programs use a look-up table that shows what percentages of CMYK inks to mix to approximate the requested PMS color. This approach only works for Pantone colors that can be accurately simulated with screen colors (many can't).

Tip: Match Pantone Colors from a Pantone Swatch Book, Not from Your Screen!

If your design includes Pantone colors, you will want to know what the colors will look like when they print. This is doubly true if your project includes multiple colors that interact with each other visually. While applications that support the Pantone Matching System provide on-screen representations of each color, check the colors with a swatch book as you work, to get a better idea of what they actually look like. Even on a calibrated monitor with licensed Pantone calibration, the screen colors aren't *exactly* right.

Pantone Matching System books can be found at any art supply store or through your printer's ink supply company. The most common kind is a small book with color panels that fan open. A more expensive three-ring binder model with the colors as tear-away chips is also available.

Yes, these books are expensive, but so is a color Macintosh publishing system and color printing—bite the bullet and buy one. The books should be replaced at least every two years because the colors tend to darken and shift as the varnish in the inks yellows with age.

Ask your printer for advice in this area and run a proof of the image-setter output when in doubt. Don't make the classic mistake of specifying twelve Pantone colors as screen colors and then getting an ugly surprise at the print shop! A source of help is Pantone's Process Color Simulator book, which shows which colors to use and which to avoid. If you get bad results from this process or feel restricted by the number of colors that look good in print, consider using one of the two alternative systems that compete with Pantone, Focoltone and TruMatch, described later.

Keep in mind that some applications produce inaccurate on-screen renderings of Pantone colors, and some are better than others at providing accurate screen color approximations of Pantone colors. If your results look poor in the proofing stage and you used a Pantone color capable of accurate simulation with four-color process inks, look first to see if there are problems with other colors in the job, pointing to improper imagesetter calibration. If that's not the problem, then it may be that your application does a poor job creating the screen-color renderings of PMS colors.

Pantone colors can also be individually screened to lighten them. These are called *screen tints* because by regulating a color with a screen, a lighter color or *tint* is created. If you specify PMS 286 (a rich blue) to print at twenty percent instead of the default 100 percent, it will change from deep blue to a pale blue. Letraset sells a screen tint guide that shows what each color looks like when printed at screen values from ten percent on up. Keep in mind that for a variety of reasons, screen colors on the Mac often print darker than what you see in the book. Until you gain experience with spot color tints, avoid using tint values (screens) of more than 50 percent because they may appear as a muddy solid in print.

Focoltone and TruMatch Color Specification Systems

Two emerging color systems that provide reliable color on the Mac are Focoltone and TruMatch. By using one of these matching systems, process colors can be specified as screened colors within applications that support them. (Focoltone also can be used to mix solid spot colors as well, but TruMatch does not currently support solid spot color.)

These systems have built-in compensation routines for dot gain and other color publishing problems and allow color change in one percent (TruMatch) and five percent (Focoltone) screen increments. Using these systems provides reliable color specification for screen color. Unlike specifying percentages of CMYK and hoping for the best on output, both of these alternatives offer precise control over color, which can then be matched on press with a Focoltone or TruMatch swatch book. As with the Pantone Matching System, you should check the screen representation against the book, because the monitor version of the color may not accurately represent the selected color. The Focoltone System swatch books are pictured in Figure C-4 in the *Color Section* of this book.

Other Sources for Spot Colors

Instead of using Pantone or Focoltone to choose a spot color, you can directly specify a custom color to be mixed at the print shop or through a custom color house. Custom color shops (often called labs) employ technicians, gifted with an accurate eye for color, to mix inks to your specifications. By buying this service, you can get exactly the color you want. This is useful for obtaining a color in between the choices in the Pantone

System. Custom ink is more expensive, but in some cases may be worth the price and the wait. On the downside, if you plan to use the color in the future, you may need to have it mixed again, and it may not match exactly.

There are also other spot color ink systems in local use around the world, such as the TOYO system from Japan. (TOYO is gaining in popularity in the U.S. and is supported in Letraset's ColorStudio.) As printing technology improves, Pantone will probably see increased competition from several color systems, in addition to Focoltone and TruMatch.

Be aware that if you intend to print your job at a quick printer, the shop may use a custom spot color system with as few as eighteen colors. Other kinds of printing technology, such as silkscreening, use a different set of standards and can't match the PMS spectrum very well. Before you specify a color for a special kind of reproduction, make sure you ask about these limitations.

Should I Use Spot Color or Screen Color?

The choice to use spot color or screen color is a decision that depends largely on the job and your budget. If you are including process color images in a job, then using screen color may make sense, since you've already inked the press for this kind of work.

If your job does not entail process color photos and you only need an extra color or two, then spot color makes more sense. It will be less expensive to ink one or two colors than the four stations required to employ screen color. Not only are spot colors better looking, especially when used in large, solid areas, but more possibilities are available. Using spot color, awkward issues such as dot gain and moirés are eliminated because screens are not employed. Ink coverage can be a problem when printing large areas of ink as solids, however. This problem is discussed further in Chapter Twelve.

If your job is graced with a big budget, as we mentioned before, you can use both spot and screen colors. Larger print shops have six-color presses. These presses allow you to use four colors for process color images and screened colors, plus the other two stations for spot color solids or for applying effects such as varnishes. If you need more colors than this, or are working with a shop with only a four-color press, then your job will have to be run through twice to apply extra colors. This will increase your printing bill substantially at most shops because twice the press time is required to run the job.

Other Color Models

In addition to the color models and processes explained in this chapter, there are other models in use on the Macintosh. Hue, saturation, and brightness (HSB) and hue, saturation, and luminance (HSL) are available in addition to RGB and CMYK. These systems are used in retouching and color separation programs and in page layout programs. Unlike RGB, which is based simply on increasing or decreasing the output of each of the three color guns in a monitor to achieve different colors, these systems work by adjusting the following:

- **Hue**   Hue is the individual color, for example, red, pink, or peach.

- **Saturation**   The amount of color is described as saturation. The strongest saturation is intense, the weakest pale.

- **Brightness or Luminance**   Brightness is the measure of light reflected from a color. Colors low on the brightness scale tend to be dull looking.

The advantage of the HSB and HSL models over RGB is that they produce more colors perceptible to the eye. Whereas RGB offers a huge number of color choices, the eye has trouble differentiating many of them. The color relationships within the RGB model are not intuitive either, making color selection somewhat awkward to users not accustomed to specifying colors on video devices. For many users, particularly those painting on Macintosh color systems after working with physical media such as oil paints, HSB and HSL are more intuitive to use, and choosing and mixing colors becomes a process similar to mixing paint.

To output images created using RGB, HSL, or HSB, the image is converted to CMYK colors and then separated into individual colors, one color at a time, at the imagesetter. It is up to the quality of the software to determine the accuracy in this conversion.

In summary, the best way to become familiar with the various color models is to work with them. While they may seem quite technical, once you start moving color slider bars around in your programs, you will quickly understand their differences.

Adding Color to Your Work

Now that you are armed with a basic understanding of Macintosh color models, it's time to learn how color is introduced and manipulated within Macintosh programs. Unlike conventional design on a drafting board, color on a computer can be introduced directly to the design and manipulated on a "what-if" basis to get the best effect and to tweak a page layout until it looks perfect. The power of color design is thus available to people who lack the experienced visualization skills that are the hallmark of professional designers and illustrators. The Mac provides the visualization for you right on screen, and no messy inks or paints are required for experimentation.

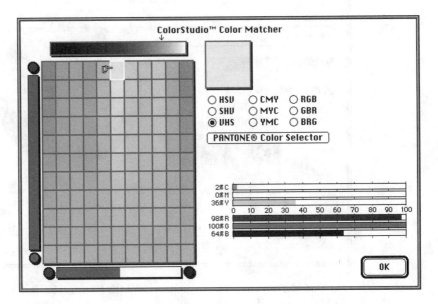

Letraset's ColorStudio supports a wide range of color models.

Color within Page Layout Programs

In a page layout program like PageMaker or QuarkXPress, color elements are usually assembled before going to the imagesetter in preparation for print. Illustrations, scans, and copy are brought together with other design elements to complete a document. A great deal of color design can be accomplished within page layout programs, in addition to importing color elements from other sources.

Within the page layout program, you define the colors you want to use. Several colors are predefined and you can use these as "markers" for spot colors. But to better see what you are doing, these are best ignored—instead, define the actual colors you plan to use on a custom palette. There is one exception to this rule: The color named *registration* is black and is output on *all* color layers at the imagesetter. This is useful for manually adding trim marks (trim marks show the print shop where to trim off the extra paper) and document control requirements, such as labels and dates, to keep track of archived artwork.

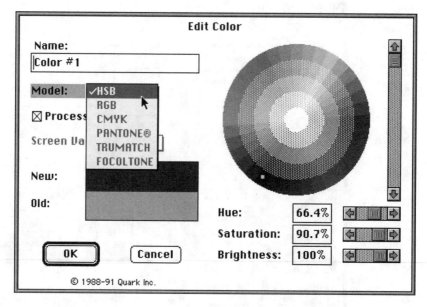

The QuarkXPress color palette supports CYMK, Pantone, RGB, Focoltone, TruMatch, and HSB color models and systems.

Choice of a palette is accomplished through a color specification menu that is included with the program. Color models and systems within QuarkXPress can be specified as CMYK, Pantone, RGB, Focoltone, TruMatch, or HSB, for example. Other page layout programs may have different choices, but they are selected in similar ways. You just select the desired color model from a pop-up menu.

In QuarkXPress, moving the large scroll bar at the right selects the desired brightness level, and then clicking within the color field makes the selection. A box shows a comparison of the selected color with the color it replaces. This is useful for making minor adjustments to colors. (For example: "Make it just a tad more blue.") The color values can also be entered by percentage in the boxes below the wheel.

Tip: Assemble a Working Palette

Because you may use the same colors over and over in a variety of publications, assembling a *working palette* can bring you up to speed faster when starting a new color publication. A working palette contains the colors you use frequently and nothing more. So, if your company's logo color is PMS 300 and you always use it and PMS 439 in two-color publications, delete all unnecessary colors from a palette and add these two. (Note that *registration* cannot be deleted, nor can the four process colors in some programs.) Then, instead of redefining the palette each time you open a new document, use the "append," "copy," or "import" command within the color dialog and open the file that contains your palette; those colors will automatically become the colors for the new publication.

CMYK values are entered directly in the percentage boxes, because the color wheel does not lend itself to CMYK color selection. Pantone, Focoltone, and TruMatch colors are selected by choosing the desired model. A display replaces the color wheel with "color chips" similar to those found in the physical swatch books. The "book" can be scrolled through to display and select the desired color, or a number can be entered directly in a box.

Pantone colors can be output as either solid colors or screen colors, as explained earlier in this chapter. But keep in mind, while QuarkXPress and other page layout programs will allow you to create any PMS number from screens, many colors that can't effectively be printed this way will still be output with the rest of your job. There may be no sign of trouble until you see a color proof of your publication.

Once a color is selected, the color selection box is closed, and the color becomes one of the color selections displayed in the palette. Selected colors can be deleted or edited to create new values. In most programs, objects defined with a deleted color will appear black until they are assigned a new color.

Once selected, color can be applied to type, lines, and shapes. Colors can also be applied to black and white and grayscale TIFF images. To add color to type, lines, or shapes, simply select the object and then choose the desired color. To color a TIFF element, simply click it to make it active and then click on the desired color to make the change.

All black elements within the image will become the new color. White areas will remain white. (Black and white one-bit TIFFs are transparent where they show white in most programs. This allows background color to show through. To eliminate this problem, put the TIFF image in front of an appropriately-sized white box.)

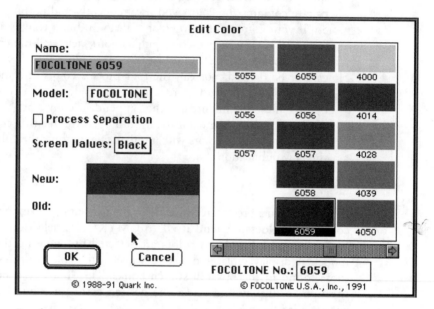

Focoltone color matching system colors are selected with an on-screen color swatch book.

Together, these colored elements can be combined with grayscale images, illustrations, scanned photos, type, and shapes to create a complete publication. The steps for adding full-color color images, such as scanned photos, are explained in the next chapter.

Color within Paint and Illustration Programs

Painting with a color palette as large as the Mac's 16.7 million colors offers you a wide range of color choices, to say the least. This may seem intimidating if you are new to color. For this reason, many paint programs provide you with palettes that deliberately limit these choices or offer the opportunity to build your own palettes of fewer choices.

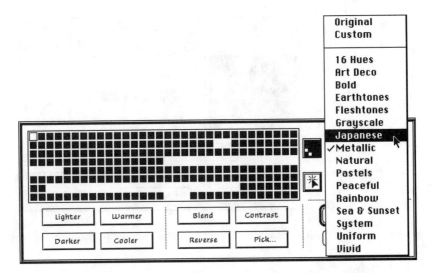

Many illustration and paint programs, such as PixelPaint Professional, provide a series of predefined color palettes to make choosing colors easier.

From within an illustration program, custom color palettes can be defined in much same way they are created within a page layout program. Once an object is clicked, a color is selected from the palette of defined colors. You can fill a box with color, fill its outline, or both. Different colors can be used for the outline and interior fill. These programs also allow the creation of color blends and gradations—a process that takes considerable time when handled conventionally, but takes only a couple of seconds within a Mac illustration program! (**Note:** Large areas filled with PostScript color gradations may take a long time to image at the service bureau.)

Color within Painting and Retouching Programs

Painting, retouching, and color separation programs work similarly when it comes to specifying and using color, although retouching and color separation programs may employ a different toolbox and offer a variety of color management features not found in paint programs. Retouching programs may also provide direct support for Pantone and Focoltone—features not found in all paint programs.

These programs employ a color palette that allows you to select from one of several color models and then "pick" a color from an area of graduated colors by clicking on the shade you prefer.

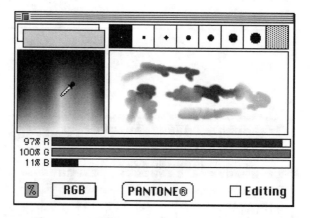

ColorStudio's eye dropper tool can be used to choose a palette color.

Tip: Change the Color by Throwing in the Bucket

Most painting and retouching applications will allow you to replace one color with another by using the paint bucket. Simply select the color you desire and move the paint bucket's tip to the area where the color should change; then click. While it may take a minute or two, the original color for an entire area will be replaced with the new one. This works best in many programs at 100 percent magnification. At higher or lower magnifications, some popular programs won't spill paint precisely where you click.

In the case of sophisticated paint programs, an area is provided that allows you to mix colors just like an illustrator or painter does with conventional paints. The colors can overlap or be added together to form a new color. The eyedropper tool is clicked on the desired color combination within the mixing area, and that mix becomes the new active color.

Color retouching and paint programs provide two layers of color. The foreground layer provides an ordinary painting surface. And, if a non-white color is selected, there is also a background layer that simulates painting on colored paper. If the "paint" is erased from the foreground, then the background "paper" color shows through.

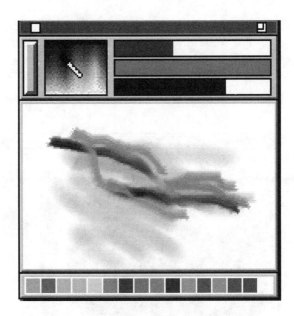

Color mixing area within PixelPaint Pro

Check Colors to See If They Will Print

While you must convert RGB images to printable CMYK colors before going to print, you may not like the results of the conversion. The most problematic colors are RGB colors that are more intense than can be printed with CMYK inks. If you have substantially increased the color saturation of a washed-out photo and it has a "neon" look in some of the stronger color areas, check it for printability. (This can be a problem with paint images as well, because brilliant colors seem like obvious choices for brightening up an image while viewing your work on the monitor.)

- **Doing It in Photoshop**   You can check a suspect color by picking it up with the eyedropper within Adobe Photoshop and opening the color picker. If the color is unprintable, a warning triangle will display with an exclamation point. If you click on the triangle, Photoshop will substitute the closest printable color. This triangle also shows when you pick an unprintable color for painting or retouching.

- **Doing It in ColorStudio**   ColorStudio offers a CMYK preview that allows you to see the results of a conversion before you actually do it. This is a handy tool for evaluating the results of the conversion to printable CMYK colors without actually changing the file. For some images, rather than accepting the automatic change of "neon green" to "gas chamber green," you may want to manually change the color to something both printable and appropriate to the image.

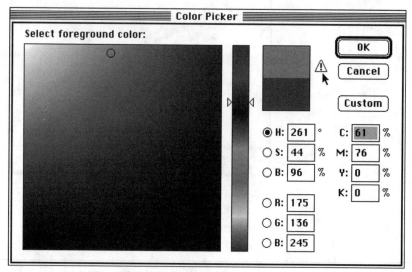

If you choose an "unprintable" color in Photoshop's color palette, a warning triangle will flash near the OK button.

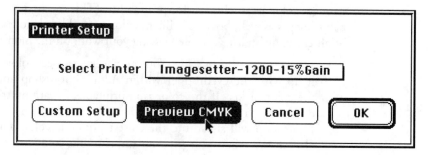

ColorStudio allows easy previewing of the colors that will be used to match the CMYK colors.

Color Calibration and Color Standards

In the idealized world of Macintosh color publishing (that's where you find yourself when talking with an imagesetter sales rep), color from scanner to monitor to print shop is accurate through the entire process. In actual practice, as you've no doubt deduced from reading previous chapters, Macintosh color fidelity has a way to go to reach this ideal state. That's not to say you can't produce accurate color, but it takes practice. Here are the basic problems:

- Color scanners shift tonal balance and hue.

- Macintosh monitors require calibration to be even vaguely accurate. After calibration, accuracy is improved but still imperfect over the vast spectrum of displayable colors.

- Extremely bright colors that can be displayed or specified on screen may not be printable (as explained in the last section).

- Application software treats color inconsistently.

- Application software uses inconsistent screen values for screens and screened colors at the imagesetter.

- Imagesetter calibration and precision varies among models and operators.

- When screens are copied during the stripping and plating process, they tend to change in density.

- Colors shift on press because of ink color imperfections.

- Printing presses differ in how they lay down ink. This variation is exacerbated by age, wear, and improper maintenance.

- Printing papers have differing textures and absorbencies that shift color. Even two shipments of the same paper may differ markedly, particularly in the case of inexpensive stocks.

There are other less serious and more esoteric issues, but this gives you a general idea of where the problems are. Fortunately, while there is no single solution for all of these problems yet, there are a variety of techniques and workarounds for some.

Among solutions, there are the Pantone System and the competing systems described earlier, which are licensed to software vendors for use in their applications. These technologies are being extended to color printers as well. Unfortunately, the Pantone system works best as a system for simple spot colors and therefore won't help with the problems associated with color scans and paint-based illustrations, although having a monitor or printer calibrated properly for screened Pantone colors helps ensure that other colors are more accurate.

Yet another solution is automatic calibrators, as mentioned already in Chapters Two and Four. The right calibration system, in theory, could be used to calibrate continuous tone images and art, all the way from scanner to print shop, although this technology remains a dream at the moment.

A third solution is to use scans of test colors and calibrate the entire system from start to finish. This works, but as soon as a device is calibrated, it starts to lose accuracy. To make this viable, someone with a good eye for color has to put in the time and effort to implement and stabilize a workable system. Some of the calibration standards available are described below.

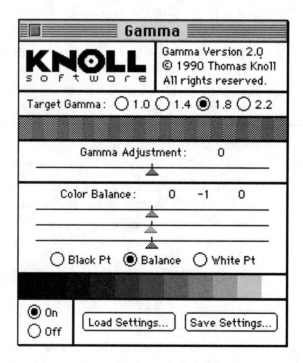

A system extension provided with Photoshop allows automatic monitor gamma correction.

Adjusting Monitor Gamma

One of the sources of inaccuracies in color monitors is their gamma—the transition from dark to light color in the midtones. Color separation programs such as Photoshop include a routine for adjusting monitor gamma. While it will not give you a color-accurate monitor, this routine will bring the brightness levels of colors displayed on the monitor closer to those that will be printed and is better than no calibration at all. To run one of these routines, carefully follow the instructions provided and keep in mind that room lighting will affect the gamma "readings."

TekColor

One experiment in color matching was developed by Tektronix, a manufacturer of color printers for both the Macintosh and IBM-compatible worlds. The system is based on a color model developed by the International Commission of Illumination (the CIE model)—a standard capable of accommodating a wide variety of color relationships and probably the most accurate model representing colors perceptible to the human eye.

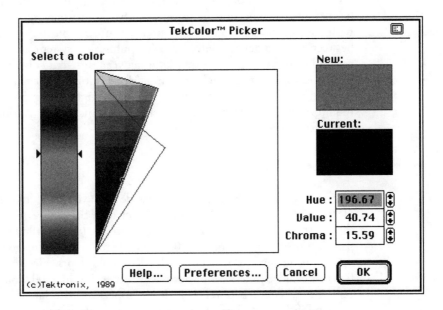

The two TekColor leaves show the color models of two devices.

TekColor is based on the premise that different devices produce colors in a distinct spectrum peculiar to the device and its technology. The system knows that the colors that can be shown on screen can't necessarily be printed on a color printer. As a result, each device has a signature "leaf." Where the leaves of two devices overlap, they share common color space, so those colors within the shared space can be reproduced by both devices. Where they do not overlap, color compromises will have to be made.

TekColor is promoted as an open standard, but its main limitation for the color publisher heading for the service bureau and the print shop is that this model is not currently applicable to color on the imagesetter. Tektronix uses this standard as a way to provide users with accurate color on their own color printers. This standard is also employed by SuperMac's Color Calibrator and Savitar's scanner calibration systems for flatbed and 35mm scanners.

Kodak Color Management System (KCMS)

Kodak is also promoting a proprietary color system. Their KCMS system allows photos and slides to be transferred from their native format onto disk with little loss of color or detail. Once transmitted, the images can be manipulated and output through software and hardware compatible with the technology. This system takes into account the differences between various devices within a color publishing system and what they can and can't do. It acts as a translator between different color models and combines them into a single, common description. Importantly, Kodak's solution takes a serious stab at producing accurate color on Mac color monitors, and it takes into account that color inaccuracy can occur anywhere from scanner to imagesetter.

Eport Color Technology

Electronics for Imaging, Inc. (EFI) has developed a new color matching technology that has great potential. Much like the device independence that PostScript provides for text and graphics (which allows the same page layout that prints on a 300-dpi laser printer to be imaged at 2,400 dpi on an imagesetter), Eport Color Technology provides the potential for device-independent color accuracy. Something like TekColor in concept, EFI's system is potentially more appealing to a larger number of color publishing equipment and software manufacturers. The Eport system uses look-up tables to establish the color characteristics of various color printing and imaging systems and software to compute the color translation from one device to another.

When installed on a Mac, Eport is called up when a color needs to be rasterized on any device and makes adjustments to the color "content" to ensure accuracy for that particular device, be it color monitor, color printer, or other device. Eport technology can also check the color against its database to see if the color is compatible with the device. The system lets the user know that a desired color is not reproducible on a specific device. At that point the user can decide whether to make changes to the color or not.

Focoltone

Focoltone, discussed earlier in the chapter as a system for color matching, is seeking to promote its own calibration standard for color images. The standard is such that an image scanned on a Focoltone-controlled scanner will produce a file that will maintain consistent color and accurate dot size (inaccurate dot sizes shift color) when output on an imagesetter. Unfortunately, as of this writing, this technology is only available on high-end prepress systems.

In addition, Focoltone also offers software that automatically compensates for dot gain on different papers in order to maintain the accuracy of colors as they are represented in the Focoltone swatch book.

Establishing Your Own Color Standard

None of these calibration standards are fully ideal or widely implemented. Since they only take into account part of the calibration problems, you may choose to either handle your own color calibration, or to combine one of the systems above with your own calibration testing. If you take this route, remember that the imagesetter must be taken into account, or whatever calibration you establish for scanner, monitor, software, and color printer will go out the window once your color publications are imaged. It also helps to send your work through a print shop familiar with your standardization efforts. This way they can help quality-control the work at the stripping and printing end of the color publishing cycle.

Now that you have been introduced to color models and color selection techniques, and are familiar with some of the things that can go wrong when color is printed, the next chapter will introduce you to the color separation process—the technical center of color publishing on the Mac.

CHAPTER

7

COLOR SEPARATION

"The purest and most thoughtful minds are those which love color the most."

—John Ruskin
The Stones of Venice

The ability to create and manipulate color publications on the desktop eliminates most of the work traditionally done in a print shop's stripping room. Unfortunately, to replace the stripping room's giant cameras, light tables, and expensive supplies with a computer, some knowledge of the mechanics of the printing preparation processes is a prerequisite. On the desktop, these processes include color separation, specifying traps, and dealing with registration issues. None of these topics are unusually difficult, and once you've seen your first color job through print, you'll have a better understanding of the need for traps, what registration is, and how to separate color documents that will sail smoothly though print.

You Are Here

At this point in the book, you already know how to scan color images and add color to your publications. You also understand the basic models for Macintosh color, and how PostScript and other systems handle many of the formerly manual tasks associated with assembling mechanicals for color reproduction.

In this chapter, we'll demonstrate how color separation is handled and how to build *traps* within your publications so that color edges meet properly when printed. This chapter also explains the steps for separating screen and process colors. Process color separations and the pitfalls associated with them are also covered in the next two chapters in greater detail. Color balancing and separating full-color images are the most complex aspects of Macintosh publishing—that's why these topics get additional coverage.

The Four Kinds of Color Separation on the Macintosh

Ultimately, Macintosh color publishing uses separate layers of film to produce each color to be printed, just like conventional color separation. However, *spot color, screen color, color illustrations, scanned images,* and *paint-type images* are all handled differently on the desktop. A summary of the four types of color separation is provided below. Later in the chapter, a step-by-step description of the four-color separation processes is provided.

1. Spot Color Separation

Spot colors are added to elements such as type, lines, shapes, borders, and bitmapped graphics by clicking on an element and then clicking on a color within a page layout program. All spot colors are separated by outputting one piece of film for each color. So, the separation of a job consisting of black, PMS 286 (blue), and PMS 206 (red) will produce one layer of film for each color (three pieces total). All the elements in the design specified as PMS 206 will appear on a single film layer ready for plating at the print shop. The same is true for PMS 286 and black. Separating solid spot color is the simplest of the four separation processes.

2. Screen Color Separation

When the four (or fewer) process colors are used to create a screen color or a screen version of a Pantone, TruMatch, or Focoltone color, the color is broken into screens that will create four pieces of film—one each for the cyan, magenta, yellow, and black inks.

3. Color Separations of Illustrations Created by Illustrator or Freehand

Illustrations created in sophisticated Macintosh illustration programs can be made up from both solid spot colors (consisting of Pantone and Focoltone colors) and process colors. The illustrations are separated as screen color and/or spot color depending on what colors were used. The color components of an illustration that use both screen color and spot color will appear as film for the cyan, magenta, yellow, and black layers, and as a separate film for the each of the spot colors.

4. Color Separations of Scans and Paint-type Images

Four-color images generated by scans and paint programs are run through a separation program included with a page layout program like Aldus PrePrint, or are processed by a standalone color separation program like ColorStudio. These images are output on the cyan, magenta, yellow, and black film layers at the imagesetter. The separations of scanned color photographs are the most complex type because it is often necessary to adjust and balance the color before separation.

The Specifics on Mac Color Separations

In the next pages, three sections will be presented for each of the four kinds of separations just discussed. These sections illustrate the process to be used and the decisions to make when using each type of separation in a publication. The three sections are:

- The Separation Process Step by Step
- Things to Consider
- Do It Yourself or Have Someone Else Handle It?

These sections provide an overview of the technical and procedural requirements for separating each kind of color image. More advanced topics and techniques for color separating images are presented in the next chapter.

Using and Separating Spot Colors—the Easiest Kind of Separations

Solid spot colors are the easiest to separate and manage successfully into print. Solid inks, unless they start taking up considerable real estate on a printed page, are also easy to print. (Large areas of solid ink can be problematic on press. See *Solids* in Chapter Twelve for more information.)

The Process of Separating Spot Colors Step by Step

Spot colors are assigned on screen within a page layout program and then separated onto individual pieces of film at the imagesetter—one piece of film for each color. The specific steps are shown in the chart.

Most page layout programs add the name of the color to each piece of film, so it's easy to keep track of the art. If you plan to handle your own trapping, you will need to build traps before heading for the imagesetter. (Traps and trapping are covered later in the chapter.)

Things to Consider When Separating Spot Colors

In applying spot color, you need to be aware of two things: 1) the number of colors you use; and 2) where spot colors touch or overlap, they must be set up to print correctly.

Spot Color Inclusion and Separation Process

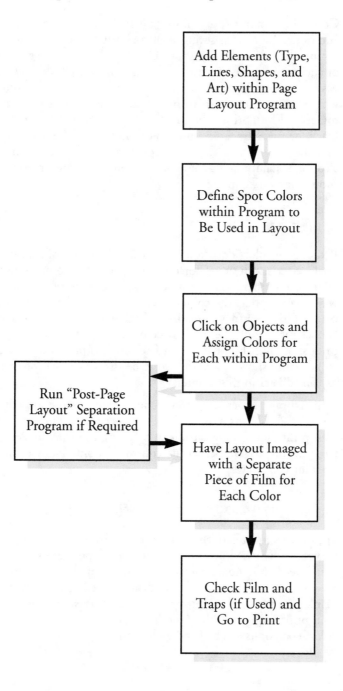

Count the Spot Colors Used

Count how many spot colors you include in a design, because each additional color adds seven to 30 percent to the printing bill, depending on the job and print shop. On the Macintosh, it's a simple matter of clicking on objects within your page layout to add new colors, so it's easy to assemble a job with 30 or 40 spot colors—something that would cost a fortune to print, *if* you could find a printer who would touch it. Most print jobs can handle two to six spot colors including black, because the largest presses can lay down a maximum of six colors at a time. Two- and four-color presses are more common. (There are also high-quality eight-color presses, but we've never printed a job at a shop that owned one.)

Trapping the Colors That Touch

If your spot colors don't touch, it's a simple matter of running film on the imagesetter and heading for the print shop. If two or more colors touch (abut) each other, you will need to assemble the publication in a special way to assure that the colors meet properly as the job goes through the press. This includes choosing whether colors should overprint or a "knockout" should be used. If colors are knocked out, then you or the print shop must build a "trap" to accomplish proper overlay of the colors so no white shows through. Don't be dismayed—all of these topics are explained later in this chapter.

If trapping issues seem too technical, discuss the job with your print shop. While it costs more and takes longer than adding trapping yourself, your print shop is fully capable of handling this for you. And, if you use a page layout program that can't control trapping, your print shop has to do it for you anyway.

Spot Color Separation: Do It Yourself or Have Someone Else Handle It?

Spot colors are relatively simple to do from the desktop. However, as we've just discussed, if your job consists of spot colors that *abut* (touch), you'll need to handle *trapping* to ensure that the colors touch just right on press without too much overprinting or a gap between them where blank paper can show through. If you aren't sure about trapping, have your print shop assemble any traps your job requires. The rest of the spot color separations can be handled by you.

Using and Separating Screen Colors

Screen colors are solid colors made up from the process colors cyan, magenta, yellow, and black, as explained in Chapter Six. They are an economical way to add extra colors to a publication already employing four-color process inks for images. Screen color choices are somewhat limited and don't look quite as good as spot color.

Screen Color Inclusion and Separation Process

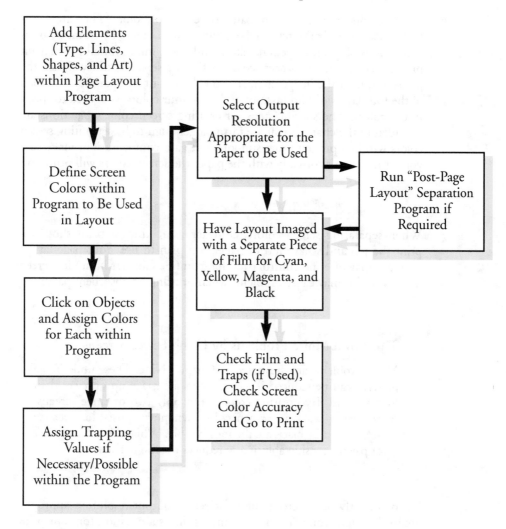

Screen color on the Mac offers one distinct advantage: While adding screen colors to publications assembled conventionally is expensive (because the print shop has to manually assemble two or more screens to create each color), on the Mac you can use as many as you want because the screens that combine to recreate the color on press are generated at the imagesetter instead of being laboriously assembled by hand. The only tradeoff is in terms of longer imagesetter processing time.

The Process of Separating Screen Colors Step by Step

Screen colors are added at the same time as spot colors. They are specified as Pantone, TruMatch, or Focoltone screen colors by number, or as percentages of cyan, magenta, yellow, and black inks. Not all page layout programs can separate process colors without a separate utility. When the job is output at the imagesetter, screen colors print as separations on each of the four layers of film (assuming that all four colors were used to specify the color). The specific steps for creating screen color separations are provided in the chart. If you are fortunate enough to be separating screen colors within a program that supports dot gain compensation, make sure you set it to work correctly with the paper the screen colors will print on.

Things to Consider When Separating Screen Colors

When separating screen colors, consider what kind of print shop will print the job and what kind of paper you plan to use. Your page layout program may offer no control over dot gain (see Chapter Nine) for screen color, and this may cause problems when printing on absorbent paper.

Tip: Avoid Moiré Problems by Using Fewer Screens

Moiré problems are illustrated in Chapter Nine. These undesirable patterns can be reduced if screen colors are made up of fewer than four screens. Try creating colors from only two or three screens. Avoid using black in screen colors whenever possible, because moirés caused by black are the most visible. While this reduces your color palette considerably, it also reduces the moiré risk factor.

To correctly print screen colors, select an output resolution appropriate to the paper you plan to use. This, again, is a question for your print shop. In general, finer screens give you more even-looking color and better color accuracy, because a larger number of smaller dots presents a more convincing representation of a solid color.

Color Separations of Screen Color: Do It Yourself or Have Someone Else Handle It?

For color separations of screen colors produced with the four process inks, things get a little stickier than for simple spot color separation. Depending on the page layout program you're using, you can either separate screen colors from within the program when the job is imaged (quick and simple) or separate them through a separation module designed to work with the program. The actual color separation is output at the imagesetter with screens of the specified values assembled into the film by the page layout or separation software. If your software is adequate, your service bureau knows what it's doing, and you can live with a little color shift, this kind of separation is fairly straightforward.

Using and Separating Illustrations from Freehand and Illustrator

The Mac's powerful illustration packages allow an experienced user to create clean, professional-looking illustrations quickly. Along with the power and relative ease-of-use of these programs, they allow you to add vibrant-colored visuals directly to the design in your page layout program with a minimum of fuss.

The Process of Separating Illustrations Step by Step

Color is added to an illustration created in Freehand, Illustrator, or other PostScript-based drawing programs by pointing and clicking, as explained in the last chapter. Colors can be specified as either spot color or screen color, and many illustrations incorporate both kinds of colors. To separate these files and successfully see them into print, you will want to carefully review each color and element to decide whether traps must be added to make them print correctly.

To do this, carefully analyze the areas in which colors touch and then follow the trapping procedures for spot color and/or screen color, as explained in this chapter. In the case of a complex illustration with colored lines that wrap around other colors in several places, you may want to print each color as a "plate" separation on your laser printer and then compare the "separations" to identify possible trouble spots requiring traps. In some cases, you may need to break lines apart and specify different trapping values for each segment where a single color crosses other colors, depending on whether the color is lighter or darker than abutting colors.

Color Inclusion and Separation Process for Computer-generated Illustrations

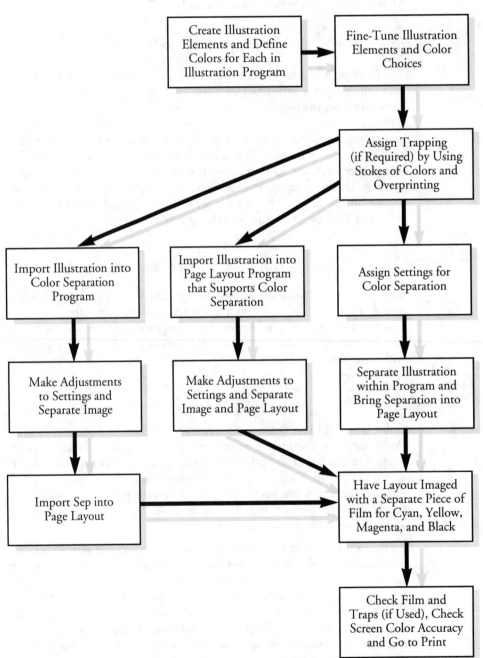

The color illustration is either separated directly or imported for separation within a program such as DesignStudio Separator or Aldus PrePrint. When separating illustrations using screen colors, set the separating program up correctly for dot gain according to the paper the illustration will print on.

The actual separation is created when the file is sent to the imagesetter to create the film. A color separation program may also be used for the job, in which case four separation files are created, plus a fifth file that contains a composite image of the file. This fifth file is placed into the page layout program as a place holder. (See the section on *DCS Separations* in the next chapter.) Depending on the kinds of colors used in the illustration, separations may be made for both solid colors and for process colors. The actual steps in the color separation of computer illustrations are shown in the chart.

Things to Consider When Separating Computer-generated Illustrations

To effectively separate illustrations created within the Mac's powerful illustration programs, you need to carefully evaluate the construction of your illustration. Complex illustrations with layers and layers of elements may not image, and trapping becomes complicated—possibly so complicated that even a dedicated print shop won't be able to figure it out. Thus, foresight and planning when creating a computer-based illustration is key to successful imaging and separation. You may want to sketch out your illustration and review it with both your service bureau and print shop before assembling a monster that defies separation.

Some color page layout programs do not recognize the colors imported from illustration programs and as a result will fail to produce film for that color. To work around this problem, recreate the color within the page layout program, using an identical name and specifications. Not all programs require this, but some do. Check with your service bureau in regard to your page layout program's ability to handle imported colors from your illustration program.

Color Separations from Freehand or Illustrator: Do It Yourself or Have Someone Else Handle It?

Color separation of illustrations developed with PostScript-based illustration programs is a little complicated. Depending on the colors specified for the drawing (both spot and process can be used), you may need to ensure that correct trapping is in place and that a specified screen color prints as close as possible to the color specified. Separation of illustrations requires some practice, but by starting with simple drawings with only a handful of traps and specifying color closely, you can master this kind of separation work fairly quickly.

Tip: Watch out for Linear Fills

One of the most stunning effects possible within illustration programs is the use of linear and radial fills that transition one color or shade to another. Creating blends and fills using hand tools takes practice and time, but the Mac makes this technique simple and easy. Unfortunately, fills that use a large number of hues or shades may image with moiré patterns, particularly on older model imagesetters. Though one part of the fill may look fine, some of the color transitions along the way may image with undesirable patterns. Color scans can suffer from this problem as well, when wide areas of smooth color transitions (such as those in a colorful sunset) are imaged. Eliminate this problem (well, almost) by avoiding large and complex areas of graduated fill; run jobs using such fills on one of the new, top-of-the-line imagesetters that incorporate superior screen angle technologies.

Using and Separating Scans and Paint-type Images

Incorporating full-color scans and paint-type images is one of the most powerful aspects of color publishing on the Mac. Unfortunately, it is also the most complicated to prepare for printing. The next chapter contains a much more detailed explanation of the color separation process for full-color scans and paint-type images. This section explains the basics and allows you to compare the degree of difficulty with the other three separation processes.

The Process of Separating Color Scans and Paint-type Images Step by Step

After a scan is corrected and sharpened, it may be separated by a package such as Photoshop or by a color separation routine included with your page layout program. Separation with a color separation program creates five files, one each for cyan, magenta, yellow, and black, and a fifth file to be brought into a page layout program. Page layout programs, using their own separation routines, separate images when the job is printed on the imagesetter. You must also set separation parameters within the program used to separate the image. This process is covered in this chapter, and more information on color separation issues is provided in Chapters Eight and Nine.

Color Image Inclusion and Separation Process
Using Color Separation Packages

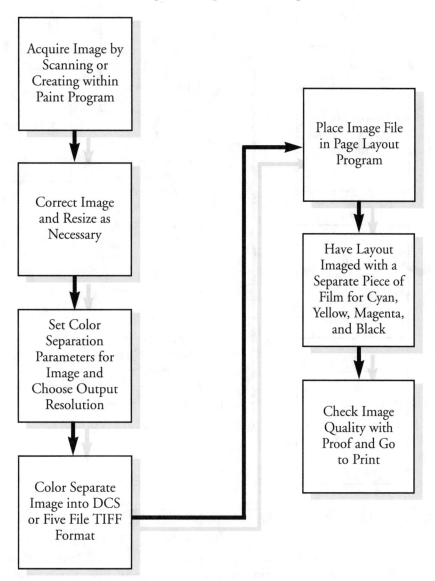

Color Image Inclusion and Separation Process Using a Page Layout Program with Separation Capabilities

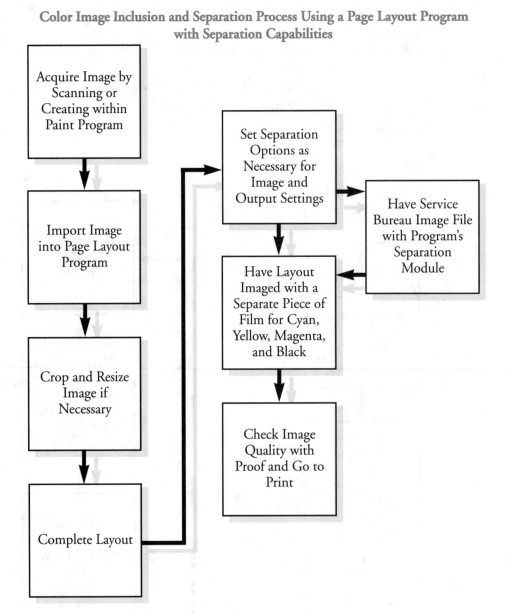

Things to Consider When Separating Color Scans and Paint-type Images

Color scans and paint images heading for four-color separation require special treatment. When you have already made color corrections and done any filtering necessary to a scan or have a completed color paint image you are satisfied with, the next step is to create color separations within a color separation product.

```
┌─────────────────────────────────────────────────────────┐
│ ▤▢▤▤▤▤▤▤▤▤  Imagesetter-2540-15%Gain  ▤▤▤▤▤▤▤▤▤▤       │
│ ┌─Printer─────────────────────────────────────────────  │
│   ☒ Device Uses Halftones   ☒ Separate Printing Step    │
│   Calibrated Medium Type  [  Coated Paper  ]            │
│   Output Option           [  Separations   ]           │
│ ┌─Screen Ruling───────────────────────────────────────  │
│     Device Resolution [2540] Units [  DPI  ]           │
│                    Halftone Screens    Screen Angles    │
│   Spot [   Dot   ]  C [133.8698] LP  C [108.4349] °     │
│   Auto LPI [ 133.9 ] M [133.8698] LP  M [161.5651] °    │
│                     Y [141.1111] LP  Y [ 90.0000] °    │
│   ☐ Use Exact Angles K [149.6709] LP  K [ 45.0000] °   │
│ ┌─Density─────────────────────────────────────────────  │
│         ☐ Multicolor Density Tables                     │
│     Density Table [ Dot Gain 15% ]                     │
│   C Min.[0]% M Min.[0]% Y Min.[0]% K Min.[0]%          │
│     Max.[100]%  Max.[100]%  Max.[100]%  Max.[95]%     │
│ ┌─Color───────────────────────────────────────────────  │
│         ○ CMY      ● CMYK                                │
│   Color Matrix [ SWOP-SkeletonBlack-290%Limit ]        │
└─────────────────────────────────────────────────────────┘
```

This ColorStudio color separation dialog may look complex, but by simply choosing the right calibration dialog for your printing requirements, the program makes most of the decisions for you. The functions shown are discussed in Chapters Eight and Nine.

Color separation programs include parameters that vary from program to program for specifying the kind of paper you plan to print on, settings for screen resolution, and a host of other functions such as undercolor removal (UCR) and Gray Component Replacement (GCR). After the files are imaged, you'll have a proof made to check that the images look crisp and no serious color shifts have occurred because of imagesetter calibration problems.

All the things you need to consider when working with full-color scans and paint-type images can't be covered in this brief introduction—that's why there are two more chapters on handling these types of images, where UCR, GCR, dot gain, color balancing, and other advanced topics are discussed in more detail.

Color Separations of Scans and Paint-type Images: Do It Yourself or Have Someone Else Handle It?

The most difficult task in color separation is achieving clean results from scanned images, particularly if you don't have access to a good quality scanner.

Both color scans and paint images tend to shift in color and take a long time to print on an imagesetter. In a scanned image, a small shift in color can cause a face to take on a greenish cast or darken shadows under the eyes to the point that the person looks like the Lone Ranger without enough sleep. Paint-type images are less troublesome because in most cases a slight color shift is less noticeable. However, you won't really know what you have until a color proof is assembled from the film output.

This level of color publishing takes good equipment, patience, persistence, and more technical knowledge than is required for the three kinds of separations described previously. It also helps to have a practiced eye for recognizing color balance, a skill that takes time to acquire. If all this leads you to the conclusion that you should practice on the other types of separations for a while before trying complex full-color separations of scanned images, you've got the right idea.

The Mechanics of Registration and Traps

When you get down to producing color separations, you must begin to be aware of the mechanical requirements of printing—and these include registration and traps. Registration is something you'll need to be aware of so that you can check it on proofs and ultimately on press. Trapping can be handled by your print shop, although doing it yourself saves time and money. When you assemble a color document on the Macintosh (or conventionally for that matter), these two requirements must be considered and supervised by you or the print shop to ensure quality results on press.

Registration

No one ever thinks about registration until it goes wrong. When working with multiple colors, the placement of each color on the printed sheet (paper) is critical. Where two spot colors touch, they must meet evenly and without too much overlap. The individual inks that make up process color images must also be laid on top of each other as close to perfectly as possible; otherwise the image will appear soft (out of focus). Getting the colors down at the right relationship to each other is called registration—colors must *register* correctly with each other, or the printed piece will look fuzzy or incompetent or both.

Registration errors can begin on the Mac with software bugs or design mistakes, be incorporated by problems in the imagesetter transport mechanisms, or result from mechanical problems at the print shop. The most common problem is caused when the press plates for several colors are incorrectly aligned on the press.

A four-color press has four stations—one station for each color of ink. When paper is run through the press at high speed, there may be imperfections in the adjustments at a station so the press fails to lay color down exactly where required. An error as tiny as 0.05" is unacceptable in a quality job. In the case of high-volume newspaper and magazine jobs, more misregistration is expected.

Registration errors are also caused by paper changing shape as it travels through the press. Less expensive papers printed at high speeds may stretch substantially. Between paper stretching and press adjustments, press personnel are constantly checking the register and making minor adjustments while each job is run.

Because registration errors can be caused by a lack of precision in older or poorly maintained imagesetters, inconsistencies within imaging media, and a variety of mistakes on the part of the designer and the print shop, it is important that color publishers always be on the lookout for problems.

Registration and Process Color

Registration materially affects four-color process images and screen color. In the case of images created with all four process colors, just a dot or two of shift among the four plates will make a color image appear soft. Several dots' worth of shift makes the edges of the picture look like colored shadows and calls attention to the individual process colors. The illusion of continuous tone will be lost. Because of this, process color jobs are often run with the tightest press tolerances and the most on-press supervision. Printing process color jobs may cost you more, simply because they are run on a print shop's best press by its most experienced personnel. The best equipment provides the tightest control over registration, and that's vital to producing quality process color publications. Figure C-5 in the *Color Section* of this book shows an example of normal registration of a four-color image and misregistration of the same image.

Registration and Page Layout Programs

Page layout programs are capable of adding *registration marks* to your job automatically when the job is printed on paper for proofing and on the final film for the job. These are target-like concentric circles bisected by horizontal and vertical lines. When your film is output there will be a registration mark on each layer at exactly the same place. When your print shop assembles your job, they line up these marks to see where each color goes in relationship to the others.

Tip: Avoid Using Screen Colors to Create Fine Type and Lines

As you now know, screen colors are made up from dot patterns that print together to create a design element. If you use screen colors from two or more of the process colors to print fine type or lines, it's difficult to get them to register properly. Use solid spot color if possible, or a single process color, either solid or screened, instead. This way there will be no registration problems possible, because the shift of the press plates or paper won't make much difference if the color moves slightly in relationship to other colors.

In most page layout programs, this option's default setting is **Off**. To turn the registration marks **On**, click within a box in the print dialog. It is usually necessary to leave the registration mark **Off** for printing proofs on a printer that produces only 8½" by 11" paper, because adding registration and trim marks to a job turns an 8½" by 11" job into output measuring approximately 9½" by 12". If you want to see the registration marks, set the print options in the page layout program to tile the job (print several pages that you glue back together to make one page), because the trim and registration marks push the complete image off the edges of the page.

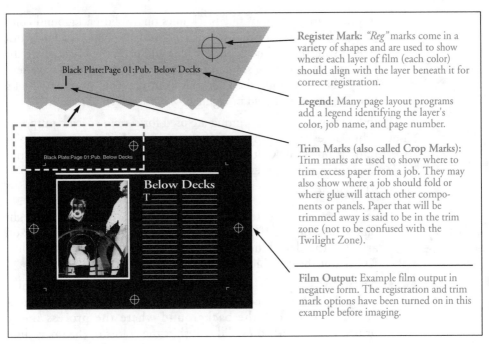

Register marks and trim marks

Knockouts and Overprinting

When separating documents with solid spot colors or where spot colors touch screen colors, you should be aware of two options that will materially effect the results of your work—knockouts and overprints.

- **Knockouts** Knockouts are a commonly used technique to keep colors from printing on top of each other. A knockout is used when one color covers another. The space where the second color will go is "knocked out" of the background color. For example, if you print red type against a gray background, the gray is *knocked out* so it doesn't show behind the red, which would create an ugly brown. This allows the red to be printed onto white paper rather than on top of gray ink. Figure C-6 in the *Color Section* demonstrates knockouts and overprinting.

- **Overprints** Overprinting is the term used when you print one color on top of another. In the case of a solid PMS 115 (yellow) overprinted on a solid PMS 285 (blue), a green of sorts is the result. Mixing colors with overprinting is a risky business, but overprinting has a specific purpose useful to color publishers. For example, if you plan to print a map made of fine black lines on a solid background color of light blue, overprinting the black covers the blue and looks just fine. If you were to knock out the blue and print the black where the knockout was, and registration shifted on press, you would have serious problems keeping the knockout from showing. An example of a knockout error is shown in Figure C-7 in the *Color Section*.

Both knockouts and overprinting are used for certain specific purposes. But within page layout programs, if you incorrectly set your spot color specifications or "Print Option" choices, you may accidentally overprint colors and get unexpected results as a consequence.

Use knockouts for:

- Light Colors Overprinting Darker Colors   If you print a light blue square on a dark blue background and overprint one color on another, the dark blue will turn the light blue into a dark blue. Knock out the dark blue instead.

- Adding Process Color Images   If you place a process color image, like a scanned photo, on top of a solid colored background, knock out the background where the process image prints. If you don't, the solid will shift the colors of the image into something undesirable.

Use overprinting for:

- Printing Fine Lines and Text in a Dark Color over a Lighter Color If you are printing a hairline black border on top of a light solid color, overprint the black so that you won't have to worry about registration problems. This is particularly useful for print jobs that finish on presses without tight registration, such as web presses and inexpensive quick-printing units. If you are printing dark type on top of a light color, overprinting makes it clean and readable and eliminates registration problems.

- Printing Large Areas of Dark Colors over Light Colors   Depending on the job, you may want to avoid registration problems by overprinting all dark colors on top of light colors. Be careful to make sure the top colors are dark enough, however, or the background colors will alter the top color. Ask your printer if you're not sure.

- For Generating a Third Color   If you print two colored inks on top of one another, a third color is generated at no extra cost. If you are considering using this money-saving solution, discuss it with your print shop. They can show you what the new "color" will look like and help you get the best results. You may want to have a proof of the colors assembled to see what the results will look like before proceeding. *Never overprint three or more solid colors!*

Baiting and Setting Traps

As explained earlier in the chapter, registration problems for print jobs occur when colors don't lay down on paper precisely where they're supposed to. Since there is some misregistration in every job, a process for compensating for the error when two colors abut has been devised, called traps (also called *grips*). Traps are used to ensure that minor misregistration does not create problems on press.

> ### Tip: Your Printer Can Tell You What to Trap
>
> An ongoing dialog with your print shop is required before your project is imaged. Your discussions should include what to trap and how much trapping to use. The printer's suggestions will make the job go smoother and in the process you'll get a free education on trapping.

In its simplest form, trapping is the process of making one color overprint the edges of another ever so slightly, so if the register shifts and the colors move away from each other on press, there is enough "slop factor" left so a gap of white paper (called a *leak*) doesn't show through. The amount of overlap is kept to a minimum acceptable to the job, because a registration shift in the other direction will increase the overlap, causing too much of the color to overprint—resulting in a muddy line where the colors meet.

Using traps is like an on-press insurance policy. Within a number of color Macintosh programs you can now specify your own traps rather than relying on your printer to build them for you.

Traps are assembled with the lighter color overprinting the edges of the darker one. The reason for this is simple. Depending on the kind of inks used on press and their degree of transparency, printing the edge of a light color over a dark color creates a new color halfway between the two in value, and it is barely noticeable by the eye. Printing a dark color over a light color creates a new color that's darker than the original color. This new color is very noticeable. An example of trapping and trapping problems is shown in Figure C-8 in the *Color Section*.

Definition: Traps, Trapping, and Trapping Traps

In the world of color printing, words sometimes change their meaning. In the printing world, a *trap* is assembled so that the press operators can trap to it, i.e., so they can adjust the press registration to make the colors go down where they should with just the right amount of one color overprinting the edges of another.

Trapping from a press point of view refers to how well one wet ink adheres to another as a job runs through the press. If a press person says there is a problem with ink trapping, it means that: 1) the adhesion quality of the ink is insufficient; 2) the press speed must be reduced; or 3) that the paper is not absorbent enough for the inks used.

Which word should you use? We've used the word "trapping" for years to describe the creation of a "trap;" though technically incorrect, no print shop has ever commented.

Trapping Scanned or Paint Images that Abut Spot Colors

When scanned images and paint-type illustrations are added to documents or publications, the design often calls for the images to be surrounded by or abut a spot color. To make this kind of image print properly against a spot color, a trap needs to be established so the image will overprint slightly on the edges of the abutting spot color. This is usually handled by having the spot color choke the image. Depending on the software you use to assemble the trap, the color must be set to overprint the edge of the image, not the knockout, or the overprinting will not occur. If the same spot color must knockout in other places in the publication, you can handle the knockouts manually to achieve both overprinting and knockouts or you can create two specifications for the spot color in the color definition dialog in your page layout program (if it has one). One definition of the color should be set to knockout and the other definition should be set to overprint.

Choking and Spreading

To trap colors there are two techniques that can be employed: *choking* or *spreading.* The process of spreading makes a colored object such as a headline slightly larger than the knocked-out background color, so that its edges slightly overprint the inside edges of the background color. Choking is just the opposite. Instead of the headline becoming slightly larger to partially overprint on the background, the background's inside edges are slightly enlarged to overprint the outside edges of the headline.

The amount to spread or choke an object varies depending on the paper and press the job will be finished on. The degree of choking and spreading is usually specified in points—the same measurement used to specify type sizes. One point is 1/72 of an inch. (For precision fanatics, there are actually 72.27 points to an inch.) Examples of choking and spreading are shown in Figure C-9 in the *Color Section* of this book.

To conventionally achieve chokes and spreads, printers use a stat camera and slightly overexpose the film, or place a layer of clear material such as acetate between the subject and the film. The acetate slightly thickens the lines, effectively creating a choke or spread as desired.

On the Macintosh, programs that support trapping do the same thing in software. They add thickness to lines or edges to create a spread or choke. Because the Macintosh handles this chore in software, a great deal of precision is possible and the results are predictable.

Should You Choke It or Spread It?

The basic rule when building traps is that the lighter color should overprint the darker, as explained earlier in the chapter. So, your choice of using a choke or spread is based on which color is lighter. A dark object, such as a headline, printed against a light background, will require that the light background choke the dark headline. This way the lighter color overprints the darker. If a light object, such as a headline, is printed against a dark background, then the headline is spread against the dark background. This causes the lighter color to overprint the edge of the darker color.

What about Trapping Screen Colors?

If screen colors touch spot colors, you will need to keep trapping in mind, because the spot color may shift in relationship to the process colors that make up the screen color. Or, when working with screen color, if one color is made of screens of black and cyan, and another made up of magenta and yellow, a trap must be added, because with registration shifts these colors may not line up properly. You can get around this problem by adding percentages of other process colors to eliminate the need for traps. For example, if your layout contains one color composed of black and cyan abutting another color made up of magenta and yellow, adding a small percentage of magenta to the first color will eliminate the need for a trap. Of course, this shifts color slightly, but by choosing colors carefully it works quite well.

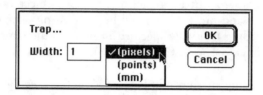

Photoshop can automatically trap edges of process color images.

One person we worked with handles his entire ski apparel catalog on the Mac with no traps whatsoever by using this technique to handle screened colors. It allows him to use a page layout program he likes (PageMaker) that doesn't currently support trapping on the desktop.

Traps can also be added to a process color image where two very different looking colors meet. Talk to your printer before using this kind of trapping. On a quality job it may not look good.

What If Two Colors Look Equally Dark?

What should you do if you need to trap two colors that appear similarly dark? After clicking to select one of the colors, open the program's color picker and study the values. Then select the other color and note the color specifications. Colors with heavier proportions of black, magenta, and cyan are darker than ones with less of these inks. Yellow, under 50 percent, can be ignored completely.

If the color is a screen-based Pantone, Focoltone, or TruMatch color, look in the physical swatch book (not the one on screen) and study the component inks used to create the colors. Solid Pantone colors can be evaluated by their component inks as specified in the Pantone swatch book.

Trapping, Choking, and Spreading within a Page Layout Program

Some page layout programs handle the trapping process automatically with little conscious intervention on your part. QuarkXPress, the first general-purpose DTP program to provide this feature, automatically sets the traps for you without any effort on your part. When you start the program, you tell QuarkXPress how much overlapping of color is required for the job you are working on. This value is specified in points.

Further adjustments can be made as colors are specified or through the trapping palette that can be left on screen as you work.

```
┌─────────────────────────────────────────────────────────────┐
│                   Application Preferences                     │
│  ┌─Guide Colors──────────────────┐    ☒ Live Scroll          │
│  │ ☐ Margin  ☐ Ruler  ☐ Grid     │    ☒ Page Grabber Hand    │
│  └───────────────────────────────┘    ☒ Off-screen Draw      │
│  ┌─Trap──────────────────────────┐    ☒ Auto Library Save    │
│  │ Auto Method:   ✓Absolute      │    ☐ Low Resolution TIFF  │
│  │                 Proportional   │    ☒ 256 Levels of Gray   │
│  │ Auto Amount:                   │    ☐ Calibrated PANTONE®  │
│  │ Indeterminate:  0 pt           │                           │
│  │ Overprint Limit: 95%           │            Slow─Fast      │
│  │ ☒ Ignore White  ☒ Process Trap │  Scroll Speed: ⇦▮▮▮▮⇨     │
│  └───────────────────────────────┘                           │
│  Pasteboard Width:   1|0%              ┌────────┐ ┌────────┐  │
│  Reg. Marks Offset:  6 pt              │   OK   │ │ Cancel │  │
│                                        └────────┘ └────────┘  │
└─────────────────────────────────────────────────────────────┘
```

QuarkXPress allows overprinting and trapping default values to be set in a "Preferences" dialog.

QuarkXPress traps against the background color. This means that if you draw a blue box and **Send It to Back** and then draw a red circle in front of it, the red circle is trapped against the background blue box. If the blue box is darker than the red circle, QuarkXPress will spread the red circle's edges over the blue box in the amount you have specified. If the red circle is darker, QuarkXPress will choke the blue box so its edges slightly overlap the red circle.

QuarkXPress can also be used to manually or automatically overprint colors. When you specify a new color or "edit" an existing one, you can specify that this color will overprint rather than [knockout and] trap. As explained earlier in the chapter, overprinting is useful for printing dark colors on top of lighter colors because with overprinting there are no registration problems. QuarkXPress can also be set to automatically choose the colors to be overprinted. If you enter a value representing a shade in the **Overprint** Limit field in the **Preferences** menu, any color that's dark or darker than the value entered will automatically overprint without requiring further specification on your part.

```
┌─────────────────────────────────────────────────────────────┐
│           Trap Specifications for TRUMATCH 45-g7             │
│  Background Color      Default                               │
│   Indeterminate        Automatic  ⇧    ┌──────────────────┐  │
│   Black                Automatic       │      Auto         │  │
│   Cyan                 Automatic       ┌──────────────────┐  │
│   Magenta              Automatic       │    Overprint    ▷│  │
│   TRUMATCH 1-a5        Automatic       ┌────────┐┌─────────┐ │
│   TRUMATCH 26-a5       Overprint       │ Trap:  ││         │ │
│   TRUMATCH 41-f1       Automatic       └────────┘└─────────┘ │
│   Yellow               Automatic  ⇩   ┌──────┐    ┌────────┐ │
│                                       │ Save │    │ Cancel │ │
│                                       └──────┘    └────────┘ │
└─────────────────────────────────────────────────────────────┘
        ┌──────────────░░ Trap Information ░░───────────┐
        │ Background :  ┌Default┐        Overprint   ?│ │
        │                                              │
        │ Text :        ┌Default┐        0.144 pt    ?│ │
        └──────────────────────────────────────────────┘
```

In Quark, individual colors can be selected to trap differently than the defaults set in the **Preferences** dialog. A floating palette for trapping can also be used.

Manual Trapping on the Desktop

Can you build traps within a program that doesn't support trapping functions? Well...sort of. You can build traps where a simple object such as a circle or square covers another color. Where the spreading of one color over another is desired, place a solid white shape (called a mask) on a layer between the two objects you want to trap. The mask should be slightly smaller than the shape in front to create a "spread." This technique can also be used with a single line of type, to a limited degree, when your publishing requirements don't require high-quality precision. Use reversed-out white type of a slightly smaller size (but with more letterspacing) to create a spread of sorts. When you image your "separation," don't turn on the knockout function, because you want the colors to overprint each other with the mask accomplishing the knocking out manually. An example of manual trapping on the desktop is shown in Figure C-10 in the *Color Section*.

Should you plan to attempt this technique, it works best within a page layout program that allows precision placement of elements by measurement, not just by eye or ruler. Unless your needs are very simple, this technique should not be used for anything above newsprint-quality printing.

Trapping with Illustration Programs

Trapping is accomplished within illustration programs by using the program's built-in capabilities. When specifying color, you can also specify the weight (thickness) of lines that will surround the objects and type that you add to your drawing. These lines can be used to spread or choke objects within the drawing.

To create a trap, specify a line width at the thickness that will meet your printer's recommendation for the amount of trapping required. If your job will print on newsprint, a trap of four points might be required, and you would specify a line of similar width. This "trap line" should be set to overprint by turning the **Overprint** option **On** in the color dialog. (Only this line should overprint, not the other colors!) Then when the job is output, this line will overprint, creating a trap. How you specify the line determines whether you create a choke or a spread. The following explains how chokes and spreads are created.

- Chokes   To choke a light background against a dark object, specify the trap line as the outside edge of the object and assign it the background's color. When the file is printed, the trap line around the object will become part of the background color and overprint on top of the object's darker color.

- Spreads   To spread a light object against a dark background, specify the trap line as the outside edge of the object and assign to it the same color as is used for the object. This way when the file is printed, the trap line around the object will overprint the background color.

Once these traps have been "set," you can import the illustration into your page layout program for separation at the imagesetter. **Note:** Illustrations can also be separated without going to a page layout program; use the print routines or color separation module included with them. (Consult your manual for details.) Never build traps in both your illustration program and your page layout program. If the page layout program recognizes the trapped colors in the illustration, this will result in double trapping and unsightly dark lines. Examples of choking and spreading within Adobe Illustrator are shown in Figures C-11 and C-12 in the *Color Section* of this book.

A Special Note about Color Separation and Page Layout Programs

Be advised that the information in this chapter is not applicable to all page layout programs capable of color separation on the Mac. Some programs claim to have color separation capabilities, but really handle only spot colors in a limited manner. Others handle the entire process, including traps, reducing the need for an expensive color separation program. However, some produce unpredictable results or force you to use default options for dot gain and screen angles, even when they aren't appropriate.

The best way to understand and use programs for separation is to carefully evaluate their capabilities before purchase and, if possible, run test separations. Test all the kinds of separations you plan to use, both now and in the future, including spot color, screen color, color illustrations from Freehand and Illustrator, and separations from color scans. Keep in mind that to be fully effective, the program must produce reliable results on a properly calibrated imagesetter—so it is best to run proofs at your service bureau.

If you are using a page layout program with "limitations," consider printing separations directly from the illustration or paint application used to create the images. Most illustration and paint programs, and all color separation programs, are capable of generating adequate separations of individual images. In turn, the print shop can strip these into the film produced by the page layout program before plates are made.

Putting It All Together

At this point you have been introduced to all the major desktop processes in color publishing on the Mac. Color separation, in its four variations, is one part of a complete path of color publishing processes that involves designing your piece, adding color, scanning and incorporating photos, creating color images with illustration programs, producing film with the imagesetter, and reviewing proofs.

The last item in the color publishing path—proofs—has been mentioned a number of times, but not yet discussed in detail. You will usually make preliminary proofs on a laser printer before sending your job out to the imagesetter to check alignment, design, and typography. After separating a document using process color, however, you should also have a color proof made at the service bureau to check colors and look for shifts. (Your service bureau should be able to produce such a proof in house if they handle color jobs. Color proofs are discussed in detail in Chapter Ten, the chapter that describes how to work with your service bureau.)

If color shift is obviously present because the process colors are all much deeper than expected, have the service bureau calibrate their imagesetter, check the chemistry in their film processor, and rerun the job. If, on the other hand, you have compensated for dot gain (see Chapter Nine), then colors will appear lighter in the proof. The more dot gain compensation, the lighter the proof's screen color and process color images will appear. A proof of a job with twenty percent smaller dots because of dot gain compensation will create a proof with colors that are twenty percent lighter.

If, on the other hand, the colors in the proof appear within a few percent of what you expected (some shift is inevitable), and everything else looks okay, you're ready to pack up and head for the print shop!

In this chapter you've looked at the four kinds of color separation possible on the Macintosh. You've also had a chance to see what mechanical requirements you must fulfill to produce each kind of separation. In addition, you have seen the entire color publishing process on the desktop put together from concept to color separations. In the next chapter, we'll look in depth at the color separation of four-color images and the mechanics of process color separation.

CHAPTER
8

CORRECTING AND SEPARATING COLOR SCANS ON THE DESKTOP

"I received a Cromalin proof from a separation of an illustration of Pinocchio. Due to the dyes [paints] used by the illustrator and how they separated, it looked like Pinocchio had a bad skin condition."

—An Art Director's Complaint in the
Designer's Guide to Print Production

The printing of simple black and white line art, and even the printing of some shapes filled with solid color, has been around for centuries. But, because of printing technology limitations and press inaccuracies, nothing but very crude color reproduction was possible. A miracle of twentieth century technology was the invention of an expedient process for separating color images into a format compatible with the offset lithographic printing press.

Today, full-color reproduction has become commonplace, with the very best print shops capable of color separating and printing images that look as good as continuous tone photographs. The most recent development, and one obviously central to this book, is the ability to handle the full-color separation process on a desktop-based personal computer—in this case, the Apple Macintosh.

You Are Here

You read about the four kinds of color separation in the previous chapter and learned how to apply traps and why registration accuracy is critical to color printing. In this chapter, we'll take a closer look at the most time-consuming, technically involved, and expensive process in color publishing: separating full-color images for printing.

The ability to complete full-color separations of scans or paint images from the desktop is relatively new—and until recently we would have recommended against it. Attempting such a task, except for simple illustrations created with Illustrator or Freehand, would have resulted in less-than-acceptable results for most applications, especially for quality printing.

Creating useless color separations is both time consuming and expensive—all you get for your trouble is a stack of film, completely worthless except for its minute silver recovery value. But now, because of advances in software development, and with training, practice, and a knowledge of the limitations of the technology, relatively good four-color separations can be achieved from the desktop. To help you achieve these ends, this chapter introduces the steps of the color separation process in detail, and the next chapter covers additional technical aspects of color separation.

Considering Color Separating Images on Your Mac?

By handling your own color separations, you save money because the high cost of purchasing outside color separations is eliminated. Also, when you image a job with the color separation imbedded in the film, all your print shop needs to do (after providing you with proofs) is assemble the film sheets into a plastic mask. This mask is then used to burn plates ready for press. This eliminates nearly all of the stripping process, which requires several days for conventionally processed color jobs and accounts for five to twenty percent of a typical separation and printing bill.

Handling color separations yourself provides complete freedom in managing your documents and more control over your schedule. Just as page layout programs eliminate the time wasted waiting for typesetters, desktop color separation software eliminates working around a color separation house's busy schedule and gets the job on press faster.

Within limits, color separation is relatively easy to accomplish on the Mac, using the new, powerful programs that are hitting the market. These programs automate many aspects of the separation process and provide reasonably consistent results without requiring extensive technical knowledge on your part. However, you must be willing to take the time to build the necessary color skills and not be easily frustrated by occasional surprises and problems. If you rely on one of the well-engineered software packages for creating separations, start with clean scans, aren't extremely critical about quality, and don't mind rerunning film occasionally, you can begin from Day One by including small four-color separations of scanned images in simple publications.

The Mechanics of Process Color Separation

As you read on, you may notice that we've covered some of following basic information on color separation before. We're repeating it here to refresh your memory and to establish a basis for the more technical aspects of the discussion that follows.

As you know by now, to print a black and white photograph with its "continuous tones" (transitions from light to dark that appear continuously smooth to the naked eye), the image must first be broken down into a series of dots for reproduction on a lithographic press. This process is called halftoning. As explained in Chapter Five, halftone dots vary in size according to whether or not they represent light or dark areas of an image. Larger dots allow less white paper to show through and appear dark or black. Smaller dots allow more white paper to show through and consequently appear as light grays.

A similar halftoning process is used to reproduce continuous tone color images on lithographic presses. Three colors (cyan, magenta, and yellow) when combined as dots of different sizes on press, are capable of representing much of the visible spectrum. These colors can convincingly recreate continuous tone color images, such as photographs or painted pictures. A fourth color, black, is used to compensate for the fact that cyan, yellow, and magenta appear more as a muddy brown than a solid black when printed in combination. The addition of black also makes shadow areas more convincing and lends crispness to the appearance of printed images. In addition, black is used to reduce the total amount of ink printed on a sheet of paper.

To be able to reproduce a color image using this halftoning technique, the image must be separated into the four colors that will be printed separately on the press. The following describes the conceptual process of breaking an image into the four color components and then recombining these images on press.

1. The Original Image Is Broken into Four Color Components Using Filters

Separating a color photo into the process colors is accomplished conceptually by filtering the image for the content of each of the process colors. Three filters are used to "separate" color information for each of cyan, magenta, and yellow. For example, the cyan filter filters out yellow and magenta and collects only information that should print as cyan. The resulting black and white image contains all of the cyan component of the color visual. The same is done for magenta and yellow.

Three black and white images are created to represent the different filtered colors. Each image represents one of the three process colors left after filtering. So, if a point in the original visual is red and contains no cyan, this area will be white (clear film) on the cyan separated image, because no cyan is present. But on the magenta image this point will appear as black.

2. The Black and White Images Are Converted to Halftone Format

Once the information is filtered from the original visual and broken into CMY components, each of these images is broken into a halftone by applying screens, as in the process for screening an image that will print in black and white. The resulting halftones are used to create press plates—one each for cyan, magenta, and yellow. Individually, these halftone images are still black and white.

The Mechanics of Process Color Separation

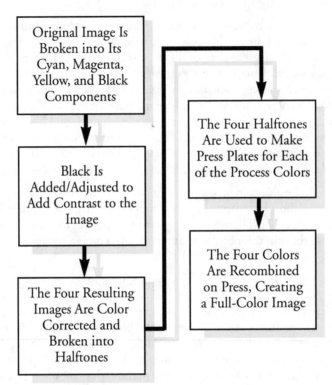

3. The Colors Are Recombined on Press

The plates made from the individual halftones are loaded onto a four-color press, and the press is inked with the process colors. Then the press is started and paper run through the press. First, yellow is laid down on the sheet, then magenta, and finally cyan is printed on top. Once the three colors are printed, the individual color components recombine visually to simulate the colors of the original image.

4. Black Is Used to Deepen Shadows and Reduce Ink Build-up

Conceptually, black is not required to produce continuous tone colors. For practical reasons, a separate image, which will become a fourth halftone for the black plate, is created to deepen shadow areas and reduce the total amount of ink on press. (See *UCR and GCR* in the next chapter for more information on black and *black generation*.)

People who are not familiar with four-color reproduction are frequently disappointed that the printed version of an image is not an exact duplicate of the original. The goal is to get as close as possible, but perfection is still beyond the limits of the technology. Only printing with true continuous tones rivals photographic reproduction. The technology for printing continuous tone color is slow, expensive, and requires a special press. The time to print using this system is measured in days, not minutes or hours.

The Conventional Separation Process

Before scanners, color separations were made with special process cameras. When people refer to conventional technology today, however, they are usually talking about the process used prior to desktop color separation programs, and conventional technology is still the standard for very high-quality printing. In color separation houses that employ this technology, images are usually scanned by an electronic drum scanner—a large and expensive piece of equipment.

To be processed conventionally, an image is converted into a format that can be wrapped around the drum and is then mounted securely to it. The drum rotates and gains speed until it reaches the RPM required for the selected resolution. Front panel controls are used to set color balance, color enhancement, and specify the number of lines per inch that will be used for scanning. This figure, ranging from 500 to 2,000 lpi, is determined by the enlargement and resolution required at printing.

As the drum rotates with the original image, a secondary drum containing the target media (film) is exposed to the scanned image with a laser. The laser passes light through filters onto the appropriate film layers. There is one film-covered drum for each of the four process colors—cyan, magenta, yellow, and black.

These scanners, owned by color separation houses and large print shops, are usually coupled with computers that digitize images, store them in memory, and present them on screen for color correction (just like the Macintosh does with less capable scanners). The electronic information gained from the original art is laundered to perform enhancements and changes before this information is burned into final target media. The finished film, if the color is satisfactory in the color proofs, is then mounted into the masks containing type and line elements that will be used to burn plates for printing.

The Color Separation Process on the Macintosh

To create a separation on the Mac, you simply save the image in EPS or TIFF format within a separation program or module. The software creates halftones of each of the four process colors and performs a number of technical tasks, such as assigning screen angles, making adjustments to ink densities and other requirements so the image will (hopefully) print correctly on press. The four halftones that represent the four process colors become part of the master art used to burn plates at the print shop and are output in position on film with the rest of the job on the imagesetter.

The Color Separation Process—Step by Step

Touched on briefly in the last chapter, the technical aspects of color separating images are covered here and in Chapter Nine. Depending on the software you own, the results you require, and your experience, you may handle the process somewhat differently than we show here. Keep in mind for your job to be printed properly, all of the following activities must occur at some point in the process.

1. Acquire an Image

Acquiring an image for separation is accomplished by scanning a photo or illustration, or by creating a paint-type color image within a program such as Fractal Design's Painter or one of many other paint programs. Images may be acquired from a wide variety of sources—but to be separated, they must be in a digital format, like scans or computer-generated illustrations or paint images. Macintosh paint programs also allow scanned images to be imported into the painting environment and extensively manipulated using paint-type tools. Scanning issues that affect color publishing were discussed in detail in Chapter Five.

Most scanned images and some paint-type images require correction to increase the sharpness of the image or to fix a variety of other problems before they can be separated. Before you make adjustments, study the image to see what kind of problems you are faced with (if any). These may include poor focus, incorrect color balance, whites shifted blue or yellow, or glitches in the scan. If substantial correction is in order, choose the filters and processes you think you'll need in addition to basic filtering and conversion from RGB to CMYK. Then to get the best results, perform the adjustments and filtering functions in the order suggested later in these steps.

2. Save a Copy of the Original Image

If you have room on disk, open the original and save a copy of it. That way you'll be working with a copy and will still have the original if you don't like the results of the "enhancements."

3. Choose the Programs for Color Separation and Adjustments

There are several programs that can handle color separations, and many of these are listed in the *Sources* section at the end of this book. Each of these programs handles color separation in a slightly different way, though the conceptual process remains the same. The file formats used by the separation programs are also important, and we'll provide more information on that a little later in the chapter.

4. Resize and Resample if Necessary

To keep file size to a minimum and reduce imagesetter processing time, you may want to reduce the actual resolution of an image. This makes it easier to transport the image to the imagesetter as well. Resampling of an image should always be completed before the rest of the adjustments (described below) are made. Another reason to resample an image is to output it on a low-resolution "proofing device" such as a laser printer.

For best results, images should be resized and resampled in the color separation program, even though resizing functions are available in page layout programs. (Refer to Chapter Five for more information on resizing images.)

Tip: Resampling down Loses Information

If you have a high-resolution image that needs to be printed as a proof on a low-resolution device such as a table-top color printer, you can save substantial processing time and get a better looking proof by sampling down. If, however, you plan to use the 400-dpi resolution at the imagesetter for your final film, *keep a copy of the high-resolution image* for this purpose—don't sample down and then sample up using interpolation—you will permanently lose detail and the image will look "flat" compared to the original image in print.

The Process of Readying an Image for Separation

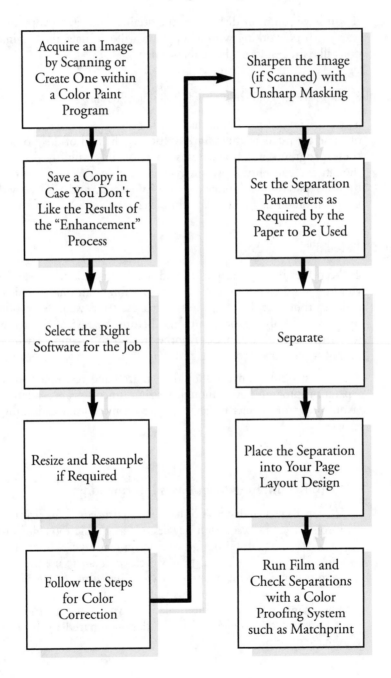

5. Follow the Seven Steps of Color Correction

Since a number of factors can affect images and shift their colors undesirably, corrections are often in order. Later in this chapter we explain the *Seven Steps of Color Correction* and lead you through the process. There is a lot to this, so don't be fooled by the small paragraph used here to describe this step. Color correction and color balancing is an art in its own right, and perhaps the single most complicated aspect of computer-based color publishing.

Color correction is done with a full-featured color separation program like Photoshop, Cachet, or ColorStudio, before the image is separated. Images that require extensive correction and retouching may not be suitable for color printing without professional (expensive) correction on a high-end prepress system or manual retouching using conventional processes.

6. Sharpen the Image

Images lose focus during scanning, and this makes them look flat. Scanned images may also lack definition and subtle detail. Because each step in the film reproduction, plating, and the printing process will exacerbate these problems, a filter is used to sharpen parts of the image to make it crisper. Again, this filtering is done before the image is separated.

Filtering of this kind isn't always necessary, or even a good idea in the case of paint-type illustrations. If a paint-type image was created on the Mac, the softening that occurs during scanning won't happen.

After the photo is color corrected, in most cases use *Unsharp Masking* (not *Sharpen*) to increase the focus if necessary. (Not all programs offer *Unsharp Masking*. Use *Sharpen Edges* to accomplish a similar adjustment.) These filters make scanned images appear crisper by enhancing changes in color or brightness to restore the sense of focus and detail that was lost in the scanning process.

The *Sharpen* filter performs the filtering over the entire image evenly. *Unsharp Masking* (USM) is the superior choice because it sharpens only the edges of objects in an image—the edges are usually the primary reason an image appears soft or out of focus after scanning. USM locates hard edges within an image and adds contrast to delineate them.

Don't over-sharpen by applying sharpening filters too many times, or your image will appear grainy and unnatural in print. Before sharpening, check the image one last time for scratches, glitches, or undesirable marks. Sharpening filters make these anomalies more apparent.

Tip: Filters Can Be Applied More than Once

The filters provided by color separation programs can be used several times to make changes. For example, running the *Soften* filter four times instead of just once creates a moody, romantic-looking image. Likewise, sharpening an image three times creates a slightly surreal-looking picture.

In addition to sharpening filters, there are softening and special effects filters, like *emboss, colorize, motion blur, mosaic,* and others, which you may want to apply at this time. Each program has a different set of filters—the best way to learn about them is to play with them and see the results on screen.

Scanned Image   The Same Image After Unsharp
Masking Was Applied

Sharpening Images: When images are scanned, some loss in sharpness occurs. While the loss is present over the entire image, sharpening areas where there are major changes in contrast, such as edges, makes images look crisp and in focus. The best filter for the job is Unsharp Masking: the second best is Sharpen Edges.

> ### Tip: Hidden Problems on Screen
>
> When correcting or retouching images, you may take a scan that looks fine and use a sharpening filter such as *Unsharp Masking.* Then, after the operation is complete, you find that a previously acceptable image now has flaws such as lint, scratches, and glitches. Where did these come from? The image looked fine before adjustment!
>
> These flaws were probably in the original scan, but in an image captured at 300 dpi, these "small" problems may be invisible on the Mac's 72-dpi screen. Then, when you used a correction routine, the computer worked with the *actual* image and turned hidden problems into ones severe enough to become visible at 72 dpi.
>
> You may feel betrayed by your retouching software if this occurs, but the problems were in the original image and would have shown up in print if you hadn't found them. If you compare the original, you'll probably find each one on the art, unless your scanner is the source of the contamination. To fix this problem, use *Undo,* retouch the spots, and then use the filter again.

7. Set the Separation Parameters

Unfortunately, after color balancing and filtering, there are other considerations that must be taken into account when color separating scanned images. (Much of this applies to screen color as well.) First, screen angles and resolution must be set for the color halftones. These are selected by you, the program, or your service bureau to avoid patterning problems. Resolution settings will also depend on the print shop and the paper you will use. A phone call to your print shop is required in most cases. Press-related issues such as dot gain, ink density, and ink build-up must also be addressed through adjustments in the separation program. These mechanical separation issues are covered in the next chapter.

8. Separate the Image

Finally, after setting the various parameters required for the job, the separation of the image can take place by saving the file as EPS (or TIFF in some programs) and selecting the **Save as Separations** option from the menu of the color separation program. This will create four or five separate files, depending on the program used. In programs where four separation files and a fifth image preview file are created, the fifth file is usually imported into a page layout program for integration of the image with the rest of the document.

For images that will be stripped in later and not incorporated into a page layout program directly, the four separation files can be sent directly to the imagesetter, or in some cases, the original image file is separated at the service bureau using their software.

If the separated image will be imported into a page layout program, tell the program to save a preview image along with the four separation files in DCS format (explained later). If you plan to use the program's color separation program, skip this step and instead place the unseparated image into your page layout program; then go to Step Nine.

9. Place the Image in Your Page Layout Design

If you are using a program that creates Desktop Color Separation (DCS) files, place the preview image within the design created with your page layout program and make any necessary crops. Keep resizing to a minimum. None is best. Move the preview image around in the design until you get exactly what you want.

If you plan to use your page layout program's separation module (such as Aldus PrePrint or DesignStudio Separator) to separate the images after placement, just place an unseparated version of the image into the layout.

When you like what you see, run a trial proof on your laser printer and then assemble the files for imaging at the service bureau.

10. Run the Film

When the design is complete and the files are assembled, the next step is to run film (the other term for outputting it) at your service bureau and have a color proof made to check for problems or surprises. Once the separations are in film, the job is ready for the print shop. Service bureau issues and the color proofing process are explained in Chapter Ten.

Color Separation Formats

As mentioned above, on the Macintosh there are several color separation format standards that you need to be aware of. Each of the formats handles the separated files in a different way. The format you use is determined by the software you work with. Programs such as QuarkXPress require that process color images be separated from within another program such as ColorStudio before they are imported into the design. The Xtension called SpectreSeps, developed by Prepress Technologies, allows images to be separated from within QuarkXPress. Other programs, such as Aldus PrePrint and DesignStudio Separator, accept images that are already separated within another program or can handle the separation of images after the entire design is assembled. As mentioned before, the finished separations are usually saved as TIFF or EPS files. These file formats were explained in Chapter Four.

DCS Format

Desktop Color Separation (DCS) is a popular format created by Quark, Inc. for handling color separation on the desktop. It is based on the assumption that a separation program will be used to color separate a scan or paint-type image into five files—one each for cyan, magenta, yellow, and black, plus a fifth file for placement in the page layout program. This fifth file is the preview image.

Most separation programs offer a choice of resolution and color information stored in the fifth file. Less color and lower resolutions mean smaller file sizes, although this fifth file is already small compared to the size of each of the separation files. The preview file can be cropped, rotated, or resized within the page layout program to fit the design requirements. If, however, you need to crop an image more than a few percent, it may be a good idea to go back to the separation program, chop the excess material there to limit image file size, and then reseparate.

With DCS, when the preview file is placed in a QuarkXPress document, for example, the positioning and size for the actual separation is established. When the separation files and the document file are in the same folder, they will image in the appropriate place on each layer of film, based on the document layout. The fifth preview file is not imaged, but provides the guide for the imagesetter to size and place the four separation files on film.

OPI Standard

Open Press Interface (OPI) is a standard created by Aldus for connecting page layout program files to color separation programs and to high-end prepress systems. Originally developed for PageMaker, this format is now supported by some other page layout programs, including QuarkXPress. When using Aldus Preprint for color separations, the program looks for images stored with OPI "tags," which are created within your page layout program by selecting "OPI" or "Print to Disk" from a pull-down menu. Once found, scanned images and Freehand illustrations can be brought into PrePrint for color separation. This same file of tagged information can be used by high-end prepress systems to link images and page layout information together for conversion, and to transfer from Mac format to the prepress system for separation and final preparation of the film. Prepress systems are explained in Chapter Thirteen.

PostScript Separations

Direct, image-only separations can be created by outputting four PostScript-only separation files on an imagesetter. The resulting film is then stripped into position using conventional stripping techniques that place the separation in a film mask in the correct place for creation of plates. Because the resulting four files will not be added into a page layout program file, no preview image is required—so the fifth file isn't needed either.

Single Files for Separation by a Page Layout Program

If you plan to use a separation program such as Aldus PrePrint or DesignStudio's separation module, which can separate images after the design is created and images are placed, simply sharpen and color correct the images and save them in an appropriate format. (Aldus PrePrint allows you to open tagged image files to adjust color and apply sharpening.) Then, let the service bureau separate the images by processing them through Aldus PrePrint or DesignStudio separation routines for you. If you need to incorporate images that require extensive manipulation through a program like Adobe Photoshop, they can be incorporated as DCS separations from other programs. (You can also create DCS separations from within Aldus PrePrint if you want to.)

When the file is imaged, PrePrint or DesignStudio Separator will apply screening as specified. The separation module recognizes whether separation of some of the images has already taken place in another program, like Photoshop, and doesn't screen or otherwise manipulate the pre-separated files. All the images, whether separated by the program at the service bureau or previously by another program, are incorporated into the correct positions on the four layers of film.

Correcting Color

In the following section, we'll look at the step-by-step process of color correction and color balancing. But before we do, there are different terms and concepts involved that you need to know. Unfortunately, while these phrases mean something very specific to a color separation specialist working in a color house, software manufacturers, in an attempt to simplify the process, may interchange phrases or lump several functions together under a single color correction command.

You'll have to study your software manuals to determine what kinds of color correction are available and how they use or combine the following terms. Here are the basic terms in color balancing—some of these you've heard already, some are new.

- **Brightness, Contrast, and Gamma—the Gray Components of a Color Image** Brightness, contrast, and gamma were explained in Chapter Five. These are the simplest adjustments to make to an image and can be handled by most color publishers from the desktop.

- **Cast** Most images have an overall cast—an unnatural leaning toward one color or another (usually blue or yellow). Cast is particularly noticeable in the highlight areas of an image.

- **Color Balance** If an image is properly color balanced, all the colors appear natural. In most cases, the colors will be matched to the original image, unless the original image is out of balance.

- **Highlights, Midtones, and Shadow** Changes can be made to an image's highlights, midtones, and shadow areas to compensate for color shifts and to bring out detail. These terms were also defined in Chapter Five.

- **Color Saturation** Images often need color saturation adjustment to enliven their color. An image's color saturation level is the amount of color present. Images with low saturation tend to be pale. Images with high saturation have full, rich color. Color saturation adjustments are described in more detail later.

- **Convert to CMYK for Printing** RGB images must be converted to CMYK for color separation if you have not already done so.

The Color Correction Steps

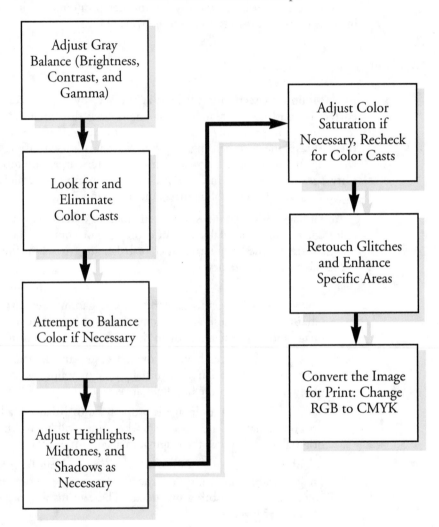

The Seven Steps of Color Correction

Though the seven steps aren't absolute, we suggest that to simplify the process you make your color corrections in the order we've specified. Skip steps that aren't required. For example, if you are already happy with an image's brightness, contrast, and gamma, don't make changes, but go on to Step Two.

1. Start out by Adjusting the Image's Gray Levels

First, don't forget to save a copy or the original image for use in case your color balancing efforts don't pan out. Then, the first order of business when color balancing is to adjust the image's gray component, because color adjustment hinges on the correct tweaking of the range of tones between light and dark. While you may not want to handle more complex tasks such as color balancing, learning to make minor corrections to brightness, contrast, and gamma should become a standard part of your color correction repertoire.

Start by adjusting the brightness and contrast sliders. Adjust gamma at this time as well, if it is available within the program you are working with. If more than simple changes to these two controls are required, try the **Equalize** control explained next.

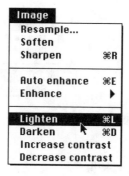

Aldus PrePrint allows you to lighten or darken an image in measured amounts.

When working with images that have extreme contrast and brightness problems, a tool that can make make your life easier is the **Equalize** command found in most retouching programs, including Photoshop and ColorStudio. This function automatically redistributes the brightness and contrast within an image over an even range. Beforehand, adjust the image to a middle gray with the brightness settings—the image should not look too light or too dark on the screen before applying the command. It's acceptable if it looks flat or lacks contrast. Then, use **Equalize** to fix the majority of gray balance problems. If the results look odd, use **Undo** and attempt the correction manually. **Equalize** can also be used on a selected part of an image. For example, if the sky in a landscape looks washed out, selecting and equalizing just the sky may fix it without altering other areas.

2. Make a Stop at Central Casting

Casts are overall shifts in color introduced during photography, photo processing, or by poorly color-balanced scanners. Cast is the tendency of almost white and almost black areas of an image to take on a particular color that gives the image a noticeable and unnatural appearance. Because the highlights are the first part of an image that are noticed, problems in this area are particularly troublesome. Study these areas to see if there is a distinct shift towards yellow, red, or blue. Cast is corrected during scanning with products such as Color Access from Barneyscan or from within a color separation program such as ColorStudio.

When correcting for cast, it's also possible to have some programs adjust color to eliminate cast by applying a Neutralize function to the entire image. This eliminates cast problems but may result in an image that is cold looking or overly neutral.

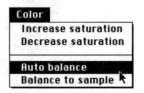

PrePrint's **Auto balance** command looks for casts and attempts to eliminate them.

3. Attempt Your Color Balancing Act

Color balancing is explained in the next section. This is where the various colors are adjusted through a variety of controls to make the total image appear natural. Hold on to your hats!

4. Now, Look into the Shadows…

If your retouching program allows you to individually adjust midtones, highlights, and shadows, these controls are useful tools for compensating for scans with inadequate contrast within the extremely dark and very light areas of an image. If your software includes these options, experiment.

First, look into the darker areas of the image and compare them with the original. Is there information in the original that is nearly invisible on screen? If so, select **Shadows** and attempt to adjust the sliders to make this detail more apparent without being unnatural. Then do the same to the light areas by adjusting the "highlights" if necessary.

5. Make the Color Saturation Adjustments

Adjusting color saturation is relatively easy if you do it in small steps and take care not to add so much color that the resulting image is unprintable. Color saturation is the degree of color richness in an image. It is possible to have too much saturation as well, when colors that should appear as quiet pastels jump off the page like neon lights instead.

> ### Tip: Severe Problems Can't Be Fixed without a Lot of Work
>
> If you are dealing with a cast that contaminates colors through the entire tonal range because of a poor original image, discolorization, or the use of an inexpensive scanner, the only way to fix such an image is laborious and may not be worthwhile. If the original image is okay, but the scanner is causing the problem, rescan on a better scanner, even if you have to go a color house or service bureau to have it done. If the image is poor, some improvement can be accomplished with color balancing, area-by-area retouching, or enhancement, but this may take more time than it's worth. Consider either getting a new photo or processing it as a duotone, where poor color won't make any difference. (Duotones are explained in Chapter Nine.)

Low color saturation can be used deliberately to invoke a mood, or take an image that screams with color down a notch in obnoxiousness. Color saturation is adjusted in retouching and separation programs. After changing color saturation levels, check that a cast hasn't been reintroduced to the image. If so, make cast corrections again.

6. Retouch the Glitches and Enhance Specific Areas

A problem common to photos and transparencies is contamination of the image by tiny scratches caused by dust rubbed across the emulsion. As explained in Chapter Three, color separation programs may also include complete painting and retouching tools. These can be used to fix scratches and other glitches, as well as to add entirely new elements to the images.

- Fixing Scratches   To fix scratches and minor glitches, zoom in on the problem area. Use the eye dropper tool to pick up the color surrounding the scratch. Then, paint the scratch over with the color, one pixel at a time.

- Enhancing Specific Areas   Often a photo will have areas that stand out darker or lighter than the rest of the image. When overall correction through gamma, brightness, and contrast won't help these areas, use the magic wand tool to pick up only the area that requires enhancement. The tolerance of the wand is set to choose only the area with the problem (see your software's manual for specifics). Then, by clicking on the problem area with the right level of tolerance, it will be selected. You can make changes to gamma, brightness, and contrast in the selected area as usual. Color and equalization changes can also be performed.

With BarneyScan software, you adjust the highlight and shadow points before scanning.

7. Correct the Image for Printing

If your image is stored as RGB color, it must be converted to CMYK format in order to print on a four-color press. This is accomplished either with a standalone color separation package, or within a page layout program's separation routine.

In addition to this step, part of the process of producing printable color separations is to adjust an image so that its tonal range can be printed. A problem with scanned images is that, depending on the paper chosen for print and several other factors, the image may contain more tonal range than can be handled on press. Transparencies, for example, have a vast range of color and brightness. The brightest area of the slide may be 500 to 1,000 times brighter than the darkest spot. When printing on paper, the brightest spot (uninked paper) may only be 60 to 100 times brighter than the darkest black ink. To be able to print the transparency properly, compensation must be made to compress the tonal range of the image into one that can be reproduced on press.

Adjusting the tonal range is accomplished by selecting the brightest point and the darkest point in an image that will be printed. The selection of these two points is described below. (For software without such correction features, compression is based on the paper you select and the percent of total ink specified. See the sections on UCR, GRC, and ink density in the next chapter to learn about this.)

- The Highlight Point   The highlight point is the brightest part of the image in which you want to maintain detail. When printed, the highlight will print as the smallest dot on press (typically five percent or less away from solid white). Levels of brightness a few percent lighter than the highlight point will not print at all (they will be white with no dots at all). For example, in the case of a close-up photo of a sailboat on a bright day, the highlight might be found in the bright folds of the sail. While the sail may be bright white, you'll still want the folds and detail to show, so a point on the sail gets set as the highlight. The sun on the chrome of the ship will be even brighter than the sail and will print as white (no dots).

- The Shadow Point   The shadow point is the darkest point in an image that still displays detail. When printed, the color that represents the shadow will print close to solid black (typically 95 percent of the way to solid black) with colors a few percent deeper printing as black (a full dot).

These points may be set either in a color separation program or by scanner software that supports "tonal adjustment." ColorStudio, for example, allows you to set both of these points. You can manually select the points with the **Black Point** or **White Point** buttons or use the **Auto** button to have the program handle the task for you.

Once the highlight and shadow points are set, the software compresses the tonal levels in between to match the limited range of highlight to shadow that can be accomplished on press. The image may look materially different after compressing its tone, because the range of tones that can be displayed on a monitor with additive color can't necessarily be printed on paper (remember that discussion from Chapter Six). If you choose a shadow and highlight point at the extreme ends of bright and dark, more compression must be used at the expense of detail. Midtones might become too light or dark as well. If you choose highlight and shadow points that are too close together, the image will have a flat look, with too much of it printing as white or black and odd-looking midtones. Learning to set the two points manually takes a little practice.

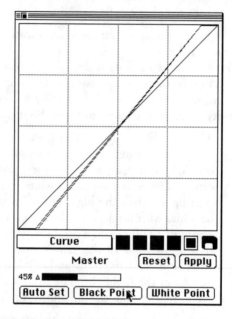

Setting the shadow and highlight points in ColorStudio.

<hr />

Meet the Histogram

A powerful tool for evaluating images and image problems is the histogram. This tool evaluates the image and then displays a histogram chart of the image's overall brightness and saturation. If the image is color, then each color component can be analyzed individually if desired.

Sometimes, after studying an image and realizing something just isn't right, you can investigate its properties through the histogram, identify the problem, and correct for it. For example, a histogram with the

Continued

lines clustered to one side or the other indicates an image that's either too dark or too light. A histogram with gaps between the lines means that colors are missing—a problem common to color images scanned on inept color scanners. If you are working with a problematic color image, selecting each color in turn may disclose a lack of green, something initially hard to spot until you develop an eye for it.

The histogram can be used for a wide range of purposes. For example, you can select one area of a scanned image that looks unbalanced and ask for a histogram of the selection. (Histograms of a scan tell you a lot about the inadequacies of a scanner as well.)

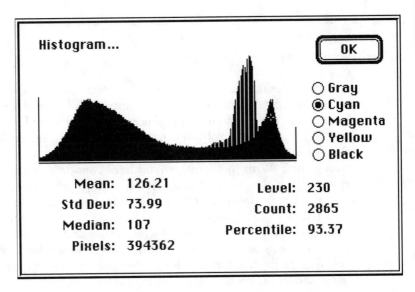

The histogram is a powerful tool for analyzing image brightness and color balance problems.

After making these specific area changes, the image should be clear, crisp, and color balanced—and ready for color separation. An example of the power of photo retouching on the Mac can be found in Figures C-13 and C-14 in the *Color Section*.

Attempting a Color Balancing Act

Just How Subjective Is Color?

Watch a Charlie Chaplin video on an ordinary television. What color is Chaplin's hat in *Modern Times?* A deep black, right? No, not really. It's the dull green of the television's screen. Your brain tells you that the color is black because that's what you expect. Other colors are adjusted as well to make the spectra appear natural. Study the grass and green trees on an overcast day. Notice that they appear greener than on a sunny day? That's because in low light levels, your eyes become more sensitive to green than on a sunny day. Is color subjective? You bet! That's why it takes time to learn to balance and adjust color.

Retouching on the Mac: Just How Accurate is It?

Accurate color retouching on the Mac is affected by a number of variables. You may want to run tests and experiment before attempting a job on a deadline or treating the process as part of a production routine. With careful control you can reproduce scanned images in print that, while not perfectly faithful to the original, look good and display strong color. With most images, you have considerable latitude between what is acceptable and the original image—unless you are printing images that require exact color matching. For example, in a catalog of women's clothing, customers will be expecting a close-to-perfect color match between the picture in the catalog and their purchase. If the actual item's color doesn't match, they may return it for a refund. If you require this degree of color perfection, use a color separation house and let them worry about getting the color right.

Even Prepress Professionals Don't Trust Their Monitors

Before making any adjustments to the color of your images, it's best to verify that your monitor is calibrated, at least by using one of the software routines included in your retouching package. While even high-end prepress systems operators don't trust the color of their expensive monitors, using calibration will at least give you some idea of the actual appearance of the image when printed. You can also analyze color within separation programs by moving (and clicking) the eye dropper tool around the image and studying the values displayed on the color palette or *Info Window* for each of the RGB or CMYK colors used.

Ideally, color correction should be performed on a computer kept in a room with lowered lights and no windows. Some professionals even paint their walls a neutral gray to reduce the subjectivity that goes along with environmental color shifts.

Tip: Check Color to Find out What You Are Dealing with

One way of investigating color problems in an image is to print separations on an ordinary laser printer. Take an image that's driving you up the wall and print its composite colors after separation. Or, print individual channels for red, green, and blue. (Output positives to the laser printer, not negatives.) Then once the "film" image is output on paper, study the problem areas to see what colors actually compose them. For example, if you are struggling with a landscape photo of a forest of pine trees in which the trees look vaguely purple, study your output. If, in this example, the magenta "plate" is contributing a lot of color to the green-blue pine trees, then you've found where the problem probably lies! Bring magenta down a notch or two and rerun the output to see if less magenta is present in the trees.

About Color Balancing Acts

Color images require accurate, or at least pleasing, color balance to attract the eye. Color balancing is more an art than a science, with considerable personal preference creeping into adjustments. For anyone but an experienced color prepress professional, color balance is achieved by starting out with a properly balanced image scanned on an accurate scanner. Correcting color is very difficult, because you may find yourself moving slider adjustments around in either RGB or CMYK mode without improving the image's color balance. In fact, the image may look worse rather than better.

Color is adjusted either at the scanner before scanning (difficult), within the scanner's software after a scan, or from within a retouching/color separation program such as ColorStudio. Color is usually adjusted by dragging sliders or scroll bars for each color. Brightness and contrast are adjusted the same way, although not from within the same dialog box.

What makes the process of learning to balance color comparatively easy on the Macintosh is that you can try any number of changes and still go back to an untouched original if the work looks less than satisfactory. Infinite experimentation is possible.

Now—Adjust Color!

Even the Flying Wallendas had get to started somewhere. You can too, by practicing. Spend a few hours in front of your monitor adjusting color until you finally achieve an improvement on a photograph's poor color balance. It doesn't matter for practice sessions whether your monitor is calibrated or not, because the knowledge you pick up will be the same, as long as the resulting "color balanced" image isn't taken into print.

Start out Easy Using Automatic Adjustments

An increasing number of programs such as Aldus PrePrint make color adjustments easy—all you do is tell the program to automatically optimize color through the **Enhance** command. The command goes to work to improve the image's color as defined in a default color correction look-up table.

This command makes a number of changes to the equalization of highlights, midtones, and shadows and sharpens the image to make the edges appear cleaner. Unfortunately, automatic correction tools may not always enhance the image the way it should be enhanced—in which case you'll have to do it manually.

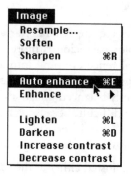

PrePrint's **Auto enhance** command will attempt to balance the overall light to dark relationships in an image.

Four Ways to Balance Color

The basic color corrections to make include adjusting brightness and contrast and then adding or subtracting the amount of red, green, or blue (or cyan, magenta, and yellow) to correct for color shift that occurred in the original image or was introduced by a scanner. In addition, the total amount of color can be adjusted to increase or decrease color saturation. Below are four methods for visually correcting these aspects of color balance.

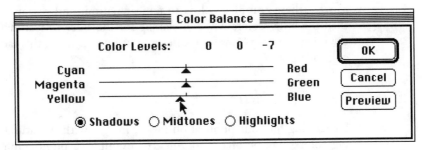

Photoshop allows individual color manipulations to highlights, midtones, and shadows using slider controls.

Match the Original Image

The standard method for adjusting color (used by color separation professionals working with photos taken by others) is to match the on-screen color of the resulting image with the original used for the scan. This only works if you were reasonably satisfied with the color in the original and if you trust your monitor's color.

The Macbeth Color Card

If you are doing your own photography or are working with a cooperative professional, get a Macbeth (or similar) cardboard color chart from a photo supply store. This card has representations of standard colors that with a little practice can be used to calibrate your photos. If your photo work consists of still-life product shots, put this card into the frame. This way the image appears at the edge of shots where it can be easily cropped out before printing. (If you shoot live-action photos of grizzly bears, however, this is difficult.)

Then, with the image of the resulting print or transparency displayed on your monitor, try to get the color of the card in the image to match the colors on the physical card as closely as possible. Do this by first matching the grays to get the brightness and contrast right, and then match the color. This method isn't foolproof, but with patience you can achieve useful results.

Match the Face Skintones

A third method that's less practical is to balance the skin colors of people who happen to be in the photo. The underlying assumption is that if you can get these complex colors to appear natural and reasonably correct, then the other colors will come along for the ride. Unfortunately, unless the image contains close-ups of evenly-lit human faces, this tactic is difficult to employ.

Work toward "Pleasing" Colors Instead of "Real" Ones

Depending on your publication needs, images with unnatural but pleasing colors may be of use to you. For example, a photograph of a light gray house may look rather dull against an overcast sky. But, by individually selecting elements of the house and the sky and adding new colors to them, you can produce a surreal but vibrant-looking separation. Color the house bright yellow and the sky a strong, deep blue. Then add colors to the landscape and the roof of the house. The magic wand tool found in most paint and retouching and color separation programs can be used to help you select areas for "color enhancement."

Tip: Experiment for Fewer $$$!

If you plan to test scanned color images before you begin printing them, consider outputting several (small) separations at the same time, by placing them on an appropriately sized page in a page layout program. Then take this one-page file and have your proof made. This way you save money by outputting multiple separations on one piece of film.

Check Your Work

After checking your work against the original and feeling satisfied (somewhat) with the results, open the unchanged copy of the image you saved before making adjustments. Compare the two on the monitor and see if your efforts look better or worse. If they look better, congratulations— you've succeeded in correcting color and have effectively put the process to work. If your "corrected" image looks worse, try again. One way to learn is to keep the original open while correcting the copy. That way you can check your work as you go.

Keep Trying

Don't get discouraged—remember that color separation professionals require years of experience before they can handle this work with accuracy. If you must color correct a basket-case photo, either have a professional do it, or after working with your color monitor and learning its idiosyncrasies, set aside several hours to experiment. Make several "corrections" and have a proof pulled for each of the different versions. Then choose the one you like best. Depending on your monitor's inaccuracies, however, none of the resulting images may be what you want. If at first you don't succeed...

Getting the Best Results from Process Color Separation on the Mac

Process color separation on the Macintosh has a number of variables that can cause colors to shift in hue and brightness and create other surprises in print. Something that looks like a nice clean image on the monitor may become murky because of imagesetter problems or poor separations produced by the software. Dots can change size and shape, resulting in color shift. Improper screen angles may produce unattractive patterning. Poor film handling by the imagesetter can introduce registration problems. Other things may go wrong as well.

To get the best results when separating color scans and paint-type images, make it easy on yourself by handling the process consistently every time, from start to finish. Handling separations the same way each time allows you to recognize mistakes and build on your experience to improve quality. Being consistent means using the same techniques, hardware, and software for your work. Use the same scanner, color separation program, settings, and page layout program. When the job is ready for the service bureau, take it to the same people, preferably a shop experienced with imaging process color jobs and known for careful imagesetter calibration (see Chapter Ten). Use one with a detail-oriented attitude focused on achieving good results.

If the film looks good, head for the same print shop and wherever possible print the job on the same press running the same kind of paper. This way you will quickly build an understanding that allows you to mentally "figure in" the consequences of carefully measured changes to color separation settings, paper stock, and resolution changes.

Keep notes on your results as well. A notebook listing each job, the settings, paper, and any problems encountered and how you fixed them, is invaluable for recognizing problems and as a reference for future work with similar requirements. This allows you to make changes systematically, and thus you can measure the exact impact of each change.

Tip: Want to Learn about Color and Color Printing?

One of the best ways to learn more about color reproduction is to study materials already in print. Pick the color supplement to the Sunday paper and study the photos. Notice how dull the color looks compared to that reproduced in a glossy magazine. Look for mistakes (common). Next, study high-quality printing in a coffee table book. And last, compare the color reproduction of your projects against what you see produced elsewhere.

Using Your Printer's Knowledge to Help You Get the Right Output

When color separating a job containing scanned images or screen colors, consult with a knowledgeable print shop—preferably the one that will ultimately print the job. Printers (the ones who remain in business anyway) naturally have an eye for problems, and you can ask for their expertise on how to set parameters for a number of technical specifications in the color separation process. If you have a responsive service bureau—one that takes the time to discuss jobs with the print shop, the more technical aspects of color separations and screen color can be handled by following their advice.

If, on the other hand, you're working with a fully booked or less-than-knowledgeable service bureau, this call to your print shop may never get made, regardless of promises. Or if it does, it will be brief, with little useful information exchanged. You should carefully question both parties to see if they understand your job and whether an appropriate amount of information exchange has taken place.

In the case of a quality print shop with a color-experienced service bureau under the same roof, the feedback between these two operations is helpful for seeing a complex Mac-based job into print. Why? Because the imagesetter operator, the stripping room, and the pressroom personnel will discuss your job, its paper, and special press requirements. Thus, they can identify any problems and correct them without running and rerunning the film (or worse, the plates).

In this chapter you have read about the basics of separating process color images. Separating color images requires practice and a concerted effort to overcome the roadblocks. If you are new to color publishing, you may initially choose to forgo the process and let experts handle it. Or, if you have the time, begin a process of experimentation to build your skills. Color separations of images destined for newsprint are relatively easy to tackle. Color separation of images destined for high-quality reproduction within an expensive brochure or annual report is much more complicated and may be beyond the level you want to master. However, as Macintosh software becomes more sophisticated and the machines faster, color separations may become more routine for the desktop color publisher.

In the next chapter we'll look at several more advanced color separation topics including screens, dot gain, moiré problems, and how to control the amount of ink thickness on press through a color separation routine. We'll also look at another kind of color separation process used for special effects—the duotone, and its close relatives, the tritone and quadratone.

CHAPTER

9

ADVANCED COLOR
SEPARATION TOPICS

"But the real answer is like the response to that old line, 'How do you get to Broadway?' 'Practice, practice, practice!' There is simply no substitute for experience in this field, and the best way to to figure out what works and what doesn't is to make some mistakes. A little perseverance definitely pays off."

— Steve Guttman
writing about Macintosh color image
separation in *Desktop Communications*

Along with the processes for correcting images before color separation, covered in the last chapter, there remain several technical but important topics to understand before you begin managing your own color separations from the desktop. While you can avoid learning how to handle dot gain, UCR, and ink density, the best way to learn the business of color is to apply these settings yourself. The newer programs are equipped with easy-to-use default settings that allow you to compensate for a variety of press problems by selecting the kind of paper you plan to print on and the amount of ink it can take. Your printer can provide this information over the phone, allowing you to get on with the process. But, if you plan to become a color publishing expert, the best results are achieved by learning what the settings do and how they affect your work.

You Are Here

In the last two chapters we've looked the process of color separating spot color, screen color, illustrations, and images on the Macintosh. This chapter covers the advanced topics that are the mechanical "nuts and bolts" of color separation, including screen angles, dot gain, ink density, and calibration issues. These are relevant both when working on the Macintosh and when using conventional separation systems. The mastery of these topics is key to making things look good in print.

Screens, Screen Angles, and Frequencies

We talk a lot about screens throughout the book. That's because the process of using screens to break images down into printable dots is a technique that makes lithographic reproduction of black and white and color images possible. Screens and screening become complicated when you start laying one screened layer on top of another, and that's exactly what is done to reproduce process color images and screen colors.

There are two aspects to specifying screens before images are separated, which will directly affect the quality of your printed images—screen angles and screen frequencies. The first and easiest specification is screen frequency. Then you must deal with the angles—and there are lots of angles to cover.

Screen Frequency

Screens are rated in lines per inch. Lpi refers to the resolution used to break the image down into printable dots. This resolution is called *screen frequency*, and you will see this term used to refer to screen resolution in page layout programs and color separation software. When you see *screen frequency*, think *lines per inch*. The higher the lpi rating, the higher the printed resolution. Newsprint images are typically printed at 65 to 85 lpi. Magazine ads print at 133 lpi, and high-quality documents such as brochures and annual reports (and the finest magazines), print at 150 lpi and higher. The kind of paper used for printing your document will have a substantial impact on the screen frequency you should use. If you aren't sure what is appropriate, your print shop can help you establish this specification. Magazines will specify the lpi rating as one of the requirements for submitting film for reproduction.

For full-color images, screen frequency is set in the color separation program. For screen colors, the frequency can be set in some page layout programs, though most programs use a default specification.

Screen Angles

Screens must be carefully aligned with each other in order to be less noticeable when printed. In the case of black and white images, the screen is usually rotated 45 degrees from horizontal. This rotation allows the eye to see the image without immediately noticing the screen.

As you can see in the example, the screen rotated to 90 degrees catches the eye with its strong vertical and horizontal appearance. The screen angled at 45 degrees is much less noticeable.

In color publishing, screen angles become complicated, because instead of only one screen as used in a black and white halftone, four screens are superimposed on each other to convince the eye that it's looking at a continuous tone photo. The finer the screens, the more convincing the effect. Each screen must be rotated so its dots don't print on top of those from another screen. Look at Figure C-15 in the *Color Section* to see the impact of incorrect screen rotations.

Halftone with 0° Screen Rotation

Halftone with 45° Screen Rotation

Screen Rotation: Screens are rotated so that the reader notices their presence as little as possible. The halftone on top has no rotation to its screen, and the dots have a noticeable horizontal and vertical pattern. The halftone at the bottom has a 45° rotation applied to its screen. As a result, its pattern is not as visible.

Screens assembled on top of other screens at incorrect angles can also create a noticeable patterning. Thus, to produce four-color images and minimize this effect, the screens are carefully rotated. But if the rotation is incorrect or doesn't take into account the limitations of imagesetter technology, then an undesirable effect occurs, called a moiré pattern.

Moiré Patterns and How to Avoid Them

For those of you familiar with Op art, a mercifully short-lived movement in the early 1960s, you've seen moiré patterns in the vibrating paintings made up of layers of swirling dots that force the eye to move around the painting without focusing on any one element.

Moirés (pronounced *more-ayes*) are a serious problem in printing—particularly to color publishers working on the Macintosh. The incorrect rotation of a screen creates the patterning. You can see an example of a moiré by placing an ordinary window screen in front of another window screen. Obvious patterning will be visible; it becomes more or less noticeable as you rotate one screen in front of the other. In print, unavoidable moirés occur when screen-like patterns such as plaid clothing and textural fabrics are screened for reproduction. Other moirés simply appear when the screen angles for the process colors are set incorrectly in the separation program. An example of a process color image reproduced with a really noticeable moiré pattern can be found in Figure C-15 in the *Color Section* of this book.

Four Moiré Solutions

Macintosh publishers can use several possible technical fixes to the moiré problem. Two of these have unpromising names—*Odd Screen Angles* and *Irrational Screening*—but they represent big improvements in dealing with the moiré problems associated with PostScript-based publishing. Because all of the solutions, except *Odd Screen Angles*, are based inside the RIP processor (part of the imagesetter), we suggest you talk to prospective service bureaus to see what they offer based on their imagesetter configuration. **Note**: If the service bureau offers none of these solutions, ask the operators how to best set your screen angles, or whether you should turn off screening altogether and let the SB handle the settings.

Odd Screen Angles

To reproduce process color images and prevent moiré patterns, screen angles must be placed precisely. Until recently, imagesetters lacked the precision to handle this exacting requirement, and problems occurred on a regular basis. Running color separations on an older imagesetter invites this problem.

```
┌─────────────────────────────────────────────────┐
│ ▓Custom Printer Setup▓                           │
│                                                  │
│        Device  [ Imagesetter-2540-25%Gain ]      │
│                                                  │
│    Paper Type  [ Coated Paper ]                  │
│                                                  │
│    Device Res  2540  DPI        Gamma  1.8        │
│                                                  │
│   Cyan     [ 160.6437 ] LPI   [ 108.435 ] Degrees│
│   Magenta  [ 160.6437 ] LPI   [ 161.565 ] Degrees│
│   Yellow   [ 169.3333 ] LPI   [ 90 ]      Degrees│
│   Black    [ 179.6051 ] LPI   [ 45 ]      Degrees│
│                                                  │
│              Auto LPI   [ 160.7 ]                │
│                                                  │
│   Recommended Image Resolution: 321      DPI     │
│  ────────────────────────────────────────────   │
│   Output Option  [ Separations ]                 │
│                                                  │
│   Spot Function  [ Dot ]              ▶           │
│                                                  │
│   □ No Undercolor for Pure Black                 │
│                          [ Cancel ]  [[ OK ]]    │
└─────────────────────────────────────────────────┘
```

Notice the unusual screen angle and lines-per-inch settings. These help eliminate moiré patterning in process color images.

To work around the limitations of imagesetters, programs such as
ColorStudio developed specially tested "odd" screen angles that produced
the best results across a wide range of imagesetters. The program actually
prints each color (cyan, magenta, yellow, and black) at slightly different
screen frequencies (lines per inch) as well. The combination of odd angles
and different frequencies provides a good chance of getting clean results
without moiré problems, even on older imagesetter equipment. These
"odd" angles are usually the default settings within programs that support
them.

Accurate Screen Angles

Another recent fix for moirés is the use of patented imaging technology
that allows process color images to be printed on an imagesetter with an
accuracy closer to conventional separations done with screens. Moirés are
rarely a problem with conventional color separations, so a process that
more closely duplicates the screening process used in a color separation
house reduces the chances that noticeable patterning will occur.

Accurate screen angle technology is based on the idea that the limitations of process color separation on an imagesetter are tied to the rigid

grid format used to create digital halftones that comprise each color layer of the separation. By calculating the cells for large groups of dots, instead of placing one dot at a time, a grid can be rearranged to vaguely resemble traditional screening.

Tip: Leave the Color Separation Software Settings Alone!

This is perhaps one of the most important tips in this book. If you are learning the basics of color publishing and handling separations within a program that allows changes to the screen angles (they all do, but these settings may be hidden unless you look for them), *don't make changes to a color separation program's default settings* until you learn more or are specifically directed by your service bureau to change them. Otherwise, moiré problems will most likely be the reward of your efforts.

The positioning of screen angles should be left alone for other reasons as well. As you saw in the black and white halftone example, a screen rotated at the wrong angle is considerably more noticeable than one that is correctly positioned. For this reason, yellow is angled at the most noticeable angle because it is the lightest and hence least noticeable color. If you change the screen angle settings, be aware that rotating a color other than yellow into a position where its lines run vertically will make it very noticeable.

Keep in mind that the engineers who write these programs spend substantial time analyzing the settings to find ones that will cause the least problems for the widest variety of print jobs. If you mess with their work, you will have to go through the same experiments they did to learn how to get optimal results and reduce precision problems common on Mac-driven imagesetters. This will result in an excellent education on color separation and screen angle considerations, along with costly bills for useless film and proofs. Still feel like changing those screen angles?

Irrational Screens

Another recent fix is the use of patented imaging technology that allows the screens for each of the process colors to be placed *irrationally* (arbitrarily) in relation to each other. Developed by Linotype-Hell, this technology also allows color separation screens to be imaged in a manner similar to those created by conventional processes. The "smart" software in the irrational screening process allows the dots that make up the separations to be placed where they should go to eliminate moirés.

Flamenco Screens

Another screen management technology that can eliminate moiré patterns is *Flamenco screens.* These screens make life easier for some color publishers—particularly those working with newsprint and its inherent misregistration.

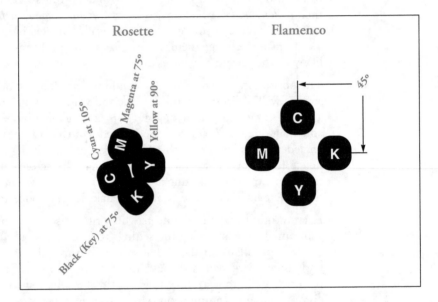

By rotating the screens for each of the CMYK colors, traditional rosettes arrange the dots of the four process colors like petals on a flower. The dots overlap slightly. Flamenco screens arrange the dots of the four process colors in a more orderly fashion using 45° screen angles. Using flamenco screeens, the dots don't normally overlap, thus reducing registration problems.

Standard screen technology uses rosettes—clusters of dots made from the four process colors. Instead of using screen angles to create traditional rosette patterns, Flamenco screens simply print dots in a vertical column, using a simple pattern. Because there's no rotation of screens, there's no possibility of moiré patterning!

Flamenco screens have a special advantage for newspaper publishing. A standard misregistration problem in printing newspapers occurs when one color of a rosette prints on top of another (instead of across or next to it). This results in a murky image. Using Flamenco screens, misregistration becomes less of a problem. When the Flamenco screens are printed slightly out of register, it does little more than make the image appear soft.

Dot Gain and Color Publishing on the Mac

One of the most serious and pervasive color publishing problems, whether using the Macintosh or conventional techniques, is dot gain. Screen colors, halftones, and color separations are made up of dots. If these dots change shape or size, the color they represent changes because larger dots create darker colors and smaller dots create lighter colors. When four colors are used to create an image, a shift in dot size may change the color of someone's face or make a sweater advertised as "red" appear in print as an ugly purple. In extreme cases, the gain may be so significant that the resulting color looks nothing like the original. Dot gain is particularly a problem for illustrations, color scans, and paint images, because while you may be able to live with a shift in a screen color, a photo that has darkened significantly may be unacceptable for publication.

Dot gain (and loss) comes from four sources:

- Incorrectly calibrated imagesetters
- Improper developing of imagesetter-produced film
- Reproduction of film at the print shop
- The process of laying ink down on paper. Ink spreads slightly during printing, particularly on absorbent papers, and dots enlarge as a result.

While there's little you can do directly about any of these sources of dot gain, there are ways of minimizing them, including the methods below.

Calibrated Imagesetters

Use a service bureau that regularly calibrates its imagesetter with a calibration program—such as Color Calibration Software for PostScript Imagesetters from Technical Publishing Services, Inc. of San Francisco or other such packages. (Newer high-end imagesetters don't need calibration.) On press, dots almost always become larger, but an imagesetter can be miscalibrated to produce dots that are too small as well as dots that are too large. If you don't use a service bureau that calibrates its imagesetter regularly, expect problems with dot gain.

Checking Imagesetter Calibration and Using Densitometers

To a large degree you're at the mercy of your service bureau. However, when it comes to imagesetter calibration and film processing chemistry problems, you can keep tabs on things to some degree by adding test swatches to your page layout and measuring them with the shop's densitometer. (If the bureau doesn't own and use a densitometer, then you are using the wrong service bureau.) To do this, add a screened box outside the trim marks to create a screen of each of the process colors and tints of solid colors. Specify these boxes as 50 percent screens. Label each screen as 50 percent. If you want to check the entire range to uncover nonlinear screen reproduction (common), include boxes made from screens ranging from ten to 90 percent at ten percent intervals.

When the job is output, each patch will appear on the negative of each process color as a black screen. Before accepting the film, put it on a light table, and after allowing for the amount of dot gain compensation applied and any transfer function used, measure the film with the shop's transmission densitometer to check the *actual* screen values. Remember, when checking a negative, screen values flip—a *negative* image of a 70 percent screen should read 30 percent. If the values are more than a few percent off, then there's either a problem with your page layout program, or more likely, the imagesetter needs calibration (or the film processor's chemistry is out to lunch).

Continued

About Densitometers

A powerful tool, which is standard within print shops and should be standard at any service bureau handling color work, is the *densitometer*. This measures how "dense" a black and white or process color is. At print shops, a pressperson takes density readings of cyan, magenta, yellow, and black to see how much ink is actually being laid down on the page. At the service bureau, a densitometer is used to ensure that the imagesetter is calibrated, so a 42 percent screen, when output to film, really measures close to 42 percent.

There Are Three Kinds of Densitometers

Programs such as SpectrePrint Pro and Color Access have densitometers in software. Photoshop handles the task with the **Get Info** window, and ColorStudio shows densities within the **Palette** window when you click on a color with the eyedropper tool. As you move the densitometer across the page, a read-out shows how much cyan, magenta, yellow, and black ink are being used to create a color. A shadow area measuring 370 percent total build-up will obviously require correction to reduce ink density before printing.

The other two kinds of densitometers are physical devices you can hold in your hand. The first kind is used on press to measure printed colors and color within color proofs. It is called a reflection densitometer, and most of the ones we've used look like large black staplers. This tool is used to measure color against a solid (reflective) background that light can't penetrate.

The second kind of densitometer is a transmission densitometer. It is used to measure light passing through a transparent medium such as film. (Good transmission densitometers are expensive.) This kind of densitometer is used by service bureaus to verify the integrity of their imagesetter calibration. In addition to transmission densitometers used to record densities of screen in film, others are available that record CMY colors in transparencies. This type of densitometer is used by color separation houses to evaluate incoming images in order to see what kind of correction is required.

Continued

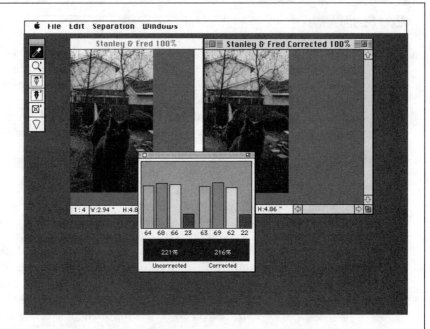

SpectrePrint Pro's densitometer can be used to investigate color density problems and compare the results of the program's **Auto Correction** command, as shown in this example.

Keep in mind that densitometers also require regular calibration. This is often accomplished with a test strip of film or other calibration standard provided by the manufacturer. Without regular calibration, a densitometer is as accurate as a meat scale with a butcher's thumb on it. Tiny, hand-held densitometers may not be very accurate either.

How to Use a Reflective Densitometer   To use a reflective densitometer, you select the process color to measure and then place the tip of the densitometer over the area you want to test. Pushing down on the densitometer's body (this densitometer hinges like a stapler in operation) brings its sensor nearly into contact with the paper or proof. A reading of the density then appears in the window as a percentage of the measured color. On press, a 50 percent screen of magenta should read close to 50 percent; a number larger than 50 percent indicates dot gain. A smaller number indicates dot loss.

Continued

> *How to Use a Transmission Densitometer* To check your film at the service bureau, first get a zero reading by placing the film on a light table and clicking on a clear area with no image; this allows the instrument to establish a reading for clear film. Then click on the area to be read. If you are measuring negatives, remember that a twenty percent screen will read as 80 percent because the image is inverted.

Develop the Film Properly

Explained more thoroughly in the next chapter, film requires accurate developing with special chemicals. Some service bureaus run film and paper through the same developer designed for paper output—this causes changes to dot size and shape, because the weaker chemicals used to develop paper won't remove the appropriate amount of imaging material from film. Old chemicals or incorrect developer temperatures can cause similar problems.

Control of Reproduction at the Print Shop

At the print shop, the reproduction of art work on film causes the duplicated dots to change shape slightly. Inept shops may overexpose the film as well. Give your print shop film that they can directly make into plates instead of paper output, even for low-resolution jobs. Also ask the shop what you can do to minimize the number of duplication procedures in processing your art.

Laying Ink down on Paper with Skill and Accuracy

In an offset lithographic press, inks are applied to paper after being transferred from the plate to the *blanket*. During this process, dots of ink increase in size. When applied to the paper, ink may spread out slightly through pressure as the sheet travels though other inking stations in the press and as it soaks into the paper. You can avoid much of this problem by carefully choosing paper and by press-checking your jobs (explained in Chapter Twelve). On press, you can work with the pressperson to increase or decrease the amount of ink being applied by each station of the press. Decreasing the amount of ink being applied reduces dot gain.

Reducing Dot Gain Problems from within Software

Much as traps and trapping account for expected misregistration problems, some dot gain is inevitable and can be dealt with through software adjustments. Dot gain caused by absorbent papers can be reduced by using better paper, but if your job is printing meat ads on newsprint, you can't tell your supermarket client to switch the ad to a magazine that uses an expensive coated paper—instead, you have to compensate for the inevitable.

Tip: Eliminate Dot Gain or Loss at the Imagesetter

Most page layout programs lack dot gain compensation controls. While you can compensate for dot gain in process color images from within color separation programs, screen color specified within the page layout program may offer no such control. A solution is to run the job through a bureau that can compensate for dot gain within the entire job by adjusting the software they use to calibrate their imagesetter. If you take this route, you don't need to adjust compensation within your separations, or think about it at all, except to find out from your print shop how much the service bureau should use. Handling dot gain/loss this way requires a patient, well-equipped service bureau, but that's the kind you should be working with anyway.

Dot gain compensation can be accomplished within software programs that support dot gain by changing the values to fit the job. It is handled by specifying an "assumed percentage" of dot gain. If your assumed dot gain is ten percent, the dot sizes will be reduced by the imagesetter when the job is imaged, to compensate for this amount of gain on press. Then, when the job is printed, the smaller dots will spread out as the ink soaks into the paper, and the expected dot size will be regained.

To understand how to set these percentages, it's best to get feedback from your print shop. Your printer can tell you the amount of expected dot gain between the receipt of film and the printed sheet as it comes out of the press and dries. Keep notes on what percentage works best for each paper you work with. If your guess is within one to five percent of perfect, you can fine-tune on press by having the press people adjust the amount of ink laid down on the sheet.

Tip: Don't Apply Dot Gain Compensation Twice

If your page layout program compensates for dot gain, either make the compensation there (particularly if your layout includes screen color), or make the compensation within your color separation programs and set any dot gain settings to zero within the page layout program or the program's separation module. But don't compensate both in a color separation program and in a page layout program, or the image will print too light on press.

Ink Density and Color Publishing

When printing four-color process jobs, there can be too much build-up of ink on the paper as it passes through the press. On press, each of the process colors is laid down on the sheet in varying amounts—from none to 100 percent. This means in theory that as much as 400 percent ink could appear in one place on a sheet of paper, although a smaller percentage is the realistic maximum depending on the press and paper used. This percentage is a measure of *ink density*. If your document uses dark colors, there can be quite a build-up of ink on a sheet of paper.

In theory, cyan, magenta, and yellow can produce black and the spectrum of grays, but in practice, because of ink density problems, black is used to create convincing grays and blacks.

Depending on the quality and kind of paper you are using, some sheets can handle large build-ups of ink gracefully, and others such as newsprint cannot. In minor cases, colors mixed from two or more colors, such as fleshtones, may become flat-looking or muddy. In extreme cases, the build-up may be so severe that color images take on a mottled look from excess ink crystallizing on the uneven surface of a fibrous sheet. Color shifts unnaturally too when dots touch dots and blend. The resulting mess may become very dark in appearance.

Color separation programs provide software-based densitometers to evaluate color density within color images. Changes must be made to the image to bring the total ink down by setting parameters for total ink density within color separation programs. Ink can also be reduced by setting UCR and GCR adjustments, described next.

UCR and GCR

Because an undesirable build-up of ink is a standard problem in process color printing, two routines have been developed to control and reduce the total amount of ink used. By keeping the ink density down to a level compatible with the paper and the press, jobs finish with cleaner looking color and the ink dries faster, resulting in fewer problems such as *doubling* and *off-setting* (explained in Chapter Twelve).

The two systems for keeping ink density in line are *undercolor removal* (UCR) and *gray component replacement* (GCR). UCR and GCR are applied just before a process color image is separated. Most color separation programs on the Mac automatically apply one or both of the systems during separation. The values selected by these applications are determined when you tell the program what kind of paper you plan to use for printing or by how you set them manually.

The novice color publisher should initially use the default settings and then study the results when reviewing the color proof. However, to get the best results from UCR and GCR, you may want to handle these settings manually or at least have a say in the degree to which they are applied. Your print shop can provide you with advice on how to set the controls for a particular job and paper. Unfortunately, these controls may vary between programs, in both their usefulness and the effect they have on your work.

Both UCR and GCR adjustments affect how black is used on press. Each works somewhat differently and achieves different ends. The idea behind both systems is that printing both black and the other three process colors partially duplicates the amount of ink that needs to be laid down on paper. Because both black and the process colors can be used to produce grays, by removing the process colors used for this purpose and replacing them with black, cleaner looking color can be achieved with less ink build-up. By replacing three inks with one, there is less build-up on press. (It takes much less black ink to make up for "black" produced by combining the process colors.)

The focus of both of the UCR and GCR controls is *black generation*, i.e., how the black plate is used to replace CMY inks and how much is replaced. Depending on the compensation applied, black generation may not begin until a certain percentage of process color ink is present. Black generation is handled by the color separation program or by a separation module included with a page layout program.

Undercolor Removal (UCR)

Undercolor removal helps clean up shadow areas and bring out detail by reducing process ink only in areas of an image where equal parts of cyan, magenta, and yellow combine to create black or gray. UCR locates areas where equal amounts of the process colors (CMY) are used to create a gray or black. It then replaces the process colors with an appropriate amount of black. Doing most of its work in the darker areas of an image, UCR does not change areas with unequal amounts of process colors. Because replacing the three process inks is unnecessary until a certain ink build-up is achieved, UCR is usually set so it doesn't "kick-in" until a specified amount of ink density is reached. In most color separation programs you can set this threshold according to the paper you are using and the kind of press the job will run on.

Gray Component Replacement (GCR)

Rather than substituting black ink for the grays and blacks created by equal amounts of CMY inks, GCR cleans up neutral tones such as flesh-tones by removing their underlying gray component. While these colors may not appear to contain any gray, they usually have at least some percentage of all three CMY inks (equivalent to a gray). By using GCR, this gray component is replaced with black, thereby reducing ink build-up. Unlike UCR, which mostly substitutes black for the darker areas of an image, GCR affects colors in highlights, midtones, and shadows. As a result, it can make a more noticeable improvement in the overall appearance of a printed image than UCR can.

UCR and GCR and Your Color Separation Program

These tools are not only technical but are difficult to use, because they require experimentation within your separation program to understand their impact on a printed image. Each separation program is different in the control it offers you for these functions, ranging from a simple GCR on/off button to a complete range of curves and algorithms. Some programs allow you to individually control the functions within the shadow, highlight, and midtones.

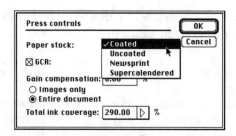

Automatic PrePrint UCR/GCR Settings

Tip: Don't Apply GCR or UCR Twice Accidentally

Be careful when using UCR or GCR to ensure that these processes are not applied to an image twice. For example, if you have an image professionally scanned, the scanner operator will probably have performed this operation on the scan after ascertaining what kind of paper you plan to print on and asking other questions. If you then separate this image within a color separation program, these processes may be applied twice, causing undesirable color shifts on press.

The process of specifying GCR or UCR generally involves three decisions, although more options be available or necessary. The three choices include:

- **A Choice of the Process You Want to Use**   You choose either UCR or GCR. (Most programs allow you to choose *either* UCR or GCR, whereas ColorStudio wraps both controls into one function.) Gray component replacement provides the best results for most kinds of images, but not all programs support it. To learn how to set these controls for a particular software product, read the manual and show your printer the options available. An experienced printer can tell you how to set up the parameters for a particular paper and press.

- **The Specification of the Maximum Amount of Ink Density**   You can choose the maximum amount of ink that will appear on the printed sheet according to the selected paper and the kind of press used. Your print shop can provide information in this regard.

- **The Specification of the Point When Black Generation Begins**
  Most programs give you the option of setting the threshold ink density where black begins to replace process colors.

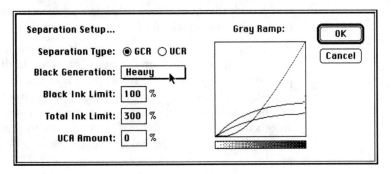

Photoshop **UCR Settings** dialog

Transfer Functions

While it's not a good idea unless you really know what you are doing, you can use a *transfer function* from within color separation programs to "commandeer" the imagesetter. The transfer function is used to compensate for known dot gain/loss problems and allows you to manually adjust for it. Thus, if you plan to image a file on an imagesetter that prints a 70 percent dot as 77 percent dot, you can compensate for it with the transfer function. Within Photoshop, compensation is available in ten percent increments. By clicking the **Include Transfer Function** in Photoshop's color separation dialog, the transfer data is maintained within the file.

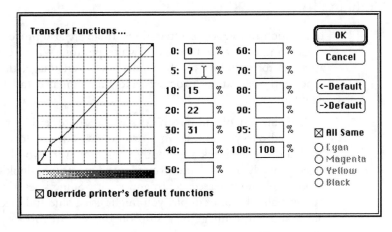

Photoshop **Transfer Function** dialog

After discussing it with your service bureau, use the transfer function for the following situations:

- A Problematic Imagesetter   If you are dealing with an imagesetter that has clearly quantified calibration problems, the transfer function can be used to selectively correct for miscalibration.

- Printing on Problem Papers   Some papers can lose or gain dot size unevenly over the tonal range. For example, if your job will print on a highly absorbent stock, you may want to increase the dot sizes slightly for the very lightest colors. While ink tends to spread on these papers, a really tiny dot may soak in so much that it is absorbed into near invisibility. If you add size to these dots through the transfer function, the colors will appear closer to normal when printed.

- Special Effects   Because the transfer function can be set deliberately to produce unusual results, special (and not so special) effects are possible with it. For example, by setting the function to image all midtone dots lighter than 50 percent to image at 30 percent and setting midtone dots darker than 50 percent to image at 70 percent, the output will have no true midtones. Instead, a posterized effect will be added to the image. Unfortunately, the only way to learn how to apply the transfer function to achieve useful and interesting results is to experiment. Unless you have direct access to an imagesetter or a lot of spare time and money, use the effect filters in Photoshop and ColorStudio instead of the transfer function for special effects.

Duotones, Tritones, and Quadratones

In addition to four-color separations, there are also processes for creating elegant multiple-tone black and white photos. Where color separation attempts to reproduce all the colors within an image, the duotone, tritone, and quadratone processes add more tonal detail to a black and white image.

The simplest of the possibilities is the duotone. Duotone images are composed of—you guessed it—two colors. These colors may consist of black and a gray, black and another color, or even two blacks. Duotones, when properly handled and printed, produce striking-looking images that appear to have increased depth and clarity. Sometimes a two-color effect can be realized. For example, you might use a blue and black to recreate a black and white image of a ship on the sea. In this way, the sea may appear in the gray-blue of the ocean while the ship still looks mostly black and white.

Duotones can be created conventionally or specified through a program such as Photoshop. When creating duotones conventionally, two pieces of film are exposed—one for each color. Typically, one piece of film is exposed to capture a photo's highlights and the other exposed to capture shadow detail. It is somewhat of a hit-or-miss affair unless you are working through an experienced color separation house.

Within Photoshop, you can assign inks and a highlight-shadow curve for each color within the duotone. Much as in the conventional process, you can use one ink to handle the midtones and highlights and a second ink to print the midtones and shadow areas of the image. Best of all, you can make changes to the duotone settings and then preview the results on screen immediately. Because this wasn't possible with conventional techniques, duotones were often surprises in the past.

Photoshop can produce duotones, tritones, and quadratones. After setting up the image, it can be immediately previewed on screen.

Tritones and quadratones work much the same way as duotones, but they use more colors. In the case of a tritone or quadratone, the first two inks may be used in a duotone. The third (and fourth) ink may be used to add a tint to the photo. For example, to make a tritone that looks old-fashioned, a sepia-colored ink can be used for the third color. This combination provides the richness and exceptional depth of a duotone, while the third color makes the print appear old-fashioned or antique. Experiment for best results!

Note: While halftones can be printed credibly by a quick-print shop, duotones, tritones, and quadratones require precise registration and will appear foggy or soft if the registration slips. Duotones are easier to print than a tritone or quadratone because there are only two plates to keep in register, rather than three or four. If registration problems are a possibility because of the kind of press or paper used, use a simple halftone instead.

Definition: PPDs, LPDs, APDs, and PDXs

When working with color publishing products, you may run across file names like PPDs, LPDs, APDs, and PDXs. Short for PostScript Printer Description, Letraset Printer Description, Aldus Printer Description, and Printer Description Extension, these are printer drivers. They are used by the application to set up a job for the kind of printer (or imagesetter) it will print to. These files tell the application what the output device is capable of. For example, a laser printer can't print at 1,270 dpi on 22" wide paper, but the application has no way of knowing that unless the correct PPD is selected.

When getting a job ready for output to an imagesetter or when readying a PageMaker publication to go to Aldus PrePrint, make sure the correct driver is selected, or surprises may ensue at the imagesetter. Most applications prefer that you select the correct driver while you are assembling your color project. The application uses the "knowledge" of the output device to determine parameters for a variety of functions.

Changing Channels

One of the tools for manipulating images is the *channel function* found in image-retouching and color separation programs. A channel is analogous to a plate used on a printing press. A black and white image has one channel. An RGB image has three channels—one each for red, green, and blue. A CMYK image has four channels, one each for cyan, magenta, yellow, and black. Because these programs treat each color as an independent channel, it is possible to make changes to one color only without affecting the others. This is useful in looking for color problems and casts where one color component predominates.

Channels can also be used to compare two images and make their color match better. For example, if you have two photos that will print next to each other and have very different looking color, individually comparing the channels side by side will show you how to adjust individual color channels to make them look more similar. (If close-ups of faces are in either photo, check the results of your work with a color proof. Similar color doesn't necessarily mean natural-looking color.)

Channels are also useful for checking the results of duotone processes. Because duotones (and tritones and quadratones) have individual channels for each color, after processing you can open up the individual channels to check that one color isn't too dominant or solid looking. In the case of a duotone where shadow areas look murky, you may find too much of both color components present. Remedy this by lightening one or both colors, or reprocess your duotone with new parameters.

Channels are also useful for creating special effects, combining two images into one, and simulating "color separations." To accomplish four-color separation for a product that only supports spot color separation, save each CMYK channel's information into separate files and combine them in the page layout program as carefully positioned images on four color layers. (Kids, don't try this at home!)

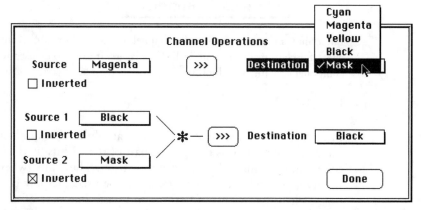

ColorStudio's channel operations, dialog controls, color channels, and mask operations.

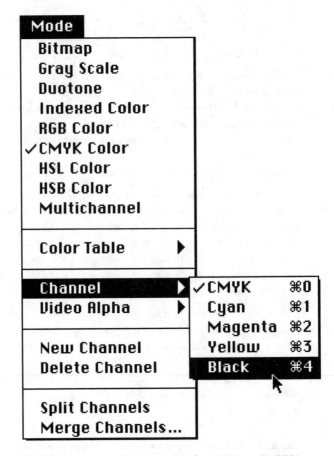

PhotoShop allows you to view the channels of an RGB or CMYK image, to check for color problems with individual layers. It can also be used to check the component channels of duotones and to view masking layers.

Masks and Channels

In addition to the standard channels, an alpha channel is available in some programs. This is the unused part of the 32 bits used to specify full color and contains eight bits of information. These bits (when used) can specify a grayscale mask. This mask can be used to apply color changes, isolate elements in an illustration, and paste one part of an image into another image. The specifications for this alpha channel can be stripped away from the image and stored separately from the image file. The mask can then be used for future work that requires similar masking. Refer back to the masking example in Chapter Three if you've forgotten how a mask works.

This chapter has further explained the mechanics of color separating process color images on the Macintosh. In the next chapter we will look at how to choose and work with a service bureau. You will also learn what these organizations can do for you, find out about their equipment, and pick up tips to help you get the best results from them.

COLOR SECTION

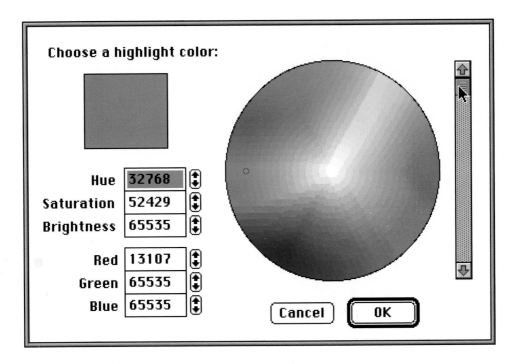

Figure C-1   The Mac's default color models use both RGB and HSB, as demonstrated in the Color Picker.

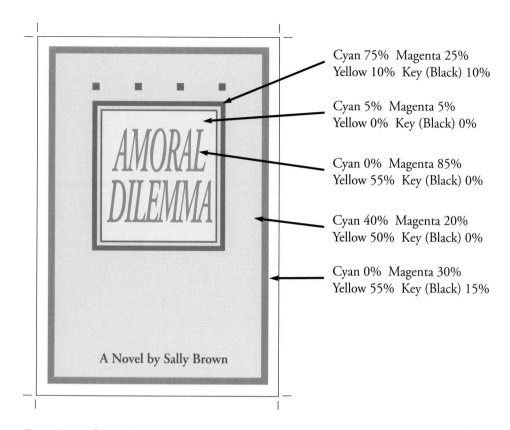

Cyan 75% Magenta 25%
Yellow 10% Key (Black) 10%

Cyan 5% Magenta 5%
Yellow 0% Key (Black) 0%

Cyan 0% Magenta 85%
Yellow 55% Key (Black) 0%

Cyan 40% Magenta 20%
Yellow 50% Key (Black) 0%

Cyan 0% Magenta 30%
Yellow 55% Key (Black) 15%

Figure C-2   If your design uses two, three, or four of the four process colors (cyan, magenta, yellow, and black), you can create other "solid" colors for use in your design by combining screens of these colors to create a new color.

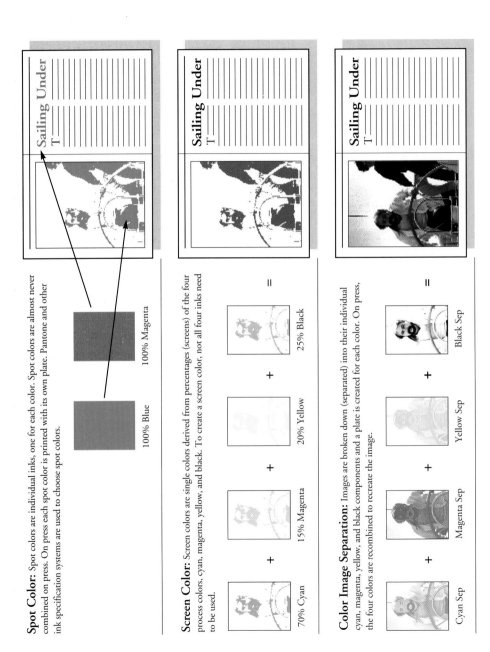

Figure C-3 Spot versus screen color

Figure C-4   The FocolTone color matching system is designed for computer color specification. It supports both spot and process colors.

Normal Registration

Misregistered CMYK Colors

Figure C-5   When a process color image is out of register, it has a soft appearance.
Note how the misregistered colors are visible around the edges of the image.

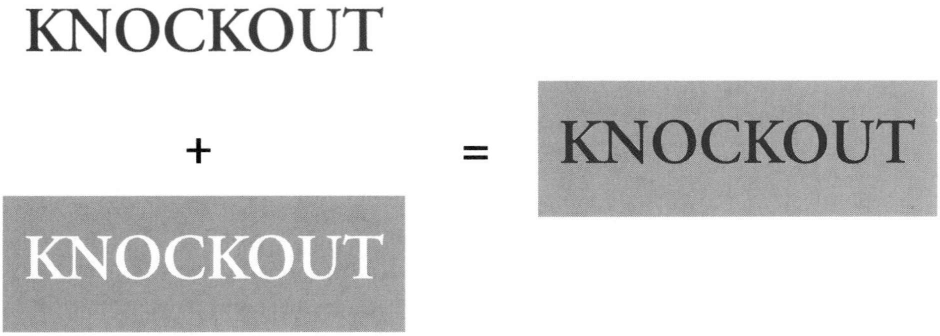

KNOCKOUT

+

= KNOCKOUT

KNOCKOUT

Knockout: When one color is knocked out of another, both colors print on blank paper. Without a knockout, one color printing over another would create a new, potentially dark color from the combination. Registration is critical when knockouts are used because blank paper may show through where the colors fail to meet. Trapping is used to fix expected registration problems when using knockouts.

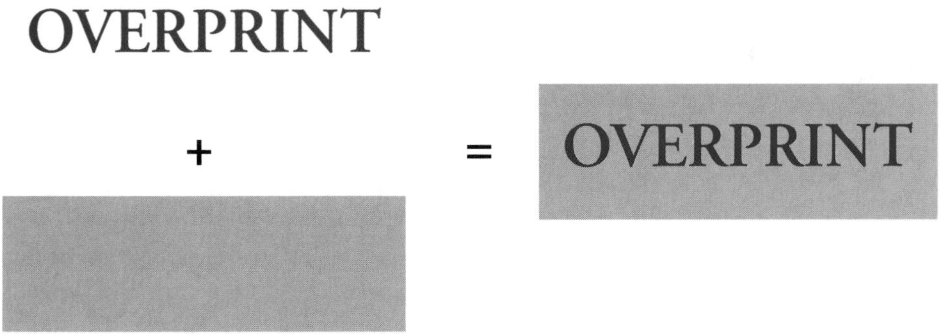

OVERPRINT

+

= OVERPRINT

Overprint: When a dark color prints on top of a light color, overprinting may be used if the light color doesn't appreciably change the dark color. Registration is not critical when overprinting is used.

Figure C-6   Knockouts and overprinting

KNOCKOUT ERROR

Knockout Error: Knockout errors are quite noticeable in most cases. Sometimes, however, they appear as a deliberate "special effect."

Figure C-7   Knockout error

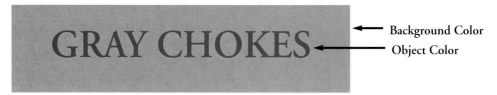

GRAY CHOKES ← Background Color / Object Color

Choking: In this example, the lighter gray chokes the darker blue.

GRAY SPREADS ← Background Color / Object Color

Spreading: In this example, the lighter gray is spread over the darker blue.

Figure C-9   Choking and spreading

NO TRAP

No Trap: Without trapping, colors that abut may not meet on press. This error becomes more noticeable when using papers prone to change shape and with jobs run on high volume presses such as web presses. Jobs without traps, but with abutting colors are said to have "butt-fitting" colors, which few printers are willing to handle.

IDEAL TRAP

Ideal Trap: The ideal trap is determined by the paper and the press the job will run on. In most cases, the edge of one color will barely overprint the other. This compensates for minor shifts in registration on press or because of paper characteristics.

TOO MUCH TRAP

Too Much Trap: When excessive trapping is used, the slight overlap of one color onto another is increased to the point that it is noticeable and distracts the reader.

Figure C-8   No trap showing gap, ideal trap, too much trap

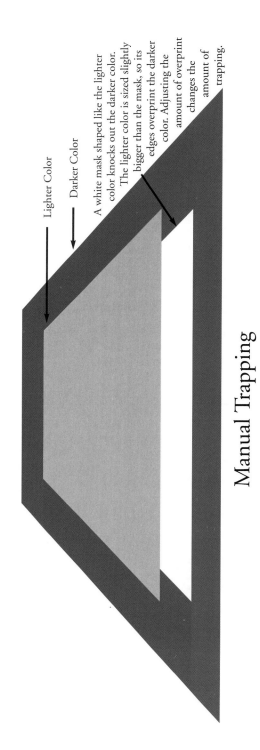

Lighter Color

Darker Color

A white mask shaped like the lighter color knocks out the darker color. The lighter color is sized slightly bigger than the mask, so its edges overprint the darker color. Adjusting the amount of overprint changes the amount of trapping.

Manual Trapping

Figure C-10 A white "mask" can be used to assemble a simple trap in programs that don't support trapping.

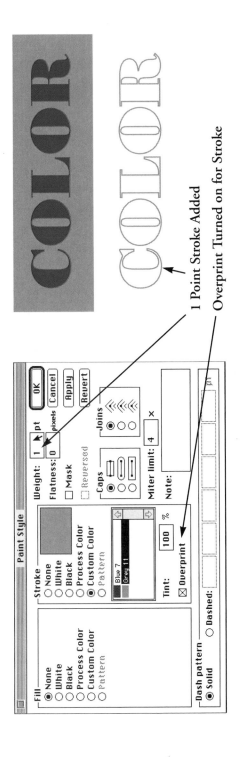

Figure C-11   To choke the lighter color over the darker, a one-point "stroke" (outline) of the background color is added to the object (*not* to the background). This line is then set to overprint. As a result, the gray knocks out for the blue, but the gray outline overprints, effectively creating a trap. The stroke is made thicker or thinner, depending on how much trap is required.

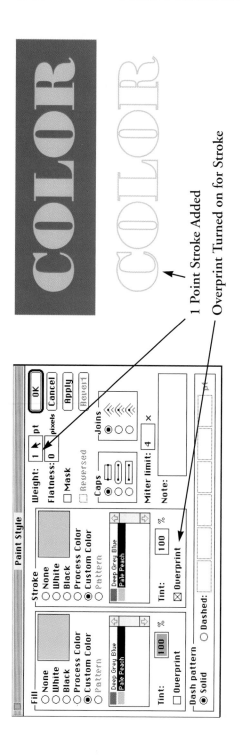

1 Point Stroke Added

Overprint Turned on for Stroke

Figure C-12   To spread the lighter color over the darker, a one-point "stroke" (outline) of the object color is added to the object. This line is then set to overprint. As a result, the blue knocks out all of the peach except for the overprinting outline, effectively creating a trap. The stroke is made thicker or thinner, depending on how much trap is required.

Figures C-13 and C-14   In this amazing example of Mac-based retouching, John Knoll used Photoshop to retouch the damaged Polaroid photo (above) and create an image that looks like new (below).

Figure C-15   Screens are rotated in process color reproduction so the dots of the four process colors do not print on top of each other. At the left, the screens are all at 0 degrees to each other, which creates an unacceptable image with dots printing on top of one another. The enlarged image on the right shows normal angles applied to the screens, so the colors will print appropriately.

Figure C-16   Moiré patterning in an image

Figure C-17   Color test strip

CHAPTER

10

CHOOSING AND WORKING
WITH A SERVICE BUREAU

"...there are two issues in calibrating imagesetters: You need to achieve a good film negative maximum density without disrupting the tints from the imagesetter. And you need to maintain that calibration, even though different programs try to disrupt it."

— Howard Fenton
writing in the prepress magazine *Pre-*

The first computerized typesetting equipment became available in the 1960s. These systems allowed an operator to key in text and add symbols and control codes to specify kerning, letterspacing, italics, justification, and a number of other typesetting tasks. Once the text and codes were entered, the text was imaged inside the machine by shining light through wheels with cut-out letters representing a font. The light formed an image on photographic paper.

As the technology advanced, the text was rasterized on a monitor and the light from this screen exposed the paper. Once paper was exposed, it was removed from the machine within a light-tight canister and then developed in a standalone processor. The most powerful of these machines, still sold today, allow the typesetter to add rules (lines) and shapes, and provide complete on-screen design functions. The most sophisticated systems ultimately became high-end prepress systems, discussed in Chapter Thirteen.

Today, instead of an operator sitting at a console and adding type and design elements, the graphics work is carried out on a Macintosh computer that is separate from the imagesetter. And, unlike traditional systems that were driven by direct computer commands with little flexibility, today's imagesetters are PostScript-based, making them capable of rendering a much wider variety of fonts and design elements, including halftones and color separations. Imagesetters are not limited to files created on the Macintosh either. Any computer capable of producing PostScript code can produce image-capable files on one of these machines, although Mac-driven systems are the most common.

You Are Here

In the last three chapters, we looked at the processes used to create the color separations for your job and covered many of the issues that can affect color quality produced from files created on the Macintosh. This chapter explains how to use a service bureau for the imaging of your film after your design is complete.

The Service Bureau Process

A service bureau (also referred to as an SB for purposes of brevity) is a business that charges Macintosh publishers a fee for time on their expensive equipment for imaging graphic files. The heart of a service bureau is the imaging equipment—a system that takes PostScript code as input and converts it into a format that can be used to expose film and produce a "hard copy" of the file. The film, once processed, can be taken to a print shop for direct conversion into press plates.

In most of this book, we have talked about the imagesetter as a singular device. To accomplish the minor miracle of PostScript rasterization to film, the imagesetter system, in fact, has four components:

1. A Macintosh Computer

A Macintosh computer is used to handle the downloading of files. The client's file (you are the client) and any of your own special fonts are installed on the hard disk. Once the file is installed, a print sequence is initiated, much like printing to an ordinary laser printer. If film is run, the **Invert Image** and **Flip Horizontal** options must be clicked inside of Apple's **Print Options** dialog, and resolution and screen setting adjustments may be necessary. If the file must be color separated at the time of printing by a program such as Aldus Preprint, it is performed at this stage. Depending on the job, the equipment used, and the resolution settings, the imaging process may take from five minutes to several hours.

2. The RIP

The RIP (raster image processor) reads and rasterizes the PostScript code into a high-resolution image. This is the brains of the imagesetter, with its own 68030 or 68040 microprocessor or faster RISC-based processor such as the MIPS R3000. The RIP accepts the input from the Macintosh and creates the image that will be drawn on film in the imagesetter. The RIP looks like a box not much larger than a Macintosh Quadra 900 and may stand vertically on the floor or sit horizontally on a shelf. (When your file is processed, it's called "getting ripped" in the business.)

3. An Imagesetter

The imagesetter receives an image from the RIP and draws it with a laser onto either film or print paper, depending on what is loaded by the operator. The target media is stored in a light-tight canister and, after imaging, is removed for processing while still stored in the canister. The imagesetter is wired to the RIP processor. Some imagesetters can be connected to a PostScipt-based RIP processor and a conventional computerized typesetting system at the same time. Imagesetters are similar in size and shape to a medium-sized office copier.

The Imaging Process Step by Step

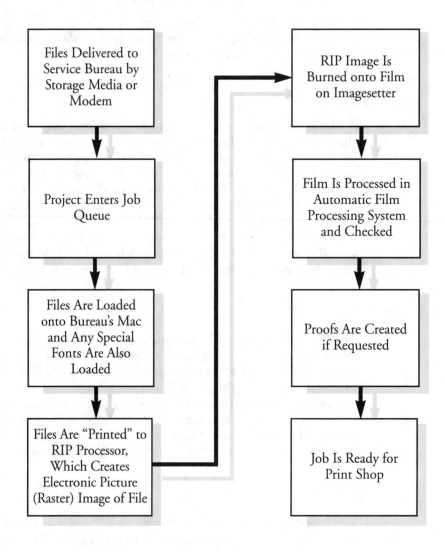

4. A Developing System

Once imaged, the film canister is removed from the imagesetter and its contents run through a film processing system. The processor develops the image captured on the photosensitive material and chemically stabilizes it. Processed film emerges from the processor in a continuous sheet, which the operator cuts into pages or individual jobs. A film processor is [yet another] box-like machine manufactured in several shapes and sizes.

Once the job is complete, the film is checked by the operator and packed into a protective envelope or paper bag, ready for the customer.

The Service Bureau's Services

Different SBs offer different levels of service. There are, however, a minimum number of services that you will require for color publishing. You will need a bureau that offers:

- **High Resolution Imagesetting**   Color work that involves screens requires an imagesetter capable of adequate resolution for the job and paper; it should be a current model and properly maintained. The SB should also have a processor for developing negatives with suitable chemistry. (More on this topic later in this chapter.)

- **Color Proofing**   When running jobs with screen color or color images of any kind, you will need a color proof made of the job to verify quality—at least until you become experienced and know you can rely on a particular service bureau (as well as your software and skills). Ask to make sure the SB can do this for you—many don't.

- **A Color Scanner (Optional)**   If you don't plan to do your own scanning, work with a bureau that offers quality scanning at a reasonable price. It's best to have the same service bureau do the scanning and handle the output. That way if something goes awry, they may try to help you fix it instead of blaming the trouble on the company that scanned the image. Some bureaus use an outside color house for their scanning. This arrangement can often work well.

- **A Color Publishing Guru**   One of the most important "services" required by Mac-based color publishers is an on-staff person(s) who really knows color publishing on the Macintosh and is experienced with printing as well. This person should be familiar with all the major product platforms and understand the pros and cons of using various settings and file formats. The person should be willing to help you solve problems, provide advice, and tell you how to specify your parameters for best results. It helps if this person also has the patience of a saint.

The Four "Kinds" of Service Bureaus

Loosely speaking, there are four kinds of service bureaus that offer Macintosh file imaging. Different bureaus have varying levels of publishing expertise, and not all SBs are cost effective for all jobs. Carefully choose the bureau for your job to get quality results while keeping costs down.

1. "The Small Shop" Service Bureau

While in the early 1980s many families and small business owners were opening video stores that ended up in bankruptcy late in the decade, a few visionaries opted to set up and run service bureaus. The best of these small SBs offer quality work and friendly advice to all comers. If you find a small, congenial service bureau with color experience, it's often a comfortable place to do business. You may even get a homemade cookie while you wait for your job.

The downside of these SBs is that their equipment may be limited, and because most jobs they encounter may be simple, they may lack direct experience imaging color files.

2. "The Print Shop" Service Bureau

A growing number of print shops are scrambling to add imagesetting to their service repertoire. The idea behind this extension is that jobs brought in for imaging may "accidentally" find their way into the print shop and bring in customers who might otherwise print elsewhere. With the right shop, this arrangement works out well, because the people manning the imagesetter receive "hands-on" feedback from the press room and learn how to set up jobs for success on press.

When considering such an arrangement, evaluate the quality of work in the press room separately from the work of the service bureau. We've worked with a number of these shops and found that many are great printers, yet run mediocre service bureaus. Of course, there are also bad printers who run great service bureaus. Look for one that rates highly as both a print shop and a service bureau, and your color publishing work will go smoothly from desktop to print shop.

Tip: One Kind of Shop to Avoid…

The worst kind of service bureau is the "we just follow the directions" kind that really believes all you need to know about imaging is found in the imagesetter hardware manuals. These installations are typically old typesetting shops that just purchased an imagesetter, or they may be owned by someone who read in an entrepreneur's magazine about the mountain of money to be made running a service bureau and decided to "cash in."

These problem bureaus are usually oriented to running black and white jobs on paper and handle film infrequently. They may have purchased the cheapest imagesetter and RIP they could get their hands on, without enough memory to image so much as a 8" by 8" grayscale image. Most of the time these operations won't know the first thing about dealing with or fixing problems. (All problems are your fault, not theirs.) Unless your work includes only type and line art, steer clear of these places.

How to Recognize This Kind of Shop: These organizations are recognizable when you ask a loaded question such as, "What tools and techniques do you use to calibrate your imagesetter and maintain film processor chemistry?" If this question produces a dumbfounded response or, "We change the chemicals every month or two," make a fast exit, stage left.

3. "The Mill" Service Bureau

In every major American and Canadian city, a handful of service bureaus are taking on the lion's share of the business by working multiple shifts, running four or more imagesetters, offering perks such as free pickup and delivery, and reducing job turnaround time from 24 hours to just four to six hours. Because these shops handle so much traffic, your job may not get the special attention it needs. However, since these people crank out color work all day, they keep their equipment in top shape and know a hundred workarounds for problems.

If you have already developed a workable color publishing methodology to the point where you regularly produce reliable results, these operations will offer you good service, quick turnaround, and reasonable prices. However, if you've heard stories of people receiving an envelope of blank negatives from their job, it was probably imaged at one of these bureaus, where the operators are too busy to check the work or make a phone call to the customer to help solve the problem.

4. "The Color Shop" Service Bureau

During the 1970s, a large number of companies specializing in computer-based color separation were established. Many of these operations take on color separation as well as offering high-end prepress services. Naturally, as the interest in Mac-based publishing increased, most of these companies purchased Macs and an imagesetter and began offering imagesetting services. This not only brought them new business and customers, but jobs that became hopelessly entangled in imagesetter or software problems could be rectified on the prepress system or they could be repaired conventionally at the facility (for a price).

Because these shops know color inside and out, the ones we've worked with in this category have been more expensive than a mill-type shop—but the results, when it comes to color, have been superb. These companies already know more about color and color separation than most print shops, plus they understand the ramifications of dot gain and ink density on press. They also have a complete range of color proofing systems and color problem-solving routines.

Aside from the slightly higher cost, the only downside of working with these shops is the typically slower turnaround. Most of them are accustomed to a four-day turnaround on color separations, so a four-hour turnaround on your file will seem hurried to them, and they'll charge you rush charges as a result.

Finding Service Bureaus

While it may sound trivial, service bureaus are often difficult to locate. At this writing there is no listing in the *Yellow Pages* for *Service Bureaus* or *Imagesetter Services,* so SBs masquerade under other categories in the phonebook. Look under *Desktop Publishing, Typesetters,* and *Printers. Desktop Publishing* is usually the easiest place in the phone book to find service bureaus, but not every phone directory includes this category (yet). In the case of print shops owning imagesetter services, we've run into more than one that offers imagesetting only to customers printing jobs at the shop.

A fourth place to look is under *Color Separation.* These listings will mostly be the more expensive color shops described earlier in the chapter.

Most of these shops own imagesetters and can help you. A few color shops do not offer imagesetting services yet, but the owners will usually know where you can get quality services elsewhere. Sometimes a color house will advise against imaging your film from the Mac. In the case of complex, high-quality color images, they're sometimes right. That's why we've included information in Chapter Thirteen on taking Mac documents into a high-end prepress system.

A Service Bureau Problem

Because some service bureaus think of their work the same way a clerk working in a 24-hour copy center does, they provide a low level of service. "Put the file up. Image it. Chop off the film and charge the customer. Job complete; next customer please. Sorry, we don't have time for questions. Next please." While simple typesetting jobs can be imaged in this fashion, color publishing jobs can't. You want a bureau that becomes a part of the printing process and works to ensure that your job is imaged correctly for print. They should take responsibility for their work and take pride in improving their quality and fixing problems.

Your bureau should not only take an active interest in seeing your job successfully output, but also in seeing that it makes it through print. It helps if your bureau works closely with printers to improve the SB's printing knowledge and refine their techniques to get the right results. Bureau personnel who once worked in a print shop are best because they know how film should look and what problems will cause grief down the road on press. If you're willing to settle for the kind of service offered at a copy center in order to take advantage of low prices, check the job carefully.

Choosing the Right Service Bureau

Choosing the right service bureau requires a little thought and time on your part. But, it's not that difficult if you look methodically and don't drop a complicated color job on an unknown shop without checking up on them first. Probably the best way of finding a service bureau is a referral from another publisher who already produces jobs at least as complicated as yours.

If you can't locate an appropriate shop through a referral, call several SBs that claim to handle color work and delicately interrogate them as to their experience, charges, equipment, and what kind of success they've had handling color work (if any).

Through casual conversation with the shop's operator or owner, check out the answers to the questions below.

How Much Color Work Have They Done?

A service bureau that claims to handle color may not work with anything more complex than spot color overlays. Ask them what kind of color work they've done and what kind of jobs they've tackled. Most bureaus successful at color will have printed samples of their successes. Ask to see some. If they don't have any, assume there's a reason for the lack of proof and look for another shop.

What Equipment Do They Use?

If you plan to output color separations, you want a bureau using fast RIP processors and an imagesetter with accurate film transport. Some form of moiré control is preferable as well (see Chapter Nine for more information on this topic). For color work, newer, more accurate models are the units of choice, although a recent bare-bones systems is not necessarily suitable for color.

Because imagesetter technology changes day by day, keep up to date on what models can produce appropriate results for your project. Unfortunately, if you query an imagesetter owner, they'll claim that their system employs the latest and greatest model, even if it's a Linotronic 100—a pioneering but now very obsolete piece of equipment. Read the Mac and prepress magazines to find out what's happening with imagesetters.

What Are the Basic Charges and Services?

Before consigning work to a service bureau, find out what they charge per page, how fast they turn work around without rush charges, and whether they pick up and deliver or if you have to drive the job around town yourself.

The Imagesetters You'll Meet

Imagesetters have become far more accurate in producing consistent dot sizes and density. For color work, you want the laser to photosensitize exactly the right amount of emulsion in exactly the right place. More importantly, if your job is large, you want exactly the same results in the last piece of film out of the machine as the first.

To make sure you are choosing the best imagesetter for your job, here are some pros and cons on current technologies in use by the service bureaus you'll find.

"Flatbed" Imagesetters

The majority of imagesetter systems use a flatbed system, where film or paper stored in a canister is moved under the imaging laser much like paper is moved through a tractor-fed dot-matrix printer. After imaging, the film is removed from the system and processed. The transport systems in older imagesetters of this kind are comparatively inaccurate and inadequate for color work. Newer transport mechanisms move film with greater precision than the systems in older imagesetters. This makes a big difference in producing color separations, because inaccurate film transport introduces nasty registration problems. Older, slower machines with slower processors and smaller memory capacities are not suitable for color, because they may take forever to image your file. In most cases, this avoidable extra imaging time is charged for.

Drum-based Imagesetters

The newest and most accurate imagesetters mechanically resemble the precision film recorders used for high-end prepress systems. A drum rotates with the imaging media (film) and a laser writes the image onto the media as it rotates. Assuming the imaging media has been correctly loaded, these systems offer incredible accuracy when "writing" the image. At last, imagesetters tied to a Mac can begin to approach the accuracy of film recorders used to capture images in color separation houses.

Continued

Which Kind of Imagesetter Is Right for Your Job?

The imagesetter of choice for each project is selected according to the kind of job, its precision requirements, and the budget. Newer imagesetters, capable of high degrees of precision and handling larger film sizes, are more expensive than older and less capable equipment. Because these systems cost more to purchase and run, the extra charges are passed on to customers.

Simple spot color work, even with traps, can be run on almost any system, unless the colored objects are very small and the trap "walls" thin. For example, a job with traps less than a point in width could go awry on an imagesetter with registration problems due to inaccurate film transport, but almost any other project with larger traps would image adequately for press.

Once screen color or process color images come into the picture, more precision is required, because of the potential for inaccurate dot size (a function of calibration) and because placing dots on register on all the color layers becomes imperative. And, as resolution increases, superior accuracy of both dot precision and registration become increasingly critical.

For newsprint work, where registration shifts regardless of accuracy and where color fidelity changes with the absorbency of the newsprint running through the press in any particular second, a properly calibrated imagesetter of almost any model (with reasonably accurate film transport) can provide adequate results. Registration problems are endemic to this kind of publishing, so the "small" shifts made by imagesetters are minor in comparison to what will happen on press because of the stock stretching as it passes through the press.

How Do They Calibrate Their Imagesetter?

Imagesetters are devices that must produce the correct-sized dots in all the right places to reproduce accurate color. The only way to get this kind of accuracy is through regular calibration with the right software tools and the use of a well-tuned densitometer to check the accuracy of screens. Some newer machines don't require calibration, but the film produced can still be affected by processor chemistry imbalance, so careful checking with densitometer is still mandatory.

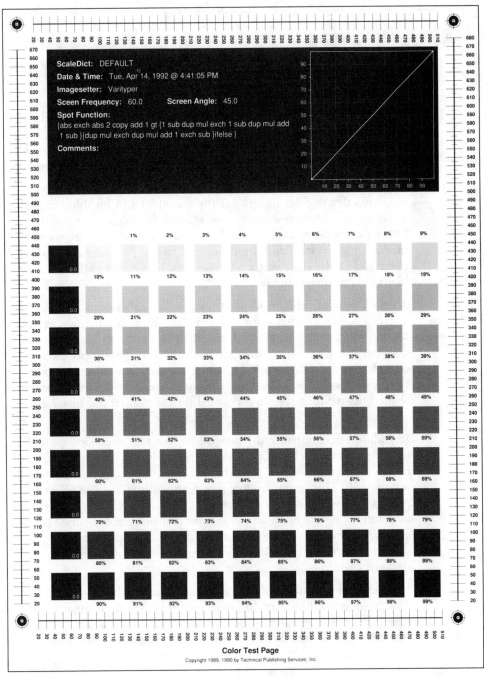

Color Test Page
Copyright 1989, 1990 by Technical Publishing Services, Inc.

This is an imagesetter system test page produced by an imagesetter calibration product called Color Calibration Software for PostScript Imagesetters. Each screen on this page can be checked for accuracy with a densitometer.

Imagesetters and Calibration

When imaging film that incorporates screens, the accuracy of the imagesetter used to image the screens is vital. Since all color publishing projects above the spot color level use screens for tints, screen color, and reproducing full-color images, the majority of color publishing projects must image on a calibrated system. While the newest and most expensive imagesetters maintain accurate calibration automatically, without care, other models may produce dot sizes that are incorrect.

Imagesetter calibration is complex in itself. While dot size may be properly calibrated for imaging at (for example) 133 lpi, film imaged at higher or lower resolutions may suffer from inaccurate dot sizes. Other factors throw calibration off as well, even for imagesetters with inherently accurate calibration. Some software packages attempt to commandeer the imagesetter and use their own values, and different kinds of films image differently.

To work around calibration problems, special calibration software is installed. Once internal software calibration is established, a sheet of test film is output. This film is manually measured with a transmission densitometer, final adjustments are made, and its density (solidness of dot, measured as D-Max and D-Min) is checked as well. At this point the imagesetter is "in calibration," at least temporarily, for jobs running at the lines-per-inch specification used for the calibration. Imagesetter test pages must also be checked for banding problems, however.

In addition to calibrating the imagesetter, the film processor must be inspected and the chemicals replaced regularly. As jobs are run, the chemicals become weaker, removing less emulsion from the film passing through. This results in dots that change shape and can affect the process even more severely than an uncalibrated imagesetter. Stories of long runs of negatives on an imagesetter that produced accurate color on a carefully calibrated system early in the run, but produced progressively less accurate color later in the run, are probably explained by depleted chemicals.

Different brands and kinds of chemicals produce different kinds of dots. So does the film used for imaging. Because both of these factors change dot size, even slightly, color shift will occur if the film brand is changed without recalibrating. The best calibration results from set-

Continued

ting up the imagesetter based on tests performed on the same kind of film and constant chemistry. That way, if the dot values conform on a printed test sheet that has been imaged and processed with the same materials, then the entire system is in balance. Software-only calibration doesn't take into account that dot shapes can change size after the film is imaged or that the imagesetter's laser may be changing over time in its output strength due to age. The resulting calibration is only as accurate as the weakest link in the chain.

One of the reasons you should work through a bureau that routinely produces complex color work is that they most likely keep their equipment in tip-top shape and check the entire system's calibration on a regular basis.

How Do They Maintain Adequate Chemistry in Their Processors?

Film requires more processing than resin-coated paper. A shop that tells you they process both media the same way is telling you to go elsewhere, because under-processed film shifts color and may not properly "open up" screens. This results in blotchy-looking color and halftones on press. Film is best handled by a bureau with separate processors for paper and film. The chemicals in processors must be changed regularly as well. Weak chemicals also produce undesirable color shifts because the film is under-processed.

What about Extra Charges?

Some bureaus charge delightfully low fees for individual sheets of paper or film and then make it up with extra charges. (See *Service Bureau Charges* later in this chapter.) In some cases the extra charges will total more than a higher cost-per-page rate at another shop.

What If There's a Problem?

Some service bureaus regard problems as a challenge and love to put their brainpower to work solving them. Others simply ship you work with obvious errors and a bill. An unethical few will allow you to run and rerun a job without lifting a finger to solve your problems, because they make money on each pass through their system. These bureaus may know exactly what's wrong but will not tell you. You want the first kind of bureau, one that cares and provides personal service, for any kind of color work.

What Services Are Available?

Check to ensure that the service bureau can produce color proofs in house. If they claim to handle a lot of color work but are unable to produce color proofs, this is indicates that: 1) they do less color work than claimed; or 2) they don't like assembling proofs because of the poor quality of their color output. Look elsewhere.

What Font Libraries Do They Own?

A service bureau should own a full library of Adobe fonts at the very least. A big bureau may own more than one complete library. A bureau with limited font selection is one that probably handles few professional-quality jobs, meaning they have limited experience.

> ### Tip: Avoid Self-service Service Bureaus for Color Work
>
> Some service bureaus have you load your files onto their equipment and output the job yourself to their imagesetter. Skip this arrangement for color work, because you need your service bureau's expertise to help you get the job output correctly. Also, when printing a color file with separations, this process may take so long that the people behind you in the job queue get miffed with the wait.

Do They Regularly Use the Software You Use?

You'll want a service bureau that regularly handles work assembled with the same software you use. That way, if there's a problem, they may have the knowledge and experience to fix or work around it.

What File Formats Do They Accept?

If you plan to send large files for imaging, how does the SB prefer to accept color publishing jobs? Can you do it by modem or do they prefer multiple floppy disks with compressed contents, optical disks, or SyQuest cartridges?

Use the questionnaire we've provided to evaluate a prospective service bureau. And, when you ask questions, do it on the phone and try to make the tone conversational rather than confrontational. That way you won't alienate bureau personnel before you meet them.

When you've found what appears to be a knowledgeable bureau, send them a simple job to test turnaround time and see how they perform. A few bureaus are all talk and slow action, so giving them increasingly complicated work allows you to see how well they perform—without committing a large, complex job to a company that can't really handle it.

If you do have a job that must be rushed through and you haven't selected a service bureau, consider using a color house. These companies often charge a little more, but most of them have the experience to ensure that color work is done correctly.

What to Take to the Bureau

When preparing to take your work for imaging, it's important that you take everything the SB will need to image your files. Otherwise you may have to make the same trip twice. If you don't take these precautions, your job may image with components missing. We have provided a checklist for this purpose. Make a photocopy of it and tick off the boxes before you go. It will provide you with a method of ensuring that everything you need goes with the job. If they don't have a job form for you to fill out, the list can be used by your service bureau as an information tool that provides details about the project.

Basically there are four groups of items that should accompany your job and a few things that don't need to make the trip at all.

1. The Page Layout

If your job includes a design done in a page layout program, you will obviously need to include this file. In addition, if you are using older versions of QuarkXPress, you must include your XPress Data, or your SB can't image the job correctly, and many bureaus won't so much as try. All disks should be labeled with the names of the files, your company name, your name, and your phone number.

Checklist for Locating a Color-capable Service Bureau

Service Bureau Basics

Bureau Name _____ Phone # _____ Years in Business _____

Imagesetter Brand(s) _____

Model (s) _____

Standard Job Turnaround Time (Hours) _____ Free Pick-Up/Delivery? ☐

How much does a sheet of standard film cost per page? $____Paper? $_____ Self Service? ☐

What font libraries do they own? Adobe ☐ Bitstream ☐ Other _____

What formats do they accept files in? Floppy ☐ Modem ☐ Optical ☐ Tape ☐ Cartridge ☐
SCSI Device ☐ WORM ☐

What compression/decompression routines do they use? _____

What page layout software do they work with on a day-to-day basis? PageMaker ☐
QuarkXPress ☐ DesignStudio ☐ Multi-Ad Creator ☐ Posterworks ☐ Ventura ☐
FrameMaker ☐ Quoin ☐ Other: _____

What color separation packages do they use? Photoshop ☐ ColorStudio ☐ Aldus PrePrint ☐
Cachet ☐ Spectreseps ☐ SpectrePrint Pro ☐ Color Access ☐ Other _____

Color Experience

None ☐ Spot Color ☐ Screen Color ☐ Color Illustrations ☐ Process Color Images ☐

Will they show you printed samples or proofs of their work? Yes ☐ No ☐

What percentage of paper to film do they run? Paper _____% Film _____%

Imagesetter Calibration and Processor Chemistry

How do they calibrate their imagesetter? (Some newer models are partially self calibrating.)

_____

How do they maintain accurate processor chemistry?

_____

Do they have separate processors for paper and film? Yes ☐ No ☐

If not, do they change chemicals for film? Yes ☐ No ☐

Other

What do they charge extra for? Overtime ☐ How is it charged? _____

Other extra charges _____

What is their policy if problems occur? _____

What color proofing systems do they offer? Matchprint ☐ Color Keys ☐ Cromalin ☐
Other: _____

Do they offer color scanning services ? Yes ☐ No ☐
What kind of scanner(s) do they use? _____

2. Image Files

All images included in your publication, including scans, illustrations, and color separations must be included. Otherwise, when the page layout file is imaged, a low-resolution preview image will be substituted (unless the bureau stops the job). The only exception to this rule is MacDraw-type illustrations. These are imbedded into the page layout, and including them just takes up extra disk space.

> ### Tip: Use the Latest Version of Application Software
>
> In order to avoid problems when you take a job through to imaging, use the latest version of all software products to create the page layout and process scans and illustrations. Otherwise your file may not image or may image with unexpected errors because of changes in the application software's design.

3. Fonts

If your job uses any custom fonts that you created with Fontographer, you must provide these along with your files. If your job includes standard fonts that the SB doesn't own, they must purchase them. (Fonts are software with a license that states explicitly that you may not give them to any other party, even your service bureau.) Or, save your job as PostScript files with the fonts imbedded. **Note:** If your job uses Bitstream's version of a font and your bureau uses Adobe's version, type will shift within your page layout. The SB should have the same version you use.

4. A Proof of the Job

When imaging a job, particularly one with possible problems, it helps the service bureau if you provide them with a proof of the job produced on whatever kind of PostScript printer you have access to. Proofs show the imagesetter operator what your job should look like, so if there is a problem they can spot it and make corrections, or at least give you a call to determine what to do.

> ### Tip: Bring the Correct Files
>
> Since it's possible to create file name aliases that are the same as the file itself so that the icons appear identical, don't make the mistake of including an alias instead of the real file. More than one service bureau has spent time trying to image a file that was really only an alias of the original.

5. Written Information

While the better bureaus provide a detailed form for you to complete in order to provide the information needed to image your job, many bureaus don't. You can either use the form provided earlier in this chapter or write out a list of specifications relevant to your job. Your SB needs to know the following:

1. The name of the file to be imaged.
2. How many pages it contains.
3. The names of all fonts used.
4. The names of all placed images.
5. How large the output should be (letter, tabloid, etc).
6. How much resolution you want used (dots per inch).
7. The screen to be used if any is required (lines per inch).
8. How fast you want the job turned around (rush or regular).
9. What kind of output media you want—film or paper.
10. What kind of page layout software was used and the version number.
11. Do you want a negative or positive output?
12. Do you want color separations or single-page output?
13. Your name and phone number.
14. Any special instructions you want carried out.
15. The kind of color proof you want to see.
16. Where you want the job delivered. (You may want to have it sent to your print shop instead of your office.)

With all these components listed, the service bureau can easily check that fonts weren't substituted, images were correctly output, and that your work was imaged on the correct media.

Service Bureau Charges

The cost of imaging jobs depends on five factors:

1. The kind of output media. Film costs more than paper.

2. The number of pages run. Remember, for process color, four sheets of film are required for each page and one sheet for each spot color in addition to black.

3. The size of the pages, with tabloid costing more than letter-sized output.

4. The time required to image the job.

5. Extra charges for special services.

Before starting the design of a color job, get a firm estimate of service bureau charges to ensure that it makes economic sense to handle all or part of the job on the desktop. Because service bureau charges vary widely among shops, get a quote from two or three if it's a large and potentially expensive job—you could save a lot of money that way. Don't make the mistake of running a color job at a shop just because their prices are low, however. Color work requires well-maintained equipment and knowledge-able people. While you may save money running at a lesser shop, you may end up paying twice to have the job rerun and the problems fixed.

There are no standard rates among bureaus. One bureau may produce film output at $13 per page. Another SB down the street may charge $18 for the same sheet of film. One may offer a low per-page rate but sock you with extra charges.

When imaging complex color documents, the most obvious extra charge is for the extra time required to image each piece of film. The first price consideration to take into account is the length of time allowed for each piece of film before overtime charges are applied. Some bureaus track extra time down to the second and bill accordingly. Others turn a blind eye if they appreciate your business and your file doesn't take all day. **Note:** If your film is run out with an older and slower imaging system, you may be charged for the extra time that could have been avoided on a faster system.

A standard practice in the communications business is to apply rush charges to jobs that require fast turnaround. The reason for this is simple: Jobs that get behind schedule require people providing services (such as typesetters, print shops, and now service bureaus) to drop their other work and complete whatever tasks are required to meet the deadline. Rush charges are often justified if a vendor has to give up their weekend, Fourth of July, or work all night to complete the job. In some cases, the

---

Imaging Checklist

Use this form to ensure that you have everything needed to image your job and to communicate your needs with your service bureau.

Your Name _____ Contact Phone # _____

Company Name _____

Billing Address _____

PO # _____ Client (if any) _____

Job Name_____ Deliver to _____

When do you need it done? Day _____ Time _____
Rush charges okay Yes ☐ No ☐

When do you need it completed by? Day _____ Time _____

Submission Format: Floppy ☐ Modem ☐ Optical ☐ Tape ☐ Cartridge ☐
SCSI Device ☐ WORM ☐

Page layout program used _____ Version _____
(If QuarkXpress 2.0 or 3.0 include XPress Data files.)

File name to image _____ Page Count _____ Resolution _____ dpi
Screen _____lpi

Film ☐ Paper ☐ Negative ☐ Positive ☐ Separations (check the kind required)

Separations Required: Spot ☐ Screen Color ☐ Illustrations ☐
Process Color Images ☐

Proof Required? Matchprint ☐ Cromalin ☐ Color Keys ☐ Mac-driven Color
Copier ☐ Other: _____

Output size excluding trim zone: 8½" X 11" ☐ 8½" X 14" ☐ 11" X 17" ☐
Other _____

Placed Graphic Name _____ Graphic Format _____

Placed Graphic Name _____ Graphic Format _____

Placed Graphic Name _____ Graphic Format _____

Font Used in Document _____ Font Manuafcturer _____

Font Used in Document _____ Font Manuafcturer _____

Font Used in Document _____ Font Manuafcturer _____

Special Instructions _____

_____

entire stripping and press floor staff of a print shop may work an entire weekend to satisfy a client on a deadline. Rush charges are usually from 50 percent to 200 percent in addition to the normal charge, though they can be higher for extreme demands.

Other extra charges are often arbitrary in nature. We have been charged for downloading files over the phone, using our own fonts, and for changing the film processor over from RC paper developer to film developer. One odd bureau charged us $3.25 per page extra for files not converted into PostScript format, for reasons unknown.

Working with Your Service Bureau

Print shops always joke that when a job has problems, they get the blame. This is more than partially true, because it's at the print shop that errors and mistakes become plainly visible. Customers howl with rage when they spot a printed typo that the printer didn't spot. Of course, it's the customer's responsibility to find these errors, not the print shop's.

This responsibility has shifted somewhat onto the service bureau, because mistakes may not become apparent until the file is imaged. SBs get blamed for all kinds of problems that may not be their fault. If a file fails to print, a font is substituted, or a picture images as an empty black square on a negative, the problem may be blamed on the bureau that had nothing to do with it.

Tip: Don't Be a PITA

A service bureau operator we use frequently told us about a phrase she'd learned that describes troublesome customers. She calls them PITAs. Though it sounds like a bread from the Middle East, PITA is actually short for Pain in the A**, and is used to refer to customers who blame every problem on their service bureau or waste the bureau's time with hours of convoluted questions. Avoid becoming one of these people, and you and your job will get better treatment.

While service bureaus do make mistakes (some make more than their share), when you check a job and find problems, ask them politely what went wrong and how to fix it. In most of the bureaus we've worked with, a knowledgeable operator will study the job and try to fix the problem—even if it was something we did wrong. Usually, if there's any possibility that something was done wrong in their shop or their equipment was to blame, your job will be rerun *gratis*.

Questions and Answers

You can't expect a bureau owner who has spent five years learning the trade to answer a hundred questions in a row. These people have work to do, and the best bureaus are often the busiest ones. While this book encourages you to ask a lot of questions, do it a little at a time or pay for an hour of consulting if you need a lot of advice. If they have the time, buy the bureau owner or operator lunch. One bureau we work with charges only $45 for an hour of brain picking. That's a small fee for all the questions you can ask in 60 minutes, and it's a miniscule charge, considering that a mistake in a color job can cost thousands of dollars to fix if it makes it onto press.

Handling and Moving Giant Files

One of the logistical problems of working with Macintosh color publishing is storing and transferring massive files to a service bureau for output. While the day of the 400 KB floppy disk thankfully came to an end years ago, transferring a color document with 60 MB worth of color files is still challenging. Basically there are three options open to color publishers: modem transmission; compression; and the use of a transmission medium with more storage capacity than a floppy disk. All of these possibilities have advantages and disadvantages, described below.

Tip: Wait Till the Midnight Hour

A multi-meg scan file may tie up a service bureau's modem and computer for several hours, making them unhappy enough to bill you for the time. Instead, make arrangements to transmit by night. Assuming your service bureau is either closed or uses a separate Mac to receive files from the one that's connected to the imagesetter, sending your file at 1:00 a.m. will make life easier for everyone. Purchase a communications program that allows files to be sent without your presence, or use a macro program such as QuicKeys from CE Software to initiate the action for you automatically.

Modem Transmission

The most elegant transmission method is to dial up your local service bureau and send a file by phone while you head off to get a second cup of coffee. This method has the obvious advantage of not requiring you to leave your office, and in theory there's no upward limit on the file size that can be transported. On the downside, modem transmission obviously requires a modem, competent communications software, and at least a basic understanding of how it all works. It's also comparatively slow and may not be a viable alternative for handling large color files. If you plan to transmit scanned images, get a fast modem, because sending 10 MB worth of data to a service bureau at 300 baud takes literally days. A really large file transmitted at even a fast 9600 baud still takes hours to send.

In addition to size and speed problems, occasionally a transmitted file will become corrupt during transmission—a one-bit change to a file can cause major headaches when the job is imaged. While most of today's software guards carefully against mistakes, and errors are infrequent, they do occur.

It helps if your service bureau also uses sophisticated software on their receiving machine. If you plan to transmit files, look for a bureau that runs a computer just for receiving files (some don't). One small bureau that we work with uses the same Mac to receive and image files. Consequently, before sending a file, you must call them and tell them one is coming, so they can set up for it. There's usually an extra charge for this "convenience."

Compression

Compression is a powerful tool for shrinking giant files into manageable sizes. Compression tools are either entirely software-based or combine software with a NuBus board that requires a slot in your Mac. There are several kinds of compression systems available: general compression programs such as StuffIt; special image compression programs that are "lossless;" and image compression programs that eliminate image detail to achieve deeper rates of compression. Compression works according to one simple rule: The greater degree of compression achieved, the less data saved. Consequently, twenty-to-one compression means that when a file is uncompressed, not all of the data will be there. This causes serious problems for compressed color separations.

General compression programs are the least expensive and most convenient to use because they can be used to stuff page layout files as well as images. StuffIt—a very popular program—is provided with documentation on the disk that is accompanies this book. A commercial version, StuffIt Deluxe, can be purchased for not much more. This program compresses files efficiently and can take large images and compress them to the size of a single floppy disk.

Commercial compression routines are available for handling only images. ImpressIt from Radius is capable of shrinking image files to as little as three percent of their original size. This software uses the emerging compression standard called JPEG. JPEG compression is a standard agreed to by a number of compression system makers and is directly supported on imagesetters running PostScript Level II. This allows you to ship a compressed image that your service bureau can directly image without first decompressing it on their Mac. In addition, a growing number of image processing applications directly support JPEG. This allows you to open and save files directly in this format.

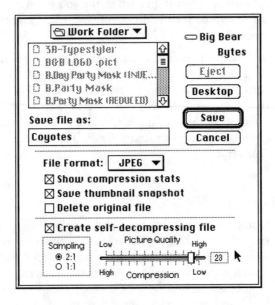

Compression programs such as ImpressIt from Radius
can reduce image sizes to make transportation easier.

Compression has three downsides that you should be aware of. First, compressing and decompressing a file takes time. One 12 MB grayscale we produced took about fifteen minutes to compress but an hour to decompress. This resulted in extra charges from the harried service bureau. Most commercial compression programs, fortunately, are much faster than the shareware program we were using. The second problem is that a damaged compressed file is usually unrecoverable. This isn't a big deal, because you can just make a new copy from your original. If, however, you follow the advice of compression software manufacturers and keep images compressed on your hard disk, a damaged file may become irrevocably lost. Third, not all manufacturers implement "industry standards" the same way. That means that a compressed file may not be directly accessible by another manufacturer's program. This can be a problem if you use one program to compress a file, and your service bureau uses another to decompress it.

Tip: Paperclips and Floppy Disks

Floppy disks are magnetic media and, as such, are subject to stray magnetic forces. Paperclips are sometimes used to attach job disks to accompanying paperwork or proofs when when sent to a service bureau. This is a bad idea because many people store paperclips in magnetic holders. A magnetized clip damages the magnetic information on the disk, resulting in errors or an unreadable disk.

Portable Storage

A third alternative is to acquire a storage medium that can be transported to a service bureau. This alternative has one significant downside: The format you choose, be it removable media such as tape, optical disk, or cartridge-based hard disk, must also be supported by your service bureau. Purchasing such a system for use with a particular bureau may also lock you into working with that SB, because they alone can exchange data with your storage "solution."

An alternative to removable media is movable media, i.e., an extra hard drive in a standalone case. To output files, you simply power your system down and take the disk to your friendly local service bureau, where they download the files directly (you can install font suitcases on this drive for convenience). When they're done, they give you your drive back. This alternative is a fairly speedy one because the files don't need to be moved, decompressed, or transmitted. But, this approach has two potential problems in addition to the risk that the drive will get stolen or dropped: 1) You may run into SCSI port conflicts at the SB, although with a drive with accessible SCSI settings, this is a minor problem; 2) if one of the Macs is a fast model (such as a IIfx) that requires special SCSI termination and one is a Mac using the original Mac II termination system, you may not be able to get the drive to talk to the other computer. Our Mac dealer's service department reports that data can also be lost or corrupted by connecting a hard disk from a Mac IIx to a IIfx or Quadra.

If you plan frequent transferring of a SCSI-based device such as a hard disk or tape system, add a short SCSI extension for the service bureau to connect to. This makes hooking up easier, and it saves wear and tear on your drive's SCSI connector.

The Best Solution

The best solution for transmitting files is probably a mixture of two alternatives. For example, compressing files and then transmitting them via modem makes a workable alternative to tying up your computer (and the service bureau's) for hours. Or compressing a large file that won't fit on a single 45 MB removable drive is a less expensive alternative to upgrading to a drive that handles 90 MB cartridges. The best alternative is to identify an efficient transport method that doesn't require purchasing anything new. If you must buy new software or hardware, choose the lowest priced path that meets your requirements and allows you access to more than one service bureau.

Proofs and Proofing

Your first line of defense against mistakes at the SB when imaging color jobs is the color proof. It allows you to check imagesetter calibration, can be shown to clients, and gives you hard evidence of problems that may dog the job on press.

If you're just getting started on the Mac, have color proofs made of every job to see how screen color and color separations look. If your job uses only spot color, you may not need a color proof of the job, although you'll want to check the traps in the document to ensure that they imaged as expected.

Keep in mind that the color you see in a proof will vary on press if you specified dot gain compensation for a highly absorbent paper stock. Images may be lighter than you'd planned, and screen color may be light as well. The more dot gain compensation you apply, the greater the color shift will be in the proof.

In addition to seeing a proof at the SB when your job is imaged, your printer may show you one as well, particularly if the print shop has assembled any component of the job. For example, if you had your color separations done by a separation house, the color separator will show you proofs of the job until you are satisfied with the color. The print shop will then assemble the job and show you a color proof as well, to verify that the job is correctly assembled. In addition, they'll probably produce a blueline proof that shows how the job will fold and specifies any die cuts.

The most popular proofing systems are described below.

Bluelines (Dylux)

A blueline is a blue (or sometimes brown) proof produced on paper. Bluelines are the least expensive and easiest of the proofs to produce. Bluelines are usually produced by print shops, not at service bureaus.

Use bluelines to proof copy and check that a job has been assembled correctly by the print shop. Blues can be used to check that trims, die cuts, and other cutting and folding processes will be carried out properly. When creating a blueline for a two-color job, most print shops will burn the second color slightly lighter so you can see a difference between the two. More than two colors can be represented through this process, but it's hard to tell the difference among the colors. Never take a blueline out into the sun. While some shops stabilize these proofs against light, they still fade quickly.

Matchprints and Cromalins

Matchprints and Cromalins are color proofs that are created from four layers of plastic representing cyan, magenta, yellow, and black. Extra layers are added to the proof to represent spot colors created with Pantone colors, although these layers may not accurately reflect the actual spot color you specify. (One Matchprint we received used a dark chocolate brown to "simulate" a pale cream color. It made parts of the proof completely unreadable where the would-be cream was overprinted with copy.)

Use Matchprints and Cromalins (called "chromes" by some) to check color within separations, screen colors, and tints of other colors. If used to show the entire untrimmed pages of a job, check them also for correct assembly. Both of these proofs are precise in rendering color because of the accuracy of the process and the lamination of the layers that removes the air space found in color keys. In some cases these proofs may be mounted to a sample of the paper that will be used to run the job, to give a more accurate impression of how the color will look. One disadvantage of Matchprints and Cromalins is that they often look better than the actual job when it's on press.

Dummies

Not to be confused with incompetent service bureau personnel, these are proofs of the physical design of a piece made up by a printer or sometimes by a paper company. They consist of a sample of the paper to be used, assembled into the format of the finished piece but left completely blank.

Use dummies to evaluate papers under consideration for an expensive job. With a dummy proof you can get a realistic idea of how your finished piece will feel. For example, if you choose a paper that's not heavy enough for a brochure project, a dummy made up from that paper will be flimsy. This shows you that another paper should be selected.

> ### Tip: Writing on Proofs
>
> Most proofs are impervious to conventional writing media. Bluelines have smooth unabsorbent surfaces, and other proofs are made of shiny plastic. Pens, pencils, and water-based felt pens won't work for marking corrections, and you do want these marks to be noticeable and clear in their intent. Two instruments that will mark on proofs are grease pencils (messy) and solvent-based markers (smelly). If you plan to print color jobs and will be responsible for checking proofs, buy a few of these pens or pencils at an art supply store.

Color Keys

Color keys are color proofs used to show the entire layout of a job. Like Matchprints and Cromalins, they consist of four layers of plastic—one each for cyan, magenta, yellow, and black. Extra layers are added to represent additional spot colors if used. Unlike Matchprints, these proofs remain as separate layers tacked down only on one side. This allows you to lift the layers and study each color individually. Color in color keys is not as accurate as that created in Matchprints, because the film material has a faint yellow tint to it.

Proofing Checklist

Use this form to ensure that you check proofs for mistakes and problems before heading into print.

Job Name _____ Date _____ Proof Created by _____

Checking bluelines and other non-color proofs

- ☐ Look for correct alignment of text, headlines, visuals, and other components.
- ☐ Check for broken type and glitches carefully.
- ☐ Reread copy one last time for mistakes.
- ☐ If second color shows on proof (as screen), check that each object in the proof is the correct color.
- ☐ Check that previous corrections have been made correctly.
- ☐ Check that all fold, trims, die cuts, and other bindery processes are correct.
- ☐ Measure the finished size of the piece.
- ☐ Mark all corrections clearly on the proof. Go over the corrections verbally as well with whoever will make the changes.
- ☐ Have another set of eyes check the proof.
- ☐ Discuss the charges (if any) and schedule for making the changes.
- ☐ Sign off that the job is "okay as is," "okay with changes marked," or "make changes and submit new proof."

Checking color proofs

Kind of proof: Matchprint ☐ Color Key ☐ Cromalin ☐ Other _____

- ☐ If the proof shows the entire layout, check everything listed above for black and white proofs.
- ☐ Check that the correct colors are used. (Color keys may substitute a related color to indicate spot color overlays.)
- ☐ Check the color in color images. Look for shifts in color, particularly in human faces, food, and fabrics.
- ☐ Check that detail is still present in image highlights and shadow areas.
- ☐ Match color images against original photo or illustration if possible.
- ☐ Check that all images appear crisp and in focus. Check that process color images are in register.
- ☐ Check screen colors and process color images for moiré patterns. Match screen colors against swatch book.
- ☐ Check the registration in the proof, particularly where colors abut each other.
- ☐ Check images for correct cropping, position, and that the right image is in the right place.
- ☐ Check that images are not "flopped" (turned backward).
- ☐ Mark all flaws, glitches, and holes in colors.
- ☐ Mark all corrections clearly on the proof. Go over the corrections verbally as well with whoever will make the changes.
- ☐ Have another set of eyes check the proof.
- ☐ Discuss the charges (if any) and schedule for making the changes.
- ☐ Sign off that the job is "okay as is," "okay with changes marked," or "make changes and submit new proof."

Use color keys to check your color job for correct assembly. **Also use** them to look at each layer of color for problems.

The Press Check

Press checks are the last stage of proofing, where the job is seen on press the way it will print. Press checks are discussed in detail in Chapter Twelve.

How to Read a Proof

Each of these proofs has advantages and disadvantages. Depending on where you do business and the complexity of your job, you may see multiple proofs. A color key and blueline may be assembled to allow you to check the job's assembly, and Cromalin proofs may be used to check color separations. Knowing what to look for is important so that you can identify errors before they make it onto press. You may also go through more than one set of proofs as problems are identified and corrections made. When you are satisfied with the job, most print shops will make you sign a stamped or adhesive-backed approval form mounted on the proof. Before taking this big step, make sure that everything is right! The checklist explains what to look for in each type of proof.

Film, Paper, or Plates?

When bringing a job to an SB for imaging, one of the most fundamental choices to be made is the kind of media you want to output on—resin-coated paper (RC paper), film, or at some bureaus, plates. Yes, some service bureaus will create plastic plates for you, and a new metal plate technology is emerging that can produce plates directly from your Mac files. Your selection will not only affect the charges for output but will affect the material quality of the job. The least expensive output medium is paper. Film is more expensive and plates vary considerably in price, with metal plates being substantially more expensive than plastic. The following are some pointers on when and when not to use each medium:

Resin-coated Paper

As the least expensive output medium, RC paper beckons. Unfortunately, RC paper is limited in the screen resolution it can handle. And, before a printer can plate, a negative must be made from the paper as well, resulting in charges that easily outweigh the initial low cost at the service bureau. Also, shooting film of paper means another generation of repro-duction has been used, resulting in resolution loss and dot gain.

Use RC paper for jobs without fine screens. RC paper is usually imaged as a positive, and it makes a good, easy-to-read proof, unlike film negatives. Any element that will be pasted down into a traditional mechanical layout should be output as RC paper, unless the printer will handle the task during stripping.

Don't use RC paper for jobs with critical registration (most color work) because it may stretch slightly and change shape with humidity and tem-perature. Don't use it for high-resolution screens or halftones either—its limit in imaging capability is somewhere around 90 to 100 lpi. Finer screens lose their dot structure on RC paper.

Film

Almost all jobs should be output on film. Film can handle extremely fine screens and is a very stable medium. With adequate storage, film output can last for decades, making it the medium of choice for jobs that may be reprinted over several years. Run correctly, it can be used directly to make plates, nearly eliminating the risk that dots will change size or shape dur-ing copying in a printer's stripping department.

Use film for all jobs that are ready for press and preferably for any job with screens finer than 100 lpi. (You can certainly use film for jobs with coarser screens as well.) Film is the medium of choice for almost all needs.

Don't use film for jobs requiring paste-up. Don't run film at a service bureau not equipped for the job—instead of using paper, use another SB.

Tip: When Is a Negative Not a Negative?

Be careful about using the words *film* and *negative* interchangeably. While in most circumstances the service bureau and print shop people will know what you're talking about, there are film positives as well as negatives. Film positives are created when you don't click the **Invert Image** and **Flip Horizontal** checkboxes within the **Options** dialog found in Apple's **Page Set-Up** menu. (Aldus Prep offers this feature as well. It's called **Invert** and **Mirror** and found in Aldus Prep's **Options** dialog.) Film positives are used for jobs that require future conversion, and occasionally plates are burned from positives instead of negatives. In the same vein, you can print "negatives" on RC paper, but you'll rarely want to.

Definition: Right-reading Emulsion Down

There are two ways you can order film—emulsion up and emulsion down. Your printer—or in the case of an ad, your media supplier—will make this decision for you. But it helps to understand what *right-reading emulsion down* means when they specify this for your job.

A sheet of film has two sides (obviously). One side is covered with a material that is chemically altered by the presence of light after processing—this is the emulsion. The other side is simply uncoated plastic. When examining film, you can identify which side is which by holding the exposed sheet to reflect light. The coated side will appear much less reflective (dull) than the uncoated side.

When film is processed for use in print, either side can be face up when it is exposed. If the wrong side is exposed, the emulsion side may be too far from the target media, because the thin layer of clear plastic diffuses light. This may alter the image. So, terminology has evolved for correctly specifying the film properties. They are:

- **Right-reading**   Right-reading means that you can read the copy, because the type is oriented normally and not backward.

- **Emulsion Down**   When a negative is right-reading emulsion down, the type should be correctly oriented and readable (not backward), and the emulsion should be on the far side of the neg, not on the side you are looking at.

- **Emulsion Up**   Film is specified as emulsion up for silk screen printing. In this case, when you can read the type, the emulsion should be toward you rather than on the back of the film.

- **Flopped**   During handling, film can be accidentally turned upside down and make it into print that way (we know because we've done it!). If the wrong side of the film is used, type will be backward, and any recognizable landmarks such as cityscapes will appear embarrassingly backward to readers.

Press Plates as Output

Plastic press plates can be imaged just like film or paper. Metal plates can be produced with a special plate imaging system. The obvious advantage of "plating" is that it removes a generation of reproduction, namely the image transfer from negative to plate. Plating technology continues to improve, but in most cases the plates should be left to your print shop, because plating is very technical business, and a lot can go wrong. Press personnel are very particular about the plates they run. If you find a foolhardy print shop willing to run your self-produced plates, and something goes wrong with the job, it will be your problem and not the print shop's.

Use imagesetter-generated plates only if they're produced by the same shop that will print the job! This way if the resulting quality is poor, you can refuse to accept the job, and the onus will be on the print shop to fix the problems and reprint for no additional charge. Avoid this route unless the shop that will output and print the job can provide credible evidence in the form of well-printed pieces of similar complexity that were plated directly from their imagesetter.

Five Common Service Bureau Problems

There are some predictable problems you are likely to encounter when working with service bureaus. Here are the five most common ones in our experience.

1. VM Error or File Fails to Image

Probably the most dreaded error in running an imagesetter, a VM error (or Virtual Memory error) has been around for a long time. It usually means that something in your project has overstepped the boundaries in the service bureau's RIP memory capabilities.

Tip: Dealing with Odd Imagesetter Results

Occasionally a TIFF or PICT file just won't print on the imagesetter and leaves a blank spot where an image should be. Or, the image produced on the imagesetter doesn't look like what you see on the screen (maddening, to say the least). You can test for this problem to some degree by inspecting proofs run on a laser printer or color PostScript printer, but something that looks fine on your printer may still not image. Deal with this problem by rubbing a lucky rabbit's foot, converting the graphic file into EPS, and then rerunning the file on the imagesetter. This simple solution solves a wide range of problems and keeps color desktop publishers from going more than half crazy. (Read also about LaserCheck in Chapter Fourteen.)

What to Do about It

There are two courses of action to consider when the service bureau simply can't make the job image: 1) go to another bureau using a RIP with larger memory capacity; or 2) simplify your job. Consider breaking large, complex spreads into single pages and running them one at a time. Or, take large separated images and illustrations out of the job and image them separately. Then have your print shop strip them back into the job. While the second approach costs more, both at the bureau for film and for labor on the part of the print shop, it's better than recreating the job from scratch.

2. PostScript Errors and Mistakes

Depending on the software you use to create a job, a number of PostScript-based problems may creep into it. (Would-be PostScript programmers take note.) These may manifest themselves in the form of a file that images but has elements missing, moved around, or drawn with odd-looking thin white lines through parts of the job.

What to Do about It

If you are using unreliable software (call service bureaus around town and ask their opinions on what to use before you buy), then you can try to image the job at another bureau and keep your fingers crossed. Choose an SB with a color publishing guru who can help you sort out the mess. Otherwise, strip out potentially troublesome elements. For example, one MacDraw-like illustration program (no longer on the market) is known to image improperly. By pulling illustrations created with such a program out of your file, the rest of the document may image fine. Then, you'll need to purchase new software and redraw those illustrations (if you can't import them into another program). Another related problem is EPS files embedded within EPS files within EPS files. Avoid constructing such files and you will avoid problems trying to image one.

3. Severe Color Shift

This is usually caused by improper or non-existent imagesetter calibration. It can also be caused by setting the dot gain parameters incorrectly, leaving an incorrect transfer function turned on at separation, or bad film processor chemistry.

What to Do about It

Check with bureau personnel before imaging your job and find out when the imagesetter was last properly calibrated and the chemicals checked. Don't take color work to a bureau that doesn't check calibration either daily or every time a job such as yours comes in the door. If the calibration looks okay, then it's time to check your settings and possibly reseparate. After checking, ask your service bureau for advice and make a list of your separation settings for them to review.

4. Long Paths

When creating illustrations in programs such as Illustrator or Freehand, it's tempting to use one long line with many control points to render a complex shape. Autotrace processes also create a long, elaborate tracing for you. The problem is that when imaged, this line may exceed the PostScript interpreter's ability to render the path.

What to Do about It

While illustration programs attempt to automatically compensate for this problem, it still occurs sometimes. If a "Limit Check" error occurs, carefully study your art and reduce the complexity of all long paths by breaking them into smaller pieces. Especially study small autotraced areas. The line may not cover much drawing acreage in such a path, but may be far too complex, running around in tiny circles and curves. Another fix is to use the **Split Long Paths** option or adjust the **Flatness** control to simplify processing and speed up output.

5. Font Substitution Occurred, Fonts Printed as Bitmaps, or Type Moved around on the Page Layout

Fonts sometimes get replaced with other fonts for a variety of reasons. All three of these problems are probably related to font substitution.

What to Do about It

Read Chapter Four's information on fonts and font problems. Discuss the problem(s) with your SB. They may be using a font with the same name produced by another company. This shifts type in paragraphs and may alter the careful kerning of a major headline. Or, you may have included a screen font in your document, such as Cairo, without realizing it. Since there is no outline font available for this cute picture typeface, the imagesetter does its best to image the bitmap of each character. Unfortunately, the results will be ugly at best.

Within this chapter you have learned how to choose a service bureau, specify a job for service bureau processing, and get final output ready for the print shop. You have also learned about proofs and proofing. In the next chapter we'll discuss printing and printers and explain how to choose and work with the right print shop for your job and budget.

CHAPTER

II

CHOOSING A PRINT SHOP FOR YOUR COLOR DTP PROJECT

"You are not an excellent designer until your designs can be printed as designed with the results you intended at the price you were quoted."

—Nancy Aldrich-Ruenzel
Designer's Guide to Print Production

Color printing is a mixture of craft, mechanics, and science. Craft comes into the formula because of the years of practice required to instinctively understand job assembly and press issues. The mechanical process of adjusting and fine-tuning a four-color press is a skill similar to that of the rare auto mechanic who listens to a balky engine and accurately pronounces a cure—without so much as lifting the hood. Science comes into the picture as new ink technologies and color standards are invented, first as theoretical research in a laboratory, then engineered for practical use on press. This process is usually completed by scientists at ink and chemical companies working hand-in-hand with experienced press personnel to iron out the bugs and problems. Without all three of these components acting in harmony, we would not enjoy the relatively low-cost and high-quality reproduction possible in a modern printing plant.

Today, in addition to evolving printing and color technology, technical pioneers are breaking down the barriers between the Macintosh and PostScript output and high-quality four-color printing. Others are working to make the Mac communicate more effectively with high-end prepress systems. The fruits of their labors are already available to the color publisher working on the Mac and willing to take the time to fully understand the mechanics of taking a color job into print. And, as hardware and software engineers join hands to tighten the Mac's control of color and improve imagesetter quality, the craft, mechanics, and science continue to improve the ease of producing quality publications on the Macintosh.

As a color publisher working on the Mac, you need to understand the differences among the print shops you can use for your jobs—and to be able to recognize those who have the combination of craft, mechanics, and science to complete your publications with the quality you require.

You Are Here

You have already read about the color publishing process on the Macintosh from desktop to service bureau. Now it's time to familiarize yourself with the print shop and see how to match the right shop to your job.

This chapter describes print shops and printing tools you'll encounter after leaving the service bureau with your film in hand. The next chapter explains the mechanics of taking a job through production, choosing paper, and checking the job on press. While it would take several volumes to fully explain the printing process, these two chapters will provide you with information and tips to give you a head start on the learning curve. The right shop will help you see your job through print correctly, while providing an education on printing, paper, and color on press.

Note on Printers and Printing

Printing is a tough business to make money in. The high annual mortality even among established shops underscores this sad fact. Many family-owned quick printers run their businesses on a month-to-month basis, barely surviving each cashflow crisis. Large print shops get hit harder than most other kinds of businesses during recessions, because companies economize by putting all expensive print projects on hold. This leaves a large shop with a big payroll and no income.

For this reason, some of the printers and shop personnel you meet are a gruff lot. Try to be understanding, but be sure that you have a least one senior person in the print shop that you can really talk to. This person should also be willing to take your side should a dispute or problem arise that is the shop's fault. Color jobs inevitably run into problems of one sort or another, so if a shop has no one that you can effectively communicate with, find another shop.

Carefully Manage the Process to Avoid Surprises

The best arrangement for taking color publishing jobs through to print is to work with a print shop that has as much experience as possible printing Mac-based color projects. When Macintosh color publishing was introduced into the already complex world of color printing, new problems and surprises were added to the standard ones. A printer experienced with desktop technology will be able to recognize errors originating on the desktop or at the service bureau, as well as those originating on press.

There are (fortunately) ways of avoiding many of these surprises. Choosing the right printer is the first order of business. Second is careful supervision of the job. Third, never rush the printing process. Too often, jobs that are rushed contain serious mistakes that might have otherwise been detected. While many mistakes are introduced in the stripping process (and the Mac reduces stripping), things can still go wrong on the desktop, at the service bureau, and on press. Careful supervision all the way through the process is the only way to bring color documents, whether originated conventionally or on the Mac, into print.

The Three Kinds of Print Shops

For the purposes of this book, we'll discuss only three kinds of printers and what they do best. In many cases a shop will overlap in the kinds of jobs it can handle. There are other printing specialties, such as engraving and silk-screening, as well, but we'll limit the topic to the kinds of printers used by the majority of Macintosh color publishers.

Quick-print Shops

The most common kind of print shop, found in almost every strip mall and city center, is the quick printer. Also known as *instaprinters,* these organizations are at the bottom of the printing quality hierarchy. Usually running a shop with limited equipment and even more limited know-how, quick printers are capable of handling two-color jobs without critical registration and without solids.

Because these printers usually run an inexpensive one-color press with little control of ink or registration, few color publishing jobs will finish in a quick printer's storefront unless bare-bones quality is all that's needed. Quick-print shops provide low prices because they run most jobs on plastic press plates (metal plates are superior and are standard in commercial and specialty print shops), take little time to set up or wash down the press, and cut corners everywhere possible. There are a few quick-print shops in every town that have the equipment and knowledge to handle more complex jobs, but these are the exception rather than the rule.

Typical quick-print projects include business cards, letterhead, and simple one-color brochures measuring less that 11" by 17" before folding.

Use quick printers for:

- One-color jobs printed on non-glossy papers
- Simple two-color jobs where colors don't abut each other
- Jobs without large solid areas of color

Matching Print Shops to a Job

Print Shop	Job Complexity	Kind of Jobs
Quick Printer	One-color jobs without solids	Simple business cards and letterhead
	Two-color jobs without abutting colors	Forms
	Jobs with low resolution halftones	Simple brochures where print quality isn't critical
	Jobs smaller than 11" x 17"	Newsletters
		Flyers
Commercial Printer	Two to four spot color jobs	Brochures with process color image reproduction specified at less than 150 lpi
	Jobs with process color images that don't require high resolution printing	More complex business cards and letterhead
	Jobs too large for a quick printer	Tabloid-style newspapers
	Jobs with a volume too large for a quick printer	Direct mail pieces
	Newsprint jobs (if they accept them)	Catalogs
	Jobs that will run on a web press	Magazines
		Posters with color images printed at less than 150 lpi resolution
		Annual reports without complex color and fancy print treatments
		Most product packaging
Specialty Printer	Two- to eight- color jobs	Elaborate brochures, annual reports, posters, product packaging, and mailers
	Job with complex registration	
	Jobs with high resolution image reproduction	
	Jobs requiring a very experienced shop, such as a six-color annual report employing fancy die cutting, foil stamping, complex registration, and hand assembly	

- Jobs smaller than 11" by 17", because most quick-print presses can't handle large paper sizes
- Jobs with halftones or tints screened at resolutions of 133 lpi or less (preferably less).

Commercial Print Shops

The commercial printer category is a broad one. Commercial shops handle the majority of printing for business, industry, and government. Individual shops are usually situated in large factory-like buildings within an industrial park. The variety of services proffered ranges from long runs of one- and two-color jobs, to newsprint work, to some brochures. Some commercial shops have four-color presses and take on the kind of work usually reserved for specialty printers, although their quality is rarely as good.

While there are fewer commercial plants than quick printers, these shops account for the majority of the printing business in most cities. Relying primarily on regular income from established accounts, a commercial shop does everything from color separation (often handled in house) to bindery. Some even perform the labeling and mailing for direct mail programs.

Commercial shops are best at industrial product brochures, catalogs, newsprint jobs, most books and manuals, and simple product packaging.

Use commercial printers for:

- Work on newsprint if they handle it
- Two- to four-color jobs run at less than 150 lpi
- Jobs run on web presses if they own one (webs are explained later in the chapter)
- Simple cardboard product packaging
- Long runs of simple jobs. While these jobs may normally head for the quick printer, an unusually long run can often be economically printed at a commercial shop that will deliver superior quality.

Specialty Printers

Specialty printers (sometimes known as art printers) are the most capable print shops, typically employing several four- or six-color presses. Specialty printers use the best equipment and hire only the most careful and experienced stripping room and press personnel. Their press people are recruited from commercial print shops only after they've honed their skills for a period of years and proven themselves capable of maintaining quality and recognizing errors that will cause surprises on press.

Specialty print shops tend to be smaller in physical size than a commercial printer's plant. Instead of the long row of presses found in a commercial shop, there may be only two or three presses and no webs, because a web can't produce the quality requirements demanded by a specialty printer. Few specialty shops do their own color separations, because they recognize that quality color is best left to a professional color separation house.

Specialty printers excel in assembling and printing complex color projects such as high-quality annual reports, elaborate brochures, color posters, coffee table books, and any color project printed at more than 133 lines per inch and up to as much as 600 lpi (rare).

Use specialty printers for any job that requires high-quality color reproduction and lots of attention.

The Printer's Equipment

When most people think of a print shop, they think of ink and presses—but there are other components of a print shop that you should consider. While the print shop of the future may consist of little more than a press or two and an imagesetter with some kind of proofing set-up, today they contain many tools and facilities. A typical well-equipped shop includes complete stripping facilities with massive camera equipment and color separation facilities. In a big plant, these may take up several rooms (or full floors in a giant shop located in a major city). Of course, in the case of a quick-print shop, all of the equipment is usually set up in an area the size of a living room.

The Stripping Room

In conventional publishing, the stripping room is where the mechanical art produced by a designer goes through a series of processes to create the film that will eventually be converted into press plates. The room centers around the camera equipment used to copy type and design elements into film. *Strippers* process the individual components of the job, add any screens required, and assemble final negatives, ready to plate. Most of this work is done on massive light tables equipped with large steel straightedges that track along carefully machined metal tables. For precision tasks, a stripper may work through a magnifying loupe during the lengthy assembly process. It is during stripping that your halftones and color separations are added to other film components, if they aren't output with film at the service bureau.

Along with integrating individual components in the negatives, strippers often assemble individual pages into "flats." A flat is constructed of the pages that will print together on one side of a sheet of paper. For example, a multi-page brochure may have eight pages printed on the same side of the paper and trimmed down later for assembly into a completed brochure. This is much cheaper and more efficient than printing two pages at a time on a smaller sheet of paper. It also helps the shop maintain better color consistency throughout the job, because colors for groups of pages can be compared and adjusted at one time.

Once the final flats are assembled into plate-sized masks, the plates are burned for each flat. In the case of a four-color job, four plates are burned for each four-color flat. Once plates are burned, the stripping room's job is complete, unless a plate proves to be defective or is damaged in the process of mounting onto the press (common).

Job Costing and Accounting

While not a part of the shop that you'll pay much attention to unless you pay your printing bills late, the accounting side of the business is vital to keeping a shop profitable. On the input side is the job costing section that takes job specifications from salespeople and creates an estimate of how much to charge before the job is accepted. Bookkeepers track how much jobs actually cost in material and labor and handle the billing of customers. Because it's easy for shops to underbid jobs and lose money as a result, accounting keeps close tabs on the estimators and salespeople to ensure that the shop doesn't run at a loss. And, since deadbeat customers are very common in the printing business, a shop may also have an active collections person working to keep the cash flowing in.

The Presses You'll Meet

There are a wide variety of presses used for commercial printing. Specialized presses are available for printing almost everything. There are presses for producing the giant panels for billboard ads and ones for printing on "unprintable" media such as cellophane and plasticized foils. Presses vary considerably in age, size, and price, as well. For example, a tiny quick printer's press, not much bigger than a floor-standing office copier, is priced between $10,000 and $40,000 and can be moved around town in a pickup truck. At the other end of the scale is the massive web press that requires custom concrete foundations, costs multi-millions of dollars, and requires a team of construction workers for installation.

Presses that are multi-color-capable are purchased by the number of stations. Each station can lay down a single color and contains an ink reservoir, inking rollers, a drum to hold and rotate the plate, a rubber blanket that transfers the image, and a mechanism that moves paper through the press. You can look at most presses and count the available stations. In addition to printing stations, presses have a paper-loading system that moves paper into the press and a stacking mechanism that handles the printed sheets at the end of the press. Paper is dried with electric heaters before being stacked. Powder that resembles coarse talcum powder is also applied to keep the slightly wet sheets from sticking together.

A five-color press made by Heidelberg of Germany. This unit is approximately the size of three passenger cars parked end to end.

Sheetfed Presses

The most common presses you'll work with in color publishing are the sheetfed presses made by companies such as Heidelberg, Miehle, Miller, Komori, Maruka, Royal Zenith, and a few others. These units have price tags of $500,000 to $2.5 million, or more. They are priced according to the number of color stations, the size of paper the press can handle, and the kind of high-tech ink control system used. Capable of incredible precision and unworldly ink perfection, these presses, in the hands of the right press operator, can print at resolutions up to 600 lpi (or, in theory, more), although most quality color work is printed between 133 and 200 lpi.

Smaller presses may be used as well. There are a number of intermediate-size machines that handle two-color work and are a notch above the machines quick printers use in both ink and registration control. A large print shop may have several full-size presses and one or two of these smaller machines for short-run two-color jobs that can be economically run on smaller sheets of paper.

Definition: Sheetfed versus Rollfed Presses

Two kinds of paper handling, used to feed presses, fundamentally define the kinds of jobs the presses are suited for. Sheetfed presses are fed by pre-cut sheets of paper. Rollfed presses use large rolls of papers. Because rollfed presses are capable of much greater printing speed, they are used for publications such as printing newspapers and high-volume, large-circulation magazines.

Rollfed presses tend to have less accurate registration than sheetfed presses because of the speed and the stretching of the paper as it runs through the press. For color publishing, you need to be aware of the nature of the press, because larger traps must be used to compensate for machines with limited registration precision.

Quick-print Presses

While small quick-print presses are sheetfed, they have little in common with the big presses described above. These are small presses, often referred to as "duplicators" by experienced press people. They offer limited paper capacity, little control of registration, and have a habit of printing a thick globs of ink rather than a thin, consistent layer. While these machines have their place, most color work requires a degree of precision beyond their capabilities. There are small presses in this category that print more than one color, but few quick printers we've used own one.

Web Presses

Webs are rollfed presses that get their name from the whizzing streams of paper that run back and forth on rollers before entering the press. This looks vaguely like a spider's web and hence the name. Printers also refer to the roll of paper going through the press as a web.

A large web press takes up two stories in a room the size of a gym. Paper feeds from monstrous rolls (you don't want to change paper too often) and winds back and forth from the ceiling to the floor several times before entering the press. Because of the high-speed paper travel, a big web uses a gas-fired oven (instead of using electric heating coils) to cook the ink onto and into the paper so it won't stick together.

Web presses are usually more economical for large print runs. If you are going to print 500,000 press sheets, it's time to start looking for a print shop with a good web press—a sheetfed press would not be economical, though you should usually let the printers' bids and the desired quality determine this choice.

Jobs and Bids

The first question that comes to mind when embarking on a color project is, "How much is it going to cost?" And for good reason, because top-quality color printing is expensive. A big corporation producing a showy seven-color annual report may spend more than $200,000 just for printing. (A seven-color job may include cyan, magenta, yellow, and black, plus two solid PMS colors and a gloss varnish.) Of course, a simple two-color brochure small enough to fit in an envelope may cost less than $1,000.

Printers put a lot of work into the bidding process. They know that unless the price is right, you may take your work elsewhere or simply cancel the project because it costs more than it's worth. On the other side of the coin, print shops have to ensure that they make money on every job. Frequently, a job shows up at the print shop's door with pictures, pages, and problems not accounted for in the original estimate. For this reason printers usually build in very specific descriptions of the job as part of the bid. If the job you deliver doesn't match this description, then expect the price to change.

What Color Publishers Pay for at the Print Shop

Printers charge to cover their expenses, including the rent, power (big presses use lots of it), labor, materials, and sales commissions. There is also a "cost of doing business." Mostly accounted for in the form of time wasted courting customers who end up taking their business elsewhere, there is also money spent on reprinting botched jobs. A shop that has to regularly reprint jobs because of incompetence or poorly maintained equipment rarely stays in business long.

Your bill is calculated by estimating how many hours will be required in the stripping room and on press. Time on a big four-color press runs several hundred dollars per hour, depending on the size of the press. This rate includes a press foreman and one or two helpers who move paper, check adjustments, and attempt to learn the trade in order to become foremen themselves. The time and the rate will be affected by the quality required for your job—rated as basic, good, premium, and showcase. The better the quality, the higher the hourly rate and the more hours required to assure that your quality specifications are met. This makes it difficult to compare one bid to another, because the quality standards might be quite different. It is important that you verify that you are comparing apples to apples when evaluating the bids of two different printers.

There are also charges for the materials your job will use. In most jobs, the largest single material expense is for the paper. Depending on the paper selection and length of the press run (the number of brochures, catalogs, mailers, or books to be printed), paper may constitute ten to 40 percent of the total cost of the job. Of course, the print shop buys paper and marks it up, so they often make money selling paper as well as on the rest of the job. There are also charges for materials such as plates, film, and ink. And don't forget shipping if the job's final destination isn't around the corner.

Get Three Detailed Bids on Color Jobs

Because color printing becomes expensive fast, you'll want to choose the least expensive print shop that can deliver the quality you need. In the case of a pricey press run, shaving a percentage or two off a big bill saves thousands of dollars. To help you do this, get three competitive bids (in writing) and compare them carefully. When requesting bids, let each shop know you are asking others for bids. This helps keep them competitive.

The bids resulting from your inquiries should be detailed. An estimate consisting of no more than "Brochure Job - 5,000 Copies - $14,236" is of little use, because you don't know if the shop took everything into account when they quoted the job. Simplistic quotes leave the door open to unexpected price increases. Your acceptance of such a bid allows the shop to claim that they didn't know in advance that your job was four-color and so they quoted on black and white. While this is an extreme example, lesser overages routinely occur and send you scurrying back to your client or boss to explain why the bill is more than anticipated.

The only exception to getting a detailed bid is when a simple job is run at a quick printer. Most small shops have no formal bidding process and often estimate jobs while looking at the work over the counter.

Should you request a written bid, unless the job is for more than several hundred dollars, they'll give you a blank stare or scribble numbers in pencil on the back of a piece of notepaper to create a "written bid." You can protect yourself, however, by making notes as you discuss the job's costs with the shop's owner.

When you've reviewed the bids and you find that all of them are priced within one percent of each other, either the shops charge very similar rates or their pricing is fixed (rare but not unheard of). When in doubt about the integrity of a quote, get a bid from a shop in another city and compare it. See *Five Ways to Save Money at the Print Shop* in Chapter Fourteen for details.

Should your job change significantly between the time it's quoted and when it's ready for the printer, have the shop you've selected do a new bid. Don't accept a verbal adjustment of, "It'll be just a couple of hundred dollars more." With color printing, an increase of a couple of hundred dollars often becomes a couple of thousand on the final bill.

Get a Schedule

If you have a realistic idea of when art will be ready for the printer and the timing is tight, ask for a schedule. Because a shop may have several one- and two-color presses, but only one four-color unit, it may be difficult to get a *press window*. (A press window is the time and date your job will most likely run. Windows change as other jobs come in late or develop problems and require extra press time.) So, while a black and white job may sail through a shop in a day or two, a four-color job may take a week or more, particularly if the four-color press is fully booked. (Presses are named by their capacity in the shops that own them. The four-color Heidelberg press will be referred to as "the four-color" in most shops.) To create a schedule, the printer will evaluate his workflow and calculate in writing:

- When the job will arrive at the shop
- When work will be sent out for outside work, such as color separation, and when the separations will be complete
- When the job will be ready to proof and how long the client has to check each one before delaying the press window
- When the job will be plated and the time and date of the press check (this date always changes); this is when you have to be there—so expect to be called at any moment
- And last, when the job will finish in bindery and be delivered.

Unfortunately some shops are far more realistic than others in scheduling jobs. So, until you've worked with a shop for a while, you'll really have no idea how well they estimate job timing. One shop we use does wonderful work at reasonable prices, typically quotes a three- to five-day turnaround for color jobs, but typically delivers in ten to twelve days. However, since we already know this, we simply add seven working days to their estimates to determine a realistic date.

Choosing the Right Printer for Macintosh Color Publishing Projects

When choosing a printer for a color publishing project, your task is to match the right kind of shop with the best price for the work at hand. If your job will finish in close to final form at the service bureau, complete with traps and separations, it helps considerably to use a print shop that prints a lot of projects originating on the Macintosh. These organizations help you identify and iron out problems that an ordinary printer won't know to look for. Unfortunately, a few shops have had experiences where a desktop-based job came out wrong in print and they got blamed for it. These printers may look on your work with disdain and suggest that they will print the job only if *you* accept responsibility for any problems. Don't agree to work on this basis—instead, find a printer with Mac experience.

Steps for Locating a Printer

Here is the process we use to locate a prospective printer:

1. Look for Shops

Identify prospective printers through referrals from other color publishers or from a service bureau that handles color work. Also consider any shop with an in-house Mac-based service bureau that handles color jobs.

2. Call and Discuss Your Job

Call the shop and discuss the project. Initially discourage salespeople who want to come out and meet you. At this point, find out whether they like taking on Mac-based color projects and what level of experience and success they have had with them. Ask them what kind of color Mac-originated projects they have printed and how complete the project was when it arrived at their shop. (If your job includes Mac-produced color separations, don't use a shop that hasn't worked with such a project previously.)

3. Visit the Shops

If you like what you hear, make an appointment to visit the shops you liked on the phone. Then meet the salesperson and review a sketch of your job. Ask to take a plant tour if it isn't offered automatically. What kind of equipment and presses do they have? Is it clean, well-organized, and well-lit, or are there piles of clutter and dirty rags laying around? What do the presses look like? Are they antiques that belong in a museum or are they modern with the appearance of regular cleaning and careful maintenance? If a job is running, watch the press personnel in action. Are they swarming like bees over the machine, checking details and making minor adjustments, or do they start the press, make a few quick adjustments, and head for a long coffee break? If you meet the shop's personnel, managers, and owners, ask yourself if you would feel comfortable working with them or whether they seem gruff or aloof. (Hurried and busy is okay.)

4. Study Each Shop's Samples

Look for work that at least equals your project in complexity and study each piece for crisp color, clean solid areas of ink, perfect registration in process color images (unless the work is on inexpensive paper), and a lack of glitches and hickies (defined in the glossary). The shop should have a number of samples they are proud to show you.

Tip: Don't Let Special Treatment Sway You

Don't be swayed by a particularly solicitous printing rep or owner. Good manners and friendly behavior are no substitute for years of experience and adequate equipment. If your job costs more than $10,000 to print, it's not uncommon for printers to use free lunches or other incentives to cloud your judgement. Be careful of such perks, because they won't get your job printed properly, and you may end up with the wrong shop.

5. Get Three Quotes and Choose

Get quotes from the three shops you were most impressed with. Don't make the final selection on price alone, but on the overall impression of the shop, its print quality, and its Macintosh color publishing experience.

Checklist for Selecting a Print Shop

Use this checklist to evaluate print shops that are "desktop color publishing compatible."

Print Shop Basics

Shop Name _____ Phone # _____ Years in Business _____
Sales representative or contact name: _____

In-House Service Bureau

Do they have a Mac-based service bureau in house? Yes ☐ No ☐

What Kind of Mac-based Color Publishing Project has this Shop Taken into Print?

None ☐ Spot Color ☐ Screen Color ☐ Mac-Produced Color Illustrations ☐
Process Color Images ☐
Who produced the final ready-to-plate film? A service bureau output the job directly using
the color desktop publisher's files and settings (Better). Yes ☐ No ☐
The print shop assembled the job in the stripping room (Worse). Yes ☐ No ☐

What Kind of Print Shop Is It?

What kind of presses do they own? (Check All) One Color ☐ Two Color ☐
Four (or more) Color ☐ Web ☐
What kind of proofs and proofing systems does the shop use? (Check All)
Blueline ☐ Color Keys ☐ Matchprint ☐ Cromalin ☐ Other _____
What services do they have in house? (Check All) Folding and Saddle Stitching ☐
Die Cutting ☐ Foil Stamping ☐
How many employees work in the shop? Small Shop 1-10 ☐ Medium Shop 11-40 ☐
Large Shop 40+ ☐
What do most of the shop's samples consist of? Cards, letterhead, and one-color jobs ☐
(Probably a quick printer.)
Two-, three- and four-color mailers, catalogs, datasheets, brochures, and newsprint jobs ☐
(Probably a commercial shop.)
Expensive-looking brochures, posters, annual reports, and product packaging ☐
(Probably a specialty or art printer.)

Rate the Shop Overall

Rate the shop from 1 to 10 on order and cleanliness _____
Rate your contact at the shop on a scale of 1 to 10 ____
Rate the shop's samples from 1 to 10 on order and cleanliness _____
Overall rating from 1 to 10 _____

If your job is complicated, and high-quality is required, consider using the highest bidder if their work and approach is significantly better and your job demands it. In some cases, a top-quality specialty printer quotes as much as ten to twenty percent more than a standard specialty printer, because no corners are cut in the work.

Three Kinds of Printers to Avoid

There are three kinds of print shops to stay away from at all costs:

1. Shops with Crusty Owners or Reps

As mentioned, many people working in printing burn out after a while and treat their work as something mundane or boring. If you find a print shop manager or owner irksome when placing an order, think how they'll be if you have a problem to iron out.

> **Tip: Just an Ugly Rumor…**
>
> In discussions with several service bureaus that handle complex color jobs, a topic came up that we would just as soon disbelieve—the deliberate sabotage of color publishing jobs originating on the Mac. Apparently there have been numerous reports of stripping room personnel damaging art or using it to incorrectly assemble or plate jobs so that the work prints poorly. The reported reason for this activity is that stripping room personnel are resentful of desktop color publishing because they believe it will take away their jobs. Unfortunately, it just might.

2. Printers Who Will Take on Any Kind of Job

When interviewing printers, if they claim they can print anything from one-color quick-print jobs to six-color annual reports, it means they'll take any kind of job even without the equipment, expertise, and integrity to handle it. They may be hard up for business because the shop's quality is low and customers don't come back. No printer has the resources to handle every kind of job, unless the company owns several independent printing facilities (rare).

A simple job that should be run at a quick printer will cost substantially more if run on a large press. While a quick printer may charge $25 an hour for assembly, a large shop charges considerably more. On the other end of the scale, no quick-print shop provides the quality required for multi-colored printing with tight registration and process color images, even if they could fit the job on their limited presses.

3. Printers That Bid Too Low

If you get three bids and two are within a few of percent of each other, but one is twenty to 30 percent less, a red flag should be raised. It may mean that you've had the job bid at two specialty printers and a commercial shop accidentally. Or, it may point to a shop with poor estimating ability. Such a shop probably has management and cashflow problems. If they aren't good at managing their estimating or are willing to "buy the job" just to get much-needed cash, assume they aren't good at printing either.

Consider Using a Print Broker

If you are new to color printing as well as color publishing, you can buy printing through a broker, an approach that can help you choose the right print shop and effectively manage the process. Found in the *Yellow Pages* under *Printing Brokers,* a broker is a person or small company that fills in as salesperson in return for a percentage of the job's price (paid by the print shop). Usually handling projects with price tags above the $5,000 level, a good broker has years of color printing experience and may have worked as an estimator in a print shop before starting out on his or her own.

The right broker knows the business backward and forward and can help you save money through a number of workarounds and elegant corner-cutting steps in the stripping room, at the color separation house (if you use one), and on press. The right broker makes the job proceed more smoothly, and since the commission is rarely much more than the printer's salespeople receive, working through a broker won't cost much more than dealing with the shop's own salesperson. As an added benefit, you get the advantage of having a knowledgeable person on your side to help you out.

When shopping for a broker look for:

- One with considerable experience in a printing shop
- One who works with a number of shops and isn't just a front-man for his brother's printing business

- One with whom you feel comfortable working
- One who has experience with color publishing projects produced on the Mac. Once a rare commodity, brokers are coming up to speed on Mac-based publishing because of demand.

The right broker will carefully study your job and recommend several shops capable of providing the required level of service at the right price. The broker will also solicit the bids and explain each one to you. Once the bids are in, your broker can help you narrow the choices to two or three shops and allow you to make the final selection. Once the job goes to press, the broker transports the art, supervises the proofing process, and ensures that the printer keeps to the schedule (tough). When the time comes for a press check, your broker will accompany you to the press check and put an experienced eye to the task. If the shop is in another city, the broker will in most cases arrange transport and accommodations and take you out to lunch or dinner. By watching a pro in action, you get a free education on choosing and working with print shops.

One Kind of Broker to Avoid

There is one kind of printing broker that you want to avoid at all costs. While most brokers are knowledgeable, honest people, a few aren't. Instead of attempting to match your job to the right press with the best price, this kind of broker matches jobs to shops that pay the biggest commissions. Because a printer must be really desperate for work to agree to these terms, it may mean the shop is so incompetent that no one gives them any business. You obviously don't want to send a job to a printer like this. You may also pay more, because the shop still has the usual manpower, equipment and material costs. And, to pay the broker's larger-than-normal fee, they charge you extra. There are three giveaways for this kind of charlatan.

1. Travel to Faraway Places

While it's common to print expensive color jobs in other cities when the right kind of quality and price can't be had locally, a broker who suggests a little shop he knows five states away may not be looking after your best interests. Unless he can explain in clear, concise terms why your job should go to this shop, steer clear. Free airline tickets and hotel are standard for such travel. Don't consider these perks to be special treatment—they are quietly added to the bill at any print shop that "pays" for transportation and lodging.

2. A Trip by Rail

If he suggests only one local shop or presents several printer's bids but attempts to railroad you into one in particular, this may indicate a "special" commission arrangement.

3. The Sky's the Limit

If you are suspicious of a printer selected by your broker because the price estimate appears unexpectedly high, quietly get the job quoted through another broker. If the second broker's price is more than five percent cheaper and the shops are comparable, there may be a problem.

In this chapter you have learned the basics of printing and print shops and how to match the right printer to your color publishing project. If you locate a shop that takes your project on and enthusiastically embraces Macintosh color publishing, the printing will go more smoothly. When visiting shops or talking to the press personnel, ask questions about the process and get their suggestions for ways to avoid problems.

Shops that work with Mac-based color publishers may also be aware of other color publishers in town you should meet with to compare notes and experiences. Once you tie into the Macintosh color publishing networks springing up in every city, other publishers will share their expertise with you and recommend service bureaus and print shops with desktop publishing expertise to make your work easier and give you better results.

In the next chapter, we'll visit the print shop while it's processing your job and see how to manage the printing process to a successful conclusion.

CHAPTER

12

PRINTING—PROCEDURES, PAPER, PROOFING, AND PRESS CHECKS

"I've been running presses in this town for over twenty years. The whole process of printing breaks down to making an enormous number of little corrections to an enormous number of little things that are always going wrong. You wouldn't believe all the things that can go wrong with a printing job on press. Lots of customers don't appreciate that. Some of them think that all it takes to run a press is enough sense to keep my fingers out from between the rollers. Sure there are sloppy printers, but often the fault lies with the customer who provides dirty mechanicals and blah photos and then expects us to work miracles."

— An Anonymous Quote in
Getting It Printed

Printing terminology is bantered about freely by everyone in the print shop and at the service bureau. Initially, it confuses everyone new to color publishing. Even designers with ten years of experience printing color jobs often have to ask what a word or phrase means. While the glossary at the back of the book will help, a print shop manager explaining that a "number two dull-coated sheet will take the solids without holdout problems while keeping the screens open," is confusing at best. In this chapter, we'll not only look at technical printing terminology, but also the entire process of taking a color publishing job through the print shop.

You Are Here

In the last chapter we looked at the various kinds of print shops and discussed how to choose one. In this chapter we cover the printing processes in more detail and have included a printing specification worksheet you can use as a checklist before contacting any printers. This sheet can be photocopied and sent to shops as a request for a bid. By answering these questions up front, you receive precise quotes because the nature of your job is clearly defined.

Another important topic we'll look at in this chapter is paper. Because different papers require adjustments to color separations on your part, the selection of paper is directly related to how you handle the design and program settings on the Macintosh. For example, if you specify a super-glossy paper for a brochure or direct mail piece, certain print shops may not be able to print on it (especially quick printers and inept commercial shops), although in most cases that won't stop them from trying. Gloss finishes are also difficult to read because of reflection. Choosing a dull-coated paper eliminates both problems. This chapter covers the basic information that color publishers should know about papers.

The Ten-step Color Printing Process

Much like creating color publications on the desktop, the process of getting a color publication printed follows an orderly series of steps from start to finish. Depending on how much of the job you handle yourself, your publication may follow the entire path, or it may skip steps and reach the print shop nearly ready for press. For example, if your job is a simple one run at a quick-print shop, the proofing phase will usually be skipped all together (unfortunately). The printing steps for color publications are discussed below

1. A Final Quote Is Made

The print shop reviews the physical particulars of the job (how many copies, number of colors and pages, halftones and color separations, kind of paper, etc.) and generates a preliminary estimate for the job.

> **Tip: Before Stepping into Print, Take a Step Back**
>
> One of the best tools for catching mistakes, if you have time, is to put a color job away for a few days, work on other projects, and then take it out again and study it. Giving your mind time away from an intense project that has become too familiar provides a second chance to identify errors and fix them before going to press.

2. Acceptance of the Job at the Print Shop

The paper or film output by the service bureau is delivered to the print shop, usually by you, so you can go over the job with the printer. The job is reviewed for problems; the quote may be revised if the finished art is different from the specifications in the bid. If everything is okay, the job is accepted by the print shop for preparation and printing.

3. Preprocessing

The job is given a docket number in order to keep track of it for scheduling and job costing purposes. The art is reviewed by the stripping staff and scheduled for stripping and press time. If color separations are required, they are sent out as soon as possible, because conventional separation takes several days if the house handling the job is busy (common).

4. Stripping

Stripping in a Mac-based job may be extensive or minimal, depending on how the color images were processed. Ultimately, the job is assembled in final negative form, ready to burn plates. At this point, you may be shown a blueline proof and one of several color proofs. If color separations are handled conventionally, you'll now see proofs of them as well.

5. Plating

The approved negatives are assembled into opaque orange plastic masks. These masks are the same size as the press plate to be created. Windows are cut into the masks to let light through to the stripped-in negatives. (Masks are used instead of plate-sized negatives because of the cost of large negs and the fact that different plate sizes would require twenty or 30 negative sizes to match all the plate options. Also, only the most expensive imagesetters can produce large negatives.) Once the masks are assembled, they're placed on top of an unexposed plate, and the image is burned with a brilliant light source. The exposed plates are then developed and carefully checked for accuracy.

6. Plating and Inking the Press

The plates are carried to the press room and carefully loaded onto the press. Care is taken so as not to scratch or bump the exposed side, or a replacement plate must be made. Inks are loaded onto the press during this period.

7. Make-ready

Press personnel load the press with junk paper left over from other jobs and start the press. During make-ready, the ink levels are brought up and balanced. Once everything looks good and the inking is stable, the clean paper selected for the job is loaded and the press is restarted. If the job will be press-checked, you will be there at this point to approve it.

The Printing Process Step by Step

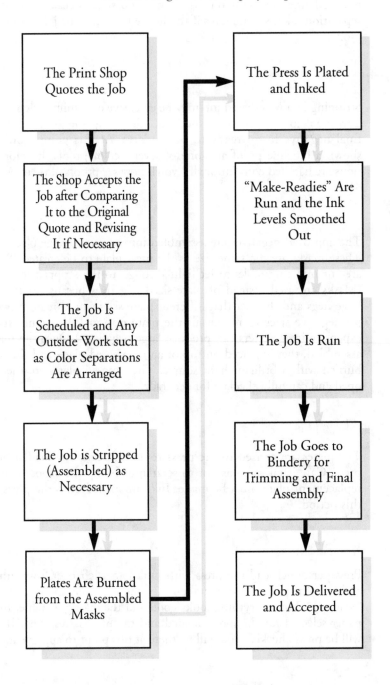

8. The Press Run

The job is run until the desired number of impressions are made. Most shops run more copies than ordered, in case some are damaged during post-press operations such as binding or bindery procedures. These extras are kept by the shop as samples, if the job is attractive, to show off the shop's skills and equipment. If the job prints on two sides, steps six through eight are repeated for the second side, after the paper has been given a chance to dry fully. (Printing the second side is called "backing up the job.") During the run, the press personnel continually check color balance and registration and top-off inks if necessary.

9. Bindery

Simple bindery tasks, such as folding and saddle-stitching (stapling), may be handled by the shop doing the printing. More complex bindery tasks, such as folding down thick paper before stapling, are usually handled by a bindery—an outside business that specializes in post-press assembly of print jobs. Special treatments such as die-cutting and foil-stamping are also completed at the bindery.

10. Delivery and Acceptance

The job packaged to be picked up or delivered to the customer (you). If the job is satisfactory to you after you have examined a few of the pieces from different parts of the box, the process is complete.

Printing Techniques and Terminology

If when you are discussing a job with a print shop, you don't understand some terminology, ask for an explanation. In the meantime, here are some of the most standard and confusing words and what they mean to a color publisher.

Reverses and Solids

Two powerful decorative techniques are *reverses* and *solids.* A solid is an area of solid ink (spot color) that covers more than five percent of a page. Screen colors that cover large areas of a sheet are *not* considered solids. A solid may be a small decorative box, or it may take up the entire side of a page (called *painting the sheet*). Solids are broken out in printing terminology, because they require special handling to achieve even coverage of the ink. Pin-holes and uneven ink application are consequences of poorly printed solids. For this reason, if you print a large black solid, your print shop may first print the area with a tint of cyan and then lay the black over that. This reduces the pin-hole risk and provides a more convincing black. Because solids require more care and effort, print shops charge extra for them.

In areas printed with solid spot colors or screen colors, reverses are areas that are not printed, allowing paper to show. Commonly used for type, a reverse can be quite striking. It's like getting a free extra color. Type can also be reversed out of photos. When reversing type, use sizes larger than sixteen points because of dot gain and other factors. Smaller type sizes may partially fill in or be difficult to read. Type reversed out of a dark color is easier to read than type reversed out of a light color because there's more contrast.

Reversed-out Type

Applying Reverses and Solids on the Desktop

Solids created within page layout programs are usually made by drawing a box or other shape and filling it with a solid spot color. Reverses are created differently within the two desktop publishing metaphors. Within PageMaker, a box is drawn and a solid color added. Then the reversing element, such as a line of type, is assigned the color white and placed on top of the solid area, effectively creating a reverse. Within programs using the box-based metaphor, like QuarkXPress, a text box is created and the text is added. Then the text box is filled with a color and the type is assigned the color "white," creating a reverse.

Tip: When Not to Use a Solid

There are three instances when you should think twice before including a solid in your work. First, never print large solid areas on highly absorbent stocks such as uncoated papers, because the ink will soak into the paper at different rates, creating blotches. Second, never print a solid at a quick-print shop—their presses lay ink down unevenly, and you will see this weakness in the printing. Third, if a page with a solid is to be folded in half along the solid, the ink may crack during the process. For example, if you print a brochure with a solid black front and back cover, the ink and paper coating may crack and show white along the fold. With handling, this defect becomes increasingly noticeable, as the cracked areas shed ink and show the white of the paper.

Bleeds and Jumping Gutters

A printing press can't lay ink all the way to the edges of the paper, because these edges must be held by the machine's *grippers* to move the paper through the press. Plus, ink printed to the edges would inevitably get onto the rollers, causing a gooey build-up. To get around this limitation, the *bleed* is used. To create a *full bleed* on an 8½" by 11" sheet, ink is printed on a larger-sized sheet of paper with a quarter-inch extra printed on all sides. The printed area measures 9" by 11½". Then, the extra is trimmed off, resulting in an 8½" by 11" bleed where the ink reaches to the edge of the paper. Printers charge more for bleeds because they often require a larger sheet of paper to accommodate the larger trim area. Anything can bleed, including solids, photos, and screen colors. Depending on the design, one, two, three, or four sides can bleed.

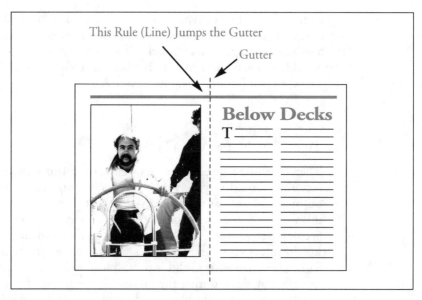

Gutter Jump

A gutter is what you are looking at between two facing pages of this book. Gutters usually require extra paper in order to center each page's contents within the finished publication. You've probably seen two-page magazine ads where the designer didn't predict the gutter's paper requirements properly when running a headline across two pages. As a result, part of a word ends up deep in the gutter, making the headline difficult to read. Gutters also become problematic if *jumps* are involved. A jump is where a photo, headline, or design element, such as a colored line, crosses from one page to the other.

Tip: Never Change Presses in the Middle of a Job

When working on a job that uses more colors on one side of a sheet than the print shop can print, never add additional colors on another press. If your job uses six colors on each side, the obvious "money-saving" approach is to print the first four colors on a four-color press and then add the last two on a two-color machine. Don't do it! Presses have very different characteristics in the way they ink the paper. Passing the job through a different press will result in colors that appear different than the four laid down by the other press.

Vertical jumps can be critical as well. If a line crosses the gutter, but its vertical position on one page is slightly higher than on the other page, it will appear to stop at the gutter and then start afresh from another position on the facing page. This kind of error is quite noticeable to readers. Printers sometimes charge extra for handling jumps, but the majority simply exercise extra caution and carefully check and recheck that the jump will print properly. Never print a piece with a jump at a quick-print shop.

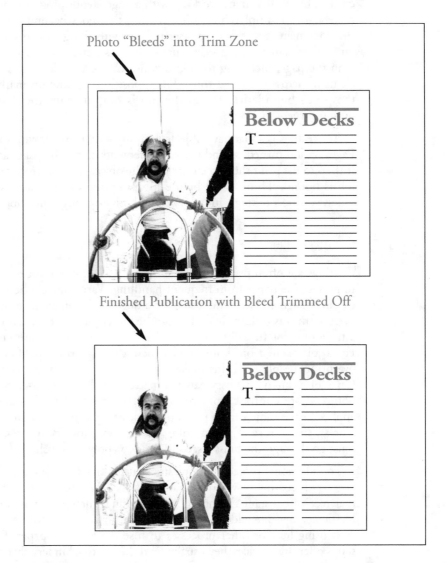

Bleed

Applying Bleeds and Jumps to Gutters on the Desktop

To make a page bleed within most page layout programs, specify the size you want the trimmed-down page to measure and then position elements that will bleed one quarter-inch off the edge of the page onto the pasteboard. Specify that registration marks be added to the job when it's output. The print shop uses these marks to trim off the edges correctly to create a bleed. If you are working with a page layout program that has no pasteboard or simply chops off anything that goes beyond the edges of the document (test this on a laser printer with tiling turned on if necessary), then handle the process manually. First, create a document larger than the page, including the bleed zone. Create the bleed by adding the elements across the bleed zone. Then, position registration marks within the page's boundaries. When the job is output, have the **Trim Mark** option turned off.

To create pages that have objects jumping gutters, work with the **Facing Pages** option turned on and place the elements across the pages as desired. It is up to the print shop to ensure that the objects mate correctly when the job is bound. Think twice before jumping photographs across gutters, unless you are working with a very careful, high-quality print shop.

Varnishes and Plastic Coating

Coatings are often used to make special elements stand out on a page or to protect the paper from frequent handling. Varnishes can be used as an elegant design element and also offer a degree of protection from scratches. A varnish is a clear "ink" that can be either glossy or dull. It often has a trace of color (usually yellow) added to it to make it more noticeable. For a job printed on dull-coated paper, a gloss varnish is often used to overprint the photos. This makes them appear richer and more vibrant. On a job printed on glossy paper, a matte varnish may be used to give the photos more contrast from the rest of the page. Varnishes are usually applied at the same time a job is printed, using a fifth or sixth station on a press. In the case of a four-color job run on a four-color press, the job must go through the press a second time to apply a varnish.

For additional protection, a plastic coating may be applied to the entire page. This coating is waterproof and adds considerable durability to pages that receive constant thumbing and handling, such as restaurant menus. Plastic coatings are added by applying thin plastic sheets to the pages and then using heat or other processes to fuse them to the paper. Few print shops offer this service; they usually send the job to a bindery that does.

Applying Varnishes and Plastic Coating on the Desktop

To specify a spot varnish within a page layout program, create a new solid color called *Varnish*. Specify it as a single solid color. It doesn't really matter which one you use, as long as it isn't specified as a process color. If your page layout program allows it, specify the color to overprint rather than knock out. Choose the object or image you want to varnish and duplicate it. Redefine it with your new color and place it on top of the object to be varnished. (For precise positioning, use the **Alignment** command if available. Otherwise, position the object using measurements identical to the object's.) When the job is imaged, a layer of film for the varnish will be output along with the rest of the job.

If you are using a program that doesn't allow individual colors to be specified to overprint, create the varnished "objects" and then move them as a group into another page layout file. If you attempt this procedure, check the film output carefully to ensure that the varnish plate lines up properly. (Because lightly tinted varnishes are not all that visible, this trick works even if the registration is a little off. Never try this imprecise procedure with a deeply tinted varnish.)

Plastic coatings are a simple matter of instructing the print shop that you would like one applied. Since a coating is automatically applied to the entire page, there's no need to create film output for this process.

Embossing and Foil Stamping

Two powerful decorative effects are *embossing* and *foil stamping*. Embossing uses a die of a logo, shape, or piece of type that is pushed into the paper to raise the surface. This creates a permanent impression in the paper.

Foil stamping uses a metallic foil that is stamped onto the page using heat and pressure. There are a wide variety of foils available in different colors and textures. Most foils are highly reflective and catch the eye before anything else on a printed page.

Both of these processes are relatively expensive and increase in cost as larger areas of paper are embossed or stamped. There is also a one-time charge to create the requisite die. (Ask for and keep the die if there's any chance you will use it again. Printers often hang on to them so that you have no choice but to bring your business to them next time you need to use your die.) Avoid stamping or embossing fine type or subtle detail, because it will disappear or transfer incompletely. The choice of paper is very important for both embossing and foil stamping.

Applying Embossing and Foil Stamping on the Desktop

Both effects are applied identically. A solid color is created as a solid and used for the object that will be embossed or stamped. This will print a plate that is used to create a die. On some papers, you can also print the area that will be stamped or embossed. If you are planning to do so, follow the previous instructions for creating a varnish plate and discuss the job with your printer.

All about Paper

Well… this section isn't *all* about paper because there are thousands of kinds of paper. Instead, we present some basics to get you up to speed selecting paper for the majority of color publishing projects. The choice of paper materially affects your job and is a major component in the success of the printing process. According to the paper you use, you may need to adjust dot gain and trapping values and refrain from certain printing processes. In addition, a paper's look and feel presents the reader with a subconscious impression of a publication's quality. Cheap papers look and feel cheap. Expensive, smooth papers look crisp and valuable.

Paper Sample Books

One way to learn about papers is to acquire books of paper samples. Paper manufacturers create sample books of their paper lines. A book may contain five to 40 paper swatches. Some of these books are beautifully invented, designed, and printed. One book, for a paper called Mohave Matte, was printed as an 8½" by 11" tourist guide to a fictitious "MojaveLand" supposedly located in California's Mojave Desert. The book was made up of artificial stills from nonexistent films, including *Lawrence of Mohave*. This highly entertaining piece also showcased how different kinds of black and white and color images reproduced on the paper.

Where to Get Free Samples

Print shops, large advertising agencies, and design houses are given *paper cabinets* from paper manufacturers. These cabinets contain a complete set of sample books covering the gamut of papers, from four-part NCR forms to the finest dull-coated sheets. Unfortunately, unless you buy or specify a large volume of paper, you will rarely be given one of these cabinets for free. You can try however. Ask your print shop for the names of several of the paper reps. Contact these people and provide a convincing case why you need a cabinet. Convincing excuses include, "I'm planning on printing 50,000 copies of 500 different brochures this year," or "I specify all the paper for the 40 catalogs we handle every quarter."

Another source of free samples is your local paper supply store. Found in the *Yellow Pages* under *Paper Distributors* or *Printing Supplies,* these retail outlets often have free sample swatch books for a wide range of papers. They may also have free samples of all their papers available to people who walk through and grab a sheet. If you take this approach, label each sheet with all of the information on the sealed packages, so you know what paper it is, its weight, and who makes it. Your print shop may also have extra books they don't need.

Tip: Never Buy Your Own Paper!

When reviewing the money spent on the printer's paper markup for a year, you may consider buying your own paper to save money. In a word—*don't.* If anything is technically wrong with the paper (common) the printer will run the job, bill you, and blame any problems, whether his fault or the paper's, on the paper.

You can't go back to the paper supplier either. Even print shops that buy paper by the ton from a supplier often can't get refunds if they accept and run bad stock. Not being a regular customer, you have considerably less leverage. Even if the supplier accepts responsibility, all they'll do is replace the paper, not pay to rerun the job.

Paper Categories and Weight

Papers are categorized by kind and weight. There are papers available for almost every conceivable chore. The kinds you will most likely use for color publishing are:

- Offset   A general-purpose paper used for inexpensive print jobs.
- Textured   Textured papers have a texture pressed into them during the manufacturing process.
- Coated Papers   Coated papers have a clay coating added during manufacturing to provide a smooth finish that takes ink evenly with little absorption.

Papers are rated by the weight of 500 sheets of a given size (the size varies within paper categories). Heavier papers within a category are more expensive than lighter papers, because more material is required to make them. When evaluating different sheets, they are rated in pounds and by whether they are *cover* or *book weights*. Cover-weight paper is thicker and stiffer than text weight. For example, an 80-pound book-weight paper could be ordered for the interior pages of a brochure. 80-pound cover-weight paper might then be used for the cover, to add stiffness and durability to the piece.

> **Tip: Paper Color and Color Publishing**
>
> Some of the most attractive papers are cream instead of white. If you plan to print color on these sheets, the sheet's cream finish will cause colors to shift into deeper registers. To work around this problem, have ink tests for solid colors done on the actual paper. For screen color and process color images, work with a knowledgeable separator the first time so you can learn how to handle this task. Don't attempt it yourself, or you may end up with a print run of muddy-looking images.

What's the Difference between a Number Three Sheet and a Number One?

Within most paper categories, each brand is described by a number. A *number one* coated sheet is the best of this category of paper, where a *number three* sheet is least expensive. **Note:** Since the paper's manufacturer assigns the number, a sheet rated number one by a manufacturer may really be a number two. Pricing is usually an indication of quality. If you compare two "number one" sheets and one is substantially less expensive, this usually indicates a lesser quality sheet. Your print shop also knows which sheets are really top-quality and which are only pretenders. Ask their advice on this.

Which Kind of Paper Should You Use?

The choice of paper is usually based on the nature of the job and its budget. From the thousands of paper kinds and brands, be assured that one can be found to meet your needs.

A New Direction

Almost unknown in the 1970s, the recent interest in the environment has made paper from recycled stock emerge as one of the most popular options for the 1990s. The variety of recycled paper is growing daily, with the "recycling symbol" evident on everything from supermarket brown bags to the tiny liner notes that accompany compact disks.

When considering a recycled paper for color publishing, keep in mind that it costs *more* than conventional papers. Unfortunately, at this writing there is no recycled stock that matches the best dull-coated papers. There are some part-recycled papers that have a reasonably smooth texture and are acceptable for mid-quality color applications. The majority of recycled papers are soft, textured papers that soak up ink like a sponge. For this reason, solids, and more importantly, screen colors and process color images, will suffer on most recycled stocks. So, for high-quality color publishing, recycled papers are not yet an option. But, with the amount of research paper mills are putting into it, a quality paper should hit the market soon.

Another way to help the environment is to print fewer copies of publications. While the more impressions made (copies printed), the lower the unit price per piece, sometimes companies go overboard in ordering and ultimately dispose of a large percentage of the print run. If you do need to throw away a large number of printed materials and don't have a recycling center to pick up or accept your waste paper, ask your print shop if they will recycle them for you. Most print shops recycle their waste at no charge through a recycling company that provides waste bins for paper. The recycler regularly stops by and picks up the waste paper. Dump excess printed materials into one of these bins instead of into an overflowing landfill. In some progressive communities this kind of recycling is mandated by law.

Offset Papers

Simple jobs without large solid areas of ink are often printed on offset papers. This stock is relatively inexpensive and takes ink fairly consistently. Offset papers are available in a range of "whites" from cream to bright white. Used for magazines, books, catalogs, and newsletters, these papers are quite versatile. You wouldn't use them in an expensive color job, however, because they are not as elegant and smooth as coated papers. For high-quality color separations, offset is not the paper of choice.

Text or Textured Papers

Textured papers come in a wide range of colors—from bright whites to nearly black. Some are available with a different color on each side (expensive). The range of textures is striking—everything from weaves to surfaces with deliberate mottling and tiny flecks of color. Textured papers are most commonly used for business cards and letterhead, but their application within brochures can brighten up a project with a limited budget. For stationery purposes, most textured papers are available with pre-converted envelopes, so all the print shop needs to do is imprint the logo and address. Otherwise, to produce envelopes, flat sheets of paper are printed and made into finished envelopes at a bindery—at a much greater cost.

Textured papers vary considerably in how they absorb ink. That makes them unsuitable for some color images and screen color. Occasionally they are used for this purpose, however, because the absorbent surface gives images an old-fashioned or unusual look. These papers are often good choices for embossing and foil stamping. Before attempting a complex job on textured paper, discuss the application with your print shop. Only certain kinds of text papers take ink evenly enough to attempt full-color printing. Some printers will refuse such work.

Coated Papers

Coated papers are used for expensive color projects, particularly those involving large solids, color separations, and screen color. Because smooth coated paper takes color the most evenly, it usually is the paper of choice for the majority of color publishing projects. (Don't print stationery on coated papers! Stamps fall off the envelopes made from it.) Like offset paper, coated papers are available in a wide range of "whites." Coated paper is also available in several finishes, ranging from dull-coated to shiny gloss. While expensive, the number-one quality, dull-coated stocks are the best papers for most complex color applications. They allow accurate reproduction of color, have a nice look and feel, and are easy on reader's eyes.

A New Paper Technology

During the 1980s a new paper technology was introduced—paper made from plastic. Costing substantially more than most wood-based papers, this material has a "perfect" finish, because unlike coated papers that must be processed and coated, this material starts out smooth. Unfortunately, these papers are difficult to print on because ordinary inks don't dry fast enough. Special inks must be used, and only a specialty printer should attempt this. The results, however, are stunning. Colors go down evenly and images have a luminous appearance. The paper feels smooth and silken and has the right amount of stiffness without feeling hard. This "paper" is uniquely waterproof as well.

Matching Paper Stock to Your Color Publishing Job

Paper	Description	Use for
Offset Paper	Smooth paper available in a wide range of "whites" and some colors. This paper takes ink somewhat evenly but not as well as the best coated papers. Offset papers are relatively inexpensive. The better grades can be used for some low-resolution process color image jobs.	Calendars, catalogs, magazines, books, and low-cost brochures.
Textured Paper	Textured papers, also known as "text," are uncoated papers available in a wide range of colors and textures (hence their name). Available colors range from bright whites to near blacks. Textured papers are also manufactured with flakes of other colors and fibers added to make the papers appear as handmade. Text papers are not usually used for process color image reproduction because their high absorbency causes serious dot gain that may be uneven over the surface of a sheet. Textured papers range in price from inexpensive to very expensive.	Business cards and letterhead. To add color and texture to brochures and annual reports, mailers, posters, and books.
Coated Paper	The best papers for taking color and reproducing process color images are coated papers. They have very even surfaces and take ink evenly. Available in grades from "number three" to "number one" (best), coated stocks are also expensive.	High-quality color projects such as brochures, annual reports, mailers, art reproductions, and posters.

Paper Properties That Affect Color Publishing

Papers have different physical properties that must be considered when selecting one for a job. Some papers shift color far more than others. Printing both sides of the wrong type of paper may allow the reader to see elements on both sides at the same time. Choose papers carefully and look to your printer for solid advice on this subject.

Ink Holdout

Ink holdout is a measure of a paper's absorbency characteristics when ink is transferred to it. Choosing a paper with a low ink holdout requires more dot gain compensation for screen color and images, because the ink soaks into the paper and spreads, making larger dots. As the color sinks into the paper, it changes and becomes darker and less lively. Papers with high ink holdout require much less compensation, because the ink dots don't spread much if the press is set up correctly. There is less color shift as a result. You can test ink holdout crudely by applying a single drop of water to several sheets under consideration and timing how long it takes to soak in and spread.

Paper and Ink Holdout

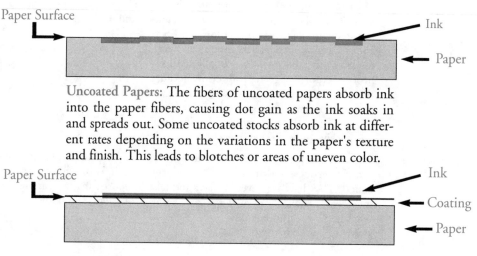

Uncoated Papers: The fibers of uncoated papers absorb ink into the paper fibers, causing dot gain as the ink soaks in and spreads out. Some uncoated stocks absorb ink at different rates depending on the variations in the paper's texture and finish. This leads to blotches or areas of uneven color.

Coated Papers: Coated papers have a layer of clay compound that stops the ink from being absorbed into the underlying paper fibers. The more heavily coated a stock, the less absorption. This results in less dot gain and more consistent application of ink over the entire sheet.

Opacity

Papers vary widely in opacity—that is a measure of how translucent they are and how much light they reflect. Stocks become increasingly opaque as they increase in weight and thickness, but using a very thick sheet simply because it's opaque makes for an ugly-looking piece of work in print. Opacity is a significant issue because of bleed-through, when a reader looking at one side is distracted by material showing through from the other.

You can compare paper opacity by using your page layout program to prepare a test page. To each sheet add several lines of black text that increase in size from ten to 36 points. Print the page on a laser printer and then place it behind the papers under consideration. The sheet with less opacity will allow you to read smaller type than one that's more opaque.

Tip: Don't Light Ink on Dark Paper

While it make seem logical that a neat effect can be created by printing a light color on dark paper, it doesn't work, because even the most opaque ink will allow some paper show-through. Even if you use a technique called *double bumping* or a *touch plate*, where the job is hit twice by the same ink, the results will still appear mottled.

Stiffness

Different paper (and weights) have varying degrees of stiffness. Stiffness is important in certain applications, because limp paper may present the wrong impression to the reader. For example, if you print a poster on too thin a sheet, it will wrinkle permanently with only minimal handling. Paper can be too stiff as well. A really stiff, thick sheet may be impossible to fold, even at a bindery.

Compare stiffness by holding up two different sheets of the same size. Grab each sheet at the bottom. The stiffer sheet will not fold over as far as the weaker sheet. Really stiff papers won't bend at all. Compare them by snapping the corners with your index finger. The sheet with more "snap" is the stiffer of the two.

A Printing Specification Worksheet

To help you specify print projects, we have included a print purchasing checklist that you should photocopy and complete before soliciting bids. By completing this worksheet, you will be able to state in clear terms what your job requirements are. This makes the bidding process easier for both you and the shop completing the estimate.

How Many Copies Should You Print?

When ordering printing, the quantity ordered directly affects the unit price. Order more copies and the cost per copy decreases, because the press set-up has already been paid for. Extra charges are made only for additional press time, paper, and binding operations. Charges for extra press time are usually negligible, because a big four-color press cranks out around 5,000 copies per hour when printing a quality job, and web presses are that much faster. The only significant additional cost is for paper, unless expensive processes such as foil stamping or hand assembly are used.

> **Tip: Use the Three Times Rule**
>
> In our experience, a brochure, datasheet, or other print project used to promote a product tends to be used approximately three times longer than estimated. So, if a client tells us that a brochure will have a one-year life span, we usually assume that enough should be printed to last two to three years, and we recommend printing a quantity to last that long. (They usually get used up long before this anyway.) The only exceptions to this rule are pieces with an obviously short lifespan, such as an annual report, an announcement of a special event, or a brochure for a product that is changed frequently.

What to Bring to the Printer

Before heading for the print shop, it's important to pack everything you need so the printer doesn't have to wait for anything. In some shops, if a job is incomplete, rather than scheduling it and beginning work, the printer may shelve your project until the missing components arrive.

Worksheet for Specifying a Print Job

Use this checklist to define the parameters of a print job. It can be used by prospective print shops to quote the job.

Job

Job Name _____ Date to Printer _____ Projected Completion Date _____

Kind of project (brochure, mailer, etc.) _____ Client _____

Service bureau outputing job _____ Phone _____ Contact _____

Deliver to_____

Finished size _____ Number of pages _____ Paper _____ Plus Cover _____

Quote these quantities Quantity _____ Quantity _____ Quantity _____

Color Comp Provided ☐ Prints Two Sides ☐ Delivered as Camera-ready Negs ☐

Stripping Required ☐

Job includes imbedded: Halftones ☐ Screen Tints ☐ Color Separations ☐

Color

(Check all that apply) Process Color ☐ Spot Color ☐ Number of Colors ____

Spot Color System _____

Spot Color Numbers (from swatch book) 1) _____ 2) _____

3) _____ 4) _____ 5) _____ 6)_____

Number of screen tints to be handled by printer _____

Traps have been included: Yes ☐ No ☐ None Required ☐

Images Not Handled on the Desktop

Number of halftones to be handled by printer _____ Sizes _____

Halftone Art Format (if print shop must process): Reflective ☐ Transparency ☐

Color Separation Art Format (if print shop must process): Reflective ☐

Transparency ☐

Number of color separations to be handled by printer _____ Sizes _____

Treatments

Reverses ☐ Number and Size _____ Solids ☐ Number and Size _____

Trimming and Saddle stitching ☐ Die Cutting ☐ Gluing ☐ Foil Stamping ☐

Bleeds ☐ Binding ☐

Other Instructions _____

_____

_____

In addition to the imagesetter output, you will need to bring any black and white or color images that will be processed by the print shop. The printer will either handle the color separations in house (if they own a scanner) or send them out to a color house. It also helps if you provide a proof or sketch of the job as well. You can use the color proof done at the service bureau if you have one. Output from a color printer also works well. Label everything with your name, company, and phone number.

If you can't provide a color comp from a color printer, create a comp of sorts from laser printer output. This comp should contain all of the elements of the job and be folded or stapled in the way the finished job will be. To indicate color, use colored pencils to draw over black type and lines. For example, if a headline is specified as TruMatch 4a (red), use a red pencil to sketch over the headline. (Don't mark colors with the kind of solvent-based markers used for manually creating comps. The solvent lifts the laser printer toner and creates an ugly mess.)

The Press Check—Use It to Ensure Quality and Fine-tune Color

The *press check* allows you to check your job and make subtle adjustments to get the best color balance. It's also your final chance to ensure that dot gain doesn't shift the color unacceptably and no other errors show up on press.

A press check is just that—you go see the job and check it on press before it runs. Press checks are usually scheduled at the print shop's convenience rather than yours. Within the trade, designers joke about press check timing. The time and date you are quoted going into a job is almost guaranteed to be the one time when the press check won't happen. In a shop that runs 24 hours (many large shops do), your printer may assemble a schedule showing that your job will be ready for a press check at 1:00 p.m. on Tuesday, but it actually occurs inconveniently at 3:00 a.m. two days later.

When you plan to press check a job, remind the print shop several times that you want to see the job on press. If you issue a purchase order, include a press check requirement. Some shops forget to call you and simply run the job when they get around to it. A shop that does this should be given no further work.

Cold Storage

When you first arrive for a press check, you are usually put in storage somewhere. There's usually a wait while press personnel complete the make-ready and achieve a color balance they think is acceptable. At shops that rarely have press checks, the process usually consists of waiting in an unused office with a cup of coffee that tastes like it was brewed during Ronald Reagan's first term. Really large shops, where checks are standard, often have a designated waiting area designed to accommodate press checkers, complete with entertainment, snacks, and beverages.

What to Look for on Press

When the job is ready for your review, in most shops you'll be taken out on the press floor. Some shops bring the press sheets to the waiting room. The former is the best arrangement because you can interact with the press personnel to get the best results, rather than having someone going back and forth relaying instructions and changes.

When *on press*, do the following as required:

Assess the Color Balance

Compare what you see on press with the color proof you approved before the job was plated. The shop uses the same proof to balance the inks. Check that spot colors are even throughout the sheet and that no pinholes (paper showing through) are visible. Check that process colors are correct as shown in the proof and that process color images appear crisp and clean. If your job uses spot colors, compare them against the swatch book, which should be kept in the press area. If you're unhappy with any of these components, bring it to the attention of the press foreman and allow him (or her) to adjust color to suit your request, if possible. See *Manipulating Colors on Press* later in this chapter.

Tip: A Last-ditch Fix for Problem Process Color Jobs

Some print shops are quite experienced mixing custom inks, in addition to handling the standard print shop tasks. If you have a problem with an overall color shift in a process color job, consider asking your print shop to try adjusting the color balance by mixing a new process color ink for one or more of the four inks. While this is a desperation tactic and you'll have to pay for the extra press time while the color is adjusted, we have used this fix successfully on more than one occasion.

Compensate for Dot Gain

If your job suffers from excess dot gain and the printer has gone ahead with it anyway, you can compensate by having the press foreman *bring down* one or more of the offending process color inks. ("Take magenta down two percent, please.") This reduces dot gain and gets colors in line, unless the problem is very severe. Inks can be brought up or down to compensate for both dot gain and loss.

Check Registration

Look to see that all trapped colors are on center with each other and that the trapping is as even as possible around the edges where the colors meet. Study the process colors and color images under a magnifying loupe to see how the dots line up. The easiest way to do this is to look at the edges of each image and the screen colors to see if they are even. If you can see stray dots of one or more colors, then the registration needs tweaking. Check all edges, not just one side. (Misregistration of this kind is described as, "Yellow is two dots off.") This is the time to get your loupe out.

Reading a Color Test Strip

Color jobs are usually printed with a special calibration bar that shows when too much ink is present for each of the four process colors. The bar is printed on a section of the page that will be trimmed away once the job is complete. The component of the bar that is easiest to interpret is the star target. When too much ink is applied, the star fills in in proportion to the excess ink. A clean, crisp star with the tiny center hole visible indicates that ink is going down correctly on the paper. Groups of other test bars are assembled along the leading edge of the sheet. Multiple bars are used because the press ink set-up may be correct on one part of the sheet and incorrect elsewhere.

Other press problems show in the targets as well. If the filled-in area in the center of the star appears as an oval instead of a circle, then dots are changing shape. (This is called *doubling*.) While a competent press foreman will see the problems and adjust the press, double check the targets yourself, particularly if you are running at a shop you haven't worked with before. Doubling makes screen colors and process color images print much darker than intended. Figure C-17 is an example of a color test strip. This figure is found in the *Color Section* of this book.

Checklist for Press-checking Color Jobs

Use this form to make sure that everything that should be checked on press is reviewed during a hectic press check on a busy printing plant floor.

Job Name _____ Press Check Date _____

Press Check Job Side #1 Press Check Time _____ Press Foreman _____

☐ Match color to color proofs.

☐ Match spot and screen colors to the swatch book (bring your own book if possible).

☐ Adjust/fix any problems found in this section with the press foreman and recheck.

☐ Look for dot gain problems that affect overall color and adjust.

☐ Check that all process color images and screen tints are in register.

☐ Look for trapping errors and adjust.

☐ Check that all process color images and screen tints are in register.

☐ Check for scratches, glitches, hickies, broken type, and offsetting, and have problems corrected.

☐ Check once more that all images are correctly placed and oriented.

☐ Read the copy, headlines, and captions once more, just in case.

☐ Verify that the correct paper has been loaded into the press!

☐ Have a press sheet cut down and check folds, trims, die cuts, and centering on the page.

Press Check Job Side #2 Press Check Time _____ Press Foreman _____

☐ Match color to color proofs.

☐ Match spot and screen colors to the swatch book (bring your own book if possible).

☐ Adjust/fix any problems found in this section with the press foreman and recheck.

☐ Look for dot gain problems that affect overall color and adjust.

☐ Check that all process color images and screen tints are in register.

☐ Look for trapping errors and adjust.

☐ Check that all process color images and screen tints are in register.

☐ Check for scratches, glitches, hickies, broken type, and offsetting, and have problems corrected.

☐ Check once more that all images are correctly placed and oriented.

☐ Read the copy, headlines, and captions once more, just in case.

☐ Verify that the correct paper has been loaded into the press!

☐ Have a press sheet cut down and check folds, trims, die cuts, and centering on the page.

Look for Scratches, Glitches, Hickies, Broken Text, and Offsetting

Study the entire page and look for fine scratches, glitches, and hickies. These marks may show in any color ink. It's possible for the yellow plate to have a fine scratch that's very difficult to see. Skim through the copy to check for broken type, where part of a word or sentence doesn't print. If you are printing a job at a printer chosen for their low price, look for a problem called *offsetting*. This is where wet ink from a printed sheet sticks to the back of the sheet above it. Offsetting results in a ghost-like image. Offsetting is a particularly serious problem if the sheet will print on two sides, because the ghost-like image will appear in the middle of the printed page.

Check That Images Are Correctly Oriented

If your printer stripped in images manually, check that none of them are *flopped* (backward). This happened to us once on a job run before the days of desktop publishing. The photo included the very readable word, "YES!" backward in the background, but no one noticed it was wrong until the press check.

Verify That the Correct Paper Has Been Loaded onto the Press

Make sure that the paper selected is the one actually loaded onto the press. Occasionally mix-ups occur, and the next job's paper is accidentally substituted on press. Or, the salesperson may have incorrectly noted the paper on the job's work order.

Have a Sheet Cut down

Before the job is run, have one of the make-ready sheets cut down and assembled into final format. This reveals any assembly problems in the document. Even a minor assembly problem can render a huge print run useless. So checking one last time is a valuable exercise. It saved one job we handled, when the print shop incorrectly assembled the pages into a complex flat. Because the problem was caught, only minor restripping and new plates were required, instead of a complete reprint.

Check Everything One Last Time!

Check other elements, such as copy, for last-minute problems. If typos or missing lines of copy are found now, they will be expensive to fix, but the repairs will be cheaper than rerunning the entire job.

Definition: Glitches and Hickies

One word that designers love to hate is *glitch*. Glitches are small (usually) black dots that creep into print projects. Originally caused by the build-up of gummy dirt from wax, rubber cement, and fate on drawing instruments, without close attention by designers and stripping room personnel, these spots often make it into print.

In color desktop publishing, glitches still creep in through the usual mechanical routes, yet because there's less manual processing, there's less opportunity for contamination. Still, glitches get into projects when you click on a page layout with the box, line, or circle tool selected in some programs. Dust and dirt on scanning surfaces and dirty developer solution in a service bureau's processor cause glitches as well. Large glitches require replating to eliminate them on press.

Hickies, on the other hand, are strictly a press problem. These donut-shaped marks are caused by a particulate getting stuck to press plates, rollers, or the *blanket* that transmits the inked image to the paper. Hickies can be remedied by the press operator cleaning the offending color station.

processing, there's less opportunity for contamination. Still, glitches get into projects when you click on a page layout with the box, line, or circle tool selected in some programs. Dust and dirt on scanning surfaces and dirty developer solution in a

Glitch
Hickey

Once you have caught and fixed any problems and adjusted the color if necessary, the press run begins. At this point you will usually be asked to sign and date the sheet that you approved. This means that you accept the way the job looks and lets the printer off the hook for errors. Take an identical sheet with you. That way, if the press foreman doubles the speed of the press after you leave and the colors in the job wash out as a result, you can compare your sheet to what's delivered and refuse to accept or pay for the piece.

If there are more sides to print, or if more colors are required than can be laid down in one pass, repeat the press check process until all of the paper is printed. On a short run in which the ink dries fast, this step may require only another hour of your time. On a long, seven-color run on both book and cover weight papers, several days may be required to complete the press checks.

Manipulating Colors on Press

While some shops get annoyed with us, we sometimes find it necessary to fine-tune color on press. By bringing process and spot colors up or down a few notches, a print job that looked dull on press can be visibly brightened. Or a screaming spot color can be taken down a notch or two. Consistent problems, such as process color images with yellow casts, can be worked around as well (sometimes).

Both spot colors and process colors can also be increased so that more ink is used. If the paper can handle the additional levels of ink, this makes the colors stronger and more vibrant. Keep in mind when adjusting process colors that when you change one to enhance (or fix) an image, it will affect any other images or screen colors printed with the new ink setting. Don't try this at a quick-print shop—their presses have rudimentary ink controls that allow little useful adjustment.

On high-quality presses, you adjust ink density to affect only one part of the page. These presses allow color to be adjusted for every two inches of paper in the direction the job travels through the press. So, you can make an adjustment to one ink area while leaving others alone.

One job we printed with large solid areas of a pale blue spot color demanded a change. On press the blue became far too dominant, because the paper soaked it up more than expected, thereby darkening the color. First, we asked the press foreman to reduce the amount of blue ink being applied to the paper. This helped, but not enough— even at the minimum ink application setting. So, to further compensate, the blue was diluted with tint base (a clear liquid used as a base material for creating colors), and make-readies were run to check the color. After several light dilutions, the blue finally looked just right. This adjustment took twenty minutes of press time and probably saved the job.

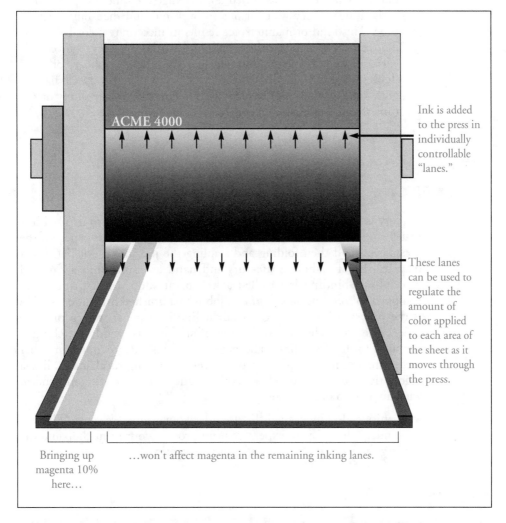

Ink is added to the press in individually controllable "lanes."

These lanes can be used to regulate the amount of color applied to each area of the sheet as it moves through the press.

ACME 4000

Bringing up magenta 10% here…

…won't affect magenta in the remaining inking lanes.

Ink Lanes: Ink can be adjusted for each "lane" on the press. This means that you can adjust a color on one part of the sheet of paper without affecting the ink levels on the rest of the sheet. Depending on the orientation of the paper as it passes through the press, this can be a powerful tool for correcting color problems.

> **Tip: Color-balanced Lights May Not Be**
>
> Print shops that handle a lot of color work have a room or booth
> with expensive color-balanced fluorescent lights that purport to be
> color accurate. They may have been when they were first installed,
> but many printers we've visited don't change the tubes on a regular
> basis. Instead, they wait for one to burn out and then buy a new
> tube. This kind of maintenance results in inaccurate color balanc-
> ing. Instead of trusting these bulbs (particularly if they're covered
> with dust), study the job under incandescent lights, ordinary office
> fluorescents, and outdoors in the shade. Most print shops will have
> both kinds of bulbs in the plant. As for sun, the average sunny day
> (unless you live in Seattle) with a few clouds will suffice.

At the Bindery

Bindery is the process of assembling the printed paper into its final format. It may consist of little more than trimming the waste paper off the
press sheets and then folding and stapling the job into a booklet. Or it
may consist of elaborate die-cuts and hand assembly into a finished
piece. Basic binding is handled at the print shop. Most printers are
equipped to *score* and *saddle stitch* a job into a finished brochure. Scoring
is the process of embossing a straight line into paper with a pressure
roller. The score allows easy folding of stiff papers. Saddle stitching is
simply a form of stapling. The pages of a finished brochure (or other
piece) are assembled and then bent over a stitching mechanism, like a
saddle fits over a horse. Then staples made from a continuous line of
wire are used to bind the job.

If an outside bindery will be used, let your printer select it. Then, if
the bindery chews up an expensive print project, your print shop and the
bindery can work it out without your intervention.

Rejecting a Job

Occasionally a print job will be unacceptable for a variety of reasons. If
the mistakes were made by you or your service bureau, then the printer's
bill will have to be paid and the job rerun at your expense. You can
attempt to make the service bureau take responsibility if they, without

question, made the mistake. If a job must be rerun, a sympathetic print shop will usually do it for their cost, plus a little pleading on bended knee from you.

If, however, the print shop made a major mistake (common in some shops), it's best to refuse the job rather than accepting it. Do this by carefully checking the job when it's delivered or when you go to pick it up. If you are in doubt about the overall integrity of the job, check samples from several different parts of the shipment. If you reject it, the printer has the option of reprinting the job, discounting the bill, hounding you with a lawyer or collection agency, or calling it a day. Then the printer can recycle the paper and refuse further jobs from you.

If the mistake is minor and your client or customers won't notice or care about it, consider asking for a discount on the run. Ten percent is the standard discount for minor but obvious mess-ups. If the problem is major but the job is still useable, then the bill should be reduced accordingly. However, the problem must clearly be the print shop's fault. If you give them an important instruction verbally, and they fail to carry it out, and this renders the job useless but properly printed, you will have to pay unless the print shop admits the mistake. That's why all instructions should be in writing and why you need to keep a copy of everything.

If you absolutely must reject a job that a printer won't reprint, try to settle the bill amicably by splitting it with them. Then find another shop.

In this chapter we've discussed the mechanics of printing and taking a job from service bureau to print and bindery. Keep in mind that there is more to printing than can be discussed here. The technical side of printing, ink, and paper is a science and craft that requires years of devotion to fully master. If you choose the right printer and learn from each job, you'll become a master color publisher with a minimum of trial and error.

We've now taken you through the entire color publishing process on the Macintosh—from desktop to print shop. In the next chapter, we'll take a detour of sorts—taking a job to a high-end prepress system for output. For top-quality work, a prepress system provides excellent color publishing results without much color publishing experience on your part—at a price that's often justifiable. We've included working with a prepress system because such systems are commonly used by Macintosh publishers for high-end publishing, though they certainly aren't a requirement.

CHAPTER

13

CONNECTING TO PROFESSIONAL PREPRESS SYSTEMS

"There are a lot of differences between Macs and Scitex systems, and I don't want to weigh you down with a lot of nit-pickey details until I get some more information from you. But the two biggest issues to take into consideration are time (which always equals money) and quality."

— Laura Haggarty on CompuServe
Responding to a Question on the Difference
between Macs and a High-end Prepress System

In the 1970s, when computers began to handle color separations in the form of million-dollar laser scanners, it became clear that the future of color publishing lay with machines rather than skilled processes carried out by teams of craftsmen. The most complicated task—color separation—took only minutes to complete on film, instead of days using cameras and filters. Once this hurdle was conquered, it made sense to bring the entire publishing process online. If color separation could be handled, why not comparatively simple tasks such as typesetting and layout on the same machine?

It was on this premise that by the late 1970s, complete color publishing systems began to emerge, based on computerized film imaging. A computer could handle every task except printing. At last an entire publishing empire could be run from a large air-conditioned room instead of requiring massive factories and giant machines.

With the introduction of the Macintosh and the Mac's rapid ascendancy as the platform of choice for low-cost color publishing, it made economic sense to bridge the two worlds—the Mac and the high-end professional prepress system. By making the two systems work together, the owners of prepress systems could take on work from a larger number of customers. For the Mac publisher, this was the answer to high-quality image processing, while maintaining much of the economy of Mac-based layout and design.

You Are Here

Connecting to prepress systems bypasses the stop at the service bureau. Depending on the jobs you attempt, a high-end prepress system may not be an option you need consider. But, if you are having problems with quality or don't want to learn advanced color publishing skills, a prepress system takes much of the responsibility for image processing off your shoulders. Of course, this simplicity comes with costs in both time and money. (What doesn't?) This chapter explains the mechanics of connecting your Mac jobs to a prepress system and provides you with the information necessary to help you decide whether this is the right option for your project.

What Is a Prepress Environment?

In this book we've referred to these systems as "high-end prepress systems" to separate them from dedicated prepress systems running on Macs and other computers. These dedicated systems are really known as *CEPS* for *color electronic prepress systems.* CEPS, when pronounced with a soft "c," is homophonous with *seps,* the industry jargon for color separations.

Prepress systems are physically large, computer-based publishing environments. Where the Mac can handle color publishing, bookkeeping, and play *Where in Time Is Carmen San Diego?* with equal aplomb, a prepress system only handles prepress tasks and nothing else. A fully configured prepress system performs much of the same kind of page layout and image manipulation that can be done on a Mac. Because these systems have faster graphics processing capabilities and are engineered specifically for creating color publications, they are much faster and more precise than a Mac when scanning, separating color images, and printing color-separated pages to film. (The time for a prepress system to print color-separated pages to film is measured in minutes, whereas the same chore is measured in 30-minute segments on the Mac.) These systems also cost substantially more than a high-end Mac installation, even if the Mac is equipped with a high-end imagesetter and scanner.

The heart of a prepress system is the operator's console. The console has two large monitors and looks like something used on the original bridge of *Star Trek's* Enterprise. One monitor is used for laying out pages and is usually monochrome. The other is an [almost] color-balanced monitor used to retouch, color balance, and edit images. The console is connected to an input device to capture images and an output device to create printer-ready film. A high-quality drum scanner is used to capture color images as the system's input. A film recorder is used to create ready-to-plate film as output. (A prepress system's film recorder is much like an imagesetter but does not require an RIP processor to rasterize PostScript code into a film-compatible format.) In some installations, the drum scanner is used for both scanning and writing the final image to film. The console is used to control the rest of the system and is capable of typesetting and page layout just like a Mac, although it lacks much of the Mac's intuitive interface and ease of use.

Unlike a Macintosh, where page layout, image enhancement, and typesetting can be accomplished with a minimum of training, a prepress system requires a skilled operator to load images onto the scanner, make color corrections, lay out pages with complex command sequences, and finally to image film. Where most Mac software is relatively easy to understand and use, prepress systems are more like running a complex metal lathe—capable of astounding precision, but requiring the eyes and experience of an expert to get quality results.

Go CEPS or Head for the Service Bureau?

Deciding to head for a service bureau or to a prepress system is a choice of time and money over control and economy. If you are new to color publishing, assembling a document on your Mac and having it completed on a prepress system provides great color image quality with a minimum of effort on your part. It frees you from scanning and color separation problems, image-retouching, color correction, and assembling traps. That sense of anxiety is eliminated while you wait to see what, if anything, comes out of the imagesetter and how much overtime must be paid for.

A prepress system can handle large, complex scanned images that make little sense even to attempt on the average Mac installation. Plus, you get the benefit of having a trained prepress professional set up, run, and color balance the scans. For these reasons, most magazines that use Macs take their output and finish the job on a prepress system. Of course, they're often lucky enough to have such a system in house, something you probably don't have direct access to.

On the downside is cost and control. While you may need to learn prepress skills you didn't know existed until you read this book, handling the entire process on your Mac eliminates the wait for your job to be processed at a busy color house. It also eliminates the large bill for their services, assuming you know how to get adequate color output at the service bureau.

We usually advise those new to color publishing to go all Mac for newsprint and magazine quality (133-lpi image resolution or less) after a few months of practice and go *prepress* or *conventional* for higher resolutions, particularly if large images are involved, color accuracy is critical, or if the job is on a tight schedule. What should you do? Use a prepress system when it makes economic or logistic sense. Then, build your color publishing skills and equipment, as explained in Chapters One and Two, until you can handle your work on the Mac and achieve the results you require. Also, go prepress if you need exact color matches, or when the film charges from the service bureau are large enough that it makes sense to pay just a little extra for better quality and less effort on your part.

Why Macs and Prepress Systems Make Good Partners

A prepress system is a very expensive proposition after the purchase price and additional costs for operator training, installation, and maintenance are tallied. (These systems require air-conditioned rooms similar to those used to house mainframe computer installations, and a dust-free environment is also preferred.) Consequently, most systems are installed in color separation houses, where it makes the most sense to put them. (A growing trend is installation of these systems at the production locations for magazines, catalog houses, and newspapers, because of a prepress system's speed and high-quality output.) The catch to using a high-end prepress system is that there are a limited number of operators who can work on a system at one time. That makes for a formidable bottleneck when multiple jobs are in progress or the production schedule is tight (common). This is being worked around with improvements in networking technology—but the throughput can still be a problem.

> **Tip: Need High Quality, Can't Afford a CEPS System, but Have a Mac?**
>
> The main economy in Mac-based color publishing is the ability to handle most of the chores a print shop's stripping room, typesetter, and color separation house would normally take care of and do them on *your* schedule. If your publication requires super high-quality color images, consider using the Mac for the part you can accomplish with ease on the desktop. Add copy, design elements, screen color, and image placeholders. Then have the color images scanned and corrected on a high-end prepress system, added to the layout to replace the "for-position images." This makes the best use of the Mac and the prepress system, resulting in optimal economy, minimal hassle, and predictable on-press results for color-critical requirements.

Even with the speed of a prepress system, only so much work can be accomplished at one time. With the cost of such a system, mundane tasks such as typesetting and page layout become impractical. Tying up a prepress workstation to type in copy on a machine that can handle high-quality scanning and color separation wastes its capabilities. That's where the Macintosh saves the day.

Mac to Prepress System to Print

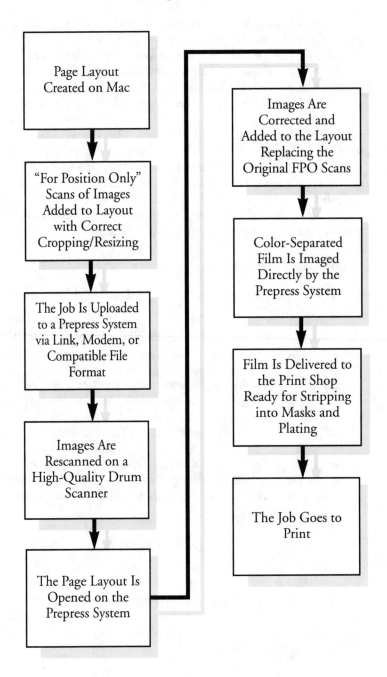

Page Layout
Created on Mac

"For Position Only"
Scans of Images
Added to Layout
with Correct
Cropping/Resizing

The Job Is Uploaded
to a Prepress System
via Link, Modem, or
Compatible File
Format

Images Are
Rescanned on a
High-Quality Drum
Scanner

The Page Layout Is
Opened on the
Prepress System

Images Are
Corrected and
Added to the Layout
Replacing the
Original FPO Scans

Color-Separated
Film Is Imaged
Directly by the
Prepress System

Film Is Delivered to
the Print Shop
Ready for Stripping
into Masks and
Plating

The Job Goes to
Print

Employing any number of Macintoshes as a front end for the more mundane publishing tasks, a prepress system can be used to handle the speed-intensive tasks that are too slow on the Mac. The Mac can be used to enter type, lay out pages, and get the publication ready for the prepress system. On the prepress system the operator can scan color images, handle complex color correction if required, and create quality color separations. Prepress systems are connected to high-quality image scanners and film recorders—offering superior quality to all but those owned by the most well-heeled Mac publishers or service bureaus. This marriage of the Mac and prepress system in a fast-paced production environment, such as a magazine, takes advantage of both systems' strengths.

Prepress Is a Pre-PostScript World

Because most prepress environments were designed in the dark days before PostScript and the Mac, these systems use their own internal format to produce film output. To transfer images back and forth between Macs and prepress systems, an interface is used to transmit (and translate) PostScript files and convert files from one environment to another.

While the Mac relies on PostScript as a mechanism to describe images and page layouts, prepress systems have a much different approach to describing pages. As explained in Chapter Four, PostScript is a language that describes elements mostly as vectors (draw a one-point line from coordinate A to coordinate B and color it blue), prepress systems store pages more like actual printed pages. Pages are stored as an image, complete with photos, illustrations and type. (Type is stored at resolutions as high as 1,800 dpi in a prepress system.) Upon output, these files recreate the page's image without the lengthy reinterpretation required by PostScript files that are saved and then imaged through a RIP processor driving an imagesetter.

Because prepress systems were an established standard before either Macintosh or PostScript, companies manufacturing these systems and third parties have scrambled to make Macs and prepress systems "talk" to each other on amicable terms. The ability to use an inexpensive Mac as a front end for a million-dollar prepress system brings more business to the company and reduces the risk that Macs connected to imagesetters will supplant these expensive environments as *the* standard for "serious" color publishers.

Unfortunately, because the Macintosh and prepress systems speak such different languages, some form of conversion must take place before a prepress system can accept and manipulate a Mac-based page layout file. There are three ways of handling this chore. The first way is one supplied (for an additional charge) by a prepress system's manufacturer. The second way is to produce a file in a format that the prepress system's Mac-like environment can interpret. The third route is to use a link created by the system's manufacturer or a third-party developer.

Using a Prepress System Manufacturer's Package

Prepress system manufacturers offer a page layout program package that directly links their prepress environment to the Mac. Scitex (pronounced *sigh-tex*), for example, provides Visionary, a software program similar to QuarkXPress that creates files in a format compatible with the Scitex environment. Scitex users create documents on their Macintosh using Visionary as their desktop publishing program. After adding type, creating the layout, and finalizing the job, the file is then *uploaded* to the Scitex, where high-quality drum scanners are used to record images and place them into the document. Once the layout is complete, it's output to film from the Scitex to a drum-based Scitex film recorder, ready for print.

Using a Prepress System Manufacturer's Package to Open Mac Files

Visionary Q (for Quark) from Scitex is capable of not only creating documents, but also of opening Quark-produced files originating from other machines. Visionary A (for Aldus) is capable of opening PageMaker documents saved in the OPI format. These variations on the program allow documents created on any Mac with one of the two popular page layout programs to be opened and uploaded using Visionary—without the Mac user purchasing the Visionary program itself.

The advantage of this arrangement is that the expensive purchase of a "front end" for a prepress system can be made by a prepress system owner. This shop can then open and upload page layouts created by affordable software on ordinary Macs. The color publisher need not purchase an expensive program such as Visionary, or an equally expensive linking software package, in order to transfer files from Mac to prepress system.

Links—a Two-Way Street

Another way of sending files from Macs to prepress systems is to use a link created by a prepress system manufacturer or independent third party. StudioLink and RipLink are two examples of such systems. Capable of translating files into a format compatible with prepress systems, these products translate text, images, design elements, and page information.

Mac Links to Prepress System and Back—A Two-Way Street

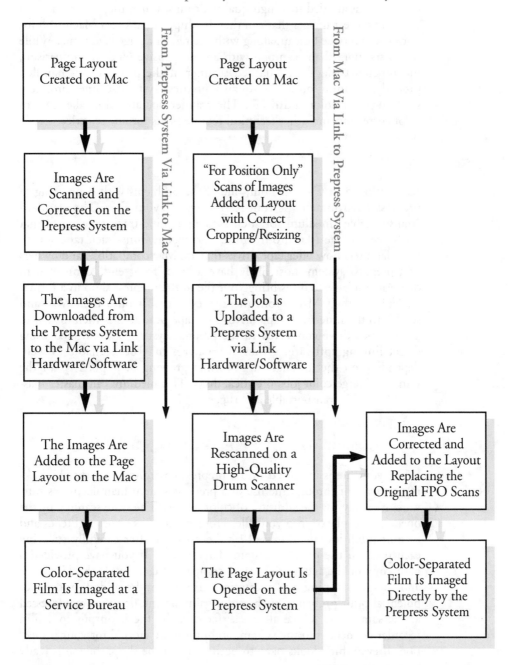

The door swings both ways with most linking software. Because prepress systems are tied to a high-quality drum scanner, they can be used to scan and correct images that can then be shipped back to a Macintosh for output at a service bureau, along with the rest of a page layout file. While this costs more than scanning with an inexpensive (and in comparison, incompetent) Mac-based flatbed scanner, if the procedure is handled properly, scanning on a high-quality prepress system scanner produces vastly superior color and detail. The scanner operator also takes care of color correction and other technical requirements for one set price.

Getting It There

As mentioned in Chapter Four, one of the problems with connecting to prepress environments is transferring page layout files. The standard "transportable" medium for such systems is nine-track tape—a format rarely seen in the Macintosh world. Fortunately, nine-track tape system manufacturers now offer tape drives that are Mac compatible, and owners of a prepress system most likely have a Mac "front end" connected to one. All you have to do is bring your file to the prepress shop in a format readable by their Mac. From there, they'll load it onto their Mac and send it to the nine-track tape drive. The tape produced is then loaded to a nine-track drive connected to the prepress system or connected using direct linking software. Other alternatives may be available as well, depending on the installation. A format growing in popularity for the transfer of large color jobs is optical disks. This medium can master massive files and is transportable and rugged.

Once the File Is Brought over to a Prepress Environment...

When your file is imported into a prepress environment, either by linking software or through the use of a prepress system manufacturer's software, it's ready for the addition of color images. These are scanned by the operator and placed into your file. Problems such as transfer glitches and incompatibilities are addressed by the operator after carefully studying each page on the prepress system's large screen. If you have provided a hard copy of the file, the operator compares this as well, checking type and image cropping and reduction. Traps may be added, and other potential print problems, such as dot gain and ink density, are addressed at the same time. Once all is satisfactory, the file is output to a film recorder connected to the system, and proofs are created for your inspection. If everything looks okay to both you and the shop, the job is ready to go to the printer.

Talk to Your Prepress Operator

Although this may now sound like shop-worn advice, you should talk to your prepress system owner or operator before showing up with a shopping bag full of images and a page layout for transfer into a prepress system. When working in a prepress environment, you must plan to get the most from your Mac, while keeping the prepress system charges in line. Since most prepress systems can replace your Mac for color publishing, you may be tempted to have your entire job handled by one. If you've read this far in the book without throwing in the towel, don't do it now! Instead, if high-quality color is demanded by your project, lay it out on the Mac following Path Three (as described in Chapter One) and have color images scanned and placed by the prepress systems after the layout is completed. This gives you the best of both worlds—economy and quality.

Before beginning a project destined for one of these systems, discuss it with the shop that you plan to use. You may find that it makes economic sense to work with a prepress system, or maybe it doesn't. You also need to find out what software and file formats the system is compatible with. If you bring in a completed file created in an incompatible page layout program, your work will need to be recreated on the prepress system—a waste of time, effort, and money.

> **Tip: Place Images for Position and Review**
>
> When working with a prepress system, feel free to scan and place color images that will be replaced with new scans when the job goes to the prepress system. The placed scans can be used in color (or black and white) proofs to show clients and managers how the job will look in print. When the job is taken over by a prepress system, these images are automatically stripped out and replaced by scans handled on a high-quality drum scanner. You may need to provide the prepress system operator with the reduction (or enlargement) of each image to make it easier for them to exactly match your comp. This can be accomplished manually with a reduction wheel, available at an art supply store, or automatically with a page layout program that allows you to specify reductions by percentage.

Shop Price

Compare the prices of the prepress houses in your area. If the quote from the prepress shop is not much more than the service bureau's and your color needs are critical, go prepress. If you don't like the color in the prepress system's proofs, ask to have it fixed (there's usually no charge for this service). At most service bureaus, you'll need to fix the color, reseparate, have new film run, and have new proofs made at your expense. This quickly tops the quote from the prepress system.

How to Choose the Right Prepress Shop for Your Project

Choosing the right shop for your project is both easy and difficult. Easy because most shops that own prepress systems are color houses with extensive experience handling complex color projects. Difficult because at a glance it's hard to ascertain how good their linking software is and how adept they are at identifying and fixing problems. Here are some questions to get answer before for choosing a shop that meets your needs:

- **What Kind of Linking Software Do They Use?**   Find out what kind of linking software they use and how long they've owned it. Ask if they've had any problems. If they say they've *never* had a problem, a red flag has been raised. Either the shop is unnaturally lucky (unlikely), or they don't handle complex color jobs uploaded from a Macintosh to the prepress system.

- **How Many Macs Do They Run to Link to the Prepress System?** A shop that handles lots of Mac-produced files will have at least several Macs handling files destined for the prepress system. Make sure the Macs are used for prepress links and not just for projects that will be sent to an imagesetter (if they own one), or as mock-ups to be recreated from scratch on the prepress system.

- **What Do Their Samples Look Like?**   Ask to see samples of projects initiated on the Mac but finished on the prepress system. A shop that takes on Mac-based publications and regularly runs them through their systems should have a variety of samples. Inspect the work for quality and study it for obvious problems that made it into print. Ask whether the images originated on the Mac or if they were handled by scanners attached to the prepress system.

- **What Is the Basis for Their Charges?**   Most prepress shops charge by the hour for time on their system. There may be additional charges for scanning and film. Before committing a job to a shop running a prepress system, get a written estimate for charges, because time is charged for in *hundreds* of dollars per hour. A job that requires a lot of time on a prepress system may be cheaper to handle conventionally.

Can This Kind of Work Be Handled on a Mac?

While a prepress system costs around half a million dollars (and up) to purchase, plus more for installation and training, a color Mac publishing system, complete with a high-quality scanner and top-of-the-line image-setter, can be purchased for less than $300,000. While the average color publisher can't afford such a system, these tools are easily within the grasp of a well-equipped service bureau or print shop interested in moving the color publishing process completely in house. There are some real pros out there handling the entire process on the Mac, with quality results.

So, what do these Mac pros use to accomplish these quality results? Well, first of all they use the fastest Mac CPUs, employing the 68040 chip or add-on accelerator boards made by companies such as DayStar and Radius to substantially increase the Mac's processing speed. A faster processor cuts the time to sharpen and color separate large photographic images—from half an hour to just minutes.

These high-end publishers also stuff their Macs with as much RAM as will practically fit and don't use virtual memory because it's too slow. More RAM means that a large image can be kept in memory. (64 MB of RAM is standard in these shops.) With enough RAM memory, color separation and image enhancement programs don't need to break large scans into pieces and swap them in and out of RAM a chunk at a time from a comparatively slow hard disk. And, since one of the other performance limiters is access to the Mac's hard disk, power Mac users employ boards called SCSI accelerators to substantially improve access times to the disk. Or they use large capacity, smoking-fast hard disks (from companies such as MicroNet) that have access times as fast or faster than 5.7 milliseconds and go around the Mac's comparatively slow SCSI interface with a NuBus card. (A typical Mac hard disk offers sluggish access times in the 18- to 35-millisecond range.) Costing more than a new car, these hard disk systems offer a gargantuan 1.2 gigabytes of storage capacity (1,200 MB). Even larger capacities are already on the horizon.

To accurately capture images, high-end Mac publishers use expensive drum-based scanners. While these scanners produce huge files, they are capable of capturing highly detailed, color-accurate images similar in quality to ones scanned by professional color separation houses.

Last, to ensure accurate color representation from monitor to image-setter, they rely on expensive monitors using proprietary color-calibration systems (not perfect, but getting there), and the most accurately calibrated imagesetters. By having an in-house imagesetter, these companies ensure near-perfect calibration and color balance at all times. They can also keep tabs on the processor's chemistry and make adjustments or replenishment as required.

All this equipment provides the ability to take full advantage of the Mac's color capability with fewer processor-speed barriers and without the limitations of inept color scanners. The results are stunning—publications created on the Mac with image resolutions of 200 lines per inch or more. This rivals the capabilities of conventional color separation, and the system still fits on a desktop!

Since we know that technology becomes less expensive and more capable over time, the prepress houses are justifiably shaking in their boots...

In this chapter we have looked at an alternative to completing jobs at the service bureau. Work completed on a prepress system finishes looking first-rate because of the superior scanning equipment employed and the color knowledge of its operator. Until recently these systems were in a class by themselves when compared to Macintosh color publishing, yet today the Mac is rapidly catching up. It's not there yet in speed, and to a lesser degree in precision, but Mac scanners, imagesetters, and software can do most of what expensive prepress systems do. It just takes a little longer.

In the next chapter we'll look at time- and money-saving tips and a hand-ful of products that can greatly increase your color publishing productivity.

CHAPTER

14

TIME-SAVING TOOLS AND MONEY-SAVING TIPS FOR COLOR DESKTOP PUBLISHING

"But gray is a color!

— Michael Beaumont in
Type: Design, Color, Character & Use

Aside from being comparatively easy to learn, Macintosh color publishing saves money by eliminating most of the manual processes required for conventional color publishing. There are several ways to save even more money in the process of producing a document, with little additional effort on your part. These tools and techniques minimize the time required between desktop and print shop by increasing productivity. We'll look at several of them in this chapter.

You Are Here

Now that you've seen the entire color publishing process from desktop to print shop, this chapter is provided to help you save money and to point out several general productivity tools. These tools cut the amount of time to produce designs on the desktop and reduce repetitive work that slows throughput for the professional color publisher. In addition, we discuss tools that can substantially reduce document assembly time.

Five Ways to Save Money at the Service Bureau

One place where you don't want to scrimp money is at the service bureau. Choosing a service bureau based solely on price is *Mistake Number One* when it comes to imaging color projects. You can, however, save money by not wasting service bureau time when there's a less expensive alternative than the obvious one-page, one-color approach quoted in a rate card. Here are five money-saving tips that don't entail risk on your part or cause problems for the service bureau.

Print Spreads

A simple trick for keeping costs down is to image more material on each sheet of film. For example, by printing two 8½" by 11" spreads side-by-side you will only pay for one sheet of film instead of two, and you'll reduce stripping charges at the print shop. While most bureaus charge slightly more for larger film sizes, this figure will still be less than imaging two pages individually.

Printing two spreads is accomplished by turning on the page layout program's "Print Spread" option. If your program lacks this feature, handle the process yourself by converting two pages into one larger page. You may want to manually add trim marks where the page divider should be.

With the advent of imagesetters that can process larger format film, you may decide to assemble all of the pages in the flat. (A flat includes all film that will print on one side of a sheet of paper.) There are programs that allow you to do this with most popular page layout programs. Some of the programs help you with this task, or you can ask your print shop for advice and measurements if you're not sure what to do.

Keep in mind when combining pages on one sheet of film that, in addition to your pages, there must be enough room for crop and registration marks around the edges of the job. And, if the pages include complex color illustrations or numerous color separations, you may run out of imagesetter memory when imaging several pages instead of one at a time.

LaserCheck—a Money-saving Tool

One of the obvious techniques for reducing the number of jobs that image incorrectly at the service bureau is printing a proof on your laser printer first. Unfortunately, jobs that print on a laser printer may still suffer problems at the imagesetter. This is because the software used to print a job at 300 dpi on a laser printer is different than the drivers that output film at higher resolutions on an imagesetter. A handy way around this problem is a product called LaserCheck.

Made by Systems of Merritt, this program makes your PostScript laser printer into a make-believe imagesetter. (LaserCheck does not run on all PostScript clones at this writing. However, it will run on some clones and true PostScript printers, including color ones.) By downloading a file to your laser printer (initialized with LaserCheck instead of Apple's printer driver), you get close to a real-world idea of how your project will image at the service bureau without risking film charges for useless output.

The program works by resizing pages to fit on 8½" by 11" paper with room for crop marks. Along with producing output for proofing, the program reports on font problems, PostScript errors, memory usage, color separation information, and image rescaling details.

Using it is easy. After downloading LaserCheck with Send PS (supplied with the program), all you do is use the **Chooser** to select the printer you want to work with, select the correct PPD (PostScript Printer Description) for the intended "imagesetter" (Agfa, Linotype, Varityper, etc.) within your page layout software, and print the file. The resulting paper output will either "image" normally, or elements that won't image correctly at the imagesetter will disappear or change on the paper output.

Now, you can change or repair the job without a trip to the service bureau for useless film. LaserCheck also allows you to determine large VM memory requirements that may crash an imagesetter or take ages to process while you are charged by the minute for overtime. Priced very reasonably, LaserCheck may pay for itself the first time you discover a color job that won't image correctly. (This probably won't take long either.)

Negotiate

While most service bureaus charge extra for everything but using their restrooms, some prices are worth a little negotiation. For example, if you are running a large color job at a bureau that's not too busy (at some point there will be more bureaus than needed in most cities), don't just accept the per-page rate and extra charges for overtime. Instead, after giving the SB operator time to review your job, ask for a flat rate on the entire project. A busy bureau may offer you one. One that's not busy will almost always provide one. Try negotiating this down further if you like. Don't, however, reduce the rate so far that service bureau personnel feel the compensation is too low and won't give your job the attention it requires.

If your job is imaged at a service bureau that is part of the print shop that will print your document, don't pay the bureau's normal rate. Instead, try negotiating a package price for the complete project, including imaging and printing. Since many print shops are hungry for printing business even though their service bureaus are busy, you may get a reduced price just so the shop gets the printing work.

You can also try getting the job quoted at several different bureaus, but unless you already have experience with each of these and know they're all quality shops, this tactic may really be comparing apples to oranges.

Run at Night

Because the files associated with color publishing can be quite large when paint-type images, color scans, or illustrations with gradient or radial blends are included, you may quickly run into expensive overtime even on a relatively fast imagesetter. If you find imaging overtime is beating your budget into the ground, consider using a bureau that will run the job at night after the shop is closed, negating overtime charges.

One progressive bureau we use doesn't charge extra; instead they guesstimate how long a job will take and if it's more than twenty minutes, they simply start it imaging at closing time. The next morning the job is complete and the customer pays the regular rate with no overtime charges. What a great way to save money with large color files!

Reduce the Resolution

As explained in Chapter Five, a common mistake made in color publishing is to assume that more resolution will provide better results in print. In the case of grayscale and color images, resolution of more than 300 dpi is generally wasted, unless the job will print at 200 lpi or more. However, if you go ahead and scan at 600 dpi just to give the image "a little extra something," you will have to transport a huge file that will go into overtime at the service bureau. Not only that, but for all your trouble, the 600-dpi image won't look any better and may crash the imagesetter if it's *really* big. Instead, scan at a resolution that makes sense for your job (also described in Chapter Five). If you have an existing image that has more resolution than you need, do a resize/resample on it in a color separation program and remove the extra dots. (This process is explained in Chapter Eight.)

Five Ways to Save Money at the Print Shop

Just as you don't cut corners at the service bureau, never cut corners at the print shop. Yes, to save money you can skip having color proofs made up of your job, but if you don't like what you see on press, it's going to cost a lot more to fix the problem than proofs cost. Another obvious way to save money is on paper. Why not print the brochure on offset paper instead of an expensive number one dull-coated sheet? Paper is what makes a print job. The one single thing you can do to improve how a job looks in print is to upgrade the paper. Downgrading paper quality has the opposite effect, because less expensive papers absorb ink unevenly.

Ask Your Printer

Before beginning a job, we have already recommended that you make an appointment with your print shop to evaluate the project for possible problems and to get a preliminary estimate of what it will cost to print. After showing the print shop a thumbnail sketch of your project and explaining the particulars, ask the shop what you can do to save money on the project. Professional printers are experts at squeezing prices because they spend so much time doing it when estimating jobs. Your printer may be able to show you a simple design change that saves big bucks. Since you probably have little background in printing, the suggestion would never occur to you without their help.

For example, a desktop-produced color box that we designed for a computer graphics board manufacturer looked like it was going to cost too much. The client was considering scrapping it in favor of a pre-formed plastic package that lacked both aesthetics and functionality. Explaining the risk to the print shop manager, he told us he would study the problem to see what he could do. The next morning he called and told us that by cutting one inch off each of four invisible interior flaps, the job could be run on a smaller sheet of paper and die-cutting could be handled by a less expensive shop using a smaller, less expensive die. This resulted in a 40-percent lower price for the printing. The client went ahead with the project.

Use the House Sheet

Many print shops have what they call a *house sheet.* This is a brand of paper the shop buys in large quantities and uses if a customer doesn't have another choice of paper. In the case of a specialty printer, this sheet may be a number one dull-coated sheet. A commercial press may use a number three matte sheet. Because of the economy of scale involved in a massive paper purchase and because paper costs as much as 40 percent of a print job, the house sheet can save you a substantial sum of money. Ask your shop if they have a house sheet. If they do, and it's one that is suitable for your project, get the work quoted on your paper choice and on the house sheet for comparison.

Take Advantage of Work and Turn

Printers have a number of confusing terms describing how paper is passed through a press. Sometimes the print shops get the terms confused when describing how two sides of a sheet will print. The one that interests us is *work and turn.* In a work and turn job, both sides of a job are printed on one side of the paper, by printing *two-up* or *four-up.* Look at the illustration to understand how this is done. To print the other side of the sheet, the printer turns the sheet over, rotates it, and passes it back though the press without replating. This saves press time and eliminates charges for two sets of negatives and plates. Ask your print shop if this technique will work for your job.

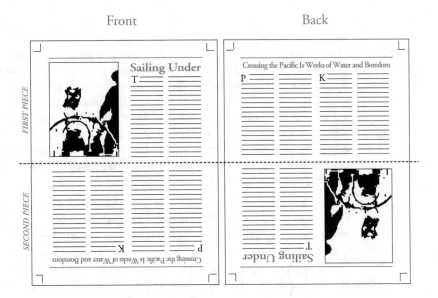

Work and Turn: Both the back and front of the job print on one side of a sheet of paper. Then the paper is turned over, rotated, and sent back through the press, where the second side takes the same image, but upside down in relation to side one. Then the job is cut apart, producing two identical printed pieces. Work and turn requires only one set of plates and one inking of the press, saving money for most jobs. In this example, only two pieces are printed at once. Any number can be printed this way, limited only by the size of the paper.

Print out of State

Printing prices vary substantially between large cities and small ones. A job might cost twenty percent more to print in New York City than in Salem, NC, where wages and property costs are lower. A little travel can save a New York color publisher a lot of money. Traveling to print color jobs at the right shop is standard within the industry. Plus, at this writing, you save the state taxes on the job as well. Unfortunately, shipping costs for a heavy project such as a catalog may negate the savings on state taxes. If you are considering an expensive job, get a quote from a shop in another city for comparison. You may be surprised at how much cheaper it is. And, a twenty percent saving on a $70,000 brochure print job easily pays for any shipping costs, even if the print shop doesn't include it in their bid.

Scrap One Color

Most color printing is done on two-, four-, or six-color presses. Keep this in mind when designing a job because using the right number of colors for a particular press can save you money. For example, if you spec a job with three colors, your printer will mostly likely run the job on a four-color press. In some shops, the four-color press will have a higher hourly rate than a two-color press, regardless of the number of stations used. By knocking off one color, money can be saved. If your job must use three colors, add a varnish or fourth color and pay only a small extra amount to use the otherwise empty fourth station on the press.

Another similar tactic used in low-cost color packaging is to print four-color images with only two colors. This is done is by having the printer study the image (usually an illustration) to determine what two colors will render it best. One four-color illustration we ran as a two-color job used a blue and an orange for the four colors. Though it sounds unpromising, the results looked similar to a four-color version previously printed in a brochure. While we handled this process conventionally (it was printed around the time the Mac 512K was introduced), it can be accomplished with the channel manipulation tools found in color separation programs. Ask your printer which colors will work best for individual images.

Gang Print Jobs

A commonly used money-saving process is to print more than one item at a time on a sheet of paper. It sometimes happens that a job doesn't make efficient use of a sheet of paper, resulting in almost half of it being trimmed off and wasted. If you have another project that uses some or all of the colors of the primary job, consider printing both at the same time. This is a great opportunity to print test color separations for upcoming jobs as well.

Six Tools That Cut Color Publishing Time

Many Macintosh color publishers are being asked (pushed might be a better word) to bring their work online within a busy production environment. Publishing is usually a hurried affair with everyone from clients to managers clambering for greater speed in order to make tight due dates. Because of the rush deadlines, almost anything that will speed up the process should be considered. Here are several of our favorites for increasing throughput on color publishing projects.

DeskPaint/DeskDraw

A pair of desk accessories from Zedcor that we use frequently are called DeskPaint and DeskDraw. Sold together as a package with both a desk accessory version and an application version of both programs, they provide both a full-color painting environment and a drawing program. Best of all, since these programs are DAs, they are instantly accessible from within any application. For example, if you import a scan into a page layout program and see a flaw that needs repair, you can open the scan within DeskPaint, make changes, and re-import it, without leaving the page layout program. DeskDraw is useful for constructing quick charts while in page layout programs and for making quick fixes to object-oriented PICT files.

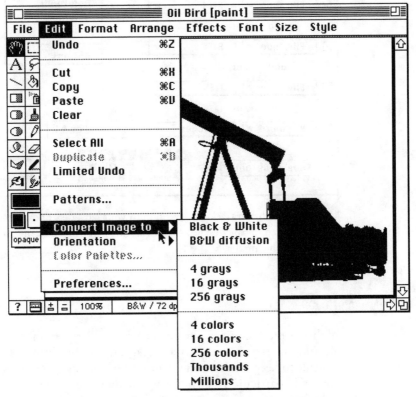

DeskPaint allows instant image file format and color mode conversions.

DeskPaint can also be used to convert paint-type documents from one file format to another. For example, a PICT-based paint document created within Studio/32, a popular full-color paint program by Electronic Arts, can be instantly converted to a TIFF file without leaving your page layout program. DeskPaint also allows conversion of documents from black and white to greys and supports color and resolution changes—useful functions for conversions on the fly. While not as powerful as professional paint programs or photo-retouching packages, DeskPaint is inexpensive, convenient, and easy to use.

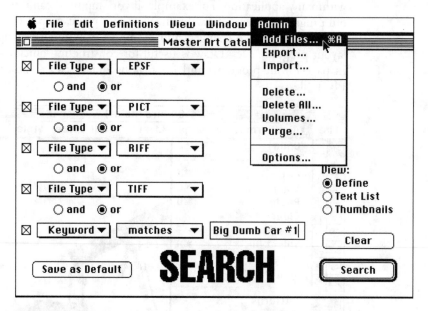

Multi-Ad Search can track images on both your hard disk and on media not currently mounted on the desktop such as archived floppy disks, optical disks, and other removable media.

Multi-Ad Search

Within a production environment where a large number of scans and illustrations stream through a workgroup of Macintoshes, it becomes difficult to keep track of one item stashed among 2,533 others. Finding images is particularly difficult when they are stored by a date-based archiving system or vaguely named "Tony's Picture." The people who brought you Multi-Ad Creator also offer Multi-Ad Search—a product for tracking images and making them instantly available. Multi-Ad

Search can track up to 32,000 images stored on a variety of media and looks across servers for an elusive file. Once located, images can be previewed, printed, or copied. Image searches are possible using various descriptive criteria including keyword, file type, expiration date, and probable location on a server. Multi-Ad Search makes working with a substantial art collection much easier, and practically eliminates the loss of images stored on removable media or nested deep on a giant network server disk.

Programmable Tablets, Macro Programs, and the Gravis SuperMouse

One of the design solutions that makes the Mac so easy to learn is the consistent use of pull-down menus and dialog boxes. Using a simple mouse click to make a selection, this easy-to-use interface gets beginning Mac users up to speed in just minutes. Unfortunately for the color publisher who sits in front of a Mac eight (or maybe twelve) hours a day, repetitive motions moving through menu items slow throughput and quickly become irritating.

Three tools can automate publishing tasks by eliminating recurring actions through the menu dialog: programmable tablets, macro programs, and the Gravis SuperMouse. Much like the input systems on high-end prepress systems, programmable tablets not only provide on-tablet tracing of images, they can be quickly programmed with macros to automate mouse clicks and pull-down menu functions. A tablet allows you to automate 40 or more procedures appropriate to the routine work you do on any number of color publishing products.

Another alternative is macro programs. While Apple no longer includes its wimpy macro program with the Mac's operating software, easy-to-use and powerful macro programs are available for the Mac. Two programs, Quick-Keys and Tempo, can work from a programmable tablet (usually included in the purchase price) or can be used to program the F-Keys of Apple's Extended Keyboard. The Gravis SuperMouse is one of several new mouse options that offer multi-button control. Standard in the DOS/Windows world for years, multi-button mice are just beginning to appear in the Mac environment. The Gravis mouse allows single and multiple clicks of its three buttons to be interpreted as single commands or steps taking you through menus and dialogs.

With practice, all three of the tools substantially speed throughput by reducing hand-mouse-menu actions.

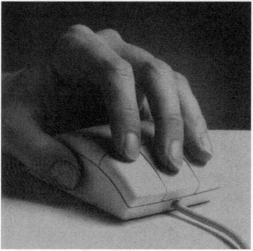

Programmable tablets and multi-button mice reduce the repetitive trips to dialog boxes and pull-down menus that can waste a color desktop publisher's time.

Adobe Streamline

We call this product Adobe "Screamline" because it traces line art quickly and provides accurate outlines of traced images. This provides a fast method for converting scans into line art for manipulation within illustration and paint programs. Unlike the familiar magic wand tool that attempts to find the edges of a single area for manipulation, Streamline finds *all* of the edges and then saves them in a format compatible with Macintosh illustration and paint programs. It's a great tool for converting 72-dpi bitmapped images into clean line art to which new colors and detail can be added, without the original's jaggy edges. (Higher resolution images work better, but what are you going to do with all that MacPaint clip art if you don't have Streamline?) The sensitivity of the edge-finding controls are also adjustable to make working with different kinds of images that much easier. For use with Illustrator, Streamline can capture the lines as Bézier curves.

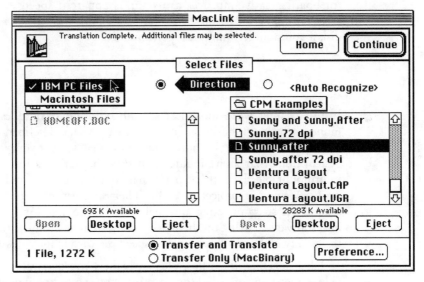

MacLink translators can help you translate some picture and most text formats between Mac and IBM PC.

MacLink Translators

If your work includes bringing images across from the DOS/Windows world or other environments, MacLink translators handle the translation for you. To use a translator, simply bring the file to your machine via network, cable provided with the software, or on a floppy disk using DOS

Mounter (also included with the program) and make the translation. Along with translating some picture formats, MacLink Translators convert files produced by most popular word processors, databases, and spreadsheets. MacLink is a two-way street. Files from your Mac can be translated into a number of other computer file formats.

Accelerators

There are a number of acceleration systems for speeding up pokey Macs. When processing color image files, you'll want all the speed you can get. DayStar and Radius provide boards that turn an ordinary Mac IIx or IIcx into a machine faster than any off-the-shelf Mac. In addition to making CPU accelerators, DayStar makes a board to speed the transfer of information between the hard drive and the Mac. Because disk-to-CPU transfers often slow Macs down even more than slow CPUs, a SCSI accelerator board greatly improves a machine's apparent speed even without accelerating the CPU. Buy accelerators for both the CPU *and* your hard disk if you want lightning-fast performance.

In this chapter we've looked at several tools and techniques for saving money in color publishing. In addition to what's described here, ingenious printers and service bureau operators may look at your job and suggest options that aren't included in this chapter. If a job's cost seems insurmountable, have the experts that routinely output and print color work review your project carefully. Their inventiveness may find a way around the steep price tag and make the job do-able. As for "labor-saving" software, arriving on the market daily are new products that improve the quality of color publishing and speed the throughput of work.

Taken together, these tips, plus any others you discover or invent, can reduce the time from desktop to print shop while keeping costs in line. Speed and low cost is what makes Macintosh-based color publishing viable, by bringing freedom of the *color* press to so many people, including you.

You have now finished reading about of basics in the world of Mac color publishing. With the information you've gained, and the references that follow to guide you, we hope all your publishing explorations on the Mac will be more colorful.

SOURCES

The first part of this chapter is a general reference to the types of products discussed in the book. Product types are listed on the left, and the companies that produce or distribute the products are listed on the right. Because Macintosh products are evolving rapidly, version and model numbers for products are not listed in this section.

A section on *Company Resources* is also provided. The listings have been organized alphabetically because many companies produce more than one type of product. The company listings include mailing addresses and telephone numbers, so you can request more information.

There are many more suppliers of Macintosh products than those listed here. We have only included products and companies with which we are familiar. Because new products are constantly being released for the Macintosh and product names change, these listings are not comprehensive.

For reviews and listings of new products, refer to the Macintosh and publishing-oriented magazines listed in the section that is titled *Useful Publications for Macintosh Color Publishers,* included after the product and company listings.

Note: A listing in this book should not be construed as an endorsement or recommendation for any product or service. Listings are provided for the sole purpose of assisting the reader to locate more information about the types of products and services mentioned in the book.

Hardware Products	Company or Source
Accelerators	Daystar Digital, Inc.
	Dove Computer Corp.
	MacProducts USA Inc.
	Micron Technology, Inc.
	Radius, Inc.
	Siclone Sales and Engineering
	Total Systems
Color Calibration Systems	Radius, Inc.
	RasterOps Corp.
	SuperMac Technologies
Color Copiers	Canon USA, Inc.
	Eastman Kodak Co.
Color Copier Controller Fiery ColorLaser	EFI (Electronics for Imaging, Inc.)
Color Monitors and Display Card Systems	Apple Computer, Inc.
	Barco Video and Communications
	E-Machines, Inc.
	MegaGraphics
	Mirror Technologies, Inc.
	NEC Technologies, Inc.
	PCPC (Personal Computer Peripherals Corp.)
	Radius, Inc.
	RasterOps Corp.
	Relax Technologies, Inc.
	Seiko Instruments USA, Inc.
	SuperMac Technologies
Imagesetters	Agfa Corp.
	Linotype-Hell
	Monotype Inc.
	Optronics
	Varityper

Hardware Products	Company or Source
Continued	
Macintosh Computers	Apple Computer, Inc.
Mass Storage Systems	
Optical Drives	Eastman Kodak Co.
	(Kodak Electronic Printing Systems)
	La Cie Ltd.
	MicroNet Technology, Inc.
	Microtech International Inc.
	Mirror Technologies, Inc.
	Pinnacle Micro
	Relax Technology, Inc.
Removable Media and Large-Capacity Hard Drives	CMS Enhancements
	Corel Systems
	Cutting Edge
	Data Enhancements, Inc.
	GCC Technologies, Inc.
	Hard Drives International
	La Cie Ltd.
	MacLand, Inc.
	MacProducts USA, Inc.
	MicroNet Technology, Inc.
	Microtech International Inc.
	Iomega Corp.
	Pinnacle Micro
Silicon Disks	ATTO Technology
CD-ROM	Apple Computer, Inc.
	Mirror Technologies, Inc.
	NEC Technologies, Inc.
Modems	Abaton (Everex Systems)
	Apple Computer, Inc.
	Dove Computer Corp.
	Hayes Microcomputer Products, Inc.

Hardware Products
Continued

Company or Source

Mouse, Multibutton Programmable
Gravis SuperMouse   Advanced Gravis Systems

Prepress Systems, Dedicated   Scitex America Corp.
                                           Linotype-Hell
                                           Crosfield Lightspeed

Printers
Color Printers   Hewlett-Packard Co.
                                           Iris Graphics Inc.
                                           Kodak Electronic Printing Systems
                                           Mitsubishi Electronics America
                                           NEC Technologies, Inc.
                                           Océ Graphics USA, Inc.
                                           QMS Inc.
                                           Seiko Instruments USA, Inc.
                                           Sharp Electronics
                                           Tektronix, Inc.

Laser Printers, Black and White   Abaton (Everex Systems)
                                           Apple Computer, Inc.
                                           Epson America
                                           GCC Technologies, Inc.
                                           Hewlett-Packard Co.
                                           LaserMaster Systems
                                           Océ Graphics USA, Inc.
                                           QMS Inc.
                                           Seiko Instruments USA, Inc.
                                           Sharp Electronics
                                           Tektronix, Inc.

Scanners
3D Scanners   Canon USA, Inc.
                                           Truvel

Hardware Products	Company or Source
Continued	
Scanners cont.	
33mm Scanners	Barneyscan Corp.
	Eastman Kodak Co.
	Howtek, Inc.
	Microtek Lab
	Nikon Electronic Imaging
Drum Scanners	Howtek, Inc.
	Linotype-Hell
	Optronics
Flatbed or Overhead Scanners	Abaton (Everex Systems)
	Agfa Corp.
	Apple Computer, Inc.
	Epson America, Inc.
	Hewlett-Packard Co.
	Howtek, Inc.
	La Cie Ltd.
	Microtek Lab
	Mitsubishi Electronics America
	Sharp Electronics
	Truvel
Tablets	CalComp
	GTCO Corp.
	Kurta Corp.
	Wacom Inc.

Software Products	Company or Source
Backup System	
Retrospect	Dantz Development Corp.
Calibration Software	
Color Calibration Software	
for PostScript Imagesetters	Technical Publishing Services
Radius PrecisionColor Calibrator	Radius, Inc.
RasterOps CorrectColor Calibrator	RasterOps Corp.
ScanMatch	Savitar Color Communication
Clip Art	
650-Megabyte Clip Art Disk	Media Clip-Art
Canned Art: Clip Art for the Mac	PeachPit Press
ClickArt	T/Maker
Cliptures	Dream Maker Software
Collector's Edition I and II	Adobe Systems, Inc.
Digit-Art	Image Club Graphics, Inc.
Images with Impact!	3G Graphics
Metro ImageBase Electronic Art	Metro ImageBase, Inc.
Professional Photography Collection	discimagery
Totem Graphics	Totem Graphics
Color Image Retouching	
ColorStudio	Letraset USA, Inc.
Photoshop	Adobe Systems, Inc.
Color Matching Systems	
TekColor	Tektronix Inc.
Kodak Color Management System	Eastman Kodak Co.
Scanmatch	Savitar, Inc.
Eport Color Server	EFI (Electronics for Imaging, Inc.)
Color Separation Packages	
PrePrint (bundled with PageMaker)	Aldus Corp.
ColorStudio	Letraset USA, Inc.
Photoshop	Adobe Systems, Inc.
SpectrePrint Pro	Prepress Technologies
Cachet	EFI (Electronics for Imaging, Inc.)

Software Products	Company or Source
Continued	
Color Specification Systems	
Pantone Color Formula Guide	Pantone, Inc.
TruMatch	TRUMatch, Inc.
Focoltone Colour System	Focoltone USA
Compression Programs for Images and Files	
DiskDoubler	Salient Software Inc.
ImpressIt	Radius, Inc.
StuffIt Deluxe	Aladdin Systems, Inc.
Drawing Programs, Object Oriented	
DeskDraw	Zedcor Corp.
MacDraw II	Claris Corp.
Super 3D	Aldus Corp.
SuperPaint	Aldus Corp.
File Access Tool	
CanOpener	Abbott Systems
File Management for Graphics	
Multi-Ad Search	Multi-Ad Services, Inc.
Font Design, Editing, and Special Effects	
FONTastic Plus	Altsys Corp.
Fontographer	Altsys Corp.
FontStudio	Letraset USA, Inc.
LetraStudio	Letraset USA, Inc.
Smart Art	Adobe Systems, Inc.
TypeAlign	Adobe Systems, Inc.
TypeStyler	Broderbund Software, Inc.
Font Outlining Technology	
ATM (Adobe Type Manager)	Adobe Systems, Inc.
TrueType	Microsoft Corp.
Fonts	
	Adobe Systems, Inc.
	Agfa Corp.
	Bitstream Inc.
	Image Club Graphics, Inc.

Software Products
Continued

Company or Source

Fonts cont.

ITC (International Typeface Corp.)
Linotype-Hell

Grayscale Retouching
Photoshop
Digital Darkroom
ImageStudio

Adobe Systems, Inc.
Silicon Beach Software/Aldus Corp.
Letraset USA, Inc.

Illustration Software
Illustrator
Freehand

Adobe Systems, Inc.
Aldus Corp.

Image Outlining/Autotracing
Adobe Streamline

Adobe Systems, Inc.

Imagesetter Simulation Software
LaserCheck

Systems of Merritt, Inc.

Page Layout Programs (Professional Level)
DesignStudio

Framemaker
Multi-Ad Creator
PageMaker
PosterWorks
QuarkXPress
Quoin
Ventura Publisher

Letraset USA, Inc.
   /Manhattan Graphics
Frame Technology Corp.
Multi-Ad Services, Inc.
Aldus Corp.
S.H. Pierce & Co.
Quark, Inc.
Quoin Publishing Systems, Inc.
Ventura Software

Painting Programs
DeskPaint
Oasis
Painter
PixelPaint, PixelPaint Professional
Studio/32

Zedcor Corp.
Time Arts Inc.
Fractal Design Corp.
SuperMac Technologies
Electronic Arts

Software Products	Company or Source
Continued	
PostScript Interpreter	
Freedom of Press	Custom Applications Inc.
Prepress Software and Links	
(See also Color Separation Software)	
RipLink	Screaming Color
Scitex System	Scitex America Corp.
StudioLink	DuPont Imaging Systems
Scanning Software	
SpectreScan (enhanced scan features)	Prepress Technologies
Screen Saver	
After Dark	Berkeley Systems, Inc.
Shading and Color Rendering	
Swivel 3D	Paracomp, Inc.
Telecommunications	
MicroPhone II	Software Ventures, Inc.
Smartcom II	Hayes Microcomputer Products Inc.
White Knight	FreeSoft Co.
Translators	
MacLink Plus/Translators	DataViz, Inc.
Utilities for Productivity	
QuicKeys2	CE Software Inc.
Suitcase II	Fifth Generation Systems
Word Processing Software	
with Some Color and DTP Features	
Nisus	Paragon Concepts, Inc.
Word	Microsoft Corp.
WordPerfect	WordPerfect Corp.

Company Resources

3G Graphics
11410 N.E. 124th St.
Kirkland, WA 98034
(206) 367-9321
(800) 456-0234

Abaton (Everex Systems)
48431 Milmont Dr.
Fremont, CA 94538
(415) 683-2226
(800) 444-5321

Abbott Systems
62 Mountain Rd.
Pleasantville, NY 10570
(914) 747-4171
(800) 552-9157

Adobe Systems, Inc.
1585 Charleston Rd.
P. O. Box 7900
Mountain View, CA 94039
(415) 961-4400

Advanced Gravis Systems
7400 MacPherson Avenue
Burnaby, Britsh Columbia
Canada V5J 5B6

Agfa Corp.
200 Ballardvale Street
Wilmington, MA 01887
(508) 658-5600

Aladdin Systems, Inc.
Deer Park Center
Suite 23A-171
Aptos, CA 95003-4723
(408) 685-9175

Aldus Corp.
411 First Ave. South
Seattle, WA 98104
(206) 622-5500

Altsys Corp.
269 W. Renner Rd.
Richardson, TX 75080
(214) 680-2060

Apple Computer, Inc.
20525 Mariani Ave.
Cupertino, CA 95014
(408) 996-1010
(800) 776-2333

ATTO Technology
1567 Sweet Home Rd.
Amherst, NY 14221
(716) 688-4259

Barco Video and Communications
1500 Wilson Way
Smyrna, Georgia 30082
(404) 432-2346

Barneyscan Corp.
1125 Atlantic Ave.
Alameda, CA 94501
(415) 521-3388

Berkeley Systems, Inc.
1700 Shattuck Ave.
Berkeley, CA 94709
(415) 540-5535

Company Resources

Continued

Bitstream Inc.
Athenaeum House
215 First Street
Cambridge, MA 02142
(617) 497-6222

Broderbund Software, Inc.
17 Paul Dr.
San Rafael, CA 94903-2101
(800) 521-6263

CalComp
2411 W. La Palma Ave.
Anaheim, CA 92801
(714) 821-2000
(800) 225-2667

Canon USA, Inc.
One Canon Plaza
Lake Success, NY 11042
(516) 488-6700

CE Software Inc.
P. O. Box 65580
West Des Moines, IA 50265
(515) 224-1953

Chinon, Inc.
660 Maple Ave.
Torrance, CA 90504
(213) 533-0274

Claris Corp.
5201 Patrick Henry Dr.
Santa Clara, CA 95052
(408) 727-8227
(800) 544-8554

CMS Enhancements
2722 Michelson Drive
Irvine, CA 92715
(714) 222-6000

Corel Systems
1600 Carline Ave., #190
Ottawa, Ontario
Canada K1Z 8R7
(613) 728-8200

Crosfield Lightspeed
47 Farnsworth Street
Boston, MA 02210
(617) 338-2173

Custom Applications Inc.
900 Technology Park Dr.
Building 8
Billerica, MA 01821
(508) 667-8585
(800) 873-4367

Cutting Edge
97 S. Red Willow Rd.
Evanston, WY 82930
(307) 789-0582

Dantz Development Corp.
1400 Shattuck Ave., Suite 1
Berkeley, CA 94709
(415) 849-0293

Data Enhancements, Inc.
31328 Via Colinas, #102
Westlake Village, CA 91326
(818) 879-2700

Company Resources

Continued

DataViz, Inc.
35 Corporate Dr.
Trumbull, CT 06611
(203) 268-0030

DayStar Digital, Inc.
5556 Atlanta Hwy.
Flowery Branch, GA 30542
(404) 967-2077
(800) 962-2077

discimagery
18 E. 16th St.
New York, NY 10003
(212) 675-8500

Dove Computer Corp.
1220 N. 23rd St.
Wilmington, NC 28405
(919) 763-7918
(800) 622-7627

Dream Maker Software
7217 Foothill Blvd.
Tujunga, CA 91042
(818) 353-2297
(800) 876-5665

DuPont Imaging Systems
65 Harristown Road
Glen Rock, New Jersey 07452
(201) 447-5800

EFI (Electronics for Imaging, Inc.)
950 Elm Avenue
San Bruno, CA 94066
(415) 742-3400

E-Machines, Inc.
9305 S. W. Gemini Dr.
Beaverton, OR 97005
(503) 646-6699
(800) 344-7274

Eastman Kodak Co.
343 State Street
Rochester, NY 14650
(716) 724-4000
(800) 445-6325

Electronic Arts
1820 Gateway Dr.
San Mateo, CA 94404
(415) 571-7171
(800) 245-4525

Epson America, Inc.
2780 Lomita Blvd.
Torrance, CA 90505
(213) 782-0770
(800) 289-3776

Fifth Generation Systems
10049 N. Reiger Rd.
Baton Rouge, LA 70899
(800) 873-4384
(504) 291-7221

Focoltone USA
5101 College Boulevard, Suite 208
Leawood, Kansas 66211
(913) 338-0505

Fractal Design Corp.
101 Madeline Dr., Suite 204
Aptos, CA 95003
(408) 688-8800

Company Resources

Continued

Frame Technology Corp.
1010 Rincon Circle
San Jose, CA 95131
(408) 433-3311

FreeSoft Co.
150 Hickory Dr.
Beaver Falls, PA 15010
(412) 846-2700

GCC Technologies, Inc.
580 Winter St.
Waltham, MA 02154
(617) 890-0880
(800) 422-7777

GTCO Corp.
7125 Riverwood Dr.
Columbia, MD 21046
(301) 381-6688
(800) 344-4723

Hard Drives International
1912 W. Fourth St.
Tempe, AZ 85281
(602) 967-4999
(800) 767-3475

Hayes Microcomputer Products, Inc.
P.O. Box 105203
Atlanta, GA 30348
(404) 441-1617

Hewlett-Packard Co.
19091 Pruneridge Ave.
Cupertino, CA 95014
(408) 725-8900
(800) 752-0900

Howtek Inc.
21 Park Ave.
Hudson, NH 03051
(603) 882-5200

Image Club Graphics, Inc.
1902 Eleventh Street S.E., Ste. 5
Calgary, Alberta
Canada T2G 3G2
(403) 262-8008

Iomega Corp.
1821 West 4000 South
Roy, UT 84067
(800) 456-5522

Iris Graphics Inc.
Six Crosby Drive
Bedford, MA 01730
(617) 275-8777

ITC (International Typeface Corp.)
866 Second Avenue
New York, NY 10017
(212) 371-0699

Kodak Electronic Printing Systems
23 Crosby Drive.
Bedford, MA 01730
(617) 276-6612

Kurta Corp.
3007 E. Chambers
Phoenix, AZ 85040
(602) 276-5533
(800) 44 KURTA

Company Resources

Continued

La Cie, Ltd.
19552 SW 90th Ct.
Tualatin, OR 97062
(800) 899-0143
(503) 691-0771

LaserMaster Systems
7150 Shady Oak Dr.
Eden Prairie, MN 55344
(612) 944-9457

Letraset USA, Inc.
40 Eisenhower Dr.
Paramus, NJ 07653
(201) 845-6100

Linotype-Hell
425 Oser Avenue
Hauppauge, NY 11788
(516) 434-2000

MacLand, Inc.
4685 S. Ash Ave., Ste. H-5
Tempe, AZ 85282
(602) 820-5802
(800) 333-3353

MacProducts USA Inc.
8303 Mopac Expy., Ste. 218
Austin, TX 78759
(512) 343-9441
(800) 622-3475

Media Clip-Art
1879 Old Cuthbert Rd., Unit #10
Cherry Hill, NJ 08003
(609) 795-5993

MegaGraphics
439 Calle San Pablo
Camarillo, CA 93012
(805) 484-3799
(800) 487-6342

Metro ImageBase, Inc.
18623 Ventura Blvd., Suite 210
Tarzana, CA 91356
(800) 525-1552
(818) 881-1997

Micron Technology, Inc.
2805 E. Columbia Rd.
Boise, ID 83706
(208) 368-3800
(800) 642-7661

MicroNet Technology, Inc.
20 Mason
Irvine, CA 92718
(714) 837-6033

Microsoft Corp.
One Microsoft Way
Redmond, WA 98052
(206) 882-8080
(800) 426-9400

Microtech International Inc.
158 Commerce St.
East Haven, CT 06512
(203) 468-6223
(800) 325-1895

Microtek Lab
680 Knox St.
Torrance, CA 90502
(213) 321-2121

Company Resources

Continued

Mirror Technologies, Inc.
2644 Patton Rd.
Roseville, MN 55113
(612) 633-4450

Mitsubishi Electronics America
991 Knox St.
Torrance, CA 90502
(213) 217-5732

Monotype Inc.
2500 Brickvale Dr.
Elk Grove Village, IL 60008
(708) 350-5600

Multi-Ad Services, Inc.
1720 W. Detweiller Dr.
Peoria, IL 61615-1695
(309) 692-1530

NEC Technologies, Inc.
1414 Massachusetts Ave.
Boxborough, MA 01719
(508) 264-8000
(800) 632-4636

Nikon Electronic Imaging
1300 Walt Whitman
Melville, NY 11747
(516) 547-4200

Océ Graphics USA Inc.
385 Ravendale Dr.
Mountain View, CA 94039

Optronics
7 Stuart Rd.
Chelmsford, MA 01824
(508) 256-4511

Pantone, Inc.
55 Knickerbocker Rd.
Moonachie, NJ 07074
(201) 935-5500

Paracomp, Inc.
1725 Montgomery St.
San Francisco, CA 94111
(415) 956-4091

Paragon Concepts, Inc.
990 Highland Drive, #312
Solana Beach, CA 92075
(619) 481-1477
(800) 922-2993

PCPC (Personal Computer
  Peripherals Corp.)
4710 Eisenhower Blvd., Bldg. A4
Tampa, FL 33634
(813) 884-3092
(800) 622-2888

PeachPit Press
1085 Keith Ave.
Berkeley, CA 94708
(415) 527-8555
(800) 283-9444

Pinnacle Micro
19 Technology Drive
Irvine, CA 92718
(714) 727-3300
(800) 553-7070

Company Resources

Continued

Prepress Technologies
2443 Impala Drive
Carlsbad, CA 92008
(619) 931-2695

QMS Inc.
1 Magnum Pass
Mobile, AL 36619
(205) 633-4300

Quark, Inc.
300 South Jackson, Suite 100
Denver, CO 80209
(303) 934-2211

Quoin Publishing Systems, Inc.
22144 Clarendon Street
Woodland Hills, CA 91367
(818) 715-7145

Radius, Inc.
1710 Fortune Dr.
San Jose, CA 95131-1744
(408) 434-1010

RasterOps Corp.
2500 Walsh Avenue
Santa Clara, CA 95051
(408) 562-4200

Relax Technology, Inc.
3101 Whipple Rd., STe. 22
Union City, CA 94587
(415) 471-6112

S.H. Pierce & Co.
Suite 323
Building 600
One Kendall Square
Cambridge, MA 02139
(617) 395-8350

Salient Software Inc.
124 University Ave., Suite 103
Palo Alto, CA 94301
(415) 321-5375

Savitar Color Communication
139 Townsend Street, Suite 203
San Francisco, CA 94107
(415) 243-3030

Scitex America Corp.
8 Oak Park Drive
Bedford MA 01730
(616) 275-5150

Screaming Color
125 N. Prospect Ave.
Itasca, IL 60143
(708) 250-9500

Seiko Instruments USA, Inc.
1130 Ringwood Ct.
San Jose, CA 95131
(408) 922-5900

Sharp Electronics
Sharp Plaza
Mahway, NJ 07430
(201) 52908200

Siclone Sales and Engineering
1072 Saratoga-Sunnyvale Rd.
Bldg. A-107, Ste. 443
San Jose, CA 95129
(408) 534-1742

Silicon Beach Software
9770 Carroll Center Rd.
San Diego, CA 92126
(619) 695-6956

Company Resources

Continued

Software Ventures, Inc.
2907 Claremont Ave.
Berkeley, CA 94705
(415) 644-3232

SuperMac Technologies
485 Potrero Avenue
Sunnyvale, CA 94086
(408) 245-2202

Systems of Merritt, Inc.
2551 Old Dobbin Dr. East
Mobile, AL 36695
(205) 660-1240

Technical Publishing Services
2205 Sacramento St.
San Francisco, CA 94115
(415) 921-8509

Tektronix, Inc.
Wilsonville Industrial Park
Wilsonville, OR 97077
(503) 627-7656
(503) 682-3411

Time Arts Inc.
1425 Corporate Center Parkway
Santa Rosa, CA 95407
(707) 576-7722

Total Systems
99 W. 10th Ave., Ste. 333
Eugene, OR 97401
(503) 345-7395
(800) 874-2288

Totem Graphics
5109 A Capitol Blvd.
Tumwater, WA 98501
(206) 352-1851

T/MAKER
1390 Villa St.
Mountain View, CA 94041
(415) 962-0195

TRUMatch, Inc.
331 Madison Avenue
New York, NY 10017
(212) 351-2360

Truvel
8943 Fullbright Ave.
Chatsworth, CA 91311
(818) 407-1031

Varityper
11 Mount Pleasant Avenue
East Hanover, NJ 07936
(800) 631-8134

Ventura Software Inc.
15175 Innovation Dr.
San Diego, CA 92128
(800) 822-8331

Wacom Inc.
West 115 Century Road
Paramus, NJ 07652
(201) 265-4226

WordPerfect Corp.
1555 N. Technology Way
Orem, UT 84057
(801) 225-5000
(800) 321-4566

Zedcor Corp.
4500 E. Speedway, Suite 22
Tucson, AZ 85712
(602) 881-8101

Useful Publications for Macintosh Color Publishers

Communication Arts (Color Design)
410 Sherman Avenue
P. O. Box 10300
Palo Alto, CA 94303
Telephone (415) 326-6040

Desktop Communications (DTP)
International Desktop
    Communications, Ltd.
P. O. Box 941745
Atlanta, GA 30341
Telephone (800) 966-9052

DesignWorld (Design Magazine)
Design Editorial Pty Ltd.
11 School Road, Ferny Creek
Victoria 3786, Australia
Telephone 61 3 755 1149

MacPrePress (Fax-based Newsletter)
PrePress Information Service
12 Burr Road
Westport, CT 06880
Telephone (203) 227-2357

MacUser (Monthly Mac Magazine)
950 Tower Lane 18th Floor
Foster City, CA 94404
Telephone (415) 378-5600

Mac Publishing and Presentation
(Bimonthly Mac Publishing Magazine)
IDC, Ltd.
P. O. Box 941745
Atlanta, GA 30341
Telephone (800) 966-9052

MacWeek (Weekly Mac Magazine)
One Park Avenue
New York, NY 10016
Telephone (609) 461-2100

MacWorld (Monthly Mac Magazine)
501 Second St.
San Francisco, CA 94107
Telephone (415) 243-0505

(MD & P) Magazine Design &
Production
South Wind Publishing Company
8340 Mission Road Suite 106
Prairie Village, KS 66206
Telephone (913) 642-6611

Pre- (Electronic Prepress Magazine)
South Wind Publishing Company
8340 Mission Road Suite 106
Prairie Village, KS 66206
Telephone (913) 642-6611

Step-By-Step Graphics
(Design Magazine)
Dynamic Graphics
    Educational Foundation
6000 N. Forest Park Dr.
Peoria, IL 61614-3592
Telephone (309) 688-2300

U&lc (Typographic Magazine)
866 Second Avenue
New York, NY 10017
Telephone (212) 371-0699

APPENDIX

A

HOW TO USE THE BOUND-IN DISK

This book includes a disk of software selected to assist you in learning color publishing on the Mac and to help you get your work done faster and with more consistent results. The disk contains a mixture of shareware and freeware programs. The freeware programs have no licensing fees and may be freely used and distributed. The shareware programs require a fee to be sent to the developer if you choose to use them.

The disk contains a shareware version of a program called StuffIt Classic. As explained in Chapter Ten, compression programs can be used to make files more compact to save disk space, reduce electronic transmission times over modems, and make it easier to transport images to a service bureau. In addition, the disk contains a variety of programs for managing color publishing tasks and an image-retouching program for experimenting with painting tools, filters, and image enhancement. All the files have been compressed to fit on a single disk with StuffIt. The UnStuffIt utility that is part of the StuffIt Classic product on Disk One can decompress the files, as explained later in this appendix.

Quick Program Summary

Here is a quick summary of each of the programs provided on the disk that accompanies this book. More information on each of the programs is provided later in this appendix:

- StuffIt Classic, including UnStuffIt   Used for compression and decompression of files. These programs are widely used and can compress all types of files.

- TermWorks   A compact communications program that supports macros. This program can be used to send files to a service bureau or to communicate with online services, such as CompuServe, to download clip art and shareware.

- Colorize   Used to add color cosmetics to applications that normally appear in boring black and white.

- Aurora   Used to customize the colors of the Mac's pull-down menus.

- Font Info Stack   Used to check fonts in your system for font number conflicts and font availability, as discussed in Chapter Six.

- TypeBook   Produces sample type pages of fonts installed in your system. TypeBook's sample pages show each selected font in several sizes and styles.

- Varityper Toolkit   Performs a variety of font management functions, including examining PostScript files to see which fonts were used and changing the default fonts that many applications open with (often the less-than-attractive typeface Geneva).

- Image   Manipulates grayscale and (256) color images. Image is provided to give you practice using paint tools and manipulating images with sharpening filters.

- Blender   Helps determine color blends and imagesetter resolution for Mac illustration programs, including Illustrator and Freehand.

- MenuChoice   Creates handy hierarchical menus that allow you to access your entire hard drive from the Apple menu. Makes placing image and text files easier when you have a page layout open on the desktop.

- PixelFlipper   Changes pixel depth instantly. PixelFlipper allows you to change from millions of colors to 256 colors much faster than using the control panels when you want to run an application, such as TypeStyler, that won't open in the millions-of-colors mode.

- PM4 Shortcuts   Provides instant (DA) access to all kinds of PageMaker shortcuts. Can be left open on screen while you work in PageMaker, if your monitor is large enough to accommodate both windows.

- HeapTool   Changes the system's "heap" size for System 6 users, as described in Chapter Six.

Compatibility

We cannot guarantee that all of the programs on the bound-in disk are fully compatible with all variations of the Macintosh. We've tested them on a number of systems and have found few problems. Still, the newest Macs, such as the Quadras, may suffer compatibility problems when running in their fastest mode. This is because, for the most part, the software was developed before Quadras were introduced to the market. Test the programs on your own system before you rely on them. Though we have done our best to assure that the programs work as stated, we are not responsible for the programs' functionality, performance, or any damages that may be incurred in their use.

The Shareware Concept

While some of the programs included on the disk are freeware or public domain software, the majority of the software applications provided are a kind of software called *shareware*. Shareware, in most cases, can be given away or distributed freely, but if you decide to use the program, you are obligated to pay the shareware fee as set by the program's author or developer. The concept of shareware is simple: pay if you like and use the program. Don't pay if you don't use it.

Shareware is a powerful concept. Individual authors can create useful programs and get them into distribution without paying for expensive packaging. No salesforce is required to sell the programs, and no expensive advertising is needed either. But, in order to encourage software developers to continue to develop useful, inexpensive software programs, it is important that shareware users send in the (usually) nominal fee. Otherwise, if shareware authors spend weeks or months developing a program and receive no money from users in return, they will think twice before developing other useful shareware programs.

Another advantage of paying the shareware fee is that for some programs you will receive a free update to the program, technical support, and a printed manual. You also get that warm feeling for being honest. The shareware fees for the products are provided in the detailed program descriptions.

How to Install the Accompanying Software

As explained earlier, all of the files provided on the disk are compressed so we could offer more software than would normally fit on one disk. The files have been compressed with a program called StuffIt—a popular lossless compression routine that can compress images, application software, and data files. To put StuffIt to work, you must first install it on your Mac's hard disk. StuffIt itself is compressed (naturally) and must be unstuffed before installation. Fortunately, StuffIt unstuffs and installs itself automatically, making the installation process completely automatic. To install it, put the disk into your floppy disk drive and double click on the StuffIt Installer. The program will prompt you with a series of dialogs, asking which files you wish installed and where you wish them placed on your hard disk, and then automatically complete the installation.

Follow the same set of steps to install UnStuffIt as well. Once this program is decompressed and installed on your hard drive, you can use it to decompress the files.

Stuffed files on disk are called archives. To decompress the archive files, launch UnStuffIt and use the **Unstuff...** command found under the File menu. The program will prompt you with a file open dialog. Simply choose the file you wish to decompress and click **Unstuff** or **Unstuff All** if multiple files are contained in the StuffIt archive. The **Unstuff All** button only becomes active (not grayed out) if multiple files are contained in the StuffIt archive.

Once unstuffed, place the files where they are most convenient on your hard disk. In the case of Aurora and MenuChoice, for example, place them in your Control Panels folder. (Note that MenuChoice will not work under System 6.) Place Blender and PM4 ShortCuts in your Apple Items folder (or install them with the Font DA Mover if you use System 6).

Documentation

Most of the programs have documentation included on the disk. This may take the form of a standalone manual that that can be read with a word processor or Teach Text (provided with the Apple system) or for the simpler programs, it may consist of a help button, available once the program or DA is open.

We encourage you to at least skim through the disk-based manuals for the complex programs. Image, for example, has a manual that explains many of the program's diverse functions, and you may learn more about image-retouching and paint programs just by reading through the relevant parts. This knowledge will assist you in choosing commercial paint and image-retouching software after you have learned the basics.

Replacement Disk

While every effort has been made to ensure that the disk has been properly duplicated and packaged in a manner that reduces the risk of damage, if you receive a disk that your Mac claims is not readable as a Macintosh disk, return it to the address below for prompt replacement. (PowerBook 140 and 170 owners should try the disk in a desktop Mac before returning it. Early PowerBooks had a defect that made them unusually choosy about the disks they could read.)

Return defective disks with your address and a copy of your receipt for the book to:

Random House Electronic Publishing
201 East Fiftieth Street
New York, NY 10022

A replacement disk will be promptly mailed to you.

The Programs on Disk

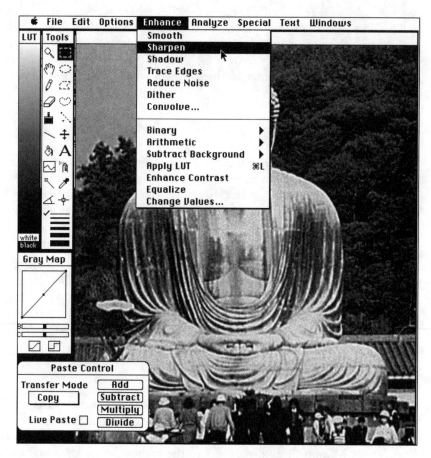

Image is an 8-bit painting and image retouching program that can help you learn the basics before you purchase expensive full-color commercial software.

NIH Image   Wayne Rasband

Purpose: Image is a powerful image painting and retouching application. Supporting grayscale and 256 colors, it allows images to be created using its paint tools, or existing images can be imported for retouching and modification. Image can also work with video. This program includes a surprisingly wide range of functionality. We have included it so that you can try out painting, filtering, and retouching tools to learn how they work. This will give you a better understanding of the technology when shopping for paint or retouching software.

Documentation: Image includes a 62-page manual on disk.

Fee: This is public domain software, and there is no fee for using it.

Contact: Author Wayne Rasband can be reached at the following electronic mail addresses:

CompuServe: 76067,3454

Internet, BitNet: wayne@helix.nih.gov

StuffIt Classic   Raymond Lau and Aladdin Systems

Purpose: StuffIt and its companion program UnStuffIt are "lossless" compression and decompression routines. They can be used to compress files and images of all kinds. Use StuffIt to compress files that will be transported by disk or modem to a service bureau for imaging. Because this is the most popular shareware compression routine, all service bureaus will own a copy that they can use to open your files. Use StuffIt also to archive image files, especially if you own a small hard disk or are trying to fit an image on a single floppy disk.

Documentation: StuffIt Classic has an excellent online help facility as well as a printable user manual.

Fee: If you like and continue to use StuffIt Classic and UnStuffIt, Aladdin Systems requests a $25 shareware fee to be sent to the address below.

Contact: A convenient order form can be printed from under the Apple menu while StuffIt is open. Aladdin also makes StuffIt Deluxe, which is a full-featured, commercial compression/decompression program. StuffIt Deluxe has many more capabilities and facilities than the shareware version. Pricing and product information is available from Aladdin Systems. If you need additional information on StuffIt Deluxe, contact:

Aladdin Systems
165 Westridge Drive
Watsonville, CA 95076
(408) 761-6200

TermWorks   James Rhodes

Purpose: TermWorks is a compact communications program that can be used to send page layouts and graphic files to your service bureau. TermWorks has a macro facility that allows you to establish an automatic log-on sequence for sending your files to a service bureau's bulletin board.

Documentation: TermWorks includes a manual on disk.

Fee: If you like and continue to use TermWorks, author James Rhodes requests a $20 shareware fee.

Contact: Send your fee and/or questions to:

Horizon Software
Attn.: James Rhodes
401 Eastwood Place
Lufkin, TX 75901
(817) 731-8254

Colorize   Neal Trautman

Purpose: Colorize allows you to change the colors of windows, text, borders, and dialog boxes of applications that normally don't use color. Colorize can make your applications much more attractive and take advantage of your Mac's color monitor.

Documentation: Colorize includes a manual on disk.

Fee: $5 is requested if you like the program.

Contact: Send your fee and/or questions to:

Neal Trautman
3700 Clinton Parkway, #1412
Lawrence, KS 66047

Aurora   Mike Pinkerton

Purpose: Aurora allows you to customize the colors of your Mac's menu bar and menus, among other things. When combined with the color selection possibilities in the General Control Panel, it's easy to create a very colorful and unusual desktop: red type on black menus, yellow on black desktops, hot pink menu names, green squares on purple. The only limit is your imagination.

Documentation: Aurora is intuitive for Mac users and requires no manual.

Fee: If you like and continue to use Aurora, author Mike Pinkerton requests that you send what you think the program is worth. He likes to call shareware "pay-if-you-use-it-ware." If you don't want to send him money, send your ideas about the cdevs and report any problems. Mike will try to send updates as they come out.

Contact: Mike's Prodigy # is HBJX46A. Send your donation and questions to:

Mike Pinkerton
2136 Owls Cove Lane
Reston, VA 22091

Font Info   Lupin Software

Purpose: Font Info is a handy HyperCard stack that lists installed fonts on your system and allows you to look for font ID number conflicts. It can also query any PostScript printer currently selected with the Chooser and report on fonts resident in ROM, on the printer's hard drive (if it has one), and show which fonts have been downloaded and remain resident in the printer's memory.

Documentation: Font Info has a explanation of its functions available as a window in the stack.

Fee: If you like and continue to use Font Info, Lupin Software requests that you send $20. You will receive updates if you send in your fee for the product.

Contact: Send your fee and/or questions to:

Lupin Software
P.O. Box 4009
Davis, CA 95617-4009
412-341-5601

TypeBook   Jim Lewis

Purpose: TypeBook allows you to choose a font (or fonts) and print a type "spec" page that displays the font in several sizes and styles. These sheets are useful for understanding the particular "look and feel" for a typeface and allow you to learn more about type and styles. TypeBook can also print to an imagesetter for creating type samples that look closer to the appearance of the type in print.

Documentation: TypeBook comes with a manual on disk.

Fee: Freeware. There is no specified fee for using this product. However, Jim offers *Pica Calculator* for a $20 fee and a utility called *theFONDler*, which manages multiple font files, for a $25 fee. If you like TypeBook, we suggest you order and pay for one of these other utilities so Jim can continue to develop such useful software.

Contact: For information, or if you want to reward the programmer in some way, contact:

Jim Lewis - Golden State Graphics
2137 Candis Avenue
Santa Ana, CA 92706
(714) 542-5518

Varityper ToolKit   Varityper, Inc.

Purpose: Varityper manufactures a line of imagesetters. ToolKit is a utility designed to check fonts imbedded in PostScript files and change the default font for application software.

Documentation: Online help is available under the Apple menu.

Fee: Freeware. No fee is required to use this product.

Contact: For information on this software or Varityper products, write to:

Mary Hughes
Varityper, Inc.
11 Mt. Pleasant Avenue
East Hanover, NJ 07936

Blender   Rick Johnson

Purpose: Blender is a desk accessory that helps you calculate the results of PostScript blends within programs such as Illustrator and Freehand. The program shows what lpi and resolution settings need to be used for a given blend.

Documentation: Blender has online help.

Fee: If you like and continue to use Blender, author Rick Johnson requests that you send $1 to $5, as you think appropriate.

Contact: Send your fee and questions to:

Graffix
Attn: Rick Johnson
2216 Allen Lane
Waukesha, WI 53186

PixelFlipper   Chris Sanchez

Purpose: PixelFlipper is a Control Panel device that allows you to change pixel depth on your monitor from within applications or anywhere on the desktop. That means that you can instantly flip into black and white for word processing or go to "millions" of colors without a trip to the Control Panel. You select which modifier keys (Option, Command, etc.) you want to use, then when you hold down the keys with the mouse button pressed, a menu pops up that allows you to choose new settings.

Documentation: Online help is available from a Control Panel window.

Fee: Shareware. If you like and continue to use PixelFlipper, author Chris Sanchez requests that you send $10.

Contact: Send your fee and/or questions to:

Chris Sanchez
630 Barr Drive
Ames, IA 50010

PM4 ShortCuts   Mark Teranishi and Paul Sorrick

Purpose: PM4 ShortCuts is a help facility for PageMaker that works as a desk accessory. By opening PM4 ShortCuts, an interactive list of shortcuts is immediately available. If you have enough space on your monitor, leave PM4 ShortCuts open while you work to learn PageMaker's shortcuts.

Documentation: None required.

Fee: Shareware. If you like and continue to use PM4 ShortCuts, authors Mark Teranishi and Paul Sorrick request that you send $10.

Contact: Send your fee and/or questions to:

Mark Teranishi/Paul Sorrick
11441 60th Avenue S.
Seattle, WA 98178

MenuChoice   Kerry Clendinning

Purpose: MenuChoice is a time-saving Control Panel device. When it is installed, items installed into the Apple Menu folder show with arrows to their right. Moving the mouse to an arrow and holding down the button produces a pop-up menu of items contained in the item. For example, a folder (or folder alias) placed in the Apple Menu folder will produce a submenu of its contents that you can select directly! This is a useful tool for opening files buried under windows on the desktop. (MenuChoice is not System 6 compatible.)

Documentation: Online help is available from a Control Panel window.

Fee: Shareware. If you like and continue to use MenuChoice, author Kerry Clendinning requests that you send $15.

Contact: Send your fee and/or questions to:

Kerry Clendinning
P.O. Box 26061
Austin, TX 78755

HeapTool   Kerry Clendinning

Purpose: HeapTool is a simple Control Panel device for solving heap problems under System 6. Because many desktop publishers have a number of inits that load with the system, System 6 doesn't always provide enough space for everything. This results in sudden crashes where a bomb appears or the screen simply freezes. Follow HeapTools directions and set the system's memory up to give your Mac more breathing room if necessary.

Documentation: Online help is included in the Control Panel window.

Fee: If you like and use HeapTool, author Kerry Clendinning requests that you send $13.50.

Contact: Send your fee and/or questions to:

Kerry Clendinning
P.O. Box 26061
Austin, TX 78755

THE COLOR PUBLISHER'S GLOSSARY

This glossary is intended to bring you up to speed on a variety of terms covered in this book and widely used in color publishing products, services bureaus, and print shops. While we've made every attempt to introduce topics and terminology in an orderly fashion in the book, if your eyes glaze over an unfamiliar word or phase, look here (in the glossary) for an explanation. Another source of definitions can be found in the excellent glossaries that accompany many color publishing software packages. For example, both PageMaker and ColorStudio have useful glossaries that cover a wide range of publishing terminology.

¼ Tone   A *¼ tone* is a gray one quarter of the way between white and black. In print a dot that is a ¼ tone is approximately one quarter the size of a dot that prints solid black.

¾ Tone   A *¾ tone* is a gray that is three quarters of the way from black to white. In print a dot that is a ¾ tone is approximately three quarters the size of a dot that prints solid black.

Abut   When two colors touch edge to edge, they are said to *abut* each other.

Acetate   *Acetate* is a clear plastic used for graphic arts, often for overlays.

Additive Color   *Additive color* is a color model where colored light is combined to create colors. A color Macintosh monitor creates color by adding the light of a red, green, and blue gun together. Red, green, and blue are the additive primaries—when added together equally they produce the appearance of white light.

Anti-aliasing   *Anti-aliasing* is a process used to eliminate jagged edges from curves and lines. Anti-aliasing may be either a process that softens edges by adding light colors or actually smooths line edges on type and curves with mathematic algorithms.

Banding   *Banding* is the obvious transition in color where an area becomes lighter or darker, and a band appears rather than a smooth, natural transition. Banding occurs in poorly designed scanners and on imagesetters with problems.

Baud Rate   *Baud rate* is a rating of modem data transfer speed based on bits transmitted per second. Faster modems have higher baud rates. When transferring files via modem to a service bureau, you want a fast modem running at 9600 baud (or more) to reduce transfer time. Slow modems run at between 300 and 2400 baud.

Bézier Curves   *Bézier curves* are a method for creating complex curved lines and shapes with infinite adjustment points. A Bézier curve can be redrawn and adjusted until it is rendered correctly by moving points on the curve.

Bindery   *Bindery* is both the process and the place at a print shop or an independent bindery where documents are folded, stapled, or die-cut, or other post-press finishing operations are performed.

Bitmapped Graphics *Bitmapped graphics* are dot structures in a computer's memory that represent images dot by dot. For the purposes of this book, a bitmap is a black and white image using one bit per pixel, although all paint-type images are really bitmaps.

Black Generation Black is used to reduce the total amount of ink on press when printing four-color process images. *Black generation* refers to the way black is added to compensate for the removal of process colors. This is controlled on the Mac within a color separation program.

Bleed Bleed is a process for allowing ink to reach the edge of a page without gumming up the press or interfering with its grippers. A bleed is created by printing on a larger-than-required sheet with the ink crossing the trim boundaries but not reaching the sheet's actual edges. After printing, the page is trimmed down so the ink appears smooth and solid to the edge of the document.

Blueline *Bluelines* are proofs with a distinctive blue color. They are used to check that elements such as copy and photos are correctly incorporated into a document and to show that folding, trimming, and other bindery processes are correctly understood by the print shop.

Bomb *Bombs* indicate that a Macintosh error has occurred. They appear on the screen as a cartoon bomb with a lit fuse. Bombs are usually unrecoverable, and the Mac must be restarted.

Book or Book Weight *Book* is used as a reference to book-weight paper. Book-weight papers are lighter than cover-weight papers and may be used for the interior pages of a book, brochure, or catalog.

Brightness 1) Images have an overall *brightness* to them. Brightness is one of the three major dimensions of color; the others are hue and saturation. Correctly adjusted, a scanned image will have levels of brightness from dark shadows to bright highlights with fairly even distribution from dark to light. 2) A reference to the appearance of a sheet of paper. Some papers are termed "bright whites" for their highly optical white finish.

Broker *Brokers* are available to help you choose and manage print shops. They receive a commission from the shop they send the job to.

Bull's-eyes (registration marks) *Bull's eyes* are marks that appear on a printed image, generally used for CMYK color separations. They help the printer align the various plates used to print the piece.

Burn *Burns* are exposures on film or press plates. For example, when film or plates are exposed to light in a print shop, they are said to have been burned. Shops can expose images more than once, creating a stronger exposure. This is called a *double burn.*

Calibrate To adjust a device (printer, monitor, imagesetter, or scanner) so it produces accurate and predictable output.

Camera-ready Jobs created from RC paper output mounted down on illustration board into mechanical format are said to be *camera-ready* if they can be directly processed into negatives by a printer's stripping room.

Cast As a result of film qualities, processing problems, or poorly color balanced scanners, images tend to have a *cast*—an overall shift in color, typically towards yellow or blue. Casts should be eliminated either during scanning (if the scanner's software is so equipped) or during color balancing.

CEPS The acronym for color electronic prepress systems.

Channel *Channels* are analogous to different plates in a printing process. A CMYK image has at least four channels, one for each of the cyan, magenta, yellow, and black layers of information. RGB, HSL, and HSB have three channels. A document may use a combination of different channels for different kinds of images that will be printed. In programs like ColorStudio and Adobe Photoshop, the channels can be selected or merged to display different aspects of the document or used to create new documents composed from only selected channels.

CIE An international color standard defined by the Commission Internationale de l'Eclairage.

CMYK *CMYK* is an acronym for cyan, magenta, yellow, and key, where key represents black. CMYK is the four-color process ink model used to render color images in print. CMY refers to the same color model, but without black.

Coated Paper *Coated papers* have a clay coating added to the wood fibers to give them a smooth surface that takes ink evenly and reduces absorption. The best coated papers are expensive.

Color Key *Color keys* are proofs used to show entire flats of a job. Produced in layers to match the process or spot colors, color keys are tacked to the mounting paper on one edge only. This allows individual layers to be lifted for inspection. This kind of proof is not as color-accurate as Matchprints or Cromalins.

Color Picker To select color within page layout, illustration, retouching, and paint programs, a *color picker* pops up to allow color selection by one of several methods. Apple includes its own color picker with Mac system software to choose highlight colors. This picker can be used or ignored by software developers.

Color Separation *Color separation* is a process that allows continuous tone color photographs to be broken into four colors (cyan, magenta, yellow, and black) for reproduction on lithographic presses.

Commercial Printer Commercial printers are usually large printing plants that handle jobs ranging from tabloid newspapers to four-color brochures.

Comprehensive   *Comprehensives* or comps were formerly hand-assembled mock-ups of color print jobs, put together by a designer for client approval before moving into print. Today, color publishers on the Mac produce comprehensives on a color printer from the same file that will ultimately be imaged for printing. These usually provide a better representation of the final printed document than traditional comps.

Continuous Tone   *Continuous tone* describes black and white and color images that have not been broken down into a format compatible with modern printing presses. They are said to be continuous because no apparent dot structure is present and color gradations are smooth.

Contrast   *Contrast* is used to describe differences in brightness or colors. High contrast describes an image with great differences in brightness and/or color. In a low-contrast image, most brightness and/or color levels appear similar to one another in value.

Cover   *Cover* is used to describe cover-weight papers. These papers are heavier and stiffer than book weight and may be used for the cover of a brochure or catalog. Cover-weight papers are also more expensive than book-weight papers.

Crash   *Crashes* are a Macintosh error condition where the system suddenly freezes and does not respond to commands from the keyboard or mouse. A bomb alert may or may not appear.

Cromalin   *Cromalins* are a kind of color-accurate proof used to check color separations or final layouts. "Chromes," as they're called in the industry, are composited from four layers of plastic that simulate the process colors and are bound together to look like a printed page. Unlike color keys, they cannot be used to view each color layer separately.

Crop   Photos are *cropped* to select only the area that is desired for print.

Crop Marks   *Crop marks* show where a photo crop should occur. Crop marks are becoming synonymous with "trim marks" that show where excess paper will be trimmed away, even if a photo is not involved.

Crosfield   *Crosfield* is a high-end prepress system.

Cyan   *Cyan* is a blue used as one of the process colors and appears as a bright, medium blue to the eye.

Default   Most computer hardware and software have *defaults* set for a variety of functions. These are the settings most likely to be used by someone not interested or educated enough to make changes. For example, the default font used by most Mac programs is Helvetica—a font that's easy to read and will neither offend nor excite anyone—hence it is assigned as the default. In color publishing there are many default settings, some of which should never be adjusted unless you are a person of experience. Others can be readily adjusted with no ill effects. In this book, we point out when default settings are best left alone.

Densitometer   To measure the amount of CMYK ink on a press sheet, a *reflective densitometer* is used. To measure a screen on a negative, it is placed on a light table and a *transmission densitometer* is used to measure how much of the light table's light can pass through the screen. Another kind of transmission densitometer is used to measure CMY color on transparencies being readied for color separation.

Density   *Density* is the degree of solid black on one spot on a negative or the amount of ink on paper. Excess ink density on press results in a variety of printing problems. Correct density on a test page from an imagesetter means that the right dot size will be produced after the film is imaged and processed.

Die-Cut   *Die-cutting* is used to create irregular-shaped paper. While regular paper trimming systems can only cut straight lines, paper can be cut into any shape on a die. This is useful for creating product packaging, cutting business card holders in brochures, and making cardboard "pop-ups" used in greeting cards and children's books.

Dithering   To compensate for the inability to accurately render an image either because of color or resolution accuracy limitations, images are *dithered*. A full-color image rendered on a color monitor capable of only 256 colors will simulate the missing colors with dithering, which looks like hatch patterns on the screen.

Dot Area   The proportion of a selected area, usually specified as a percentage, that is covered by halftone dots.

Dot Gain   When paper is printed, each dot of ink tends to spread as it is applied to paper—this spreading is called *dot gain*. Dot gain can be a serious problem, resulting in murky photos and gummed-up presses. It can also be exacerbated by incorrectly calibrated imagesetters, improperly processed film, the wrong paper choice, and excessive ink extrusion levels on press.

Double Bump   To make a color in an image really jump out or to add opacity to ink, print shops sometimes run the paper through the press twice and hit it a second time with the same plate. Printers call this a *double bump*. Talk to your print shop before specifying this procedure in a job.

Download   To transfer a file, either by modem or directly by network or cable link from a remote computer, the file is *downloaded* to your computer.

DPI   *Dpi* stands for dots per inch, a measurement of resolution. More dots per inch equals higher resolution.

Draw Images   Produced by programs like MacDraw, in a *draw image,* each component remains an individual element capable of manipulation without affecting the rest of a drawing. Draw images are saved as PICTs for export to page layout programs or for use in Macintosh illustration programs.

Drum Scanner   The best (and most expensive) scanners are *drum scanners.* Used for both Macintosh scanning and conventional separations, the image is mounted to a transparent drum. After the art is loaded into the scanner, the drum is rotated at a high speed to capture image data.

Dull-coated Paper Coated papers are sold by the kind of finish they have. *Dull-coated papers* are not reflective like gloss papers and are best for many color projects, particularly if images and type are involved. These sheets take ink evenly, and their lack of gloss allows for easy reading.

Dummy A *dummy* is a kind of proof made in the size, format, and paper of the final piece, so the client can see how the paper looks and how the flats go together before committing to a particular sheet. On an expensive job, dummies may be created from several papers for comparison.

Duotone To add more tonal possibilities to black and white (gray) images, a second color may be used to print the halftone. Thus, two versions of the image are printed on top of each other; one in the first color and one in the second. This is called a *duotone* because two colors are used. The resulting image is denser and the effect can be dramatic. However, if the wrong two colors are used, the effect can be horrendous.

Dylux *Dylux* is a tradename for blueline proofing material.

Emulsion *Emulsion* is the film and print paper coating that is light-sensitive (photo-sensitive). Because this coating is fragile, emulsion should be treated carefully. Film should be shipped with its emulsion side carefully protected from scratching.

Emulsion Up and Emulsion Down When asking for film to be output, you must request the *emulsion* as up or down. Emulsion down is most common, though a few magazines require film imaged emulsion up.

EPS or EPSF *EPS* stands for Encapsulated PostScript—a file format for storing a PostScript description of a page or image. EPS files may consist of English-like words and binary or hexidecimal data. Also called EPSF by some.

Exposure The length of time and the intensity of the illumination that acts on the emulsion on a photographic film.

Fade-out Rate The *fade-out rate* is the rate at which color being applied with computerized paintbrush tools fades out as you move the tool across the page, simulating actual brush or airbrush textures.

Fill A fill is a color, gray, or texture used to *fill* an area in an illustration or other image.

Film *Film* is transparent medium covered with light-sensitive emulsion. Film in graphic arts is like the kind you use in your camera, but it is thicker and sold in sheets. Color film is rarely used in printing applications. Most graphic art film is designed to become transparent or remain black with no grays in between. This allows better transfer of dot structures for lithographic reproduction.

Film Processor   Once film or RC paper is imaged, it's passed through a *film processor* that automatically develops it. A film processor is a standard component of imagesetter installations.

Filter   *Filters* are used by color separation programs to enhance the sharpness of images before separation. Other filters may be used for special effects.

Flat   Negatives are assembled into *flats* before a job is plated at the print shop. A flat consists of all of the pages or material that will print on one side of a sheet of paper.

Flat Color   A solid color or tint that is printed without tonal variation.

Flatbed Scanner   A *flatbed scanner* captures images from photos and drawings placed on a flat glass imaging area. Flatbeds can scan books, photos, fabric, and hands placed on the scanner bed.

Flop   When handling film (a transparent medium), it is possible to flip the film over horizontally. This is called *flopping* it. Usually considered a mistake, flopped film can sometimes be used to change the way an image appears on a page.

Focoltone Color System   Focoltone is a color system designed to compete with the Pantone matching system. The central feature of Focoltone is its compatibility with computer-specified color. Its colors can be specified as either solid spot colors or as process colors.

Foil Stamping   With the use of a custom die, *foil stamping* is added as part of a design. The (usually) shiny stamped material catches the eye and adds a texture that can't be rendered by metallic inks. Foil stamping is relatively expensive.

Folio   The page number that appears at either the top or bottom of a page throughout a publication.

Font   The complete set of characters, with a specific size, weight, and attribute, in a typeface. The term *font* is often used interchangeably with the term "typeface" in desktop publishing circles, even though this is not technically accurate.

Font ID   Macintosh typefaces (fonts) are referred to within many programs by a *font ID* number. This causes headaches when two fonts accidentally share the same font ID number (common). Apple's new font scheme asks that developers refer to fonts by name, but not all software manufacturers are following this advice yet.

Full Color   For the purposes of this book, *full color* refers to what is confusingly described as 24-bit color or 32-bit color, or is labeled in Apple's Monitor Control Panel as "Millions."

Gamma Correction   *Gamma correction* is a mathematically defined function where the midtones of an image are adjusted based on a curve rather than on a linear change in brightness or darkness. Gamma correction is a powerful tool for fixing images where one area is extremely bright but most of the image is too dark.

GCR *GCR* or gray component replacement is used to replace the gray components of process color mixes on press. This results in less ink build-up and more natural neutral colors.

Grayscale Black and white continuous tone images are scanned into the Macintosh as *grayscales* made up of four, sixteen, 64, or 256 grays. For output, grayscales are converted into a black and white halftone where dots of varying sizes are used to represent grays ranging from black to white.

Graduated Blend *Graduated blends* are even transitions in colors from one value to another.

Gutter The area where two pages of a book are connected to the spine is called the *gutter.* Gutters require extra paper so that contents of the left and right pages will align properly. Elements "jumping gutters" (images that continue from left to right on two pages) can be problematic when the job is assembled at the bindery because they have to be matched perfectly.

Halftone To print black and white images, the continuous tone must be broken down into dots. These are called *halftone dots.* The entire image is known as a *halftone.*

Halftone Cell When halftones are created conventionally, a screen is used to break colors into dots. On the imagesetter, each halftone dot is represented by a cell made up of subdots. More subdots drawn in the *halftone cell* make for a darker gray than when fewer dots are used.

Hickey On press, physical contaminates, such as particles of grit, can adhere to the press and ink transfer mechanism. Because of the way press mechanisms work, instead of the particle taking ink and printing, the area surrounding it becomes inked and prints as a donut-shaped mark. These objectionable marks are called *hickies.*

Highlight The *highlight* is the brightest element in an image that will print with dots still large enough to be seen on paper. Elements lighter than the highlight don't print and become white by letting paper show through.

Histogram *Histograms,* a type of bar chart, are used in color programs to show the amount of color used in an image across the tonal range. Histograms are an excellent tool for identifying image deficiencies.

Holdout Each kind of paper has a *holdout* rating which describes the amount of ink it absorbs. A paper with a high holdout is one that absorbs little ink when printed.

House Sheet Most print shops buy one kind of paper in bulk and use it for the majority of their work. This is called their *house sheet.*

HSB *HSB* is an acronym for hue, saturation, and brightness—one of many models for describing and representing color. An HSB image is an RGB image displayed in three channels, yet only one channel is displayed at a time.

HSL   *HSL* is an acronym for hue, saturation, and luminance—one of many models for describing and representing color. An HSL image is an RGB image displayed in three channels, yet only one channel is displayed at a time.

Hue   *Hue,* along with saturation and brightness, is one of the primary dimensions of color. Hue is the aspect of color that distinguishes it from other colors, for example "peach" is a different hue than "pink."

Imagesetter   *Imagesetters* are devices that convert PostScript code into a rasterized format for high-resolution output on film or paper. Imagesetters are used to convert page layout files into film for print. In most of this book, the word "imagesetter" is used to refer to the complete imaging system, made up of a Macintosh computer, a RIP processor, the imagesetter, and a film processor.

Imposition   When pages are assembled into flats in order to print several pages on one side of a sheet of paper, the process is called *imposition.* The individual sheets are trimmed apart after printing.

Indexed Color   When Macintosh color monitors are set to 256 colors, this is called *indexed color,* because a look-up table or index is used to define which of the Mac's 16.8 million colors are shown on screen to make up the 256.

Key   1) Part of the cyan, magenta, yellow, and key (CMYK) color model; *key* is another name for black. 2) *Keys* are also black and white line art. Also known as *key-lines.* 3) *Key* is a term used synonymously to talk about a color key, a patented color proof process.

Knockout   When two colors print on top of each other, one color is removed so that overprinting doesn't occur. This *knockout* allows the second color to print on blank paper rather than on top of another ink, which would change its color.

Layer   When working within illustration programs, images and design elements may be kept on separate *layers.* This makes it easy to get to an object that may have other objects in front of it.

Linear Fill   A color, gray, or textured fill used to paint an area from one point to another with a mathematical gradation of texture or color between the two points.

Line Art   *Line art* is made up of lines and solids with no grays or colors. It can be the basis of color art created on the Macintosh and used by a print shop as a guide for adding colors to a job.

Linotronic   Imagesetters manufactured by Linotype are called *Linotronic* imagesetters. This word is included because many people call all imagesetters Linotronics, regardless of manufacturer. In the same vein, some people refer to all imagesetter output as *Linotronic output.*

Loupe   *Loupes* include a variety of magnifying glasses used in the graphic arts to check image quality before scanning and verify process color registration on press.

LPI   *Lpi* or lines per inch is a rating of print resolution defined by the kind of press and paper a job will finish on. Higher lpi ratings mean finer resolution (more lines per inch).

Magenta   *Magenta* is one of the four process colors. It looks like a bright purple-shifted pink.

Malarkey   When files fail to image at a less-than-competent service bureau, *malarkey* is often what you will receive when you ask for an explanation or assistance.

Mask   To allow only a certain area of an image to be changed or manipulated, a *mask* is created to block the areas where no change is desired. Masks are used for a variety of assembly and production processes in publishing. Masking capabilities are built into many publishing programs. Traditionally, the masks were created out of film and other materials.

Matchprint   *Matchprints* are a color proof in which the layers for the four process colors are exposed and then fused together to create the proof. Additional spot color layers may be added as well.

Mechanical   A *mechanical* is the raw artwork produced by a designer to send a job to a print shop. Consisting of a base layer on illustration board that includes the key design elements, such as type and illustrations, clear overlays may be used to show where colors and images should be stripped in by the print shop. Traditional mechanicals are being replaced by imagesetter output on film.

Midtones   In a photo, the colors halfway between light and dark are the *midtones*.

Modem   *Modems* are hardware devices used to transmit information from one computer to another over telephone lines. In desktop publishing, they are used to send files to a service bureau.

Moiré Pattern   When one halftone screen is laid on another, a mathematical effect can occur that causes an undesirable and regular patterning. This obvious, visible patterning is called a *moiré* and has been a major source of problems in Macintosh color publishing. Moiré problems are being addressed with new software technologies to manipulate the screen angles of color separations.

Mottled   When ink is absorbed unevenly into paper, areas of high ink absorbency take on a different color than areas of less ink absorbency. This results in the variation of color that looks splotchy or *mottled*. It is avoidable by printing on superior, smooth-finished paper or refraining from the use of large areas of solid ink on paper with uneven ink holdout.

Mylar   *Mylar* is a clear plastic sometimes used for overlays when producing a mechanical in the traditional way.

Negative   *Negatives* are film or paper with the light areas reversed to dark and the dark areas reversed to light. Negatives are usually produced on film for direct plating at a print shop.

Object-oriented   Drawing and illustration programs where the elements remain separate from the background and can be manipulated individually are said to be *object-oriented*.

Offset   1) Most modern presses are *offset* litho models where water on the plate resists or offsets ink where it shouldn't be printed. 2) Offset is also the description of a press problem where the ink from freshly printed sheets offsets or transfers to the sheet on top.

Opacity   Paper is rated, in part, by its degree of translucency (or opacity). For printing on two sides of a sheet, a higher *opacity* reduces show-through from the other side.

Overprint   When two colors print over one another, this is called *overprinting*. Used mostly to escape registration problems, black type and lines are commonly overprinted on top of other lighter colors.

Page Layout Program   A software package that allows the combination of images with design elements and type. Some page layout programs provide color separation and other prepress functions. Some also offer objected-oriented drawing tools.

Paint the Sheet   When a large area of solid ink is used to completely change the color of a sheet of paper such as a brochure cover, this is called *painting the sheet*.

Paint-type Images   Paint-type images are comprised of dots or dot structures. These dots may represent simple black, white, grays, or colors. If they consist solely of black and white dots, they may also be called *bitmapped images*.

Palette   A *palette* is a selection of colors. Palettes are frequently created for groups of frequently used colors. By creating a standard palette in a publishing program, commonly used colors don't need to be specified each time a new document is started.

Pantone Matching System (PMS)   The *Pantone Matching System* is a patented process for defining colors. Pantone colors (called PMS colors) can be specified from a swatch book and then closely duplicated by a print shop from books that explain how to mix colors to match the numbered inks in the swatch book. PMS colors can also be specified in many applications as screen color, although the resulting color may not match its spot counterpart exactly.

PICT   *PICT* format is a file format that supports paint-type images as well as object-oriented drawings; PICT2 supports color.

Pinholes   *Pinholes* are objectionable tiny holes that may appear in the ink when printing solid colors.

Plates   Press images are transferred to paper by metal or plastic press *plates.* Metal plates are superior to plastic. Quality color publishing jobs are rarely printed with plastic plates.

Point   *Points* are a measurement used in the graphic arts to specify type sizes, line weights (widths), trapping values, and paper weights. There are 72.27 points to an inch, but most page layout programs measure a point as an even 1/72 inch. In measuring paper thickness, a point is a thousandth of an inch.

Portfolio   Creative professionals assemble samples of their best work into a showpiece called a *portfolio.* Portfolios take many forms. A writer may carry an armload of brochures. An animator may show up with a VCR, monitor, and a video of his work.

Positive   The opposite of a film negative is a *positive.* In a positive, light areas remain light and dark areas are dark. RC paper is usually run as a positive because it can be proofed more easily. Plates may be made from negatives or positives, but negatives are the standard.

PostScript   *PostScript* is a page description language developed by Adobe Systems and used to describe type and visual elements so they can be output on devices with PostScript interpreters. PostScript instructions are highly portable across a wide range of computer platforms and output devices.

PPD   *PostScript Printer Descriptions* (PPDs) are used to tell application software the characteristics of the output device to be used. Obviously, a 300-dpi laser printer uses a different PPD than a high-resolution imagesetter.

Prepress   The process of getting a job ready for print is called *prepress.* In the case of Macintosh color publishing, this begins with readying a page layout for output at the service bureau. It ends when the job is on press being printed. In traditional publishing, prepress involves processes like camera work, stripping, and platemaking. Many of these functions are now automated by computers and special software. Prepress is sometimes called preparation or prep.

Prepress Systems   *Prepress systems* are large, powerful, computer-based systems used to lay out pages and process images. The high-end systems are complicated to run and require a skilled operator, knowledgeable about color and color separation. Many functions of professional prepress systems can be performed on a Macintosh, but it takes longer to process the images.

Press Check   Color jobs are usually checked on press before the job is run, to identify last-minute mistakes and correct color. This is called a *press check.*

Press Window   When large (or complex) color jobs are brought to a print shop, a *press window* is scheduled. This is the time when the job will have its "day in the sun" on press. Press windows tend to shift as jobs are late arriving or as a printer's schedule faces reality when committed jobs take longer to strip and print than estimated.

Process Blue   See *Cyan.*

Process Color   *Process color* is a system of breaking down and reproducing all visible colors (in theory) in print. The process colors are cyan, magenta, yellow, and black.

Process Red   See *Magenta.*

Progressive Proofs   The set of proofs, often called progs, that show each color of a job separately or several colors in combination in their order of printing.

Proof   There are a variety of proofs available to the color publisher. Proofing systems range from black and white, to color output produced by PostScript printers connected to a Mac, to special systems such as the Matchprint used to check color. Proofs are used to catch mistakes and identify problems before going to press.

QuickDraw   The Macintosh uses *QuickDraw,* a set of screen drawing routines developed by Apple to translate its internal processes into a format that can be rasterized on a monitor or (non-PostScript) printer.

Quick Printer   *Quick printers* are small shops that handle simple print jobs, usually offering fast turnaround and low prices. Quality is not part of the service at most of these shops.

Radial Fill   A color or gray fill used to paint an area from one point at the center of a circular area to the outside of the area, using a mathematical gradation of color between the center point and the outside edge.

Rasterize   Because PostScript exists as a series of instructions rather than a digitized image, a raster image processor (RIP) is used to convert the PostScript instructions back into a picture-like format that can be output on an imagesetter. This process is called *rasterization.*

RC Paper   *RC paper* is resin-coated paper. As one of three mediums that can be imaged on an imagesetter, RC paper is the least expensive format for output. However, its economy is lost at the print shop, where it must be converted to film. RC paper can be used to proof a job. Though it is easy to proof an RC paper image, it isn't always cost effective.

Ream   500 sheets of paper.

Reflective Art   Another term used for *reflective copy.*

Reflective Copy   Art that reflects light, i.e., is not transparent, is said to be *reflective copy.* Photographic prints, illustrations, and RC paper are all reflective copy.

Registration Marks   *Registration marks* are added to color jobs at the imagesetter to show the printer exactly where each color film layer should be positioned in relationship to other layers.

Resample   To change the resolution and/or size of an image, *resampling* is used to add or remove dots through interpolation. Interpolation uses mathematics to guess the color value of new dots inserted between existing ones, and then assigns the dots the estimated value.

Resolution   A measurement of the amount of information in output, specified as dots per inch, pixels per inch, bits per pixel, or lines per inch—depending on the device and application. Higher numbers have more *resolution,* which results in more information in the output image.

Retouch   If an image has a flaw such as a scratch, *retouching* is used to manually disguise or remove the flaw. Formerly done on a light table, retouching can now be performed with special software on the screen of a Macintosh computer.

Reverse   To get a "free" color when paying for printing, objects such as type are often *reversed* out of another color or picture. For example, it is common to have white type reversed out of a black background. The type appears white because the paper shows through. Sometimes a color can be printed over the reversed area.

RGB   *RGB,* or red-green-blue, is the standard color model for color monitors and color televisions. It is based on the use of red, green, and blue electron guns that cause phosphor on a monitor's screen to glow. Different amounts of output from each gun mix together to create different colors.

RIFF   *RIFF* (raster image file format) was developed by Letraset for its page layout and image processing packages. RIFF supports both color and black and white images, though not all non-Letraset applications can read this format.

Right Reading   When an image or layout is readable, i.e., the type reads normally from left to right, and pictures are oriented normally left to right, it is said to be *right reading.* An image that is backward when compared to the original is called *wrong reading.* Right and wrong reading are specified when producing film with special requirements. Most service bureaus will know what you want without this specification.

RIP   A raster image processor or *RIP* is used to rasterize Macintosh output into a format that can be imaged on film or paper within the imagesetter.

Rollfed Press   Presses which take paper from a roll are (surprise!) *rollfed.* Rollfed presses are not as accurate in registration capability as sheetfed presses.

Rosette   When four-color images are printed, the process inks are printed in *rosettes,* shapes where a dot of each of the four colors loosely forms a circle. Rosettes are used because the dots comprising a color must print close together to be less noticeable, but not print on top of each other, which would change the colors.

Rough   A very preliminary design or layout to provide the general size and position of graphic elements. Traditionally, *roughs* were produced on tracing paper.

Saddle-stitch   Brochures and booklets that are stapled at a print shop are *saddle-stitched* by a machine that lays them under the stapler head like a saddle over a horse. The staples used for saddle-stitching come from a continuous feed of solid wire.

Samples   *Samples* are copies of print projects kept by print shops to show to potential customers. Much like a designer's portfolio, a print shop's sample supply changes as new work is printed and old work is given away to prospective customers.

Saturation   The amount of color used in an image is adjustable by its *saturation* level. Unsaturated colors tend to be pale and cool. Super-saturated colors tend to be rich and vibrant in color. Excess color saturation results in colors that are unprintable by the CMYK printing model. Saturation is also used to describe the amount of gray in a color or the vividness or purity of a color. More gray is a color of lower saturation; less gray is a color of higher saturation.

Scale   To *scale* an image is to increase or decrease its size.

Scitex   *Scitex* is a high-end prepress system.

Score   To fold heavy papers or to make light papers fold more precisely, a roller is used to emboss (*score*) a line on the page where the fold will go. This results in easier, cleaner folds.

Screen   In traditional publishing, the *screen* was the patterned glass or film through which a photograph was converted to a halftone. In electronic publishing, the term screen is often used to refer to the halftone pattern itself.

Screen Angle   When printing black and white or color images, each color is broken into a halftone with a screen. The angle of the screen refers to the direction of the lines that comprise it. Choosing the wrong *screen angle* results in noticeable screen lines, or in the case of process color images, moiré patterns.

Screen Color   *Screen color* is a color made up from screens of two or more of the four process colors.

Screen Frequency   The lines-per-inch resolution used to screen an image is referred to as the *screen frequency*. So a color separation run out at 133 lpi has a screen frequency of 133.

Screen Ruling   The number of lines per inch on a halftone screen. *Screen ruling* is also called screen frequency.

Screen Tint   Solid colors such as Pantone colors or solid process colors can be lightened by screening them; the resulting color is called a *screen tint* or simply a *tint*. For example, magenta printed as a 40 percent tint appears as a medium pink. The ink coverage for a screen tint is less than 100 percent and thus simulates shading or a lighter color.

Service Bureau or SB   A *service bureau* or *SB* is a company that provides publishing services to desktop publishers. A typical service bureau sells time on an imagesetter by the page or minute. Other service bureaus may include proofing, scanning, advice, and problem-solving as part of their services.

Shadow   Dark areas of images are called the *shadow*. Shadows often require special attention within Mac-based color publishing projects because they tend to lose detail or take on undesirable casts.

Shadow Point   The darkest part of an image that will print with a black dot smaller than 100 percent is the *shadow point*. Depending on the settings, anything darker than the shadow point prints as solid black (a full dot).

Sharpen   Because detail in scanned images may become hazy and edges may lose definition, most scans are *sharpened* before separation. Sharpening helps improve both of these problems. **Unsharp Masking** is the filter of choice for sharpening images within programs that offer it.

Sheetfed Press   A press that's fed by individual sheets of paper, as opposed to a roll of paper, is *sheetfed*.

Signature   A group of printed pages on a sheet which, when folded and trimmed, become a sequence in the publication.

Slur   A printing problem when halftone dots become slightly elongated during printing.

Soft   *Soft* is word for out of focus.

Solids   Contiguous areas of a single color that cover more than a few percent of a page are called *solids*. Solids require special attention by the print shop to avoid pinholes and uneven application of color.

Special Effects   The general term used to describe photographic techniques such as posterization, line conversion, and other filter conversions of an image.

Specialty Printer   *Specialty printers* are high-quality print shops, often specializing in four- and six-color print jobs.

Specifications   The specific and precise descriptions of the ink, paper, binding, quantity, and other features of a printed job.

Spot Color   Color that doesn't use process color separation, but instead consists of solid-colored type and design elements, is said to be *spot color*.

Spot Varnish   *Spot varnish* is the application of varnish to specific elements of a page. It is used mostly for highlighting photos and design elements. Subtle tints may be added to the varnish for emphasis.

Spread   Two facing pages in a publication. In printing, the enlargement of a color area to build a trap with abutting areas of a different color.

Star Targets   To check the amount of ink being applied to a sheet of paper and to check for press problems, *star targets* are symbols added outside the print area of jobs before printing. If problems occur, the crisp lines of a star target begin to fill in, indicating a need for press adjustments.

Station (Press)   Color-capable presses have individual mechanisms that handle ink, hold a plate and impress the ink onto paper. Each color unit is called a *station* and is responsible for printing one color. A four-color press has four stations, one for each color.

Strip or Stripping   The process of converting a mechanical into plate-ready film is the process of *stripping*. This involves taping together various pieces of film so they can be made into a printing plate. The people who handle the jobs are strippers.

Subtractive Color   Printing colors on paper with colored ink is a process called *subtractive color,* because the ink blocks reflection of certain colors by subtracting them. Thus, printing yellow on a sheet of paper is actually subtracting blue and red. Cyan, magenta, and yellow are the subtractive primaries and the hues used (with black) for process color inks. When cyan, magenta, and yellow are overprinted in equal amounts, they appear as black (actually more of a dark muddy brown), which is an absence of color.

SWOP   The ink color standards used in North America are somewhat different than those used in other parts of the world. *SWOP* is an acronym for *standard web offset publication,* the name for the North American ink color standards used for process color printing.

Tb   A *terrabyte,* which is a trillion bytes or a thousand gigabytes.

Text   Text or textured papers are uncoated stock with a physical texture added during manufacture. Text papers are often used for letterheads and come in a number of colors. Note that "text" is sometimes used as another word that describes a paper's weight; a print shop may talk about text-weight and cover-weight paper.

Thumbnails   Tiny sketches that show a layout are called *thumbnails* in reference to their size. Typically measuring larger than a human thumbnail, these sketches are used to evolve designs with headlines, copy, and actual photos and illustrations. By creating the layout in a small format, drawing time is reduced and elements simplified. This way, the overall design is easy to see without the clutter of headlines, illustrations, and multiple colors.

TIFF   *TIFF* (tagged image file format) files are in a file format used for paint-type images. This format, now in widespread use, was originally developed by Aldus for use with PageMaker.

Tint   A *tint* is a color obtained by adding white to a solid color or an alternate term for screen tint.

Tone   The range of grays between black and white or the variation in a color.

Transfer Function   The *transfer function* is an adjustment that makes an imagesetter print a dot of a specified size to compensate for calibration or accuracy problems. Set within an application program, the dot size specification overrides the imagesetter's normal dot-size specification. As an example, with this function it's possible to make the imagesetter print a 45 percent dot instead of a 40 percent dot.

Transparency   *Transparency* film is color-positive film of the kind used to make 35mm slides. (It's available in much larger sizes as well.) Transparencies have the advantage that they are processed directly into images without the two-step negative/print process used to create photographic prints. Because they are film, transparencies offer superior detail and livelier color when compared to prints.

Trap   *Traps* are assembled where one color touches another to guard against ordinary and acceptable shift of registration on press. When two colors trap, their edges overlap slightly.

Trim Marks   *Trim marks* show where excess paper should be shorn away from the side of a printed sheet. They can be added automatically by most page layout programs. Trim marks are also called crop marks.

Trim Size   The size of the final printed product after the final trim is made.

TruMatch   *TruMatch* is a patented system for specifying process colors; it allows each color to be specified in one-percent increments.

UCR   *UCR* or undercolor removal replaces process colors that will print as black with actual black. This reduces the total amount of ink on press.

Uncoated Paper   Papers without clay coating are uncoated. *Uncoated papers* tend to absorb more ink during printing than do coated papers.

Unsharp Masking   *Unsharp masking* is a filtering process used to enhance scanned images by finding edges and making them clearer. The name comes from the way this process was handled photographically in traditional publishing.

Upload   To *upload* a file is to transfer it (either by modem or through a direct network or cable link) from your computer to a remote computer.

Varnish   *Varnish* is used as a base for inks and as a coating to protect printed images. It is also used to highlight certain objects on a printed page. Varnish is applied by conventional presses.

Vector   *Vectors* are mathematical descriptions of lines in space. A vector may exist as a line that starts at point A and travels to point B with a mathematically described curve. Vectors are used by object-oriented illustration programs and PostScript to describe lines, create objects, and draw type outlines.

Virtual Memory   *Virtual memory* is a process that allows actual RAM memory to be supplemented by treating part of a hard disk as RAM. Thus, your computer behaves as if it has more RAM than it actually does. Virtual memory makes working with large images easier, but it is much slower than real RAM memory.

Wavelength   It is the *wavelength* of light that determines its color.

Web Press   *Web presses* are fed by rolls of paper. Called "webs" for short, they are used for printing long jobs, and they can process paper much faster than a sheetfed press. They are called webs because of the continuous sheet of paper that moves back and forth on the rollers that feed the press. These rolls of paper are also called webs. The press vaguely resembles a spider web.

WYSIWYG   *WYSIWYG* (What You See Is What You Get) is a central idea behind the visual display on the Macintosh. If something is true WYSIWYG, what you see on the screen is identical to what you will see in print. Unfortunately, this isn't always so when it comes to color accuracy.

BIBLIOGRAPHY

461

Aldrich-Ruenzel, Nancy. *Designer's Guide to Print Production*. New York: Step-By-Step Publishing, 1990.

Bann, David and Gargan, John. *How to Check and Correct Color Proofs*. Cincinnati: Quarto Publishing Inc., 1990.

Beach, Mark, Shepro, Steve and Russon, Ken. *Getting It Printed*. Portland: Coast to Coast Books.

Beale, Stephen and Cavuoto, James. *Linotronic Imaging Handbook*. Torrance, CA: Micro Publishing Press, 1990.

Biedny, David and Monroy, Bert. *The Official Adobe Photoshop Handbook*. New York: Bantam Books, 1991.

Campbell, Alastair. *The Graphic Designer's Handbook*. Philadelphia: Running Press, 1991.

Fenton, Howard. "DTP Color Remains a Big Question," *Pre-*. September-October 1990, 20-48.

Guttman, Steven. "What's All The Fuss About Color Prepress," *Desktop Communications*. November-December 1990, 32-38.

Matazzoni, Joe. "The Prepress Edge," *MACWORLD*, October 1991, 138-145.

Sloane, Patricia. *The Visual Nature of Color*. New York: Design Press, 1989.

White, Jan V. *Color for the Electronic Age*. New York: Watson-Guptill Publications, 1990.

INDEX